Palaces in the Night
Whistler in Venice

AHMANSON · MURPHY
FINE ARTS IMPRINT

THE AHMANSON FOUNDATION
has endowed this imprint
to honor the memory of
FRANKLIN D. MURPHY
who for half a century
served arts and letters,
beauty and learning, in
equal measure by shaping
with a brilliant devotion
those institutions upon
which they rely.

Margaret F. MacDonald

Palaces in the Night
Whistler in Venice

University of California Press
Berkeley and Los Angeles

To Norman, Kathy and Helen, with love

Acknowledgments

University of California Press
Berkeley and Los Angeles, California

Published by arrangement with
Lund Humphries, UK

Lund Humphries is part of
Ashgate Publishing

First published in 2001

ISBN 0-520-23049-3

Designed by Chrissie Charlton & Company
Printed in Hong Kong by Midas Printing Ltd

I would like to thank all the people who have helped by their advice, shared their research and offered hospitality over the years I have been working on this book. I wish to thank the many collectors, some of whom wish to remain anonymous, who have generously showed me their collections. Many individuals have helped me in many ways, and among them I thank Avis Berman; Katharine Blood and Harry Katz, Library of Congress; Elaine and Louis Dailey; Eric Denker, Corcoran Gallery; Ruth Fine and Carlotta Owens, Department of Prints and Drawings, National Gallery of Art, Washington, DC; Jay Fisher, Baltimore Museum of Art; Vivian Hamilton and Hugh Stevenson, Glasgow Museums; Hugh Honour; Collis and John Larkin; Katharine Lochnan; Paul and Elaine Marks; Linda Merrill; Martha Smith, Freer Gallery of Art, Washington, DC; Robin Spencer; Anne and Nesta Spink; Harriet Stratis and Martha Tedeschi, Art Institute of Chicago; Roberta Waddell, New York Public Library. I owe a special debt to Dr Alistair Grieve who collaborated with me in researching sites and shared much valuable information on Venice. Many dealers and auction houses have helped me, in particular *Artemis*, Fred Baker, Christie's, Thomas Colville, Kennedy's, Ewan and Carol Mundy, Phillip's, Sotheby's, William Weston and, above all, Gordon Cooke and Andrew MacIntosh Patrick and the Fine Art Society. Among the many museums, galleries and libraries whose help I value greatly are the British Museum; Art Institute of Chicago; Freer Gallery of Art; National Gallery of Art, and Library of Congress, Washington, DC; Victoria and Albert Museum. I particularly thank the staff of the Hunterian Art Gallery and Special Collections Department in the University of Glasgow, including Peter Black, Mungo Campbell, Anne Dulau, Pam Robertson and David Weston. I would also like to thank Brian McKerracher and the ever helpful Martin Hopkinson, both former staff. My colleagues at the Centre for Whistler Studies – Patricia de Montfort, Sue Macallan, Ian and Joanna Meacock, Georgia Toutziari and Nigel Thorp – have, as always, given me wonderful support.

I am grateful to the University Court of the University of Glasgow, holders of Whistler's copyright, for permission to publish excerpts from his letters.

I gratefully acknowledge a grant for research in Venice in 1993 from the Gladys Krieble Delmas Foundation, New York, and the University of Glasgow for Research Awards in 1995–7.

Thanks finally to my family, enthusiastic Venetian explorers and proof correctors, Lucy Myers of Lund Humphries, for unfailing encouragement, and Lucy Clark, also of Lund Humphries, and Chrissie Charlton for making this a beautiful book.

Margaret F. MacDonald

Contents

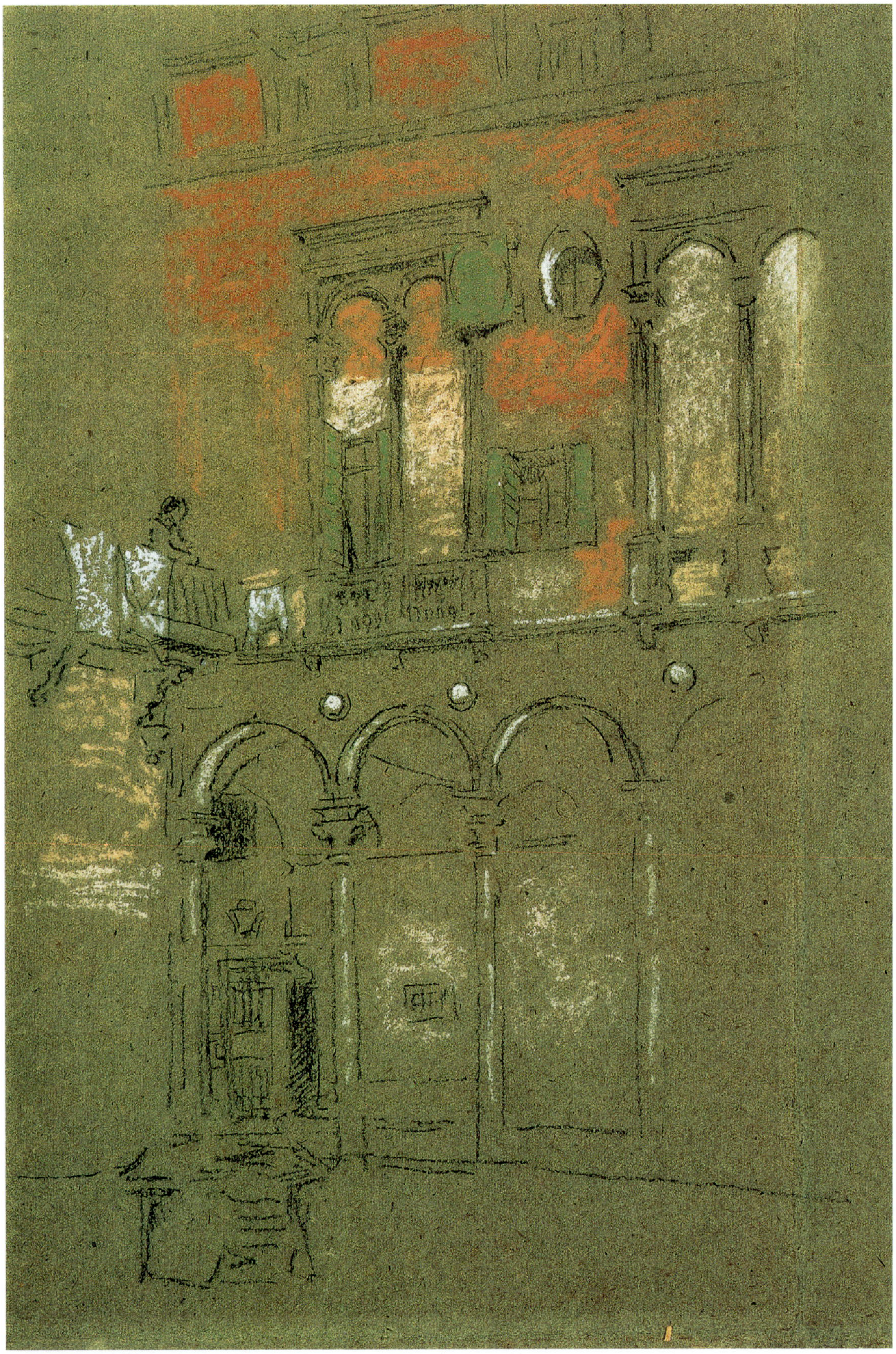

1
James McNeill Whistler
Venetian courtyard
Pastel 298-309 x 201-203 mm
Dr and Mrs John E. Larkin Jr., M.792

Preface: Visions of Venice

Venice is a unique and beautiful city. For centuries, it has inspired great artists, from Canaletto to Turner and Whistler, and writers from Byron to Ruskin and Henry James. The fourth canto of Byron's *Childe Harold's Pilgrimage* opens with perhaps his best-known evocation of Venice:

> I stood in Venice on the Bridge of Sighs;
> A palace and a prison on each hand:

His romantic view of a city in decay is memorable:

> Her palaces are crumbling to the shore,
> And music meets not always now the ear;
> Those days are gone – but Beauty still is here.
> States fall, arts fade – but Nature doth not die,
> Nor yet forget how Venice once was dear,
> The pleasant place of all festivity,
> The revel of the earth, the masque of Italy![1]

John Ruskin evoked a similar nostalgia at the beginning of his influential *Stones of Venice*: 'a ghost upon the sands of the sea, so weak – so quiet – so bereft of all but her loveliness, that we might well doubt, as we watched her faint reflection in the mirage of the lagoon, which was the City, and which the Shadow.'[2] However, several volumes of closely packed prose and diagrams followed, which ensured that no traveller lacked concrete information on what to appreciate in the architecture of Venice, and why.

On a more practical level, guidebooks to Italy by John Murray and others detailed the routes and sights, the hotels and hazards of travel. Travellers were not exactly going into uncharted territory, but they rather liked to think that, if not discovering, they were rediscovering great wonders for themselves. In Dickens' *Little Dorrit* of 1857–8, the family, *en route* for Italy, reached a mountain hotel, where the guests included an elderly lady: '"like other inconvenient places," she observed, "it must be seen. As a place much talked of, it is necessary to see it."'

The rich went to Italy to spend their wealth in the pursuit of culture and society. Artists went in pursuit of art, architecture, and the rich. The impoverished went because it was cheap. Whistler went to Venice in 1879 to escape from poverty, and there he enjoyed the society available to an artist of limited means, among other expatriates, artists and birds of passage. Travel, which had been the prerogative of the rich, was opened to the middle classes by the growth of the railway network. They flocked to the south for warmth, culture, and a mildly exotic and dangerous experience. They brought home souvenirs that reminded them of architectural and scenic beauties safely negotiated. Volumes of prints and photographs were easily affordable and adorned many a Victorian tea table. These souvenirs proved to others that they too belonged to the cultivated and leisured classes.

As for armchair travellers, they also bought reproductions of foreign scenes. Basking in the experiences of others, they were reassured by their breadth of vicarious knowledge. A volume of lithographs of Venice by a little known artist, Lessore, after paintings by William Wyld, seemed to Whistler the epitome of what he must avoid. He wrote to a fellow artist, Matthew Elden:

> Lessor's photographs [sic] can I am sure give you no idea of Venice [...] it is not merely the "Views of Venice" or the Streets of Venice, or the "Canals of Venice" such as you have seen brought back by the foolish sketcher – but great pictures that stare you in the face – complete arrangements and harmonies in color & form that are ready and waiting for the one who can perceive –[3]

Lessore's lithographs provided carefully drawn views of well-known sights, as seen by unambitious tourists on leisurely gondola rides along the Grand Canal and strolls around San Marco. Neat figures in picturesque local dress stood stiffly in the *Piazzetta* and sold wine on the Riva degli Schiavoni (fig.2).

Whistler's aim was to etch views of the city that would enable him to return and restore both his fortune and reputation; that would boil the pot but not be superficial pot-boilers. His etchings therefore include views of familiar sights like the Riva degli Schiavoni and San Marco, but also show quiet backwaters, secret gardens and lantern-lit windows, which were not in any guidebook.

Whistler was concerned that his work should not be classed with ephemeral productions geared for the tourist market: 'Mind I shall not come back with sketches of Venice after the manner of Philip's [sic] return with sketches of Spain – the whole thing with me will be just a continuation of my own art work, some portions of which complete themselves in Venice.'[4] John ('Spanish') Phillip rested his reputation on *La Gloria* (fig.6), started in Seville in 1860, completed in London and exhibited at the Royal Academy in 1864. It is a bravura painting, full of local colour: a fiesta, picturesque costumes, mantillas, sombreros, guitars, etc, and on the left, a mourning mother and her dead child. It was intended to arouse emotion, and admiration for the artist who inspired such sentiment.

At the same exhibition, Whistler exhibited *Wapping* (fig.7), which was also painted over several years, mainly on site at a Thames-side inn. It shows two sailors sitting with a young woman, against a background of sailing boats, barges and steamers. Its immediacy, vigorous brushwork and fresh colour met with a positive response from the critics. It is the nearest Whistler came to a genre painting, but the underlying realism and the somewhat ambivalent subject link it to his later work. Some years later he wrote, 'the picture should have its own merit, and not depend upon dramatic, or legendary, or local interest.'[5]

His work in Venice could not be mistaken for work done anywhere else, and to that extent it was dependent on local interest. However, the selection of views and compositions, plus the expressiveness of his line and printing, were the means he used to differentiate his work from that of others. He drew figures in distinctively Italian costume, each an individual, moving, gesturing and interacting with other real people. Whistler wrote that he had 'learned to know a Venice in Venice that the others never seem to have perceived.'[6] His vision of Venice, and the means he took to accomplish it, are the subject of this book.

I shall investigate when and why Whistler went to Venice, placing his journey in the context of his life and art; describe his life in Venice, and relations with friends and fellow-artists; examine his work, his artistic aims and techniques; explore the presentation, promotion and reception of this work on his return; discuss the significance and influence of the Venetian period in Whistler's career; and finally, let the artist speak for himself, through the letters he wrote from Venice to family, friends and colleagues. As Whistler said, 'I don't think I am doing so badly in my new role of foreign correspondent – Now it is for all of you in your turn to write me lots of news and if you can find no scandal you must invent some.'[7]

1 George Gordon Byron, *Childe Harold's Pilgrimage*, London, 1812–18, Fourth canto, verses I and III.
2 Ruskin 1853, in Cook and Wedderburn 1910, IX, p.17.
3 Whistler to M. R. Elden, nd. [15/30 April 1880], GUL E61.
4 Whistler to C. A. Howell, 26 Jan 1880, GUL LB 12/39.
5 *World*, 22 May 1878, rp. in Whistler 1890, p.127.
6 Whistler to M. B. Huish, nd. [21/26 Jan 1880], GUL LB3/8.
7 Whistler to H. Whistler, nd. [late Jan/Feb 1880], GUL W681.

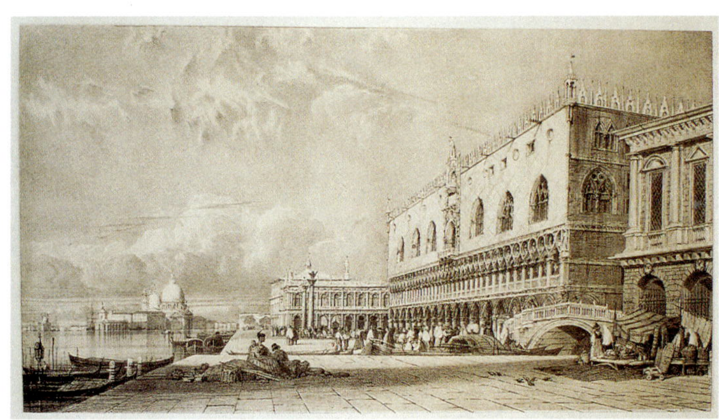

2
E. Lessore after W. Wylde
Le Mole 1833
Lithograph 173 x 311 mm
Plate 7 in 12 *Vues de Venise*
Victoria and Albert Museum

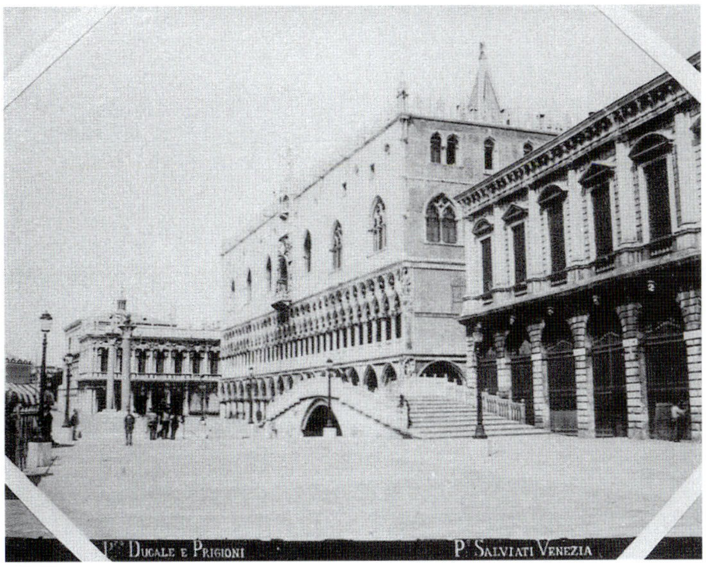

3
P. Salviati
Palazzo Ducale e prigioni 1880s
Photograph 193 x 244 mm
Private Collection

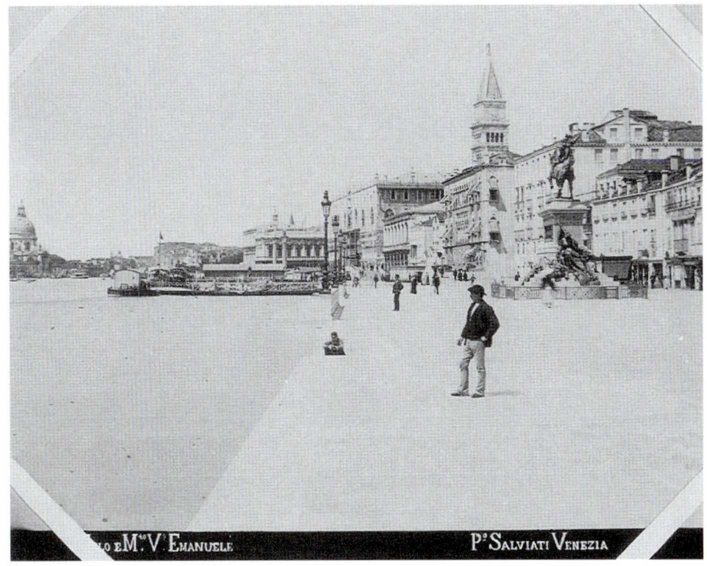

4
P. Salviati
Molo e Monumento Vittorio Emanuele 1880s
Photograph 190 x 244 mm
Private Collection

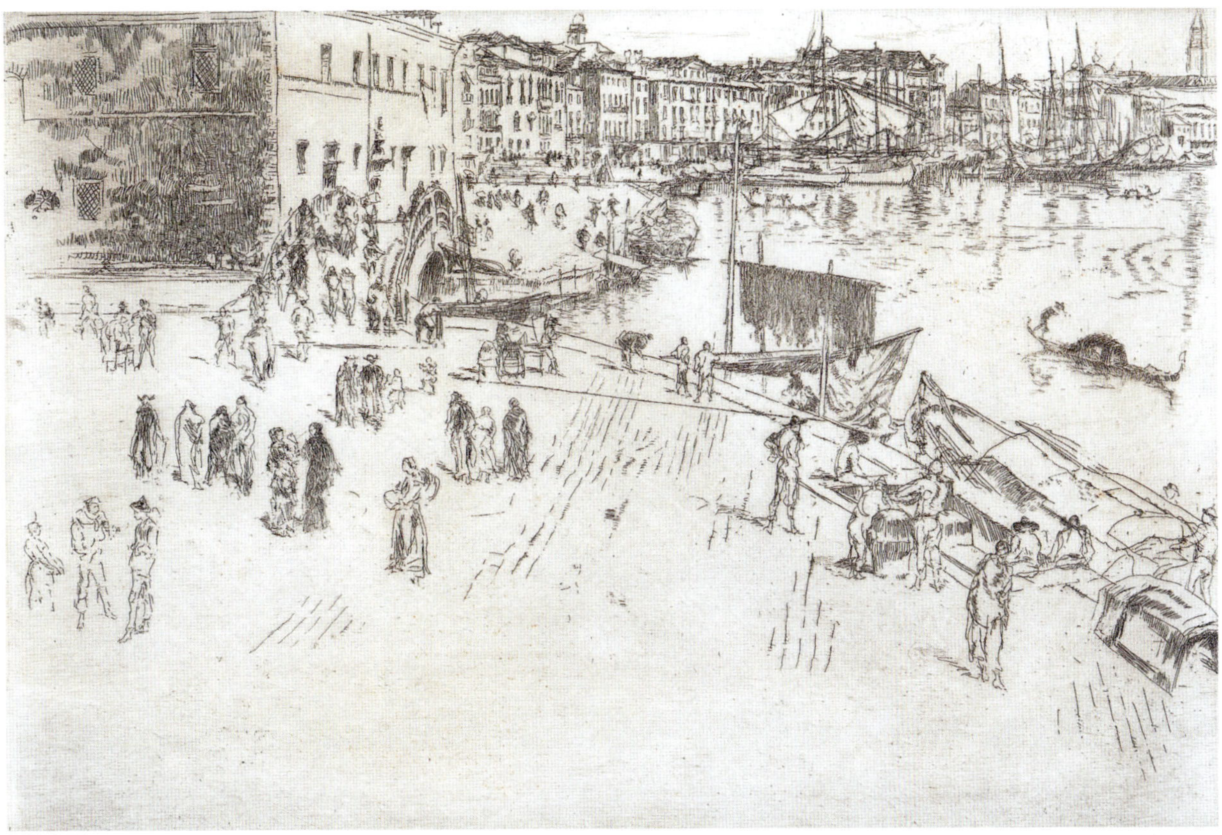

5
James McNeill Whistler
The Riva, No.1
Etching 200 x 295 mm
Hunterian Art Gallery, K.192 III

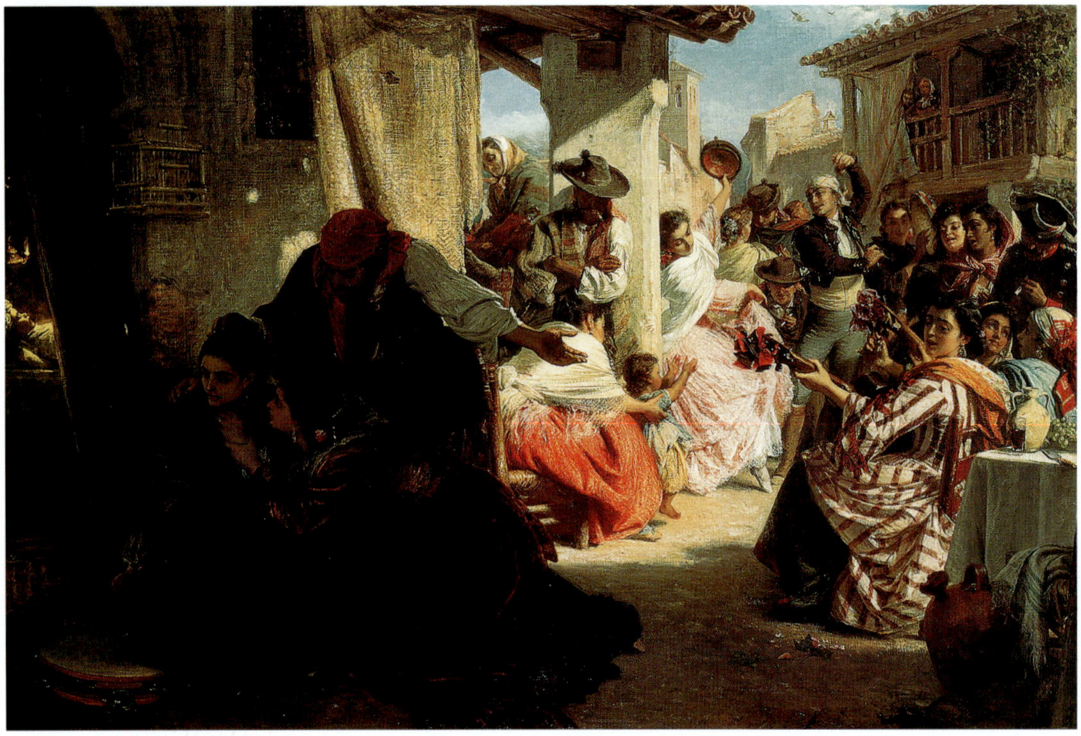

6
J. Phillip
La Gloria: A Spanish Wake 1860-4
Oil 143.6 x 217.2 cm
National Gallery of Scotland

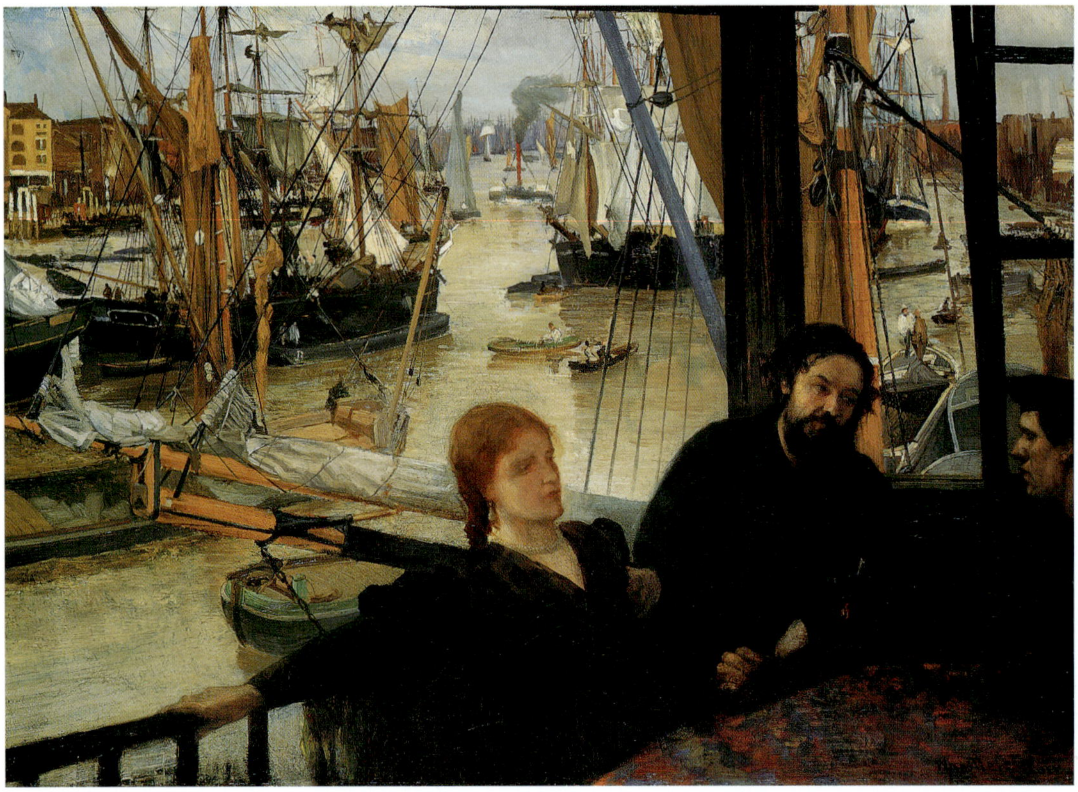

7
James McNeill Whistler
Wapping 1860-1
Oil 71.1 x 101.6 cm
National Gallery of Art, Washington, DC

1 'Arrangement in Black and White': or Why Whistler Went to Venice

In Paris on 18 September 1879 James McNeill Whistler boarded the night train for Venice. The American-born artist, long resident in London, was forty-five years old, and bankrupt. He planned a three-month stay, long enough to complete a set of twelve etchings for the Fine Art Society, for exhibition in Bond Street in December. In the end, it was fourteen months before he returned bringing back over fifty magnificent etchings and a hundred pastels, far in excess of the original commission. Venice proved a turning point in Whistler's life and art. He returned to re-establish himself in the art world of London and Paris, turning disaster and disgrace into profit and prestige.

But the story starts thirty years earlier, in 1849, when Whistler was given a copy of Mrs Jameson's *Memoirs of Early Italian Painters*, and decided to be an artist. Raphael, he wrote, was 'the greatest artist that ever was'.[1] This youthful enthusiasm was reinforced at West Point, as he copied prints after Italian Masters, an Italian view by James Duffield Harding, and an illustration to Alessandro Manzoni's novel, *I Promessi Sposi*.[2] Later he described Raphael as 'the smart young man of his period', but he retained his respect for Italian art.[3]

The importance of being an etcher

The story would have been very different if he had not joined the US Coast Survey in Washington. His accuracy and precision was based on this early training as a draughtsman and etcher. Years as an art student in Paris culminated, in 1858, with his 'French Set' of *Twelve Etchings from Nature*, printed by Auguste Delâtre (fig.8). It was published with the help of Whistler's brother-in-law, the surgeon, etcher and collector, Francis Seymour Haden. The set included figures, land- and city-scapes, uniting Courbet's Realism and Rembrandt's technique. A substantial body of work, calculated to appeal to connoisseurs and collectors, it was presented in a tasteful album which cost far more than individual etchings, so that both dealer and artist would profit.

Whistler's paintings met with mixed reactions; in 1863 *The White Girl* had a *succès de scandale* in the *Salon des Refusés* in Paris, but *Wapping* was well received at the Royal Academy in 1864. On the other hand, his etchings were exhibited and well reviewed in Paris and London and won a gold medal in Amsterdam in 1863.

Etching was a quick, direct method for sketching and hand printing in small numbers, but it was not the first choice for printmakers, dealers or collectors in the mid-nineteenth century. The Royal Academy favoured reproductive engravings, which could convey complex effects and be mechanically printed in large numbers. Haden promoted the status of his own etchings, and etching in general, by lecturing and by exhibiting his Rembrandt etchings alongside his own work. As a result, P. G. Hamerton, whose magazine *The Portfolio* was among the first to promote and publish original etchings, saw Haden, not Whistler, as the leading figure among English etchers.[4] However, Whistler's *Sixteen Etchings of Scenes on the Thames*, or 'Thames Set', started in 1859 and finally published in 1871 (fig.9), confirmed his reputation, and the first catalogue of his etchings, by Ralph Thomas, was published in 1874. By 1878, writing in the *Magazine of Art*, Marcus B. Huish of the Fine Art Society claimed Whistler and Haden as joint leaders of the etching revival.[5]

The Fine Art Society

In the 1870s several London dealers, including the Dudley Gallery, Messrs Dowdeswell and the Fine Art Society,

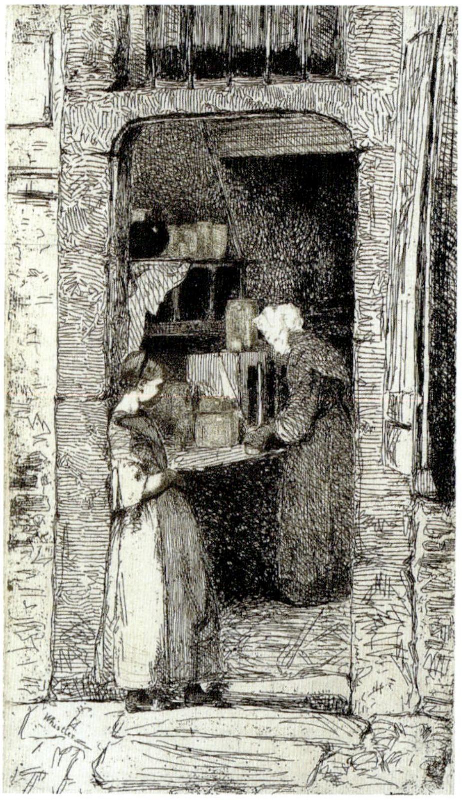

8
James McNeill Whistler
Marchande de Moutarde 1858
Etching 157 x 90 mm
Fine Art Society, K.22 III

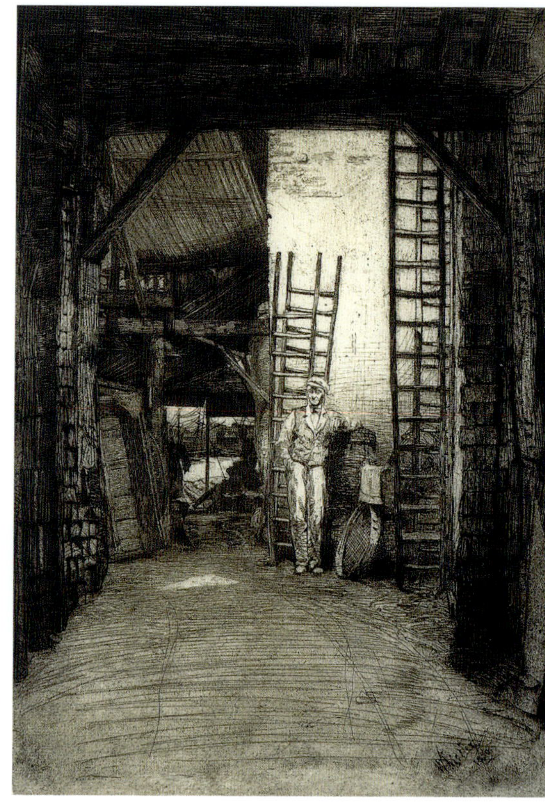

9
James McNeill Whistler
The Limeburner 1859
Etching 252 x 179 mm
Fine Art Society, K.46 II

began to exhibit and promote contemporary etchings. The Fine Art Society, founded in 1876, combined progressive, educational and commercial aims, and employed art historians and critics, including John Ruskin, to write catalogues.[6]

Huish was the managing director, a barrister turned art dealer, with an effective network of professional contacts. Forceful and intelligent, combining wide cultural interests with a flair for business, he was an influential figure in the London art world. He wrote a weekly art column for the *St James' Gazette* and was editor of the *Art Journal* from 1881 to 1893. He was an authority on oriental art, chairman of the Japan Society and author of *Japan and its Art*, and also wrote a significant study of Greek terracotta statuettes.

The Fine Art Society organised exhibitions of the work of artists like Rembrandt, whose reputation was above question, and also published contemporary prints. Their programme included mixed shows, British subjects by British artists such as J. E. Millais, work from 'exotic' locations like Italy and Egypt, and Venetian subjects by both British and foreign artists.[7] Thus, a series of contemporary etchings by an American artist living in London and of an exotic subject, like Venice, could be said to satisfy several aspects of the Fine Art Society's policy.

A set of Venice etchings: the first proposal

In 1876 Whistler decided to secure his reputation as a printmaker by embarking on a new set of etchings, and on 29 July the famous actor Henry Irving became the first subscriber for a set of Venice etchings at a cost of £52 10s. Irving's name, at the head of the list, was probably intended to attract further subscribers. He was followed by Whistler's lawyer, James Anderson Rose. Thomas Sutherland, Chairman of the P&O line and of the London board of the Suez Canal Company, came next. Sutherland also planned to accompany Whistler, but the months passed and he left for Switzerland alone. The accountant Charles J. Singleton was an early subscriber; his mistress Agnes was the sister of Whistler's ex-mistress Joanna Hiffernan. Another subscriber was the American dealer and collector Samuel P. Avery, whose Whistler etchings are now in New York Public Library. He had published the American edition of Thomas's catalogue. Several London print dealers, including Knoedler's and Colnaghi's, subscribed for sets, but were unwilling to publish the complete set.[8]

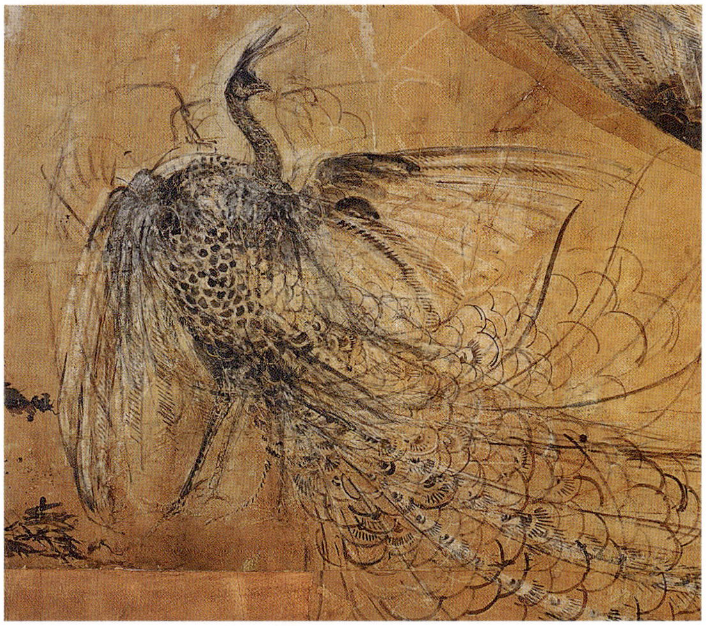

10
James McNeill Whistler
Cartoon of rich and poor peacocks (Detail of left peacock) 1876
Chalk and wash 181 x 389.2 cm
Hunterian Art Gallery

Whistler enlisted his mother to circulate copies of a prospectus among American friends, but the results were disappointing. There was, he complained, 'No rise to the list among the "crème" – filthily poor and stingy – We are disgusted – and disillusioned about all the dear Duchesses.'[9] His patrons were to be found in the professional and manufacturing classes, but few collected prints.

The Peacock Room

The Liverpool ship owner Frederick R. Leyland had commissioned Whistler to work on a decorative scheme for his dining room at 49 Princes Gate, which evolved into the 'Peacock Room', a harmony in blue and gold. Leyland wrote to Whistler on 17 August that he expected Whistler to complete the room and leave for Italy before his return to town. But instead of setting off, as he planned, for Venice with the writer and critic Lionel Robinson, Whistler visited the Leylands at Speke Hall.[10] Among the visitors to the Peacock Room was Edward W. Godwin, architect, designer, and leading figure in the Aesthetic Movement, with his bride, the nineteen-year-old Beatrice Philip, who, after Godwin's death, married Whistler. Having designed opulent sets and costumes based on research in the British Museum for *The Merchant of Venice* at the Prince of Wales Theatre, Godwin was interested in Whistler's Venetian project.[11]

Someone leaked Whistler's plans to the press. The *Academy* reported on 2 September 1876: 'Mr Whistler, who is about to start for Venice, has lately been employed in decorating the dining room of Mr Leyland's house.'[12] But Whistler had far exceeded his commission, and Leyland paid only half of the £2000 Whistler demanded. Nevertheless, Whistler continued to work until well into March of the following year, thus alienating his patron and thwarting his own plans.

The Grosvenor Gallery

By April he had other concerns; the wedding of his brother, Dr William Whistler, to Helen Ionides, on 17 April 1877, was followed by the start of the London art season. Whistler, having abandoned the Royal Academy, was delighted when Sir Coutts and Lady Lindsay established the Grosvenor Gallery. Selected works, carefully lit, hung in an opulent setting; academicians rubbed shoulders with the avant-garde, Frederic Leighton and Alma-Tadema, with the Pre-Raphaelites, Whistler and Albert Moore.

Whistler prepared a substantial contribution to the Grosvenor Gallery's first exhibition in May 1877: eight works tried and tested in previous exhibitions, including portraits of Irving and the philosopher and historian Thomas Carlyle, and his finest Thames *Nocturnes*. The result was not all that he could have hoped. His selection drew Ruskin's attention. Once champion of Turner and the Pre-Raphaelites, Ruskin was newly returned from Venice. In *Fors Clavigera*, his journal for English working men, he attacked the *Nocturnes*, accusing Whistler of 'flinging a pot of paint in the public's face', and Whistler sued him for libel.[13]

Whistler v Ruskin

The trial finally took place on 25 and 26 November 1878, but Ruskin, suffering intermittently from mental illness, could not appear. Whistler's views were widely disseminated by the trial and his influence among younger artists strengthened, but although he won the

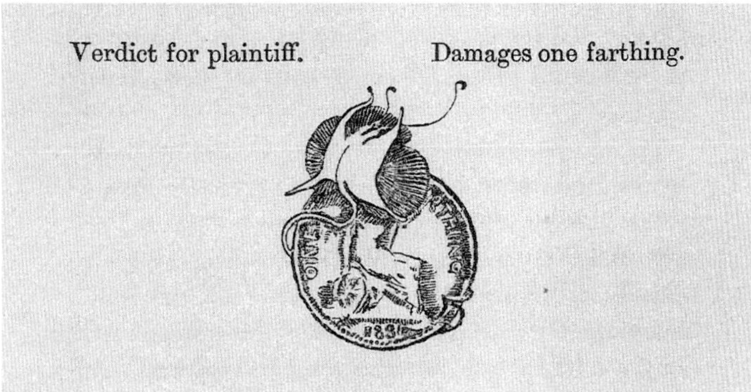

11
James McNeill Whistler
Verdict for plaintiff. Damages one farthing from
The Gentle Art of Making Enemies, London, 1890, p.19

case, he was awarded derisory damages (one farthing) and had no resources to meet costs. 'A nocturne Andante in the direction of the Sandwich Islands', wrote D. G. Rossetti ironically, 'can now alone avert the long-impending Arrangement in Black and White.'[14] What is more, despite divided sympathies, the Fine Art Society organised a public subscription and raised £385 to pay Ruskin's costs. Since Ruskin could perfectly well have afforded to pay, he was not particularly grateful.

Whistler had liberally annotated a copy of Ruskin's *Notes On Some Of The Principal Pictures Exhibited In The Rooms Of The Royal Academy: 1875*, culminating with 'THE END of drivelling immodesty!'[15] However, Ruskin's influence was still considerable. The publication of *St. Mark's Rest* in parts, from 1877 to 1884, and a shortened edition of *The Stones of Venice*, from 1879 to 1881, continued to spread his opinions. Ruskin admired the fusion of artistic, civic and moral values in Byzantine and Gothic buildings, and deplored the degeneracy of later Renaissance and Baroque architecture. In July 1878 Whistler was reading Ruskin's works and over the following year jotted down extracts from his *Guide to the Principal Pictures in the Academy of Venice*. Their views diverged, particularly on the question of the painterly, rather than moral, content of Venetian art. Ruskin, quoted by Whistler, wrote dismissively:

> Enter now the great room with the Veronese at the end of it, for which the painter (quite rightly) was summoned before the Inquisition of State [...] but you must not stop now at this picture, if you are in a hurry, for you can see the like of it, and better, in Paris; [...] And now, if you are yet unfatigued, you had better go back into the great room, and give thorough examination to the wonderful painting, as such, in the great Veronese, considering what all its shows & dexterities at last came to, and reading before it, his examination concerning it.[16]

It was the Roman Inquisition which, on 8 July 1573, examined Veronese on his substitution of a dog for Mary Magdalen in the *Feast in the House of Levi*. The idea that painterly quality was less important than historical context was anathema to Whistler. Another paragraph Whistler selected concerned the moral content of art: 'I found that I had never got to the roots of the moral power of the Venetians & that they needed still another & a very stern course of study [...]'.[17]

Whistler's public position was diametrically opposed to Ruskin's: 'Art should be independent of all clap-trap – should stand alone, and appeal to the artistic sense of eye or ear, without confounding this with emotions entirely foreign to it, as devotion, pity, love, patriotism, and the like', Whistler wrote in May 1878.[18] It is possible that reading Ruskin's didactic writings stimulated Whistler to record his own vision of Venice and to see Venetian art *in situ*.

The second proposal: 'a set of twelve etchings'

This was hopeless without money, yet Whistler faced rising costs (£2750 and up) for his new house, the 'White House' designed by Godwin, and unpaid bills for everything from coals to caviare. In October his friend, the enterprising Charles Augustus Howell, resurrected the Venetian project and printed a proposal for 'a set of Twelve etchings', *Venice by Whistler*, which 'will appear in the course of the next two months.' There was to be an edition of a hundred, at fifty guineas the set. £5250, less percentages due to Howell and dealers, would have defrayed Whistler's debts. The banker W. C. Alexander agreed to take a set and subscribers were collected right up to December when the Fine Art Society committed itself to one set, by which time the sum promised amounted to £693.[19]

In April 1878 Whistler prepared six canvasses for exhibition; 'the most important thing', he wrote to his lawyer, 'is that I should appear well at the Grosvenor'.[20] Unfortunately, the pictures were not particularly well received. Collectors were wary, commissions few, and he failed to complete those he had. Still thinking of Italy, he asked one patron, A. J. Chapman, 'If I go to Venice would you like to go in for a Nocturne of the Gondola kind?'[21]

The ingenious Howell and his mistress, the artist Rosa Corder, encouraged Whistler to print from his old copper-plates, 'and, with the plates under my fingers, I felt all the old love of it come back'.[22] He borrowed a large printing press; 'and soon I trust I shall turn some of my copper into gold! – Ultimately I hope to get together sufficient to go to Venice with, and then I might come back in about six weeks with a sum large enough to pay off nearly everything and find myself quite out of difficulty at last!'[23]

The Adam and Eve, Old Chelsea (K.175), published by Messrs Hogarth and Son, is full of graphic, almost photographic, detail. This sort of subject, said Huish, appealed 'to many who like a church or old houses'.[24] He opted for *Little Putney* (K.179) and *Fulham* (K.182), paying eighty guineas for the copperplate and twenty signed proofs of *Fulham*. A professional printer, Frederick Goulding, was to complete an edition of fifty, but sales were slow and, with etchings selling for between one and ten guineas, profits were pitiful. Seeking other outlets, Whistler sent recent etchings to the Grosvenor Gallery and Royal Academy. It was the first time he had exhibited at the Academy since 1872 and it was to be the last. But promoting etchings had little immediate effect on his disastrous financial position.

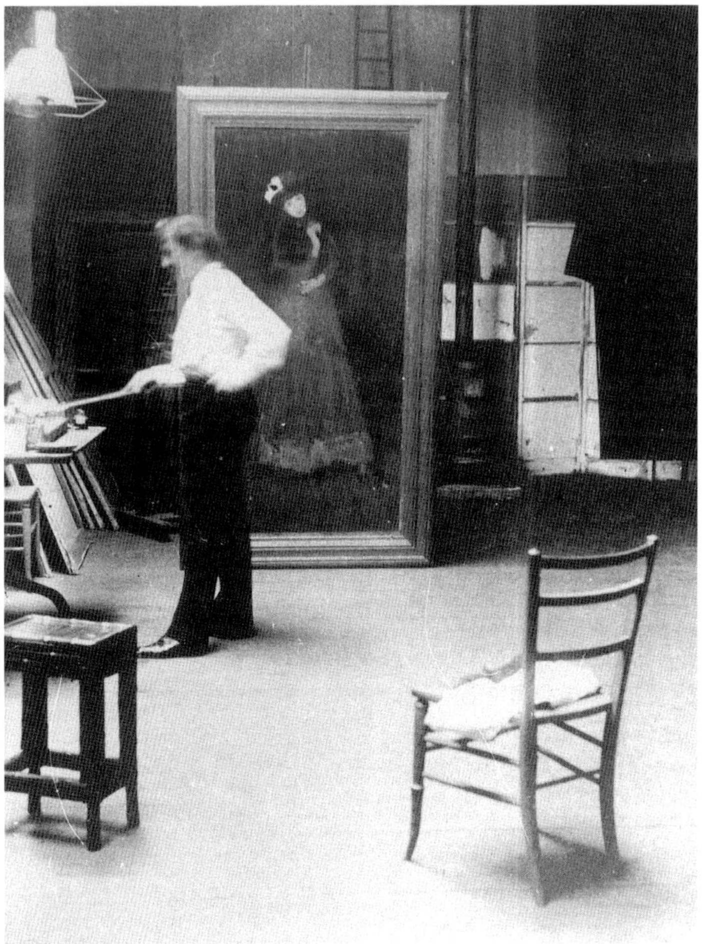

12
Whistler painting Maud Franklin 1876/9
Photograph
Glasgow University Library

Bankruptcy

The domestic situation compounded the problem. Maud Franklin, the model for some of his finest portraits, had lived with him since the early seventies. A girl with fair complexion and dark red hair, she had become an elegant woman and a sympathetic model. His family disapproved of the liaison and she was not received in Society, though welcome among fellow artists. She bore him a daughter on 13 February 1879, just as Whistler absorbed the financial implications of the Ruskin trial. Whistler's first reaction was flight, leaving Maud to cope alone; but the child was sent to foster parents, while Maud and Whistler were reunited.

By this time it was too late to retrieve their fortunes. On 8 May 1879 Whistler was declared insolvent, with debts of £4500. The bailiffs moved in. All his possessions were to go to auction and the White House sold.

The Fine Art Society to the rescue

Whistler was eager to walk away from the chaos of his affairs, and the Fine Art Society offered an escape route. Huish's second-in-command was Ernest Brown who, before joining the Fine Art Society, was working for *The Portfolio* when they published *Billingsgate* (K.47) in January 1878. Brown recalled that before his bankruptcy, Whistler 'spoke of the work at Venice he had long wanted to do', and Brown persuaded the directors to invest in him.[25] With an eye to publicity Whistler's plans were again 'leaked' to the press:

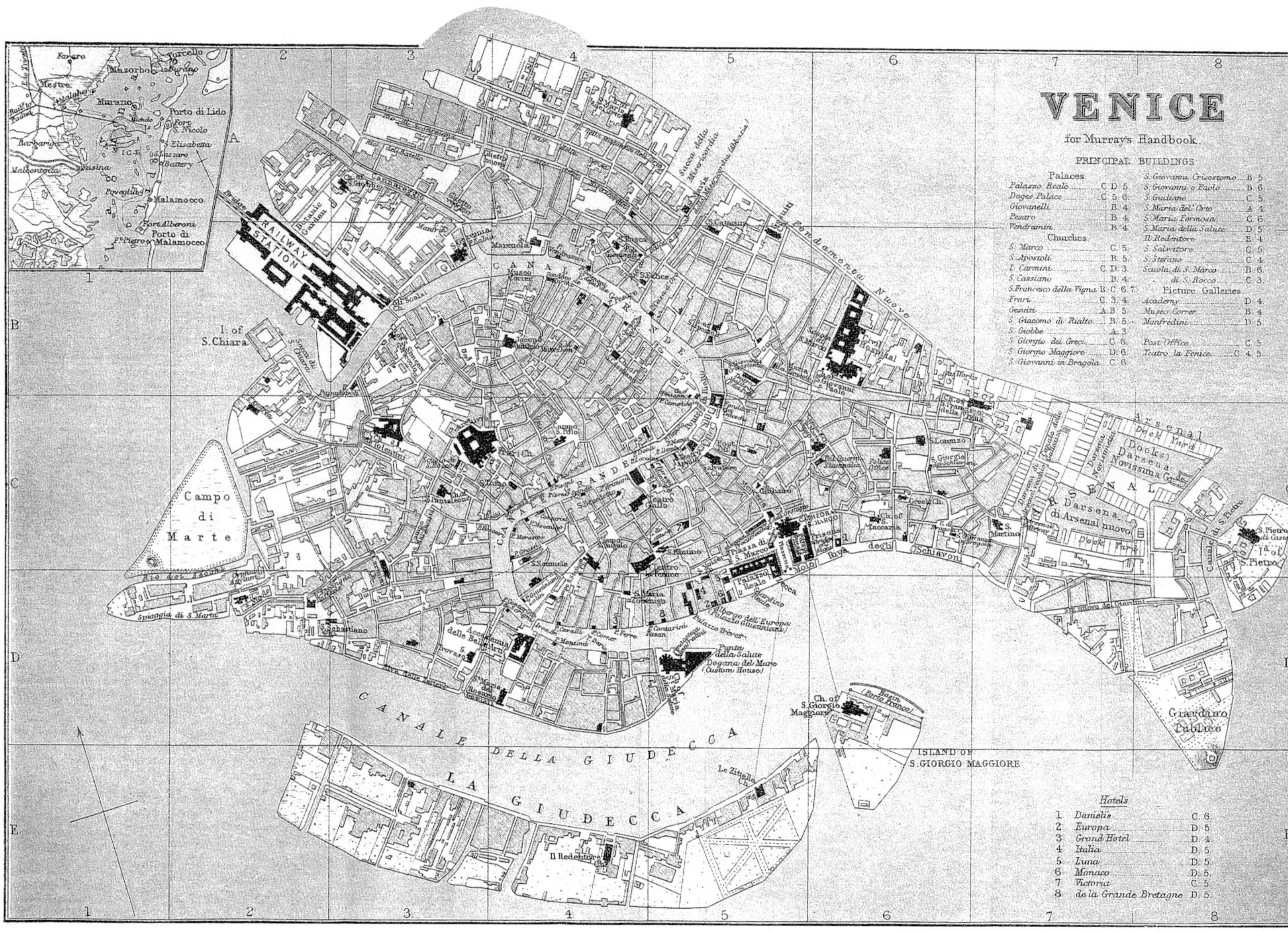

15
Map of Venice in John Murray's
Handbook for Northern Italy, London, 1876
186 x 270 mm
Mitchell Library, Glasgow

2 Whistler in Venice

At first Whistler disliked Italy. He was homesick: 'I begin rather to wish myself back in my own lovely London fogs!' he told his sister-in-law, 'They are lovely those fogs – and I am their painter! [...] I am bored to death after a certain time away from Piccadilly! – I pine for Pall Mall and I long for a hansom!'[1]

He could afford only the cheapest of lodgings. When Maud joined him he was living in Dorsoduro, on the Rio di San Barnaba, which runs west from the Ca' Rezzonico on the Grand Canal. Venice is divided into six areas, or *sestieri*. On the San Marco side of the Grand Canal are Castello, San Marco and Cannaregio. At first Whistler worked mainly in the western *sestieri*, in San Polo, Santa Croce and Dorsoduro. A favourite haunt was the Campo Santa Margarita (figs 17 and 18), with its busy market stalls and cheap cafés. An American artist, Ross Turner, remembered seeing Whistler in 'a small house with a small garden in front near the Frari [...] and a large [canvas], with a big gondolier sketched on it, stood by the door'.[2] The painting was abandoned after the model fell ill. Nearby, Whistler drew *Under the Frari* (fig.16), a view of the bell tower of Santa Maria Gloriosa dei Frari from the Ponte San Rocco.

Another American, Ralph Curtis, thought Whistler had a second floor studio in the massive Palazzo Rezzonico on the Grand Canal.[3] Many artists, including John Singer Sargent, rented studios there. Sargent, born in Florence of American parents, visited Venice annually from 1874 and arrived in September 1880 shortly before Whistler's departure. Whistler may have taken a studio in this Palazzo, but no portraits including it, or pictures of the interior or of the view, have survived. His beautiful pastel *The Palace in Rags* (fig.20) shows a room also painted by Sargent (fig.19), but it is not in the Palazzo Rezzonico.[4] It has, however, a similar decayed grandeur, which appealed to Whistler in his poverty-stricken exile.

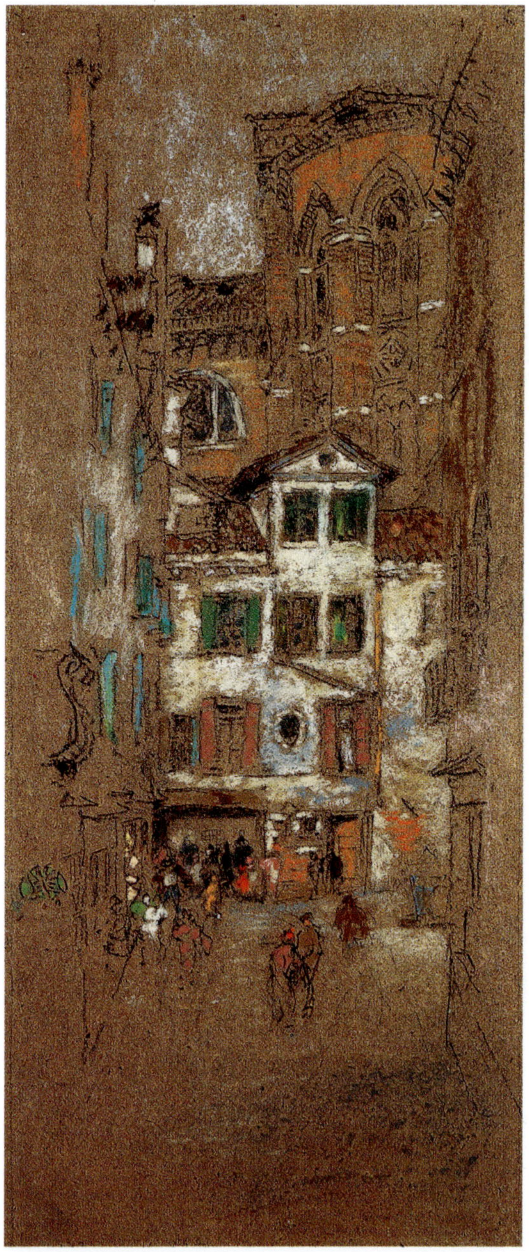

16
James McNeill Whistler
Under the Frari
Pastel 298 x 130 mm
Private Collection, M.771

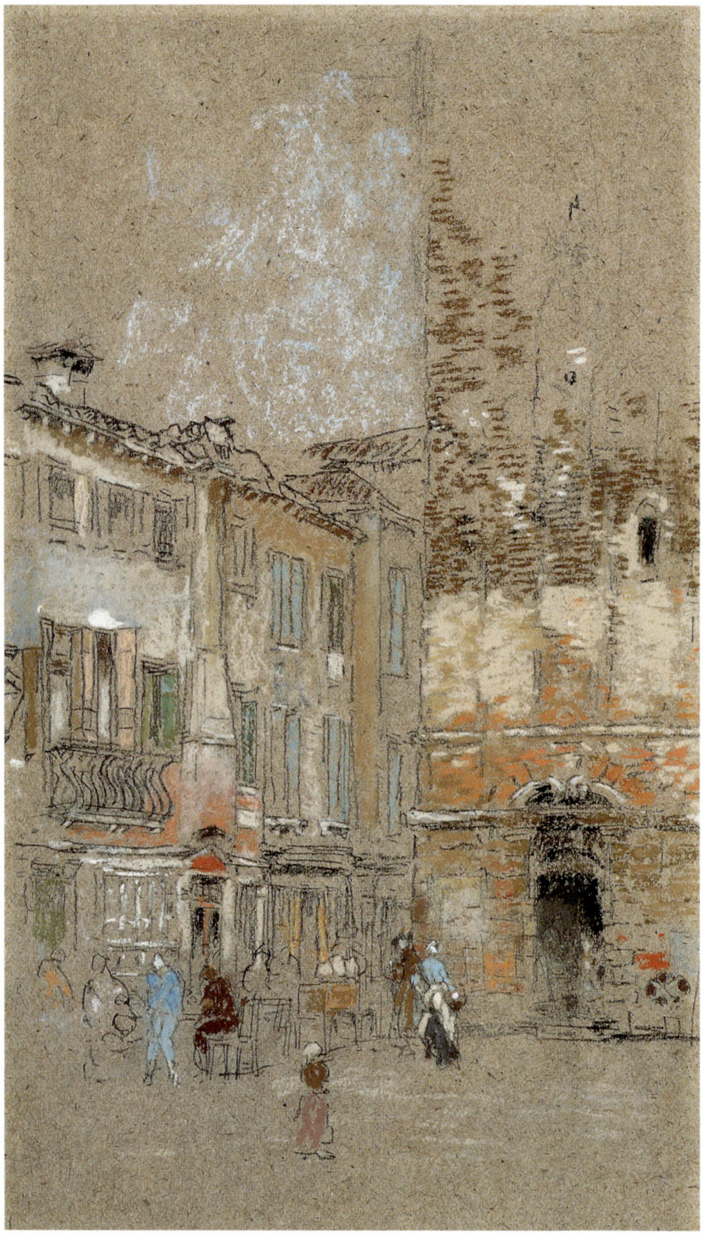

17
James McNeill Whistler
Campanile Santa Margarita
Pastel 299 x 181 mm
Addison Gallery of American Art,
Phillips Academy, Andover, M.773

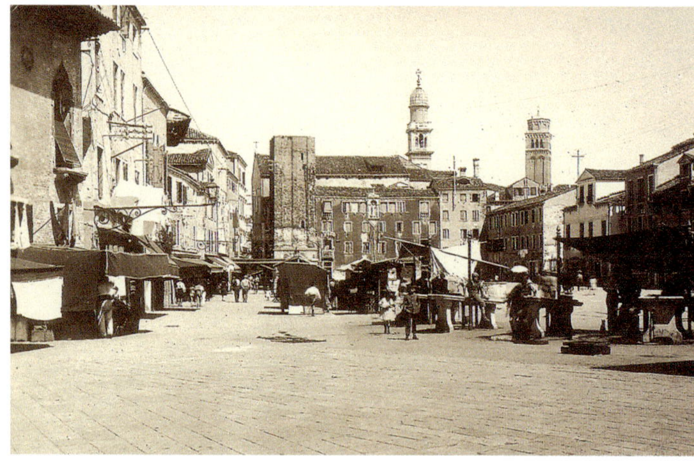

18
Campo Santa Margarita, Dorsoduro 1890s
Archivio Filippi
Photograph

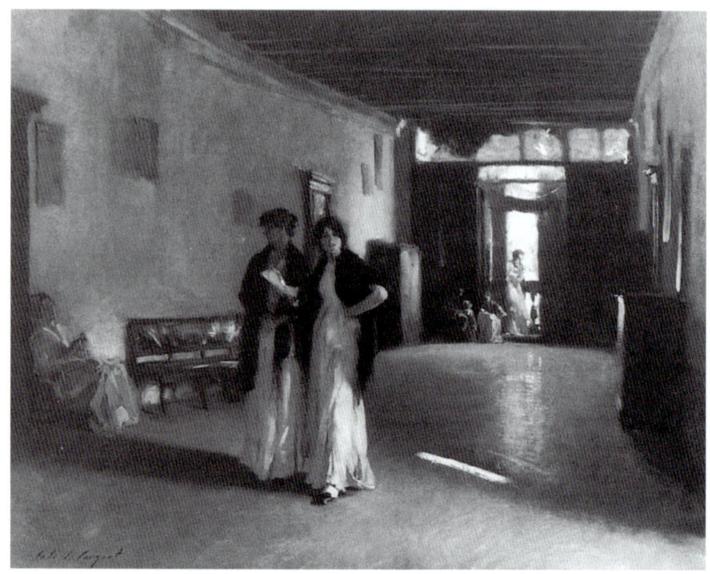

19
J. S. Sargent
Venetian Interior c.1880–2
Oil 68.6 x 86.4 cm
Carnegie Museum of Art

Whistler shared his feelings with only two people – his sister-in-law Nellie Whistler and his older sister Deborah Haden. His first letter home to Deborah is rueful: 'frozen I am and certainly feel that I also should live in conservatories with flowers and pines and the other luxuries that one is naturally meant for – the most charming people to say delightful things to you and in every way this absurd and ridiculous poverty effaced!'[5]

It was perhaps no coincidence that one of Whistler's first subjects was *The Beggars* (figs 21 and 22). At first Whistler etched a young woman and a child, who must have been hired as models since the setting was a tiny unfrequented courtyard off the Campo Santa Margarita. It can be read as a contemporary genre subject, peopled by three distinct 'types' of Venetian characters: ragged beggars, a romantic and slightly sinister man in broad-brimmed hat

20
James McNeill Whistler
The Palace in Rags
Pastel 280 x 165 mm
Private Collection, M.770

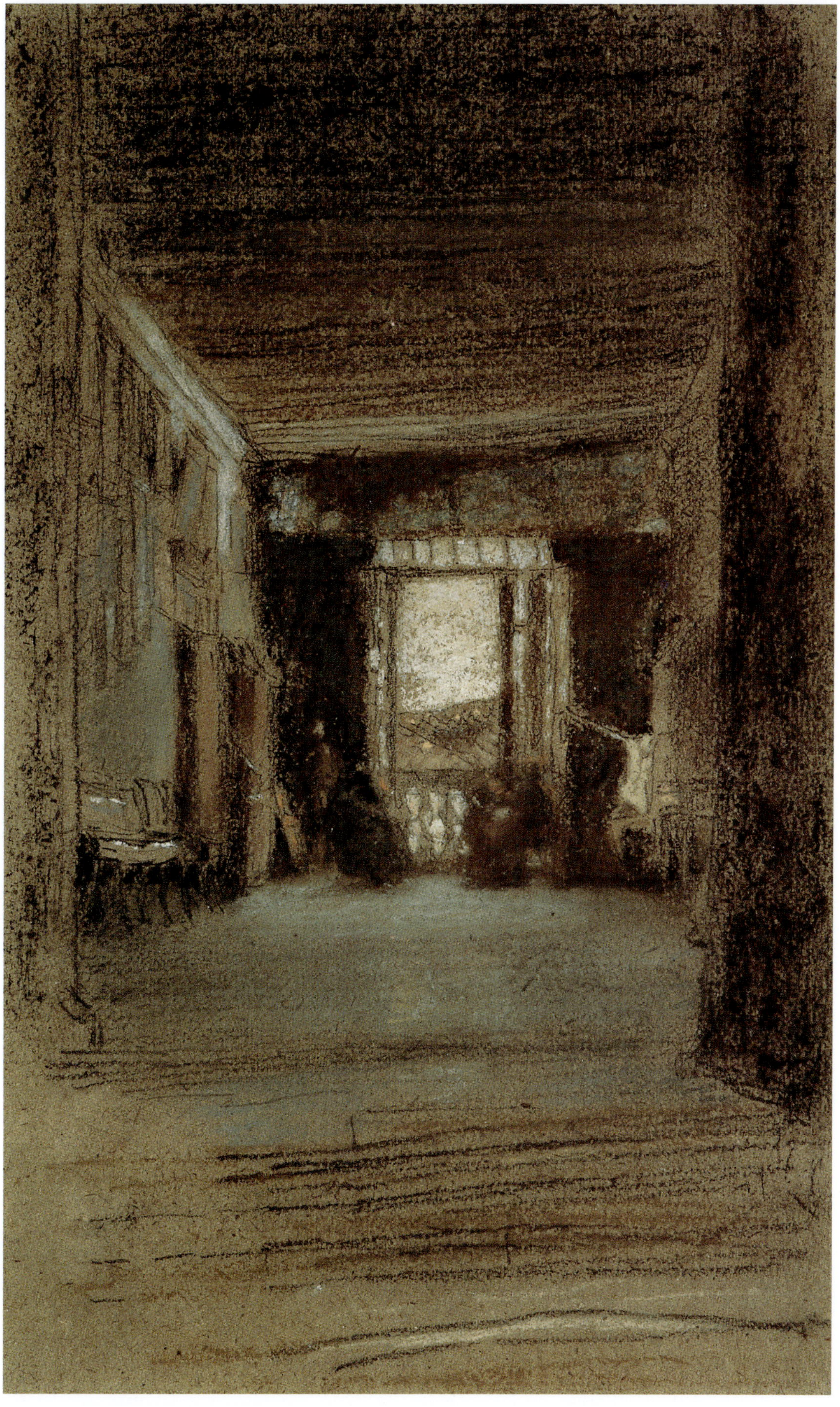

22
James McNeill Whistler
The Beggars
Etching 305 x 211 mm
Freer Gallery of Art, K.194
(first state)

21
James McNeill Whistler
The Beggars
Etching 304 x 208 mm
Freer Gallery of Art, K.194 (second state)

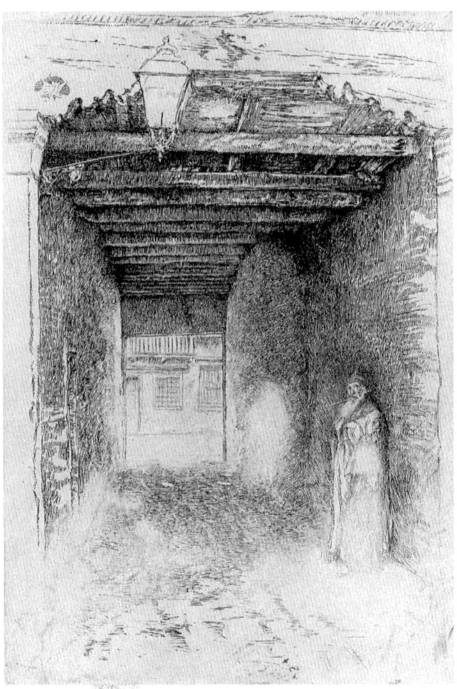

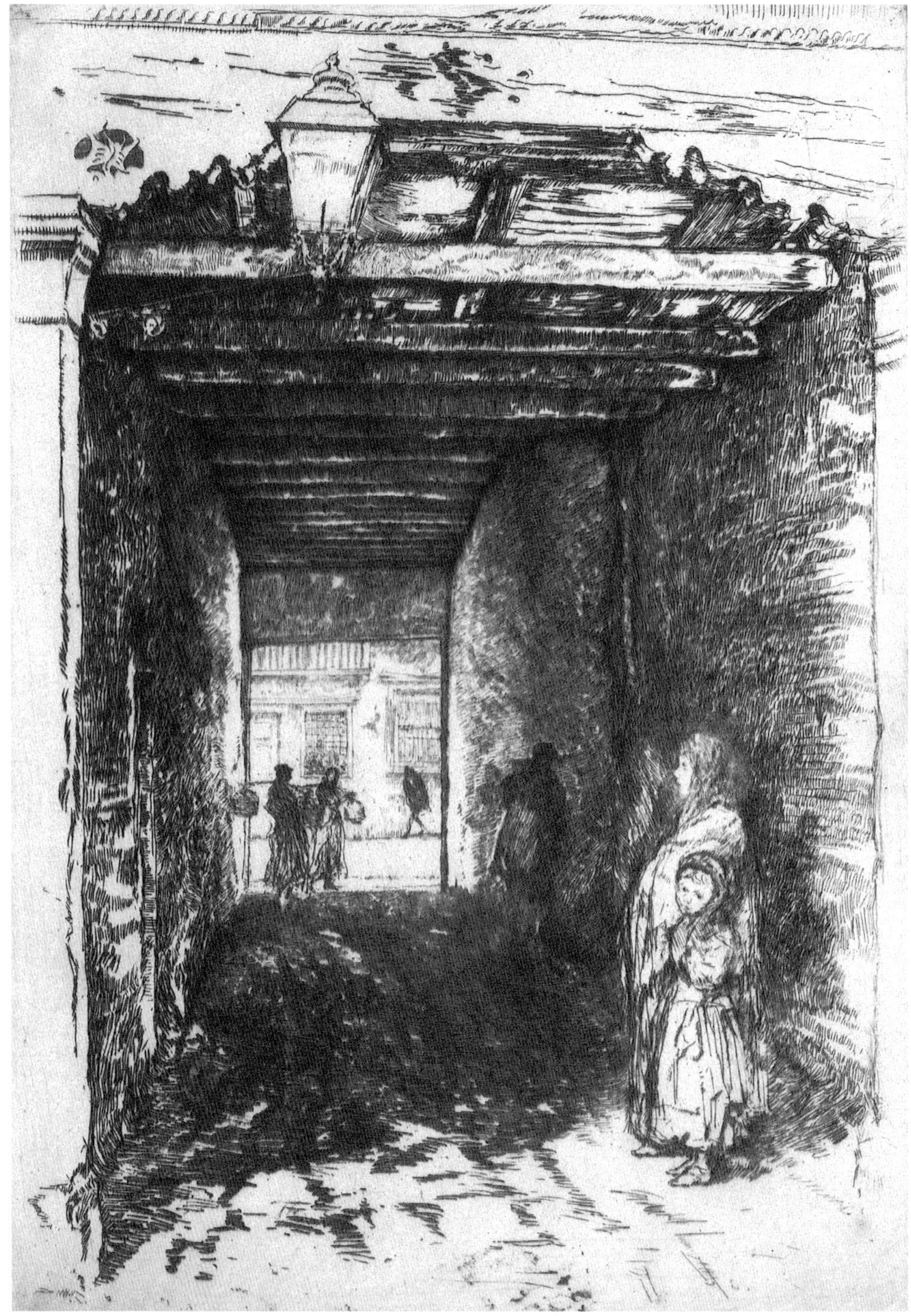

and cloak, half-hidden in a dark passageway or *sotto-portico*, and two young women carrying water, with the bright *campo* beyond. Contrasts of light and texture are emphasised by the broken, intricately cross-hatched lines with which Whistler drew the beggars and decaying bricks and beams, and the light wiry lines that depict the women. Whistler later changed the young woman to an old man, and then to an old woman with a waif-like child by her side, but the subject's sentimental appeal was denied by its treatment and by the attitude of the beggars, whose dispassionate gaze rejected sympathy[6].

Venetian Genre Painting

Whistler's attempt at genre must be seen against the background of his commission, which required twelve recognisable Venetian subjects, and of the current taste for such genre subjects. In Venice there was a large international community of genre painters and Whistler met many of them. There was Franz Léo Ruben from Munich, Martin Rico y Ortega from Spain, Eugen de Blaas, then a professor at the Accademia in Venice, a young local artist, Ettore Tito, and the Russian, Alexander Nikoljewitsch Wolkoff-Mouromtzoff (also known as Roussoff).[7] They painted Venetians, ancient and modern, wearing picturesque clothes and engaged in leisurely activities in generic Venetian settings (fig.23). Whistler's lost painting of a 'swell Gondolier'[8] could have showed just such a romantic figure.

The British painters included a young artist from Nottingham, William H. Jobbins, who lent his studio to Whistler, despite his objections to Whistler's liaison with Maud Franklin.[9] William Logsdail, who arrived in Venice while Whistler was there in 1880, stayed until 1900. By 1883 he had completed *The Piazza, Venice*, a highly coloured *tour de force*, and *Eve of the Regatta*, a mildly humorous conversation piece.[10] Less vulgar are Luke Fildes' Venetian paintings, which were brighter in mood and colour than his London subjects. They were popular in Britain and sold as engravings, although the engraved lines, with their mechanical depiction of textures and tones, lacked the expressiveness of etching. Whistler's *The Beggars* and Fildes' *The Venetian Fruit Seller* (fig.24) show a common interest in unembellished Venetian life, in compositions of stark simplicity.

Fildes, who first visited Venice in 1874, persuaded his brother-in-law, Henry Woods of Warrington, to visit Venice in 1876. Woods exhibited his first Venetian genre painting at the Royal Academy in 1877, and lived in Venice from 1878 until his death in 1921. He sent letters back to Fildes reporting unfavourably on Whistler's activities in Venice. Woods complained that Whistler borrowed 'money from everybody, and from some who can ill afford to spare it', and indeed, Whistler repaid sixty lire to Woods just before leaving Venice.[11] Woods, however, was delighted to accept Whistler's Sunday 'breakfasts' and the hospitality of the American Consulate.

The American expatriates

John Harris, who was American Consul from 1870 until his death in 1881, had a first floor apartment at 2727 San Maurizio, looking out on the Grand Canal. Whistler reassured his mother, 'Mrs Harris the wife of the American Consul has been very charming – always asking me to her house and presenting me to all her best acquaintances –' and furthermore, the painter William Graham, had, he assured her, been 'most courteous and persistent in his good services'.[12]

In midwinter, Whistler fell ill, having endured, as he told Graham, 'too many Sottoporticos for my health!'[13] Graham brought a doctor; the patient was recalcitrant, but recovered. Graham also lent Whistler his studio and canvasses, invited him to life-drawing sessions, and introduced him to a West Point Colonel who wanted a portrait of his son.[14] Whistler remembered his kindness, and years later recommended Graham's work to the Fine Art Society: 'no one has such an Artist's understanding of the beauties of Venice' he wrote, 'and you will find a freshness and delicacy in his paintings that with your wise handling ought not to prevent their selling as well as Roussoff's that contended with no such difficulty!'[15]

The Consulate provided a focus for expatriates, but the real leader of American society was Mrs Katharine De Kay Bronson. Whistler was a distant relation, his older brother George having married Julia De Kay Winans. The Bronsons, wrote Whistler, were 'most amiable and nice,' and Mrs Bronson 'the most generous woman possible'.[16] Arthur, Katharine and their daughter Edith Bronson, had settled in 1876 in the Ca' Alvisi, a modest palace with a magnificent position on the Grand Canal opposite Santa Maria della Salute. 'Venice is only really known in all its fairy perfection to the privileged who may be permitted to gaze from Mrs Bronson's balcony. How simply lovely it must be at this moment!', wrote Whistler later.[17] Browning, Henry James, and Sargent were among the guests. Mrs Bronson's house was 'the open rendezvous for the rich and the poor – the famous and the famished', said Ralph Curtis, and Whistler was her 'constant and ever-welcome guest'.[18]

Ralph was the son of Daniel Curtis (Daniel had left Boston after assaulting a judge and so sympathised with Whistler's litigious experiences). Daniel had settled in Venice with his wife, the daughter of an English admiral, and they first rented and later bought the splendid Palazzo Barbaro on the Grand Canal. Ralph was an accomplished artist, a fellow student and distant relative of Sargent and an admirer of Whistler. The Whistler he knew was dapper, entertaining and self-confident.[19]

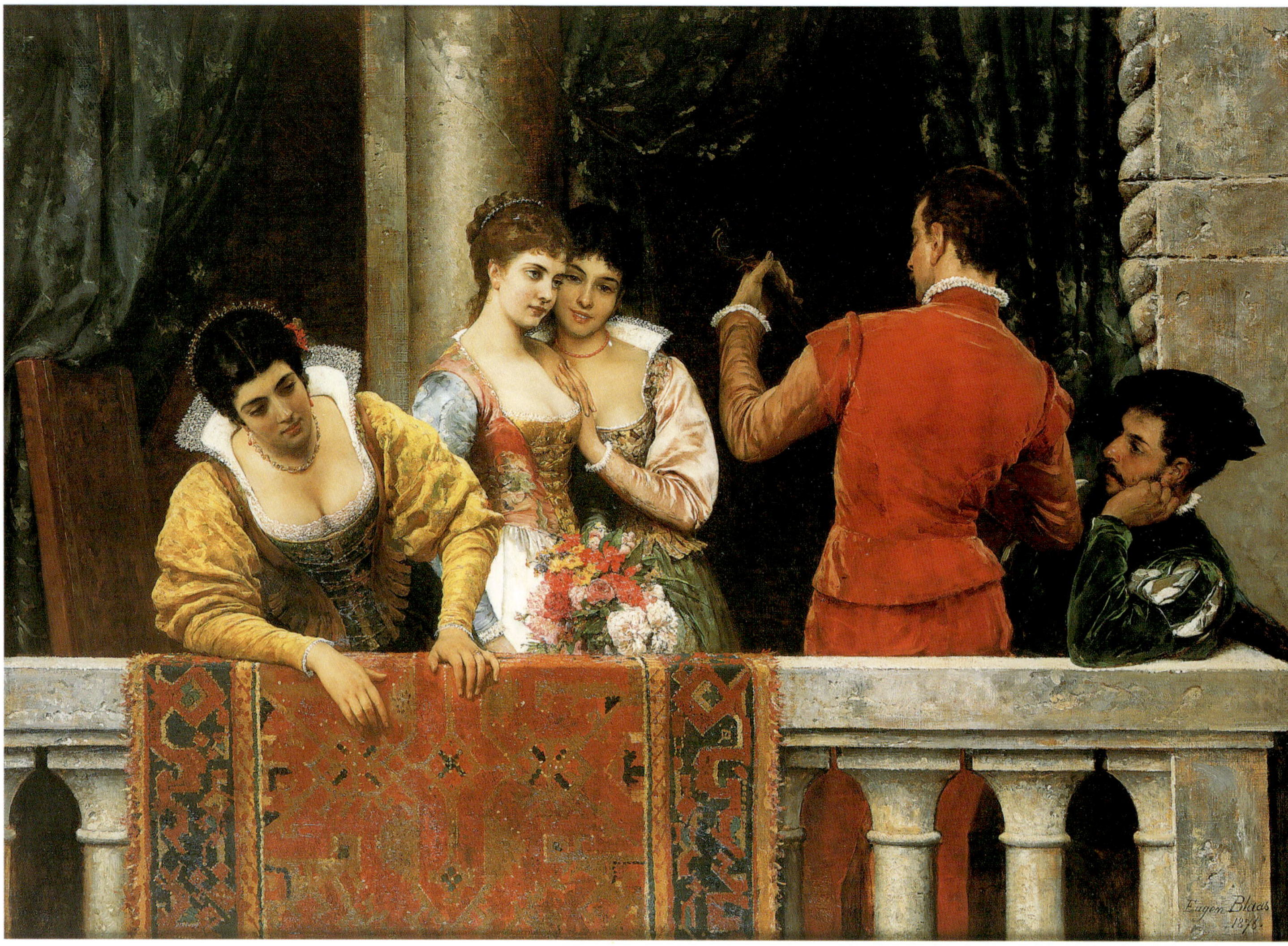

23
Eugen de Blaas
On the Balcony 1877
Oil 124.5 x 174 cm
Private Collection

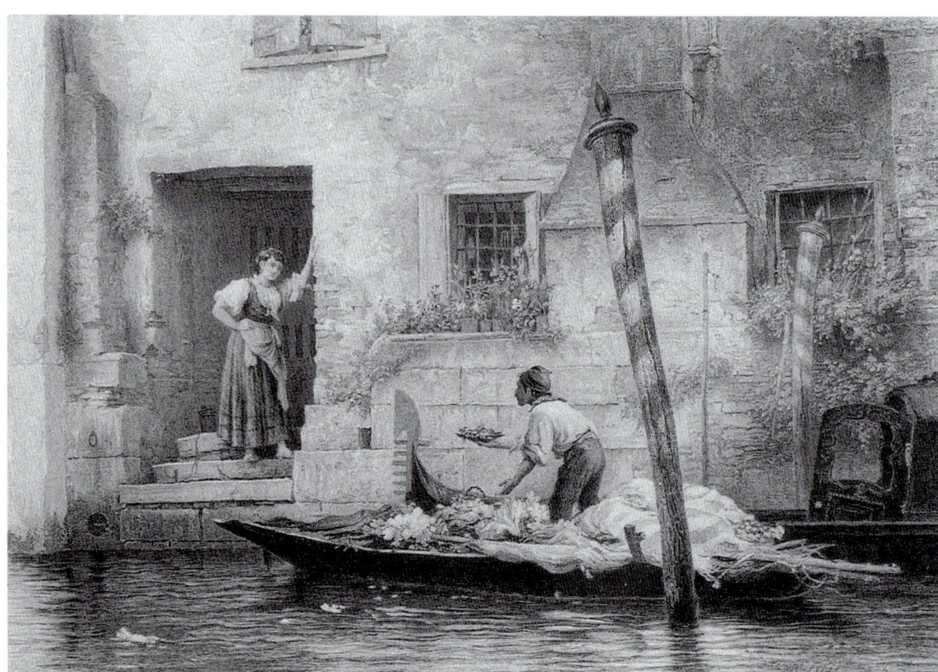

24
T. Brown after Luke Fildes
The Venetian Fruit Seller 1876
Engraving, published by Virtue and Co
154 x 253 mm
Witt Library, Courtauld Institute, London

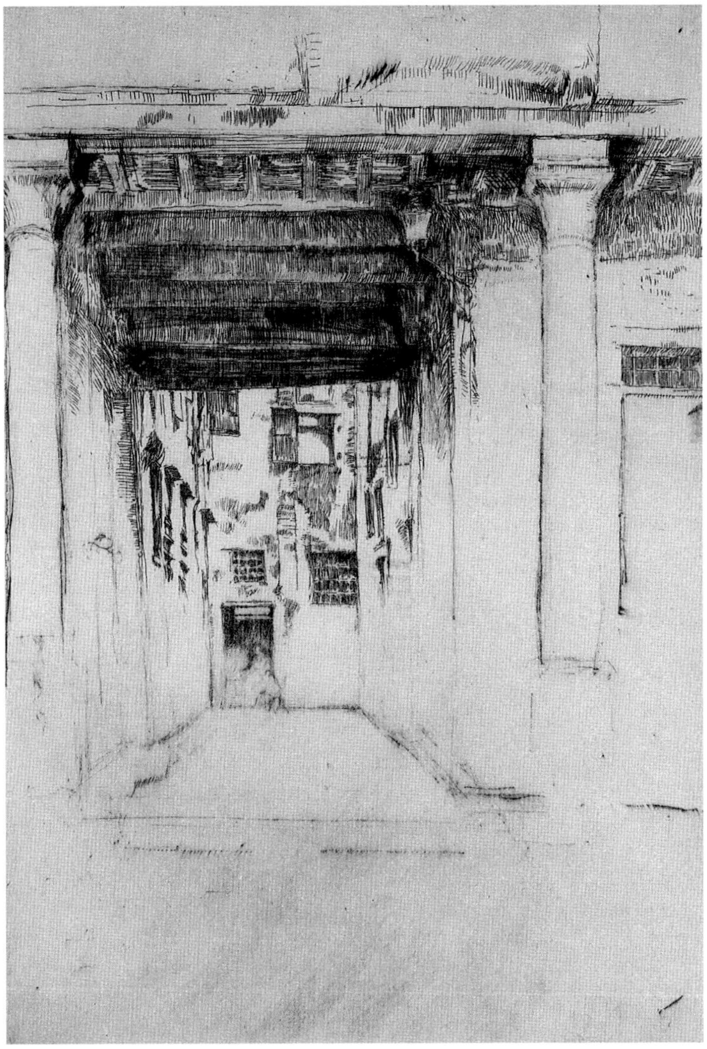

25
James McNeill Whistler
Venetian Court
Etching 291 x 200 mm
Freer Gallery of Art, K.230 II

Progress and problems

In fact Whistler was by no means confident about his progress. The Pennells, Whistler's biographers, suggested that 'the plates were not started for months after he got to Venice' because of Whistler's 'fastidiousness'. Edith Bronson (later Countess Rucellai) remembered: 'he used to say Venice was an impossible place to sit down and sketch in – he always felt "there was something still better round the corner".'[20] Even Whistler admitted, 'You are perfectly bewildered with the entanglement of beautiful things!'[21] Indeed, one winter evening he strayed into a courtyard so absolutely beautiful that it was impossible for him to draw it. *Venetian Court*, dated 1879, one of his earliest etchings, was never completed, perhaps because of this psychological block (fig.25).

The early drawings show that he ranged far and wide in search of subjects. 'We are just off to the Lido', wrote Maud on 23 October 1879, 'Oh isnt this a lovely place and such a lovely day too.'[22] *The Cemetery* (M.738) and *Campanile at Lido* (M.737), were drawn on day trips across the lagoon, to the cemetery island of San Michele in Isola and the church of Santa Maria Elisabetta on the Lido.

Everyone assumed that Whistler's twelve etchings would take three months at most, but December came and went and he had not returned. He wrote to Huish:

> The "Venice" my dear Mr Huish will be superb [...] only I can't fight against the Gods – with whom I am generally a favorite – and not come to grief – so that now – at this very moment – I am an invalid & a prisoner – because I rashly thought I might hasten matters by standing in the snow with a plate in my hand and an icicle on the end of my nose.[23]

For all his air of bravado Whistler was suffering from depression. 'I have been working too hard', he told Nellie in his next letter; 'I am just a little down on my back for the moment [...] No winter like this known for at least thirty years and at last I am getting very much depressed'.[24] Towards the end of January, 'The 57th day of hard unrelenting frost! Venetian method of counting', Whistler told the Fine Art Society, 'you might as well have proposed to etch on a block of Wenham Lake as to have done anything with a copper plate that involves holding it!'[25] Unable to etch in the bitter cold, he turned to another medium, pastel. Woods remembered Whistler for 'his remarkable energy – and actual suffering – when doing those beautiful pastels, nearly all done during the coldest winter I have known in Venice, and mostly towards evening, when the cold is bitterest! He soon found out the beautiful quality of colour there is here before sunset in winter.'[26]

His pastels were 'totally new and of a brilliancy very different from the customary watercolor' he told the Fine Art Society, 'and will sell – I don't see how they can help it – '.[27] Although they were under no obligation, the Fine Art Society agreed to exhibit these pastels and urged him to return. Their initial subsidy had long run out, but Whistler needed more time and the Fine Art Society, not being left with very much choice, agreed. Huish sent him fifty pounds on 5 February, saying, 'So I hope that now we've met all your wants you will hurry back with all your trophies'.[28]

As the artist later admitted to the Pennells, the Fine Art Society 'were used to artists who agreed to definite terms and kept to the agreement'.[29] Their doubts annoyed him and they heard nothing more for eight months. As the weather improved, so did his spirits, and he was able to work more freely. In March he wrote to his sister-in-law:

> I am worked to death – up in the morning without exageration [sic] by half past six and "at it again" – though let me tell you it is bitterly cold still in the early part of the day – But you see I have been so put back by the ice and snow that I try not to lose a moment now –.[30]

Etchings and pastels alternated as the mood took him, the weather permitted and the subject demanded. 'I am working with the kind of wildness that belongs to the sportsman!', he told Elden.[31] By May he had some sixty pastels, but the etchings were not quite ready and again he postponed his return. There was really no point in returning until the autumn season. Meanwhile the arrival of a band of American artists in May and early June lessened his isolation.

The Duveneck boys

They were led by Frank Duveneck, who was, Henry James said, 'a very good fellow', producing 'remarkably strong

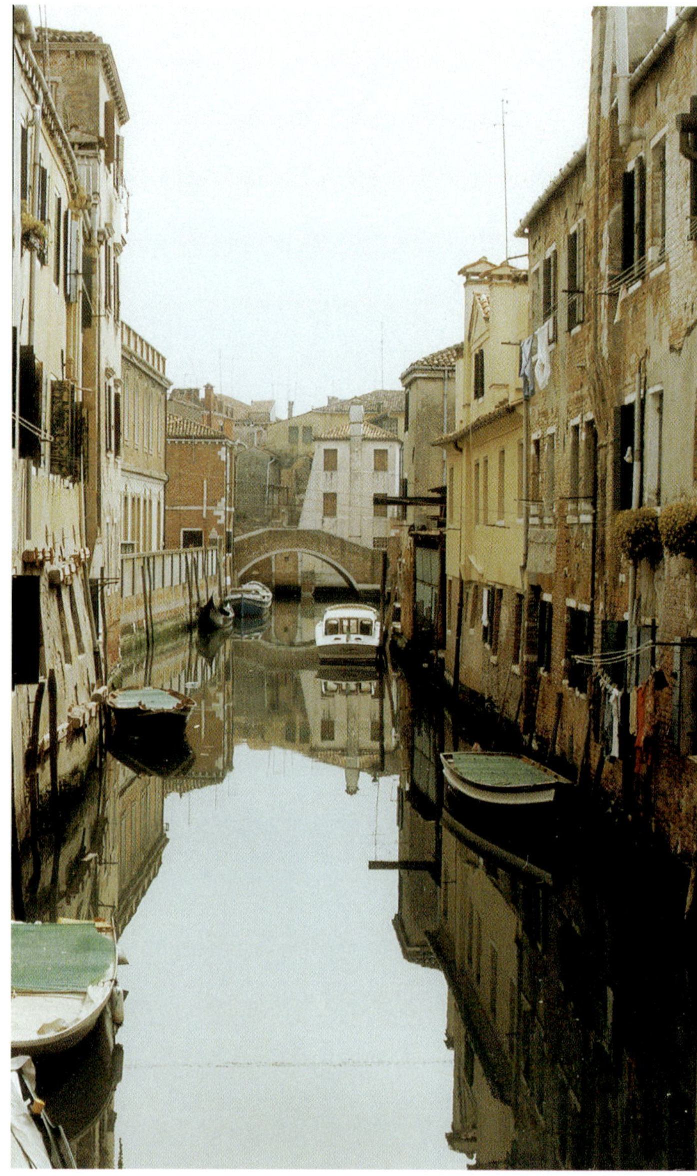

26
The Ponte Sartorio from the Ponte de l'Avogaria
Photograph

and brilliant work'.[32] Born in Covington, Kentucky, Duveneck studied art in Munich and visited Venice for the first time in 1873. He returned in 1877 with his compatriots W. M. Chase and J. H. Twachtman, and in the following year began a successful career as an art teacher.[33]

The Duveneck 'boys' were based in Munich and spent their summers in Florence and Venice. Those in Venice in 1880 included Otto Henry Bacher, Robert Frederick Blum, Theodore M. Wendel, George Edward Hopkins, John White Alexander, Julius Rolshoven, Charles Abel Corwin, and Harper Pennington. In addition Twachtman,

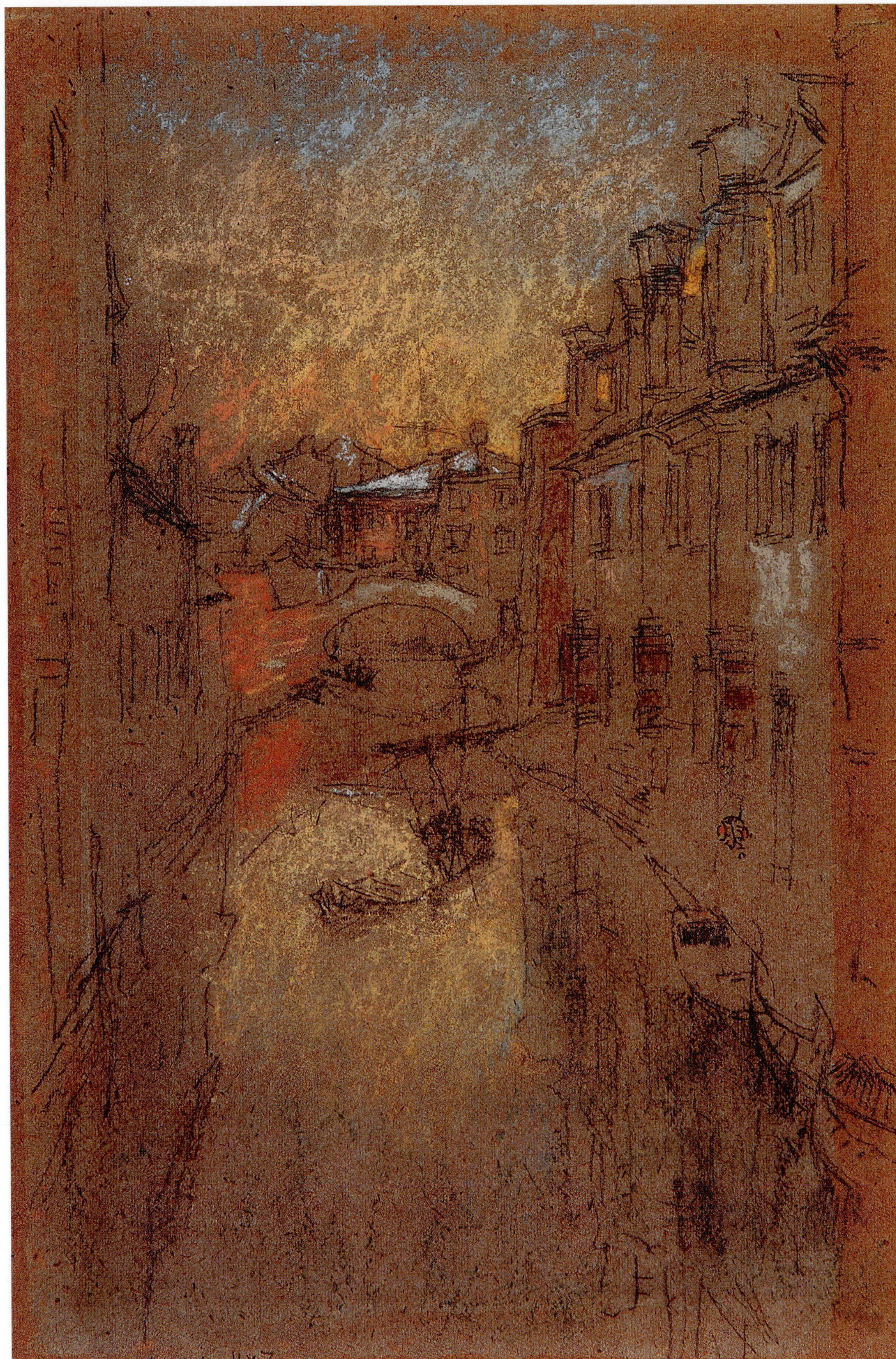

27
James McNeill Whistler
Winter Evening
Pastel 300 x 210 mm
Freer Gallery of Art, M.755

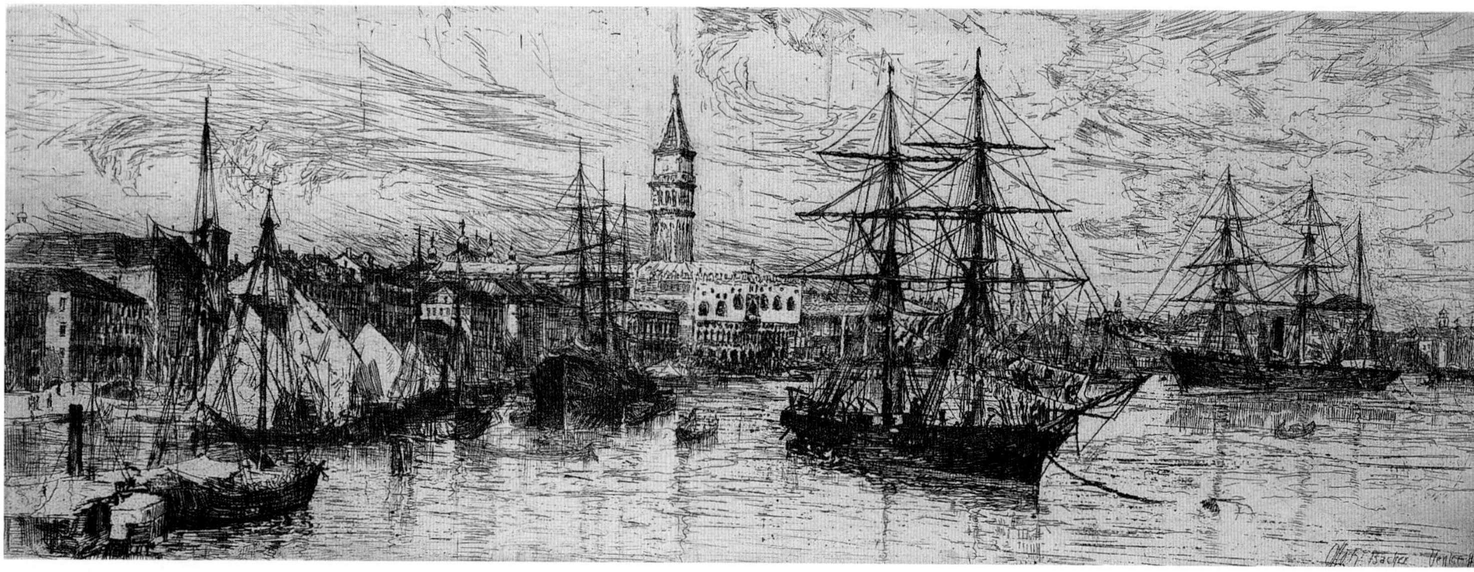

28
Otto Bacher
View from Whistler's window 1880
Etching 130 x 316 mm
Hunterian Art Gallery

whose work, with its delicate tonalism and light colours, is sometimes very like Whistler's, may have met him while *en route* to Florence in late autumn 1880.[34]

Bacher was coming out of the Academy of Fine Arts when he met Whistler with the American Consul. He described Whistler as 'short, thin, and wiry [...] curly black hair and singular white lock, high over his right eye, like a fluffy feather [...] A dark sack-coat almost covered an extremely low turned-down collar, while a narrow black ribbon did service as a tie, the long pennant-like ends of which, flapping about, now and then hit his single eyeglass.'[35] Bacher's memoir, *With Whistler in Venice*, provides a vivid first-hand account of that Venetian summer.

In June, a month after their first meeting, Whistler called on the Duveneck 'boys', who were lodging in the Casa Jankowitz on the Riva San Biagio in Castello, near the Public Gardens. Bacher records:

> He liked our surroundings, was charmed with the vistas from our windows, and asked permission to come and sketch from them [...] A few days later he came and worked from our windows and this he continued to do almost daily. Sometimes he would work from one window with pastels, and from another window would begin another subject for late afternoon work, upon which he worked several afternoons until it was finished [...] About two weeks later he decided to move from his quarters on the opposite side of the Grand Canal near the Church of the Frari, to our house.[36]

The Casa Jankowitz

On 27 June 1880 Robert Blum wrote home from the Casa Jankowitz: 'Whistler is here [...] he is busy making an etching from my window'.[37]

A substantial five-storey building, the Casa Jankowitz looked west down the Riva degli Schiavoni, and south over the lagoon to San Giorgio Maggiore. Whistler took an upper room with two windows looking towards the Doge's palace, San Giorgio, and Santa Maria della Salute (fig.28). Bacher lived in a room underneath. He collected Rembrandt and Whistler etchings and was a proficient etcher. He became both apprentice and collaborator and soon Whistler was calling him 'one of his favourite pupils'.[38] Whistler's progress was hampered by poor facilities. In January he had complained, 'The printing business itself is very primitive and difficult here and on another pilgrimage of the kind I should certainly bring out my own press.'[39] Bacher, therefore, was a godsend. From Munich he had brought good printer's ink and a printing press: 'my press (which was larger than the usual portable press)', said Bacher, 'came in for a good share of attention'.[40] A. G. Reinhardt, another student from Munich, also claimed that Whistler used his printing press.[41]

The students, at first, were rather in awe of Whistler's forceful opinions, but they soon lost their shyness, and at a banquet Whistler spoke 'at such inordinate length about the virtues of America [...] that the rest of the company threatened to do dreadful things to him if he didn't shut up!'[42] Their friendship reinforced his sense of national identity and strengthened his latent anglophobia. The 'boys' were impressed by Whistler's experience and reputation. Whistler did not intrude on their work, but he was prepared to discuss it and to give both advice and judicious praise. A monotype by Corwin shows the intense, introspective and thoughtful worker revealed to fellow artists and students.[43] (fig.29)

John White Alexander met Whistler some time in late May or June, as his wife remembered:

> He met Whistler on a very hot day. John was working in one of the little back canals and very hard at work at what he was doing. Somebody came up to him and put his hand on his shoulder and looked over his shoulder and began talking to him about his work, and it was Whistler. He sat down and practically gave him a criticism on what he was doing. From that time on they were always friends.[44]

Whistler's pastels had a great impact on the students. Their drawings changed from a dark thickly-worked style, influenced by the Spanish artist Mariano Fortuny, through the Naturalism of Bastien-Lepage, to Whistler's lighter, more decorative, topographically accurate approach.[45] As the 'boys' and Whistler worked from the same quarters and shared similar views, resemblances between their art is close. Twachtman drew small pastels of Whistlerian delicacy, showing back canals and views from the Casa Jankowitz. Blum was one of the artists most influenced by Whistler's work, particularly in pastel, and in 1882 he founded a Pastel Club. Jerome Elwell, another American in the Whistler circle, produced pastels that have frequently been mistaken for Whistler's (fig.30), and his signature is uncommonly like Whistler's 'butterfly'.[46]

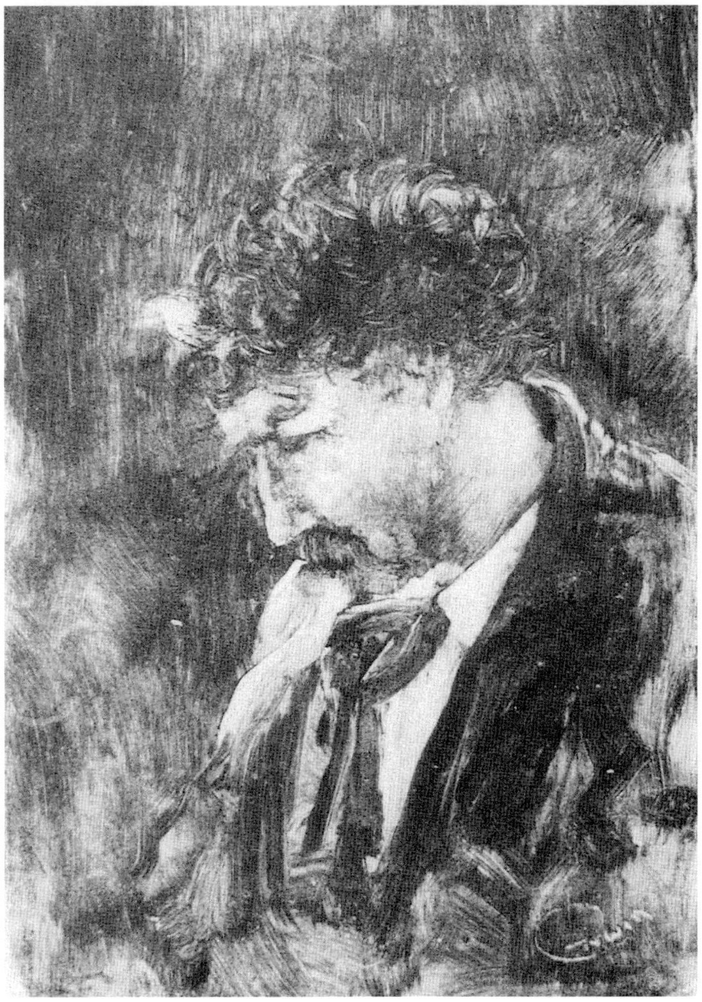

29
Charles Abel Corwin
J. McNeill Whistler 1880
Monotype 224 x 156 mm
Metropolitan Museum of Art

Bacher described Whistler as 'scrupulously dressed', wearing a monocle and holding a Japanese bamboo cane. For working, he wore an old brown felt hat, so ragged that one of the 'boys' said it was 'over-bitten'; when someone quietly repaired it, he ripped out the stitches, saying 'a darn is premeditated poverty, but a tear is the accident of a moment!'[47]

Despite their poverty, the hot summer passed in a holiday atmosphere. Whistler painted Maud reading in a hammock and gave the sketch to a neighbour, the wife of George E. Hopkins, one of the Duveneck 'boys'.[48] When in funds, or on borrowed funds, Whistler and Maud liked to entertain and gave Sunday 'breakfasts'. There was fried fish and cheap red wine, and Whistler cooked over a spirit lamp. The landlady's polenta was served *à l'Américaine* with syrup. W. Scott said that after breakfast the recent pastels were brought out for inspection.[49] Whistler valued their approval and reassured his family: 'I assure you the people – painter fellows here, who have seen them are quite startled at their brilliancy'.[50] These pastels, he emphasised, were as good as money in the bank.

Meanwhile he borrowed money. The Americans 'were quite flattered at first when he joined them', wrote Woods: 'he evidently pays for nothing [...] he is the cheekiest scoundrel out –', and he added, righteously, 'I am giving him a wide berth. It's really awful.'[51] This was not quite the whole story. In the summer, Whistler pulled proofs on Bacher's press and sent them to London to raise money, and although he borrowed money from Bacher he eventually repaid it. The last sixty-eight lire were repaid when he was back in London, with money from his pastel show.[52]

Oil paintings

Whistler also borrowed paints and an easel. Woods complained to Fildes that when Whistler was painting oils: 'He used all the colours he could lay his hands on; he uses a large flat brush which he calls "Matthew", and this brush is the terror of about a dozen young Americans he is with now. Matthew takes up a whole tube of cobalt at a lick; and of course the colour is always someone else's property.'[53] Since Whistler's few surviving oils are painted with his usual economy, Woods' 'whole tube of cobalt' would have painted an entire nocturne. However, several artists, including Duveneck, lodged on the Riva degli Schiavoni. Whistler probably spent time in their studios as well as at the Casa Jankowitz, just as he had borrowed Graham's studio and left equipment there.[54] Ross Turner and Pennington had balconies from which Whistler is said to have painted an 'upright sunset', views along the Riva 'full of figures, and with boats and a suggestion of the Lagoon' and a 'Nocturne of the Giudecca, with shipping'.[55]

These paintings have not survived, but *Nocturne in Blue and Silver: The Lagoon, Venice* (fig.31) was painted not far away, looking from the Royal Gardens south-east to San Giorgio, the Lido and the Public Gardens. Bacher records him memorising the scene:

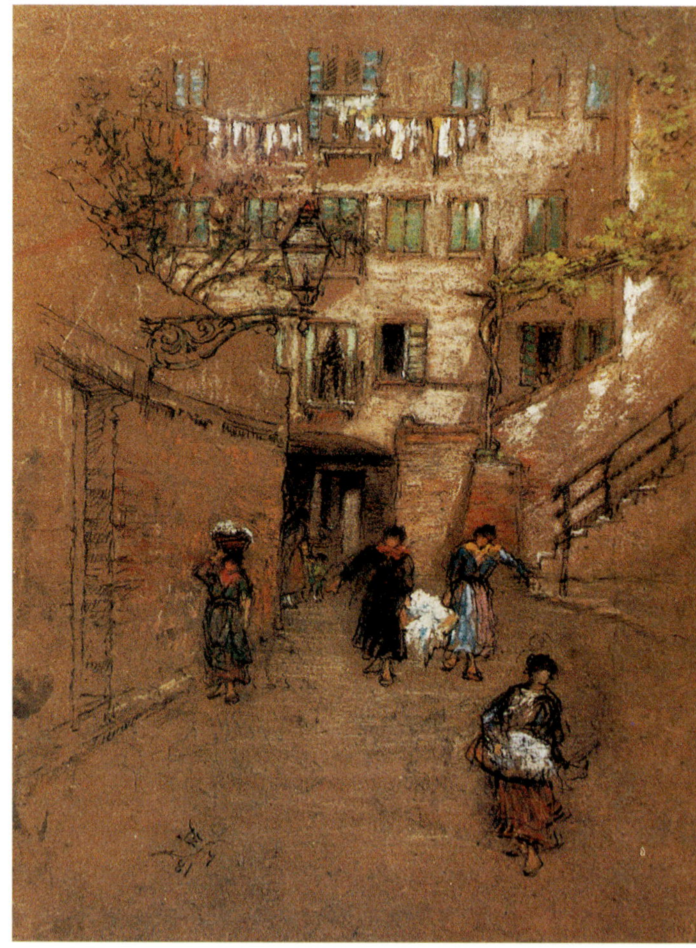

30
Jerome Elwell
Street in Venice 1881
Pastel, 260 x 173 mm (sight)
Neville Strass Collection

> Night after night he watched the gondolas pass [...] with lanterns waving in the darkness, without making a stroke with brush or pen. Then he would return to his rooms and paint the scene, or as much as he could remember, going again and again to refresh some particular impression.[56]

It is painted with thin oil washes on coarse canvas, smoothed and rubbed to create an unfocussed effect, wherein church and figures and gondolas emerge mysteriously from the enveloping misty blue semi-darkness.

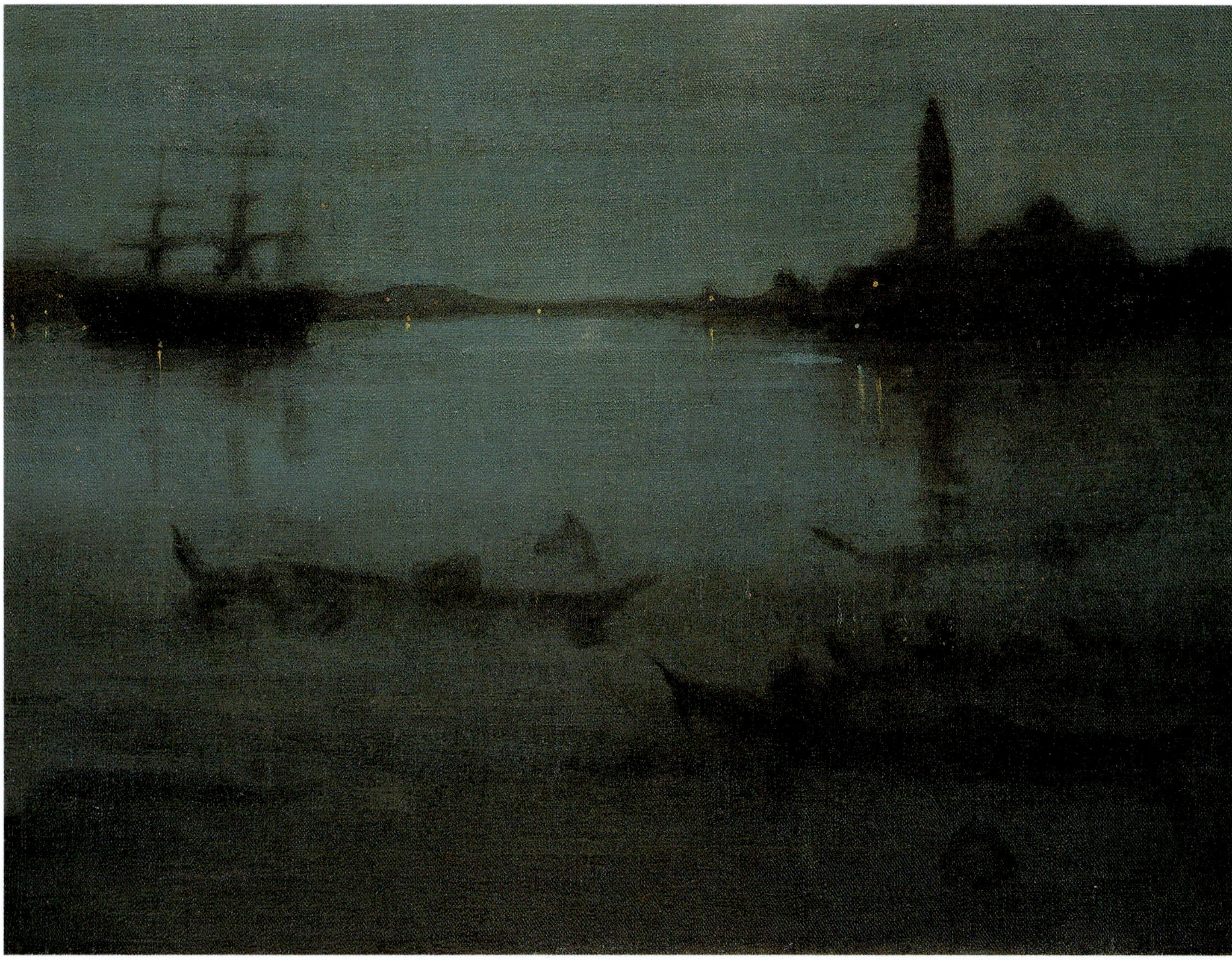

31
James McNeill Whistler
Nocturne in Blue and Silver: The Lagoon, Venice
Oil 51 x 66 cm
Museum of Fine Arts, Boston, YMSM 212

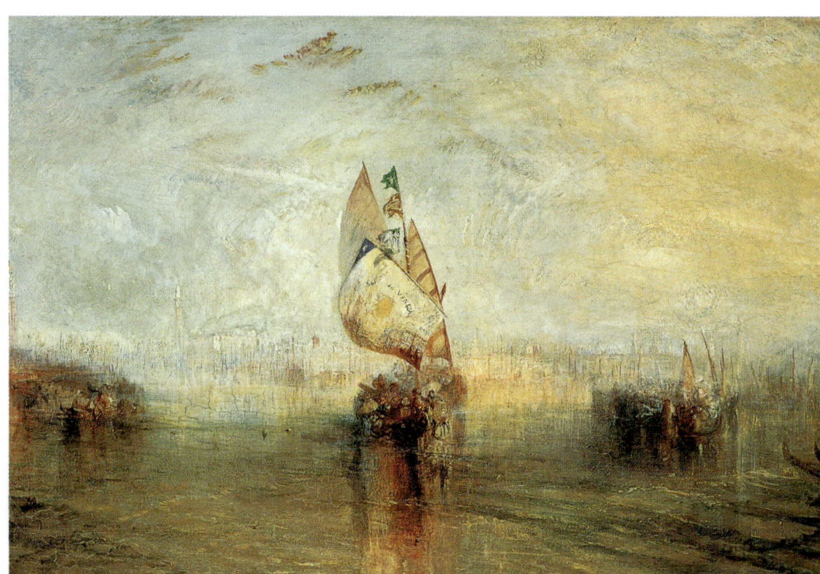

32
J. M.W. Turner
The Sun of Venice going to Sea 1843
Oil 61.5 x 92 cm
Tate Gallery

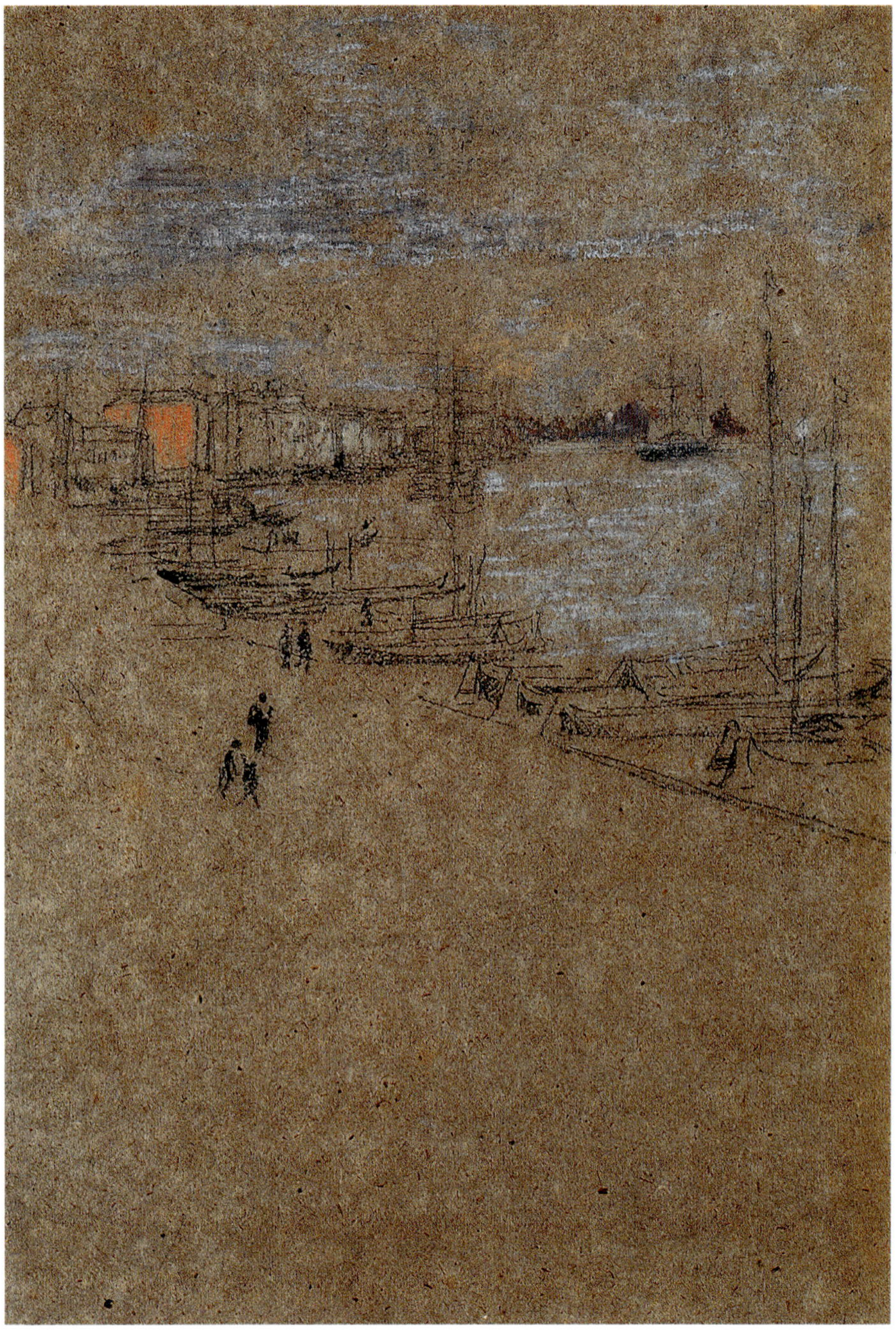

36
James McNeill Whistler
From the Café Orientale
Pastel 300 x 200 mm
Private Collection, M.751

Finally in October he asked the Fine Art Society for a hundred pounds to enable him to return, and they sent fifty, which was not well received. 'Please to remember that since the 3rd of February I have not had a penny from the "Fine Arts Society"', he wrote: '"Gird up your loins – pay your hotel bill" – (how devilish lucky I didn't ask for it!) – "and bring me a boat load of plates" – and then you scuttle the boat that was to bring them!'[69] Huish, in magisterial tones, reminded him that the original agreement was to pay him £150, and they had in fact paid him £250: 'You have neither returned in three months with 12 plates – no not in 12 months with any – Well so far you will see they have more than kept to their word – You havent kept to yours at all –'.[70]

However, it was obvious Whistler could not return without some more money, and so, on 4 November, Huish gave in and sent a further fifty pounds.[71] And then, at last, Whistler was ready to leave. He brought not just the twelve etchings of the 'First Venice Set', but forty more copperplates, several oil paintings, and those precious hundred pastels.

1 Whistler to H. Whistler, nd. [Nov/Dec 1879], GUL W680.

2 Pennell 1911, p.189; YMSM 216.

3 Pennell 1908, I, p.265.

4 Dorment and MacDonald 1994, cat.no.105, fig.79; L. Ayres, 'Sargent in Venice' in P. Hills (ed.), *John Singer Sargent*, exh.cat., Whitney Museum of American Art, New York, 1986–7, pp.49–73.

5 Whistler to D. Haden, 1 Jan 1880, GUL H20.

6 E.G. Kennedy reversed the order of these first two states (K.194 I and II).

7 Pennell 1908, I, pp.190, 268–9; W. Scott, 'Reminiscences of Whistler. Some Venice Recollections', *Studio*, London, XXX, no.128, Nov 1903, p.98; Roussoff's work included *On the Canal, Venice*, 1872, oil, sale cat., Sotheby's, London, 13 Jan 1977 (78).

8 Whistler to H. Whistler, [20 Feb/March 1880], GUL W684.

9 Pennell 1908, I, p.288; letter from Woods to Fildes, in Fildes 1968, pp.65–6; YMSM 219.

10 Birmingham Art Gallery; R. Ormond, 'Victorian Paintings and Patronage in Birmingham', *Apollo*, LXXXVII, April 1968, repr. p.244, pl.8; E. Morris, *Victorian and Edwardian Paintings in the Walker Art Gallery and at Sudley House*, London, 1996, p.284.

11 Fildes 1968, pp.57, 58, 64–7, 81.

12 Whistler to A. M. Whistler, nd. [March/May 1880], GUL W559; Thorp 1994, pp.65–8, no.23; see also Pennell 1908, I, pp.264, 268–9.

13 Whistler to W. Graham, nd. [Nov/Dec 1879], copy, GUL LB4/15; see also Bacher 1908, p.25.

14 Reminiscences sent by Graham to C. L. Freer, 3 March 1908, FGA. The *Portrait of a Boy* has disappeared (YMSM 211).

15 Whistler to E. Brown, nd. [1891/2], GUL LB9/10.

16 Whistler to A. M. Whistler, nd. [March/May 1880], GUL W559; Thorp 1994, pp.65–8, no.23.

17 Whistler to Mrs Bronson, nd. [1885/1890?], Magg's sale cat. 811, London, 1952, cat.no.539.

18 Pennell 1908, I, p.273; see also Honour and Fleming 1991, p.42; Stebbins 1992, p.404.

19 Honour and Fleming 1991, drawings by Curtis of Whistler repr. p.43.

20 Pennell 1908, I, pp.263–4.

21 Whistler to M. R. Elden, nd. [15/30 April 1880], GUL E61.

22 Maud Franklin to G. A. Lucas, 23 Oct 1879, Baltimore Museum of Art.

23 Whistler to M. B. Huish, nd. [21/26 Jan 1880], GUL LB3/8; Getscher 1970, p.116; Lochnan 1984, pp.183–4; Thorp 1994, pp.62–5, no.22.

24 Whistler to H. Whistler, nd. [late Jan/Feb 1880], GUL W681.

25 Whistler to Huish, nd. [21/26 Jan 1880], GUL LB3/8; Thorp 1994, pp.62–5, no.22.

26 Pennell 1908, I, p.263.

27 Whistler to Huish, nd. [21/26 Jan 1880], GUL LB3/8; MacDonald 1976, cat.no.86; Lochnan 1984, pp.183–4; Thorp 1994, pp.62–5, no.22.

28 Huish to Whistler, 5 Feb 1880, GUL F39.

29 Pennell 1908, I, p.264.

30 Whistler to H. Whistler, 22 March 1880, GUL W682.

31 Whistler to M. R. Elden, nd. [15/30 April 1880], GUL E61.

32 James, quoted by Honour and Fleming 1991, p.40.

33 Pennell 1908, I, p.267; Weber 1985, pp.103, 206.

34 T. E. Stebbins et al., *The Lure of Italy. American Artists and the Italian Experience, 1760–1914*, exh.cat., Museum of Fine Arts, Boston, 1992, pp.417–18; R. Boyle, *John Twachtman*, 1982, p.16.

35 Bacher 1908, pp.4, 7. The Consul, whom Bacher called 'Grist', was actually Harris; see Getscher and Marks 1986, p.102, F.7–9. See also Grieve 2000, p.106.

36 Bacher 1908, pp.13–14.

37 Weber 1985, I, p.108.

38 Bacher 1908, pp.14, 39, 91, 237, 241–3; Pennell 1908, I, p.267.

39 Whistler to E. Brown, nd. [26/29 Jan 1880], GUL F37.

40 Bacher 1908, p.9.

41 Letter from Reinhardt to E. Gottschalk, 30 Oct 1907, sent to C. L. Freer, 10 Jan 1908, FGA. See M.781.

42 Way 1912, p.39; see also Bacher 1908, pp.28–9.

43 Getscher 1977, cat.no.101, repr.; Honour and Fleming 1991, repr. p.41; see also Bacher 1908, p.287.

44 Elizabeth, Mrs J. W. Alexander, interviewed by DeWitt M. Lockman, 24 Jan 1928, J. W. Alexander Papers, reel 1727, Archives of American Art; I am grateful to Avis Berman for this reference.

45 See Theodore E. Stebbins, *American Master Drawings and Watercolors*, New York, 1976, and Doreen Bolger et al., *American Pastels at the Metropolitan Museum of Art*, New York, 1989, bibliography, pp.233–8.

46 For example, 'James A. McNeill Whistler, "Etude de Venice"', Pastel 14" x 10" in *Recent Acquisitions. Important American Paintings*, exh.cat., Bernard Danenberg Galleries, Inc., New York, Winter 1969, cat.no.32, repr. and 'J. A. M. Whistler, Venetian Scene' in *American Artists Abroad*, exh.cat., Nassau County Museum of Fine Art, 2 June–2 Sept 1985, repr. col. pl.28.

47 Bacher 1908, p.285, see also pp.19, 23, 285; Way 1912, p.40.

48 *Maud Reading, in a Hammock*, watercolour, Fogg Art Museum, M.780.

49 Pennell 1908, I, p.278.

50 Whistler to H. Whistler, nd. [Feb/March 1880], GUL W683.

51 Fildes 1968, pp.65–6.

52 Bacher 1908, p.143, see also pp.35–6, 39, 157–8.

53 Summer 1880, quoted in Fildes 1968, pp.65–6; see also Bacher 1908, p.61.

54 Whistler asked Graham to return his 'paint box portfolio plates etc', nd. [Dec 1879/80], GUL LB4/15A/1.

55 Pennell 1908, I, p.272; Pennell 1911, pp.200–1; YMSM 219–22a.

56 Bacher 1908, pp.55–6.

57 Turner Bequest 1856, Tate Gallery, London; Butlin and Joll 1977, pp.227–8, pl.389.

58 Sterling and Francine Clark Art Institute, Williamstown, Mass.; Butlin and Joll 1977, cat.no.387, pl.361.

59 Bacher 1908, p.31.

60 *Catalogue of the exhibition of pictures and drawings of Venice, including a memoir of J. Bunney by A. Wedderburn*, exh.cat., The Fine Art Society, London, Nov 1882. J. W. Bunney, *The West Front of St Mark's*, 1877–82, The Ruskin Gallery, Guild of St George Collection, see R. Hewison, I. Warrell amd Stephen Wildman, *Ruskin, Turner and the Pre-Raphaelites*, exh. cat., Tate Gallery, London, 2000, cat.no. 257, repr. p.274. See also J. Unrau, *Ruskin and St Mark's*, London, 1984, pp.208–9.

61 FAS to Whistler, 31 Jan 1880, GUL F38; *The Daily News*, 31 Oct 1879, had published a letter from Morris on the restoration; Unrau 1984, op.cit. pp.191–205.

62 Pennell 1908, I, p.270; C. Miele, 'The Conservationist' in *William Morris*, exh.cat., Victoria and Albert Museum, London, 1996, pp.72–83.

63 Getscher 1991, p.104, no.33.

64 Ritter quoted by Bacher 1908, p.281, Wagner was in Venice in Oct 1880 (R. W. Gutman, *Richard Wagner*, Pelican ed., 1971, p.568).

65 Pennell 1908, I, pp.273–4.

66 H. James, 'From Venice to Strasbourg', *The Nation*, XVI, 6 March 1873, republished in H. James, *Italian Hours*, illustrated with etchings and pastels by J. Pennell, Boston, 1909, p.54; see Honour and Fleming 1991, pp.27–8.

67 Bacher 1908, pp.258–61, 265.

68 Pennell 1908, I, p.273.

69 Huish to Whistler, 21 Oct, and reply, 25 Oct 1880, GUL F42-3.

70 Huish to Whistler, 29 Oct 1880, GUL F46; see Getscher 1970, p.30.

71 Huish to Whistler, 4 Nov 1880, GUL F47.

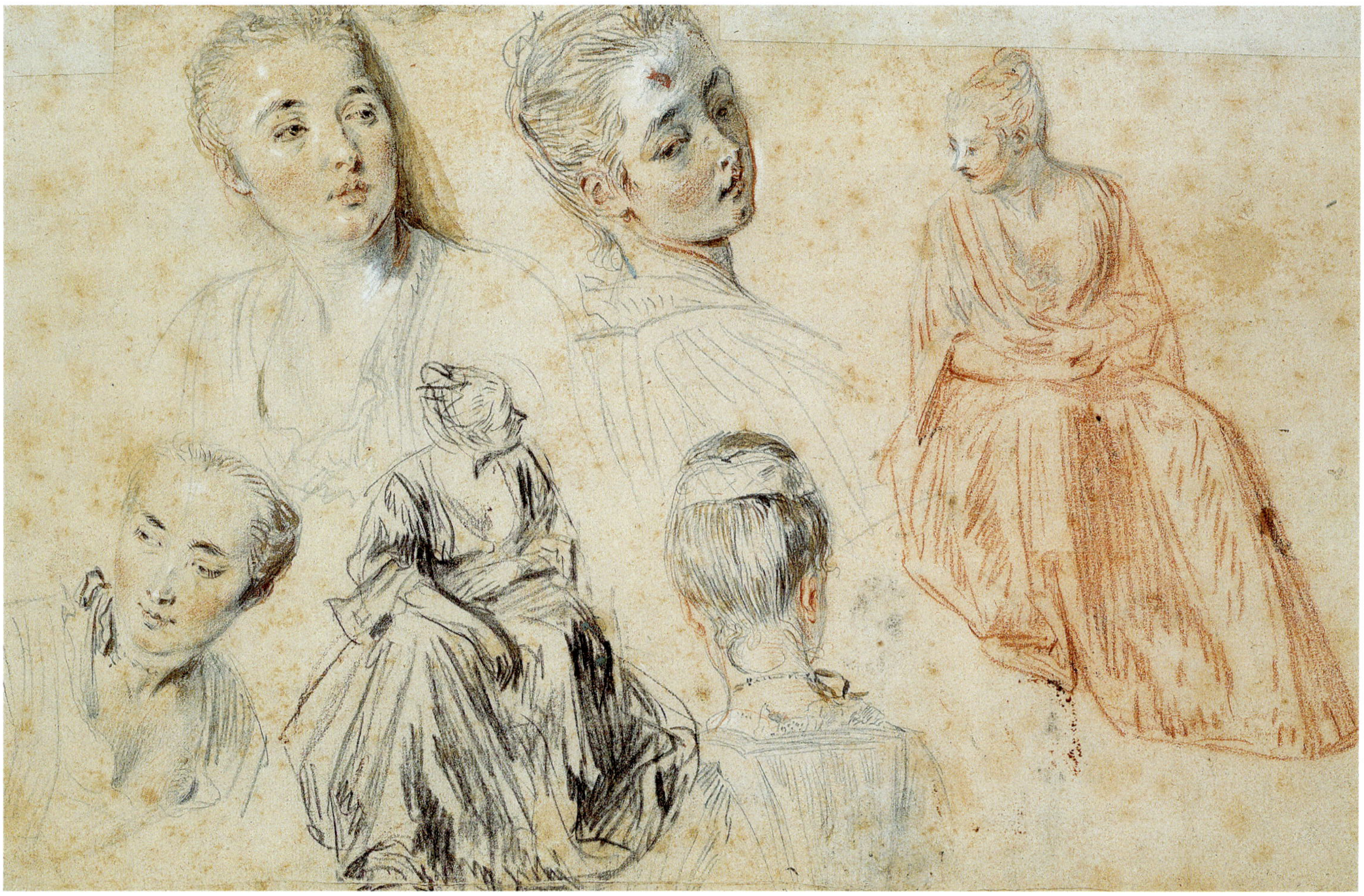

37
A. Watteau
Four Studies of a Woman's Head and Two of a Seated Lady c.1717–18
Graphite, brown wash and chalk 228 x 353 mm
Rijksmuseum, Amsterdam

3 The Pastels

'I picture to myself the joy I shall have in showing you my pastels – Seriously I think you can form no idea of their bright beauty – their merry lightness and daintiness [...] I wonder what you will say to the drawing in them all – You can't imagine what I have taught myself by all this'; so wrote Whistler to his friend, Matthew Elden.[1]

The Pastel tradition

Drawing with coloured chalks on coloured paper enables the artist to work immediately in dark outlines and white highlights, using the paper as both colour and background. This technique has long been popular, particularly in eighteenth-century France. Whistler could have seen drawings by Watteau in British loan exhibitions, or in Paris.[2] Indeed a beautiful drawing in red, black and white chalk on cream paper was owned by the Marquise de Ganay, a relation of Whistler's by marriage.[3] (fig.37)

By the nineteenth century there was a well-established academic tradition of using chalk studies as a stage in the preparation of oil paintings. In the 1860s Whistler drew figures in crayon and chalk, and created texture by rubbing the chalk lightly across the grain of off-white or beige papers. After 1865 he regularly made life drawings of women in black and white chalk on brown paper,[4] as did Albert Moore, who met Whistler in 1865, Leighton and Burne-Jones, and many others.

Whistler took a professional interest in the quality and durability of materials, and in the case of paper he responded to its colour, texture, weight and feel. He wanted paper that had a 'tooth' to catch the chalk, an irregular grain, and fibres that could be rubbed and manipulated to give contrasting textures. Cheap brown wrapping paper was ideal.

By 1870 he had started to use colour sparingly. His wonderful studies of Mrs Leyland (fig.38) were at first drawn only in black and white. The number of colours was gradually increased, first with yellow and orange, but later to include a wide range. *The Blue Dress*, for example,

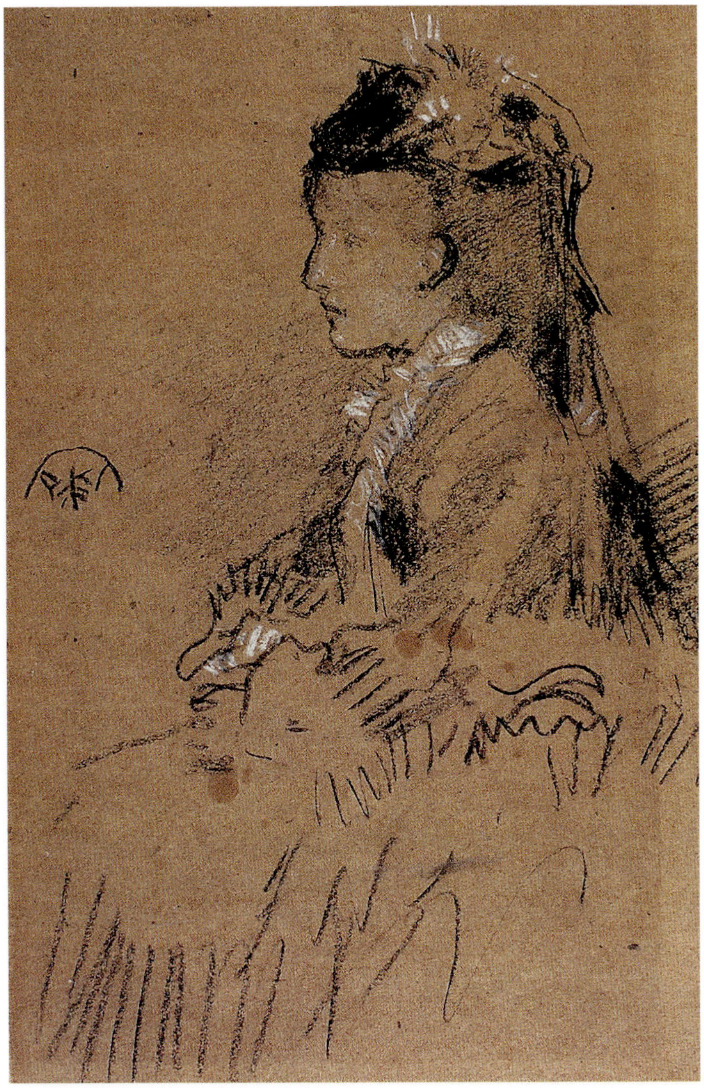

38
James McNeill Whistler
Mrs Leyland seated 1873/5,
Chalk and pastel on brown paper 277–9 x 178–80 mm
Hunterian Art Gallery, M.549

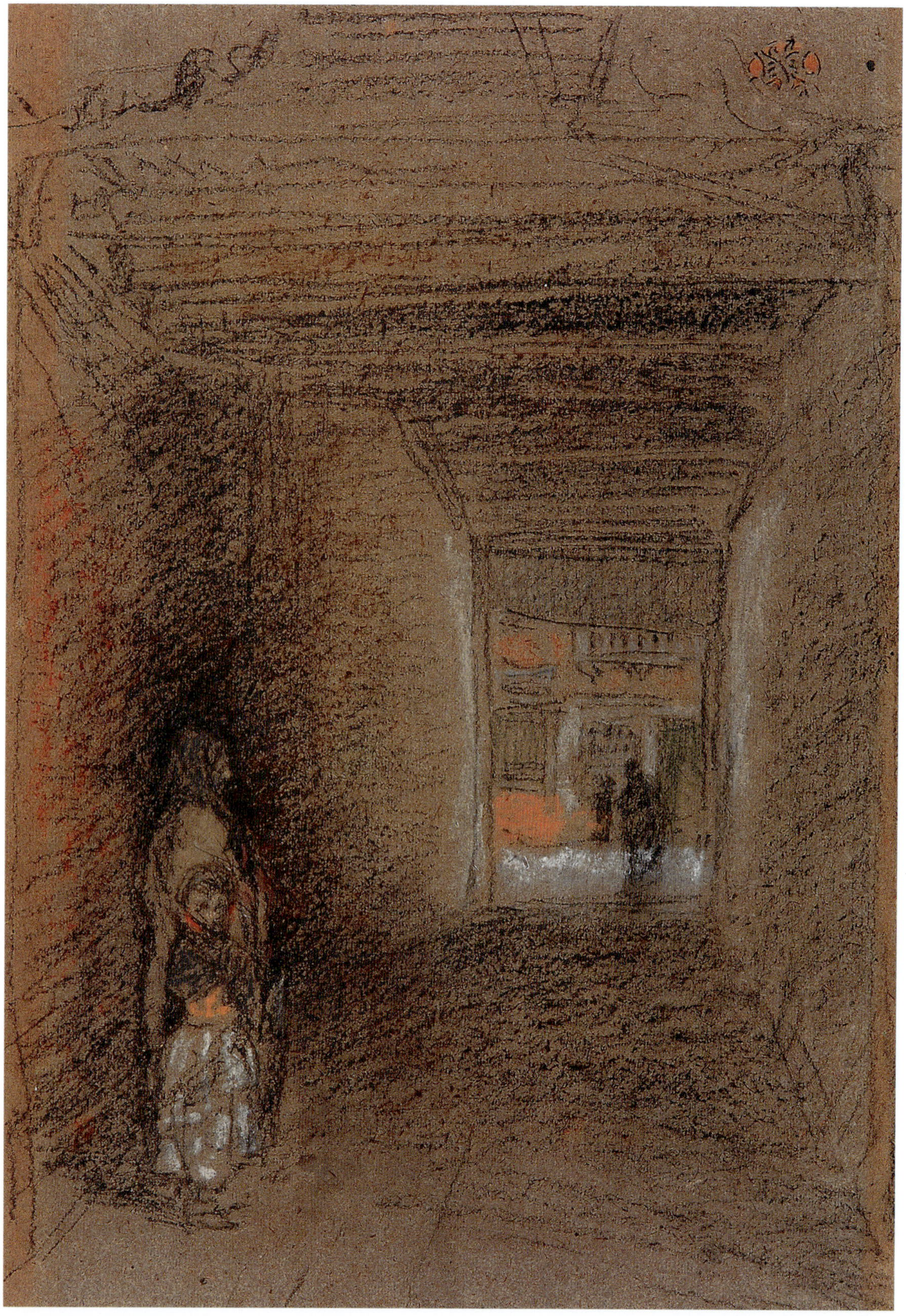

39
James McNeill Whistler
The Beggars – Winter
Pastel 300 x 201 mm
Freer Gallery of Art, M.727

is lightly coloured with pink, coral and brick-red, brown and blue. Similarly, his early studies of the Thames were minimalist notes in black and white but later landscapes were touched with orange or sepia as well. By 1878 some pastels, like *Nocturne: Battersea Bridge*, were worked with brilliant turquoise, blue and purple, sparkling with dots of lime yellow and green, chrome yellow, pink and light red.[5]

When he held his first one-man exhibition in Pall Mall in 1874, Whistler thought his pastels important enough to exhibit. He included the delicate portraits of Mrs Leyland along with vivid Thames pastels and a *Sunset*, precursors of the Venetian pastels. In the same year Monet exhibited his pastels for the first time, with the Impressionists in Paris. In *View of the sea at sunset* and other studies Monet, like Whistler, exploited the possibilities of pastel in catching fugitive effects of light, colour and movement.[6]

A whole panel of pastel drawings was sent by Whistler to the Society of French Artists in 1875, where they caught the attention, but not the approval, of the critics. The artist was considered original but eccentric, while the pastels (and pastels in general) were criticised as slight and tentative, lacking 'qualities to justify their public exhibition'.[7]

However, he continued to use chalk and pastel wherever appropriate. In 1878 he made chalk drawings of Old Battersea Bridge, *The Broad Bridge*, and *The Tall Bridge*, and redrew them on lithographic stones back in Way's printing office, for publication in the new magazine *Piccadilly*.[8] Perhaps he was thinking of brown paper drawings as preparatory sketches for prints when he put together the materials for going to Venice. Way's son remembered that his father bought Whistler 'a supply of a special brown paper, which we had been fortunate enough to find, and upon which were drawn the greater part of the [...] Venice pastels'. [9]

The decision to pack pastels and paper was natural. The medium is very convenient for small sketches. It requires no instrument (no brush or needle) or solvent (water or oil). A wide range of effects can be achieved from a few basic colours, by drawing with the tip or side of the pastel, varying the pressure on the chalk and rubbing or layering to achieve intermediate shades. Indeed, apart from its fragility, no other medium is as convenient.

Pastels in winter

In Venice, as the bitter weather closed in making etching on site impossible, he turned to pastel as more suitable for working quickly in the open air. Some pastels bear titles indicating they were done during the winter: *The Beggars – Winter* (fig.39), *The Old Bridge – Winter*, *The Giudecca – Winter; grey and blue*, *The Brown Morning – Winter*, *Campo Sta. Marta – Winter Evening* and *Winter Evening*.[10] Most date from that first winter of 1879–80, and were drawn in the *sestiere* of Dorsoduro. The two exceptions are *The Giudecca – Winter; grey and blue*, a view of the Riva degli Schiavoni from the Public Gardens, and *The Brown Morning – Winter*, which was drawn from the Casa Jankowitz and could date from as late as October 1880.

The colour scheme of *The Beggars – Winter* is restricted to white, orange and green, suggesting it is among Whistler's earliest Venetian works. It shows the same Sotto-portico de le Carrozze, off the Campo Santa Margarita, as in his etching, *The Beggars* (K.194). The outlines were incised on the paper with a sharp point (like an etching needle), possibly as a stage in completely reworking the etching, or in order to transfer the drawing onto a copperplate. In the end, it was an older woman than the figure seen in the pastel that was etched and printed for the Fine Art Society. It is a most unusual technique, and unique in his Venetian pastels.

Two other wintry pastels, *Campo Sta. Marta – Winter Evening* (fig.40) and *Winter Evening* (M.755), set the pattern for Whistler's later work. The paper provides much of the colour, set off by a limited application of coloured pastels. Whistler drew the subjects in black chalk, and then touched in areas of colour, delicately, with the sides of the pastel, or sharply, with the point. His use of line in describing reflections in canals, the brickwork of ancient palaces, and the conflicting angular outlines of the tiled rooftops, was varied and full of life. *Winter Evening* was described by a critic as 'a few scratchy lines to indicate forms, and then a luminous touch of pastel color in sky and water to give the glow of sunset'.[11] It is simple and effective.

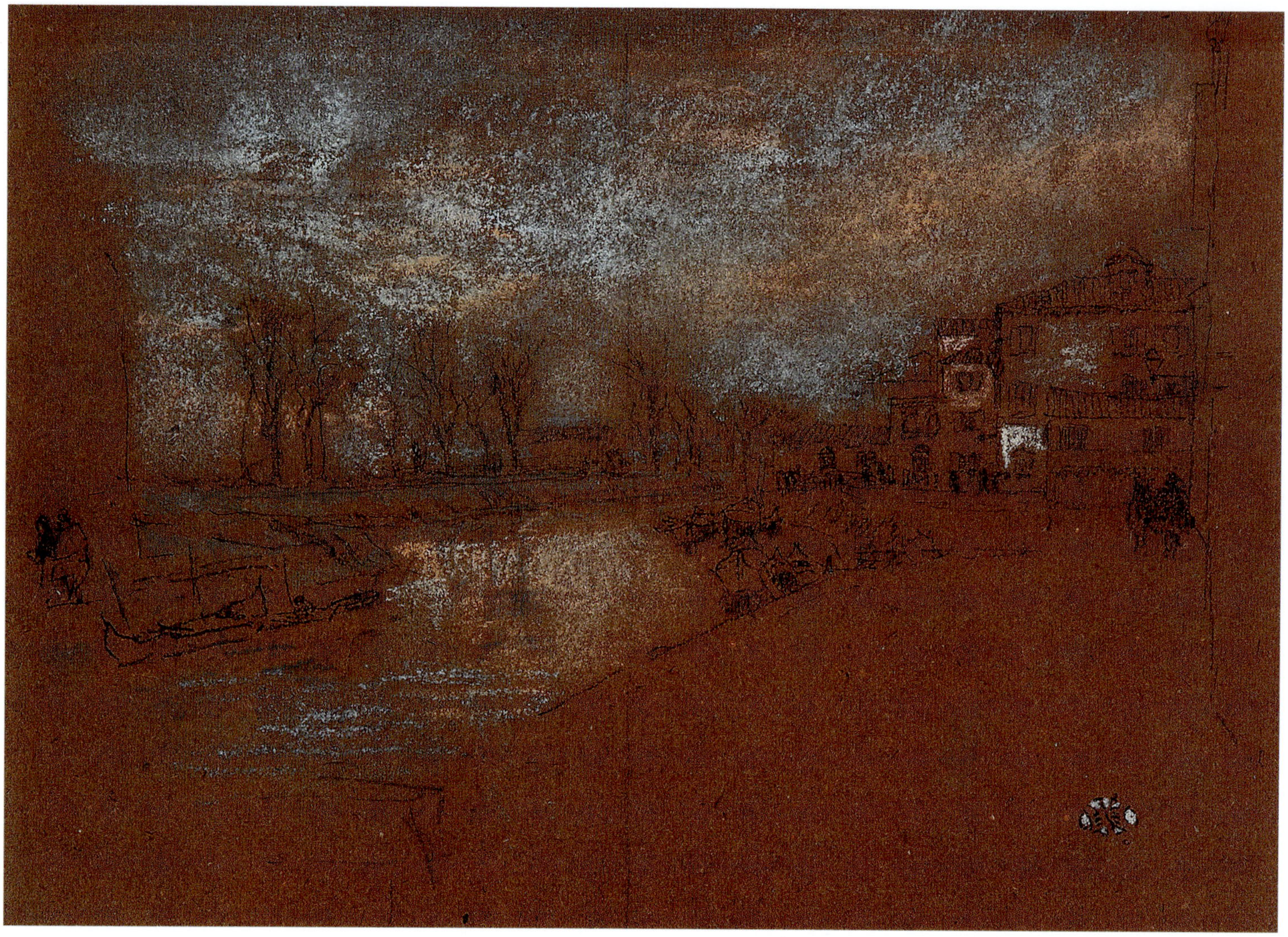

40
James McNeill Whistler
Campo Sta. Marta – Winter Evening
Pastel 206 x 280 mm
Freer Gallery of Art, M.753

Sites and titles

In *Campo Sta. Marta – Winter Evening* only three or four colours – pale pinks and blues – were added to the bare skeleton of fine, sensitive lines in black and white. However, it was the view rather than the drawing that aroused notice. It is a view north along the Fondamenta de l'Arzere to the *campo* by the church of Santa Marta, between the Piazzale Roma and the Zattere – a working class area.[12] The American artist Twachtman may have seen Whistler's pastel, for he painted almost exactly the same view.[13] Whistler called it 'Campo Sta. Martin – Winter Evening'.

This title caused controversy. 'I give up "Campo Sta. Martin"', wrote 'Atlas' in *The World*, 'I don't know what that can be. The Italian Calendar has a San Martino and a Santa Martina, but Sta. Martin is very curious.' Whistler replied, 'far be it from me to justify spelling of my own!' and went on to tell 'the story of the witness who, when asked how far he stood from the spot where the deed was done, answered unhesitatingly – "Sixty-three feet seven inches!" "How, sir," cried the prosecuting lawyer – "how can you possibly pretend to such accuracy?" "Well," returned the man in the box, "you see I thought some d – d fool would be sure to ask me, and so I measured."'[14] Nevertheless, the title is now 'corrected'.

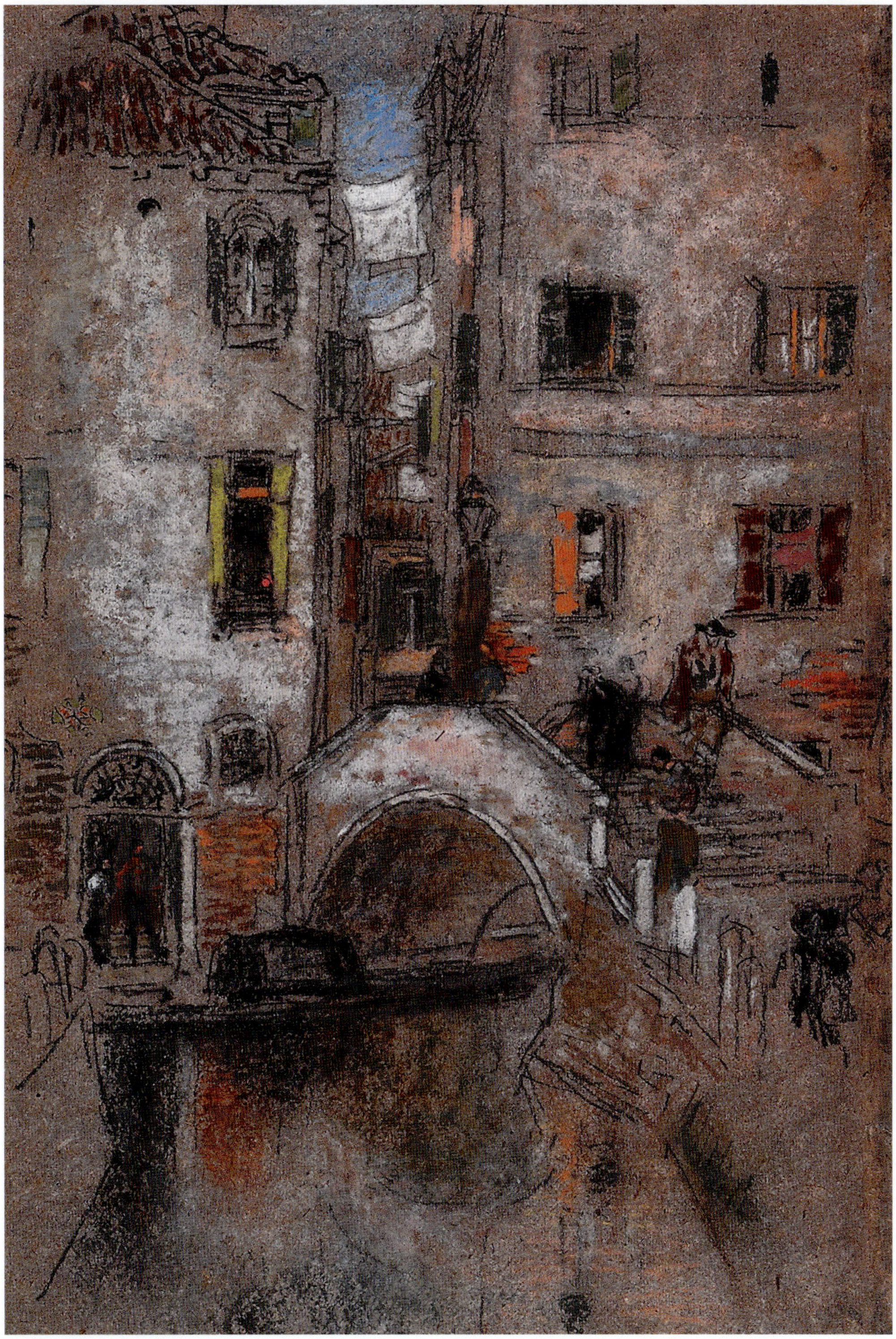

41
James McNeill Whistler
The Bridge; flesh colour and brown
Pastel 293 x 197 mm
Glasgow Museums, Burrell Collection, M.759

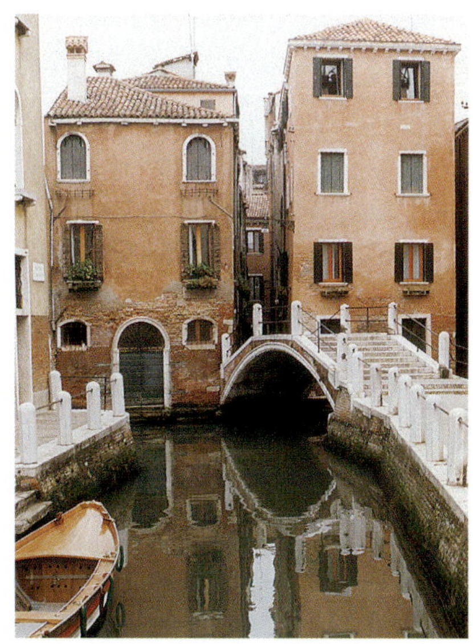

42
Ponte delle Turchette, from the Ponte de le Romite, Dorsoduro
Photograph

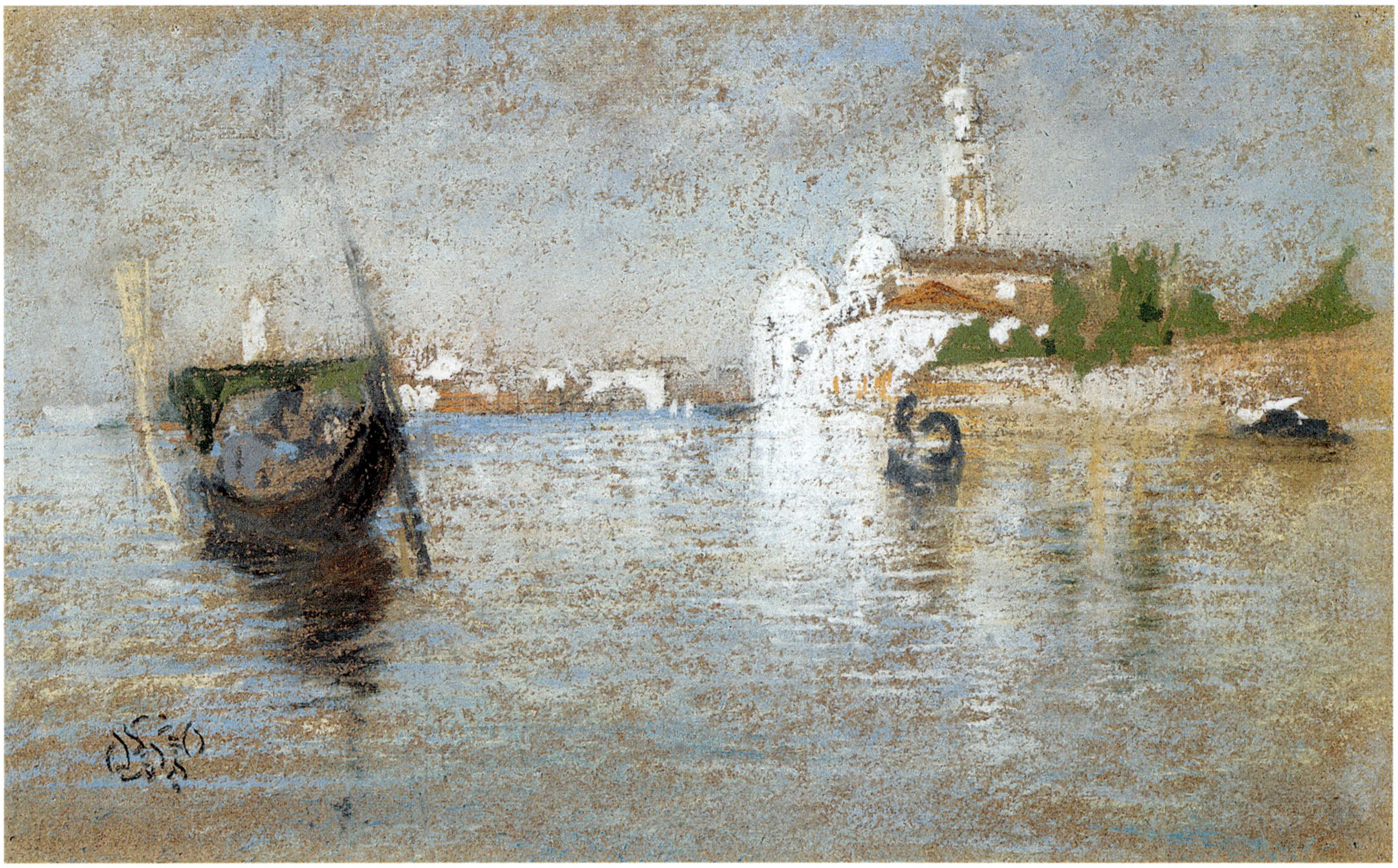

43
James McNeill Whistler
The Cemetery
Pastel 203 x 301 mm
The Frick Collection, M.738

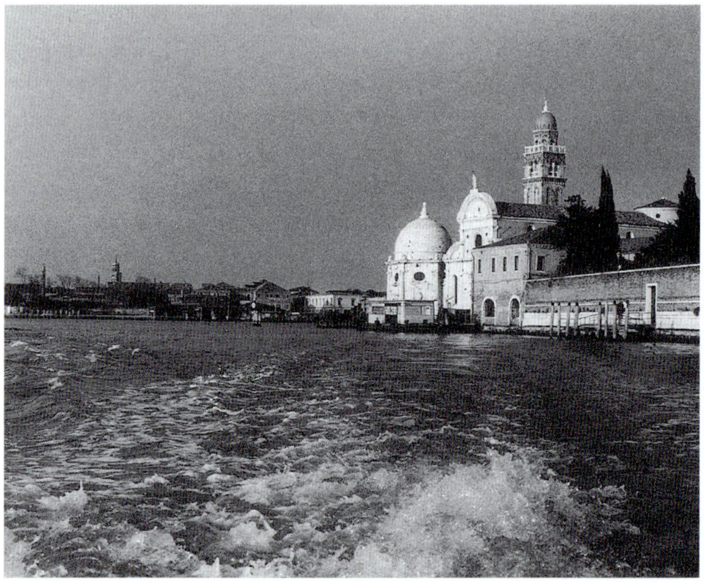

44
San Michele in Isola
Photograph

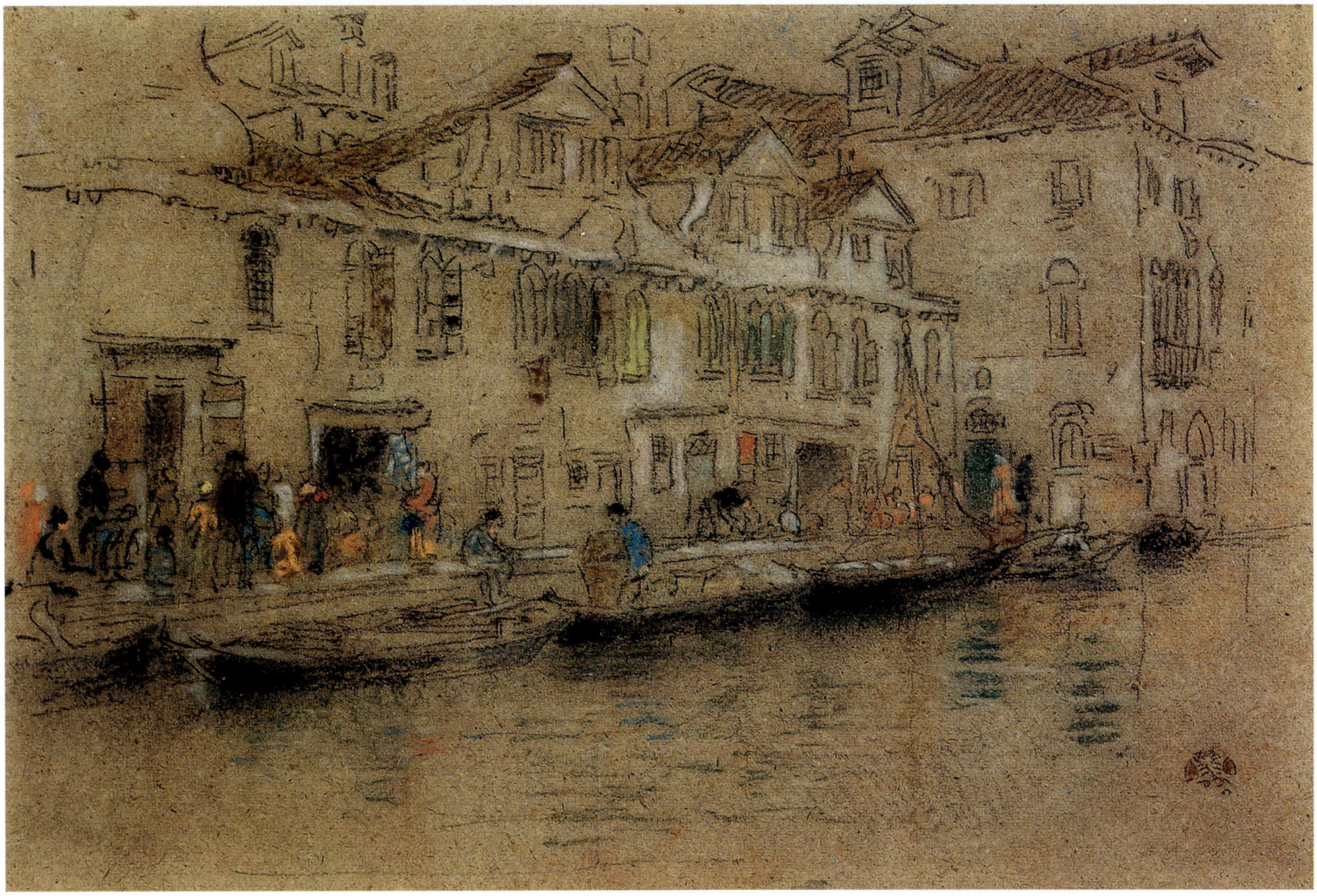

45
James McNeill Whistler
Fondamenta dei Mori
Pastel 196 x 285 mm
Private Collection, M.760

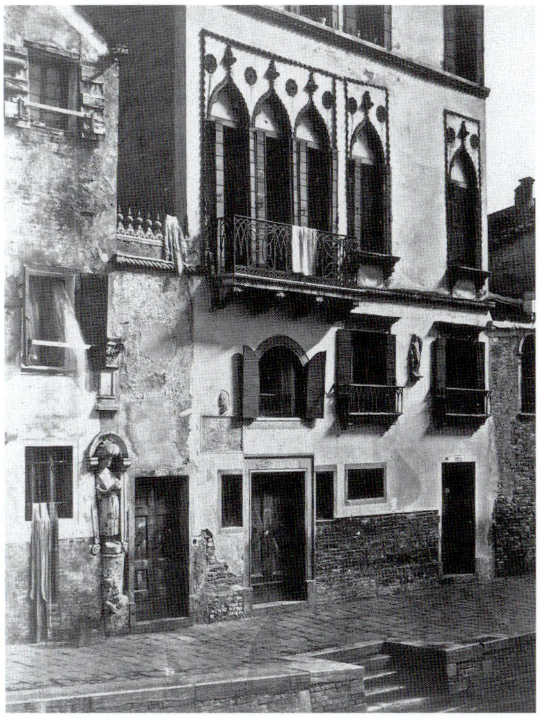

46
Carlo Ponti
Casa del Tintoretto, Venice 1852/18603
Photograph, albumen silver print 356 x 270 mm
Canadian Centre for Architecture, Montréal

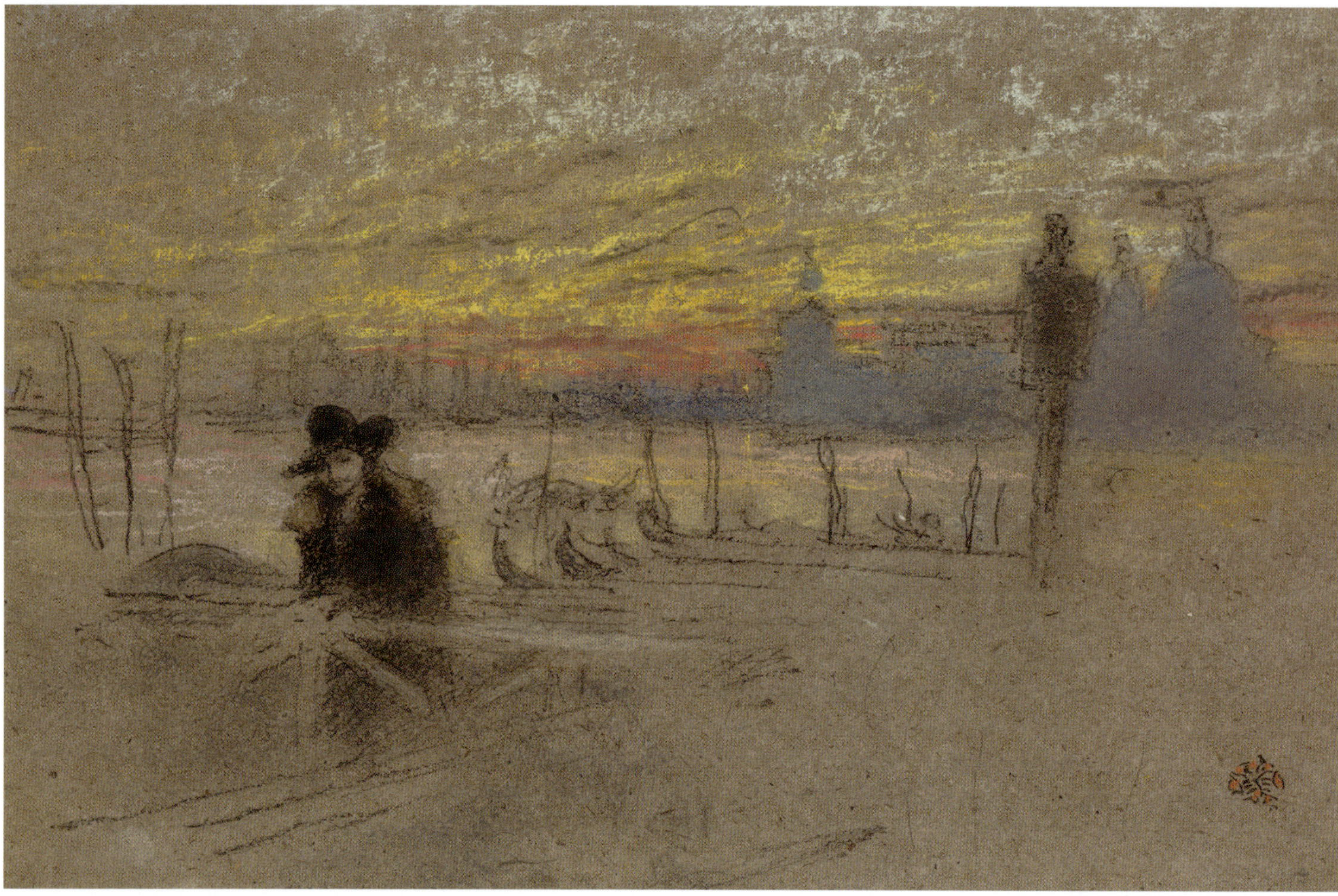

47
James McNeill Whistler
Sunset; red and gold – The Gondolier
Pastel, 192 x 285 mm
Fogg Art Museum, Harvard University, M.806

Although nearly all of Whistler's sites can be identified, his titles vary in precision, often emphasising colour or generic subjects. *Campo Sta. Marta – Winter Evening* was drawn near the site of an etching called only *The Bridge* (K.204) (although Whistler listed it privately as 'The Bridge, Santa Marta').[15] *The Tobacco Warehouse* (M.762) was actually a tenement on the Fondamenta dei Cereri, drawn from the Ponte Rosso, west of the Campo Santa Margarita. *The Bridge; flesh colour and brown* (fig.41), is a view of the Ponte delle Turchette from the Ponte de le Romite. All these probably date from early in Whistler's time in Venice.

The Cemetery (fig.43) was drawn on a trip across the lagoon to the cemetery island of San Michele in Isola. In several pastels, including *The Cemetery*, he placed a black gondola in the middle distance to lead the eye into the picture. The effect was dramatic but not entirely convincing. *Fondamenta dei Mori* (fig.45), rich in variety of line and colour, shows that Whistler ventured into the *sestiere* of Canareggio, perhaps to see the house of Tintoretto and the carved Moors' heads that gave the *Fondamenta* its name, and which are central to Carlo Ponti's photograph of the scene (fig.46).

Brown paper

The Beggars – Winter, Fondamenta dei Mori and many other pastels are on a good quality brown paper of a reddish-purple shade with a very neat fine grain, containing small fibres and occasional flecks of wood stalk. The grain is most visible on one side, but Whistler sometimes used the less grainy, more irregularly textured side and this is less distinctive. The paper is of uniform quality, although by

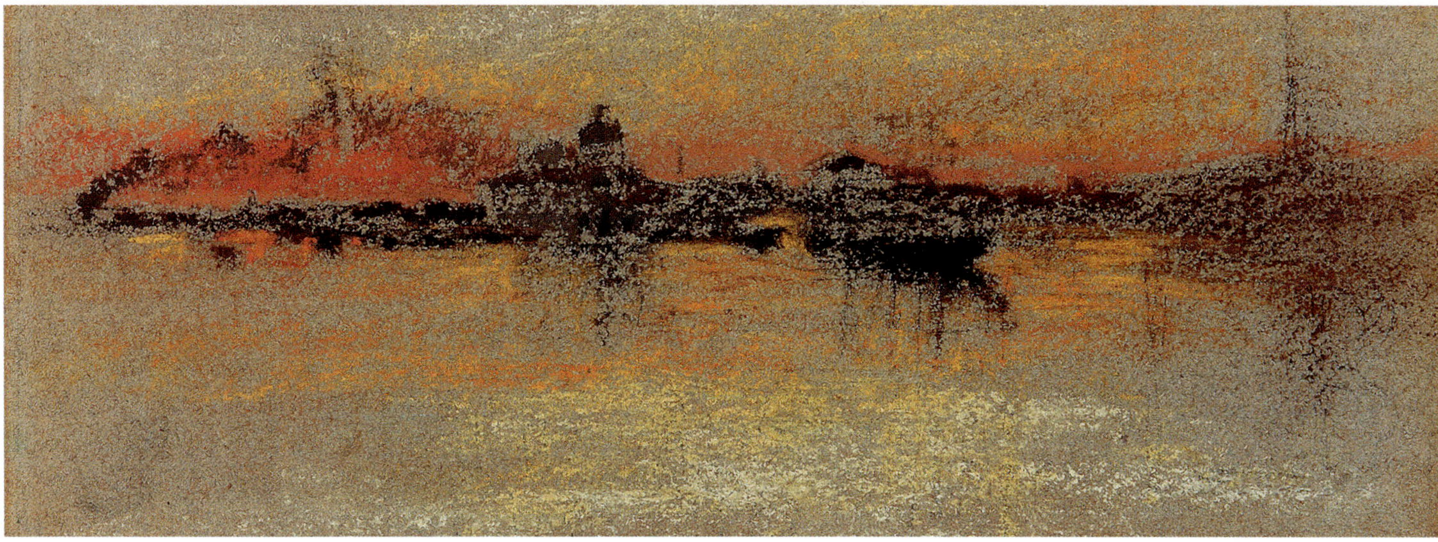

48
James McNeill Whistler
Venice: Sunset
Pastel 105 x 270 mm
Freer Gallery of Art, M.812

49
Panorama with Santa Maria della Salute and the Doge's Palace
Photograph

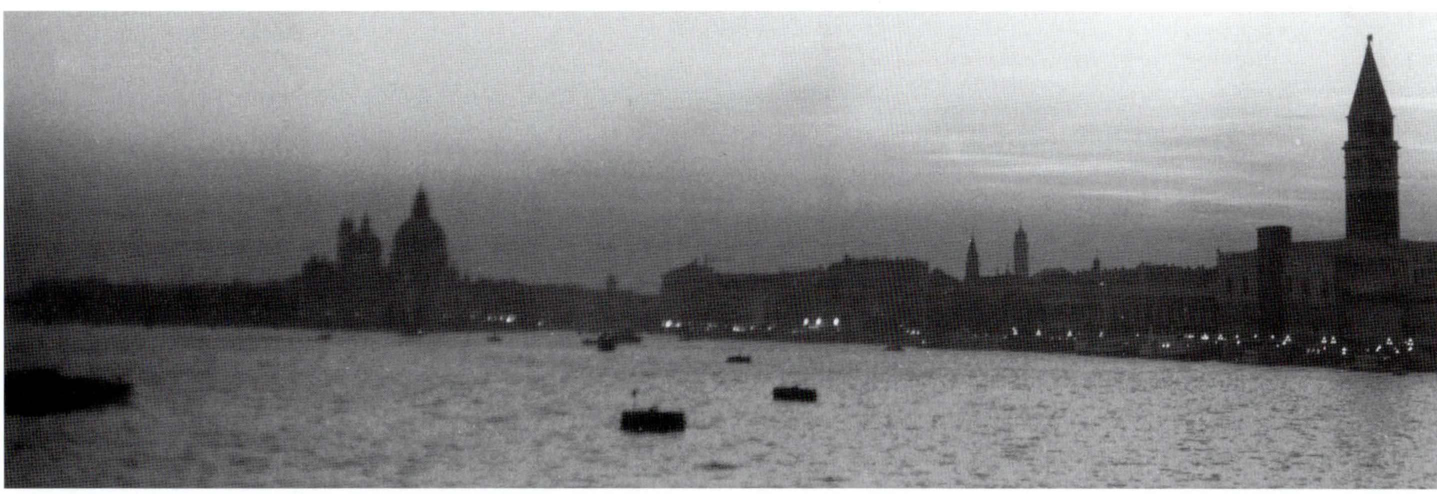

now, after a century of wear, individual sheets have darkened or lightened a little (*The Beggars – Winter* has darkened to reddish-brown at the edges, while *Campanile Santa Margarita* tends towards purple). At least thirty Venetian pastels are on this paper, and it was used only in Venice.[16] This suggests that Whistler took with him a lot of paper, much more than one would expect for someone who was supposed to be doing etchings.

Sunset; red and gold – The Gondolier (fig.47) is a classic Venetian subject drawn on this paper. The romantic black figure of a gondolier dominates the composition. Behind him, Whistler outlined gondolas moored by the Piazzetta. A lantern cuts boldly across the silhouette of Santa Maria della Salute at the entrance to the Grand Canal. The domes are soft blue and purple, rubbed into a blur against the rainbow colours of the sky. The pastel appears designed to evoke nostalgic memories of Venice. It is one of the few pastels to feature a prominent figure, and it is very much an exhibition piece, suggesting that pastels on the paper brought from London were intended for exhibition.

Some of the surviving pastels are on other papers and some in other colours. A complex and subtly coloured pastel, *Venetian canal* (fig.50), and an exceptionally bold one, *The Church of San Giorgio Maggiore* (M.805), are on

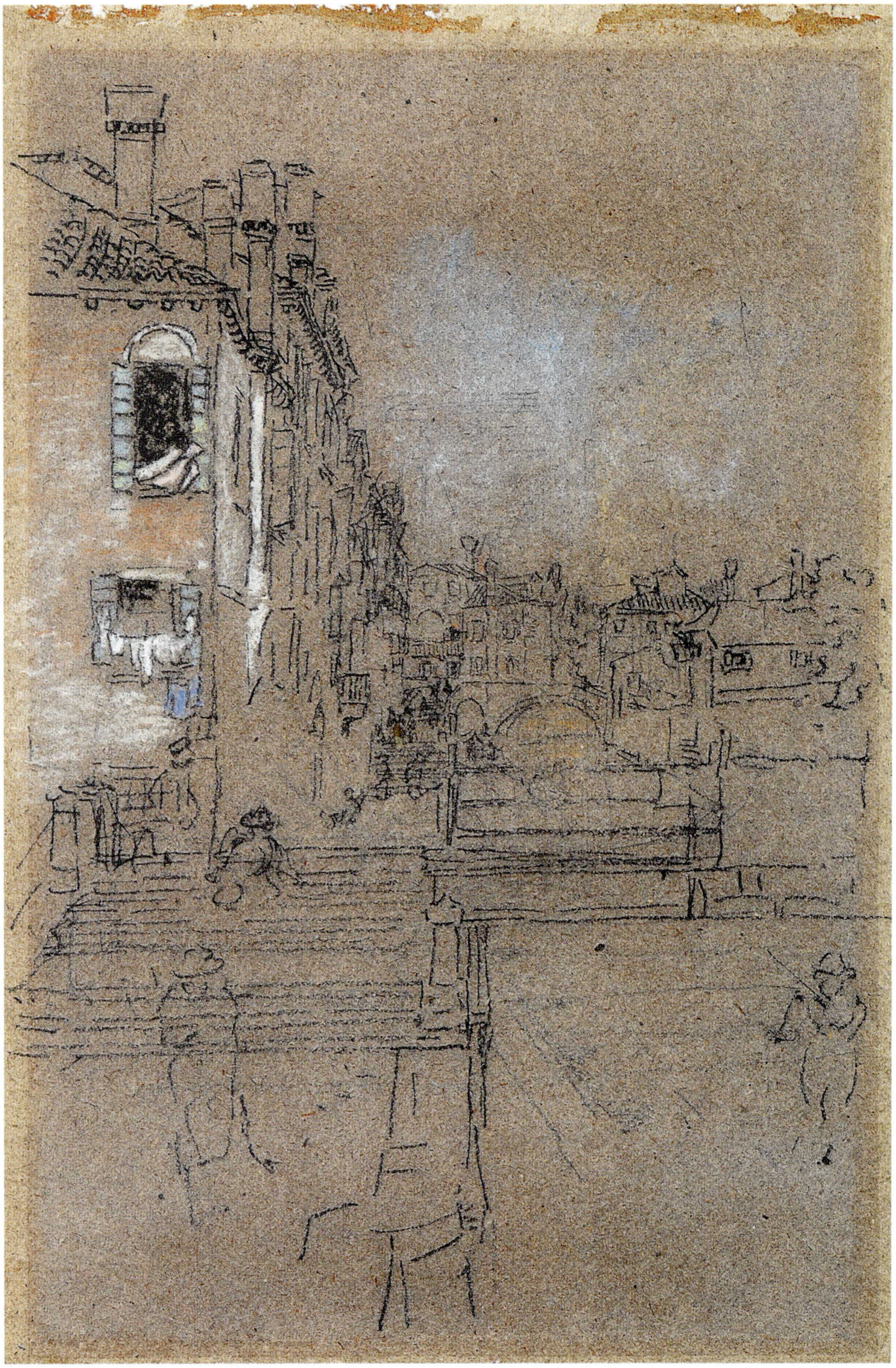

50
James McNeill Whistler
Venetian canal
Pastel 299 x 203 mm
Private Collection, M.766

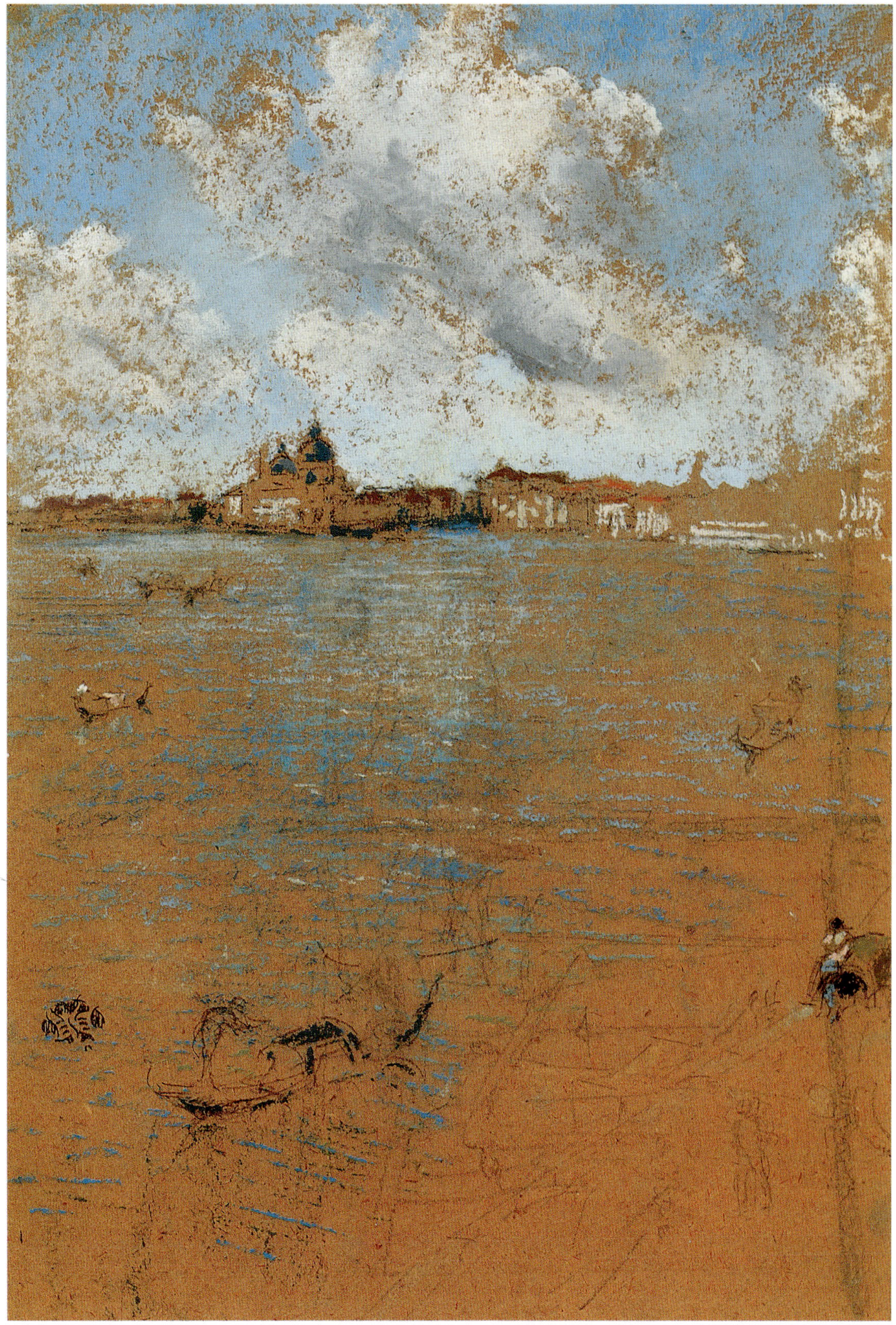

51
James McNeill Whistler
Venetian scene
Pastel 296 x 202 mm
New Britain Museum of American Art, M.744

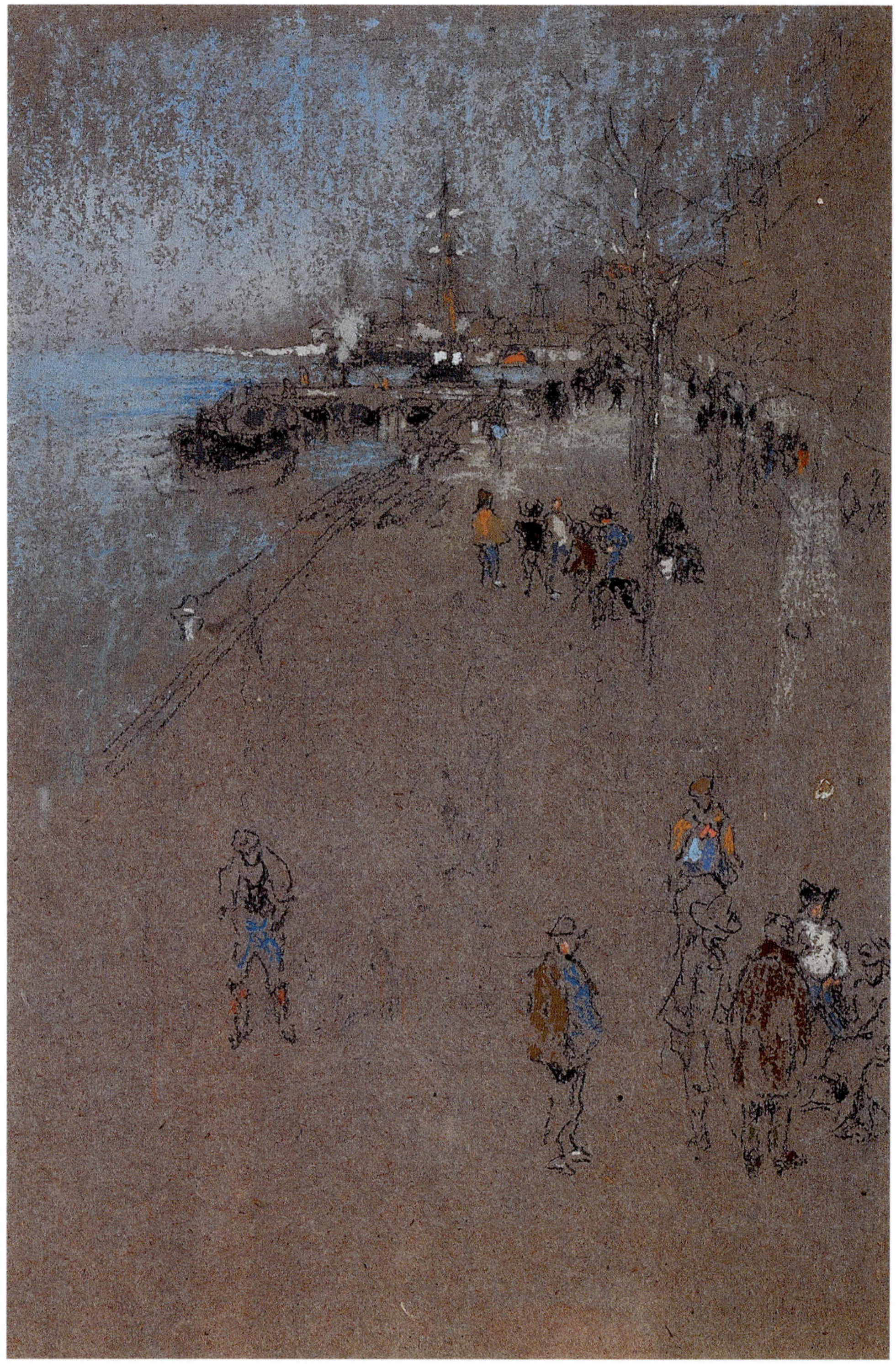

55
James McNeill Whistler
The Zattere; harmony in blue and brown
Pastel 300 x 203 mm
Terra Museum of American Art, Chicago, M.774

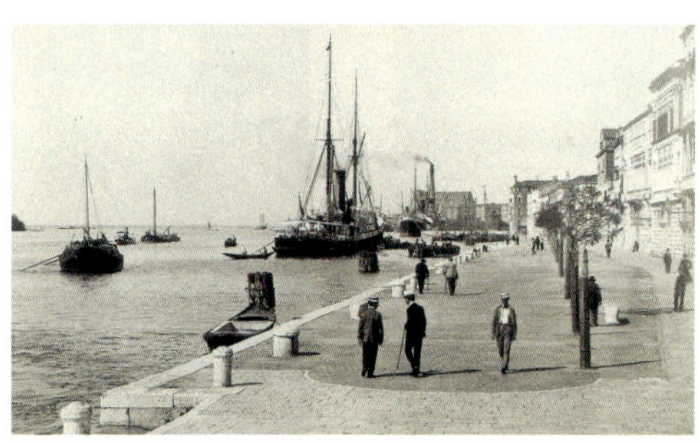

56
The Zattere 1890s
Archivio Filippi
Photograph

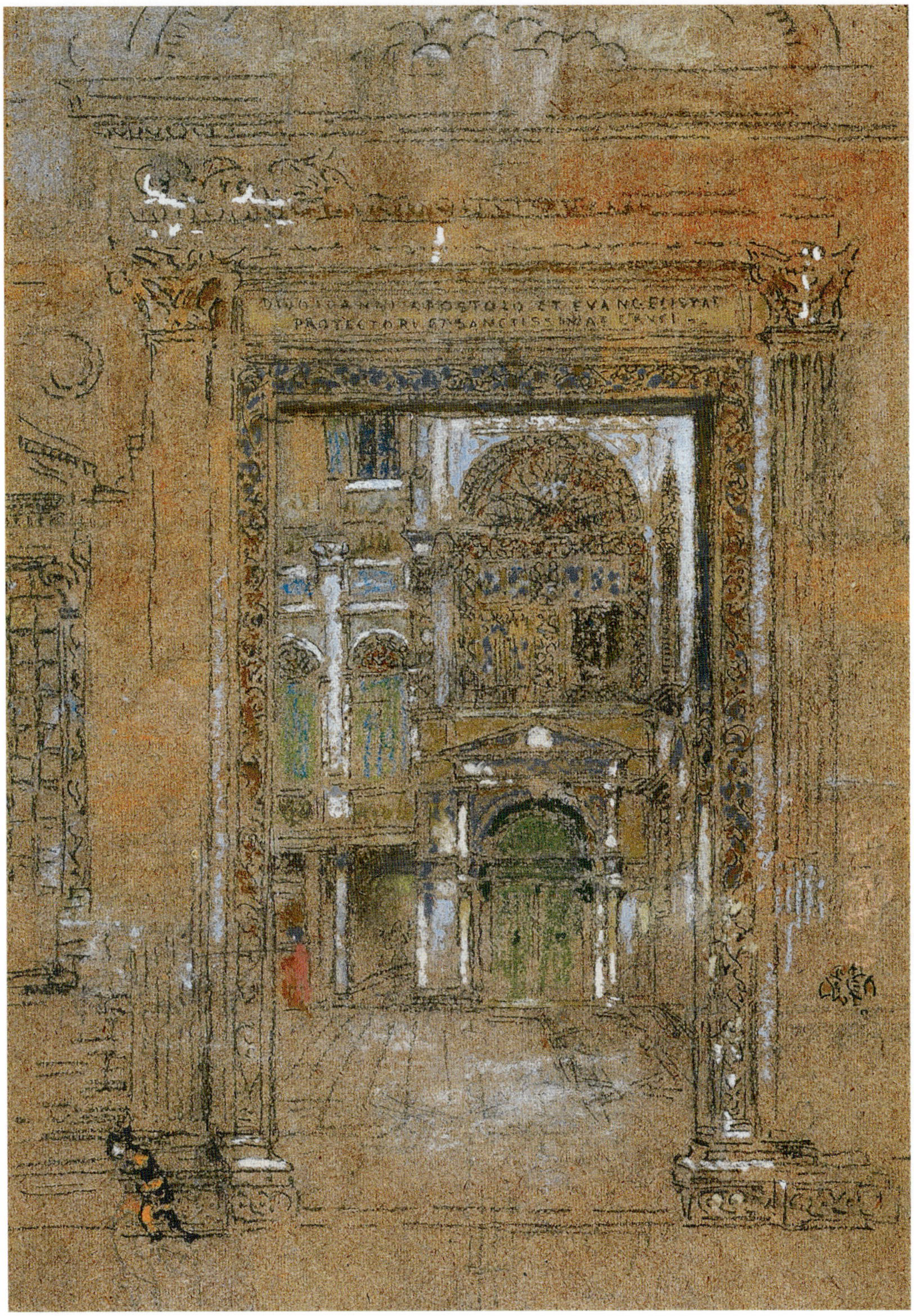

57
James McNeill Whistler
San Giovanni Apostolo et Evangelista
Pastel 298 x 201 mm
Freer Gallery of Art, M.783

58
James McNeill Whistler
Canal, San Cassiano
Pastel 292 x 171 mm
Westmoreland Museum of Art, Greensburg, M.778

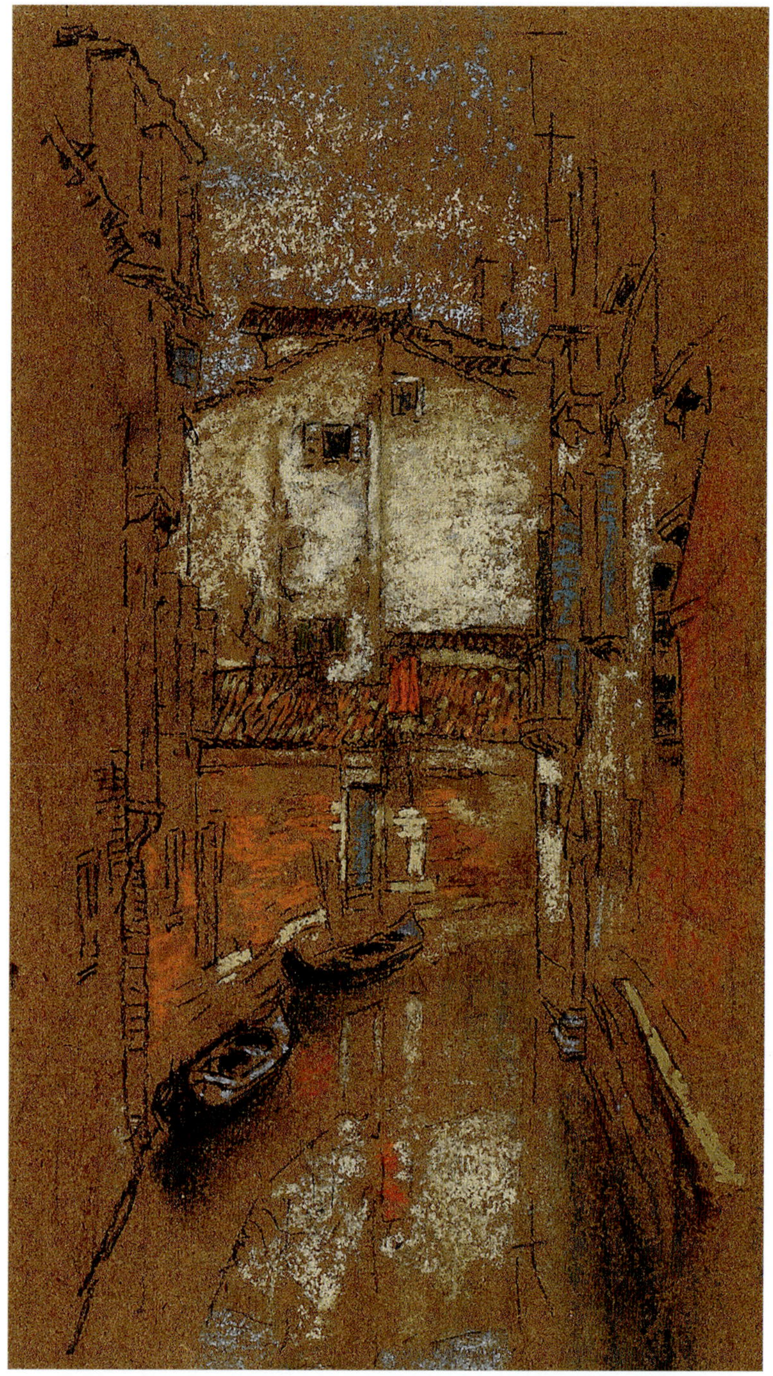

59
Rio de le Becarie from the Ponte Raspi o Sansoni, San Polo
Photograph

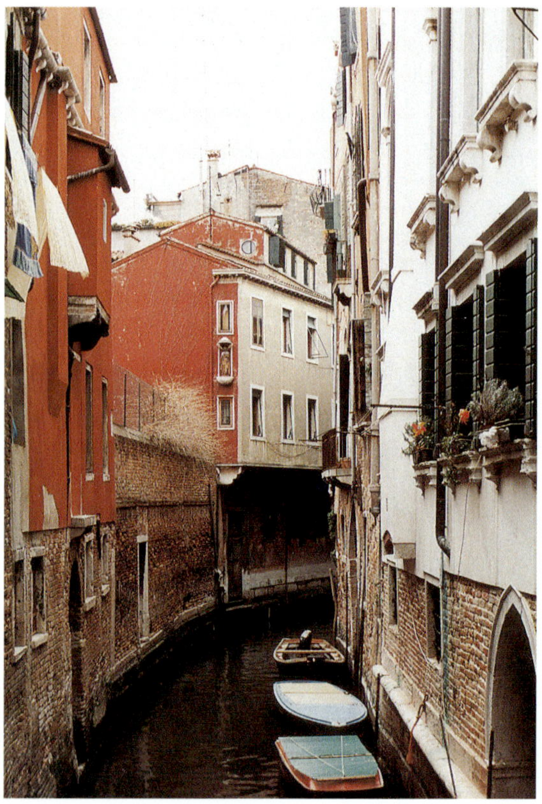

the figures and the ship on the Giudecca canal) are balanced by turquoise and a deeper blue. Touches of white, bone white, khaki and black are interspersed between more vivid colours.

Hazy scumbles of turquoise (on sky and sea) and bone white (on the quay) set off the firmly applied details. Colour is used decoratively to both enliven the surface and focus attention on the distant shipping that was, and still is, the life-blood of the city.

He sometimes used spots of bright colour to illuminate a drawing and, following a tradition popular among landscape painters (Poussin and Constable being prime examples), he would incorporate a spot of red to set off cooler colours. A red dress in *Corte del Paradiso* (M.784) provided a focal point of intense colour, brightening the sombre courtyard.

In many drawings, paler softer colours were used to great effect. One of the pleasures of using pastel is the

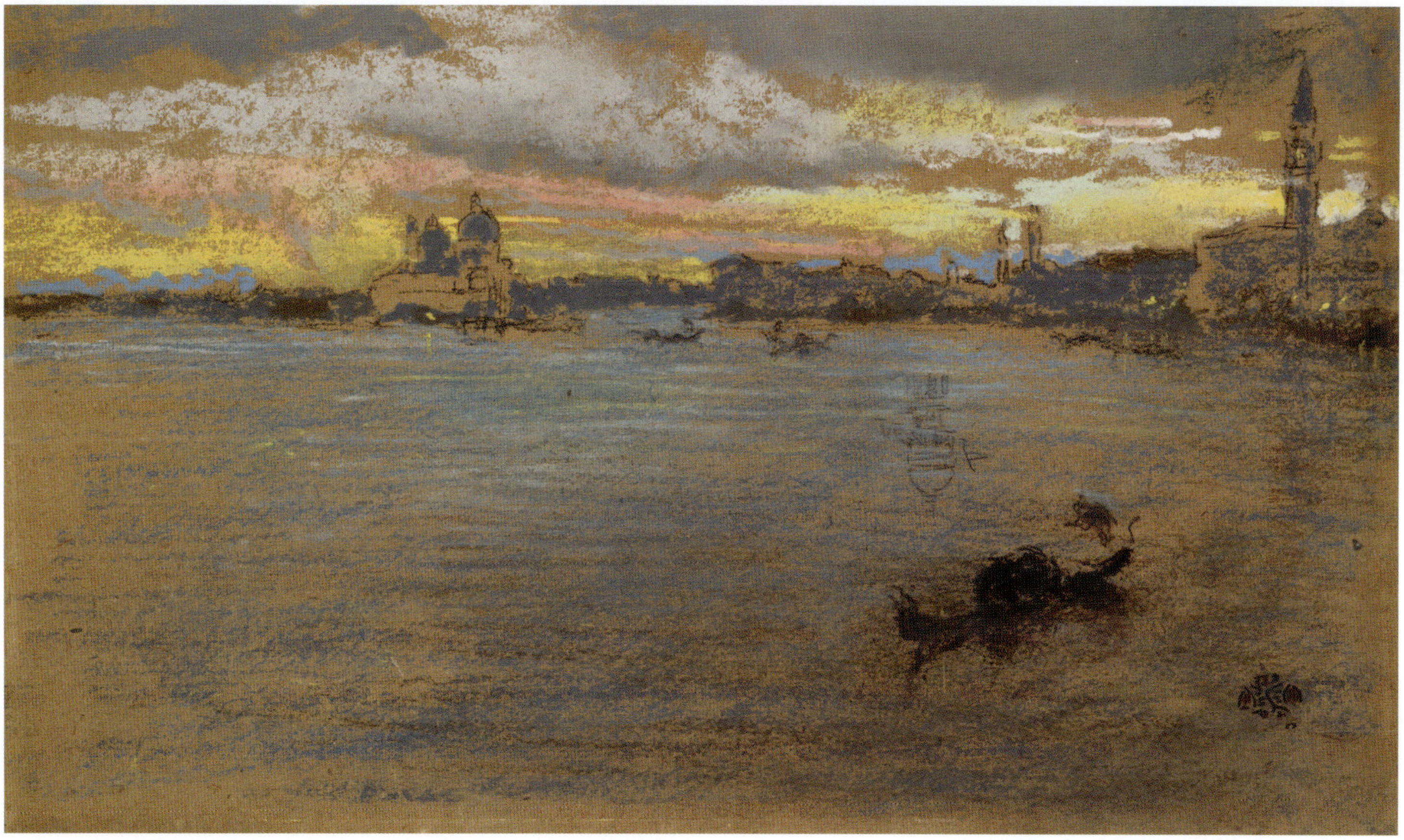

60
James McNeill Whistler
The Storm – Sunset
Pastel 186 x 261 mm
Fogg Art Musem, Harvard University, M.808.

effectiveness of subtly differentiated shades of white, off-white (white with a greyish tone), ivory (yellowish white), pinkish white, beige and so on. Several tones of each shade are available. These tones were used with precision by Whistler in describing, for instance, the superb Renaissance doorway of *San Giovanni Apostolo et Evangelista* (fig.57). The pilasters of the screen and the foliage in low relief frame a view of the courtyard of the Scuola di San Giovanni Evangelista in San Polo. Whistler's drawing is both accurate and detailed. Whistler, for once, seems to have agreed with Ruskin, who called the courtyard 'sweet in feeling'.[23] Architectural details were summarised in crisp, silvery charcoal with a fairly fine point, to give an impression of the richness of the whole.

Another drawing done in San Polo, *Canal, San Cassiano* (fig.58), is a view of the Rio de le Becarie from the Ponte Raspi o Sansoni. In it Whistler used only five colours, including a white, which through variations in pressure and texture conveys in turn clouds, stucco, marble and their reflections. Each colour can convey a multiplicity of surfaces with utter conviction.[24] Although he had eight or nine shades of green, Whistler used it sparingly. In some of the most complex drawings there is no green at all. To a certain extent, of course, this reflects the season and also the nature of the city, with its face to the sea and its private courtyards. However, an occasional splash of green sets off the warmer colours, for instance icy green shutters in *Venetian canal* (M.766) – a view of the Rio dei Tre Ponte from the Fondamenta San Marco[25] – and dark green leaves and shutters in *The Little Back Canal* (M.779). Whistler rejoiced in the vivid colours of early spring. He wrote home to his mother:

> After the wet, the colors upon the walls and their reflections in the canals are more gorgeous than ever – [...] and with the sun shining up on the polished marble mingled with rich toned bricks and plaster, this amazing city of palaces becomes

really a fairyland, created one would think
especially for the painter –.[26]

Techniques in Pastel

Pastel is not a medium for precision, like etching. Pastel employs a broad and crumbly chalk. It cannot be reworked, as oils can, without destroying the paper, and several times, instead of rubbing out an earlier drawing, Whistler simply turned the paper upside down and started again. For instance, a balcony appears upside down under *Venetian scene* (M.744) and Santa Maria della Salute under *The Storm – Sunset* (fig.60). Either he simply did not care, or he calculated that the freshness of the sketch was enhanced by the false start – for this is extraordinarily vivid, with eloquently varied strokes of brilliant colours under a grey storm cloud. It was drawn quickly to catch a passing effect, but usually Whistler worked more slowly, making each stroke count. The view of San Giovanni Evangelista took at least eight sessions (the number of pinholes is an indication of how often a drawing was pinned to his drawing board), and the pastel of the Zattere even longer, at least ten sessions.

Courtyard on Canal; grey and red (fig.61) may have taken as many as fifteen sessions. It shows a row of windows, each different in character, in a rose-red wall above a *sotto-portico* opening onto a canal. The strong T-shaped emphasis is softened by the bolder drawing of women at a well in the sloping cobbled courtyard. This makes for an unusual, asymmetrical composition.

To differentiate shapes and colours as Whistler does here requires time, patience, exquisite judgement and, as he said at the Whistler v Ruskin trial, 'the knowledge I have gained in the work of a lifetime'.[27] The skill and precision of his pastels is belied by their apparent simplicity.

Whistler v Roussoff

It is no easy matter to imitate, copy or fake a Whistler pastel. The Russian artist Roussoff arrived in Venice in late summer. Woods, who introduced him to Whistler, wrote home, 'They are very happy together and I am very glad'.[28] Indeed, some of Roussoff's Venetian views are

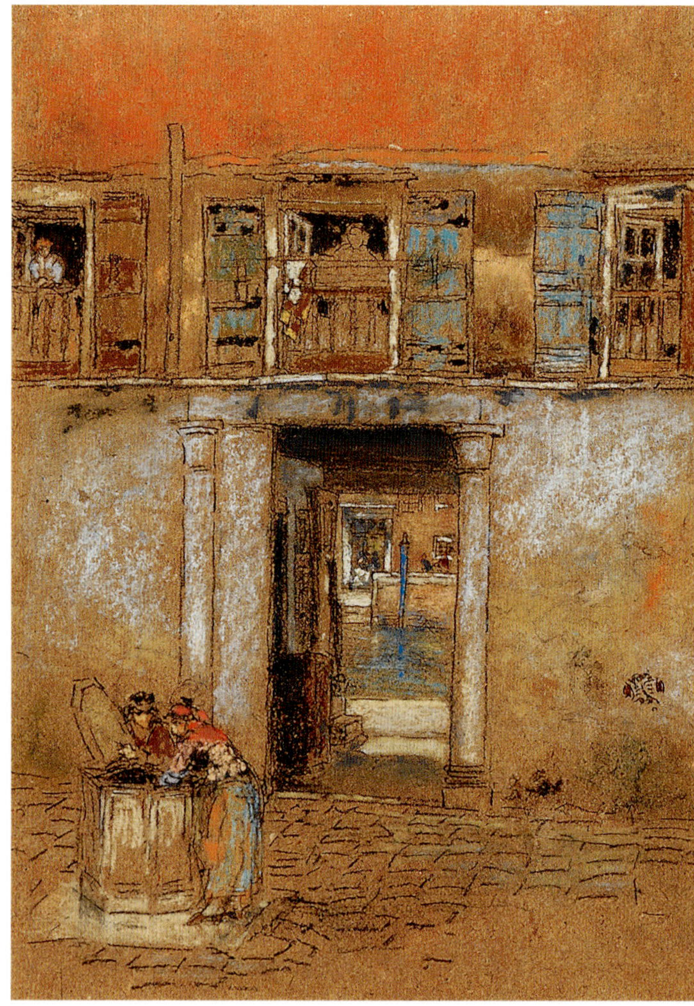

61
James McNeill Whistler
Courtyard on Canal; grey and red
Pastel 301 x 202 mm
The St Louis Art Museum, M.790

strongly reminiscent of Whistler's both in subject and format.[29] However, some rivalry arose when, one night at the Bauer Grunwald restaurant, an American praised Whistler's pastels.

Bacher tells the story from a pro-Whistler point of view. Roussoff ridiculed the pastels, 'jeeringly saying that he was willing to bet he could make half a dozen pastels as good as Whistler's, and, if they were mixed with his, nobody could tell them apart'.[30] An American friend of Whistler's bet Roussoff a champagne dinner that he could do no such thing. Whistler showed Roussoff his drawings, but after six weeks the Russian said he could not get the same pastels, so some were borrowed from Whistler. Finally, the international jury – an Austrian and a

Dutchman, Van Haanen, the Spaniard Martin Rico, Woods, Duveneck, Curtis and Bacher – met near the Casa Jankowitz, with a nervous Whistler in attendance, and unerringly told them apart.

Rico told a slightly different version of the story: that the dispute started at a soirée, the jury consisted of an Austrian, Pasini, and van Haanen on one side, Wust and himself on the other, and they identified all but three correctly, despite the minimalist simplicity of the pastels.[31]

Maud Franklin later reported a London paper saying 'Wolkoff, the Russian imitator [...] was obliged to take a course of mud baths after his defeat.'[32] Several years later, when Wolkoff/Roussoff sent some of his watercolours of Venice for sale at the Fine Art Society, Whistler wrote unforgivingly: 'I suppose they look like H–l and sell well – thereby combining virtue with business.'[33]

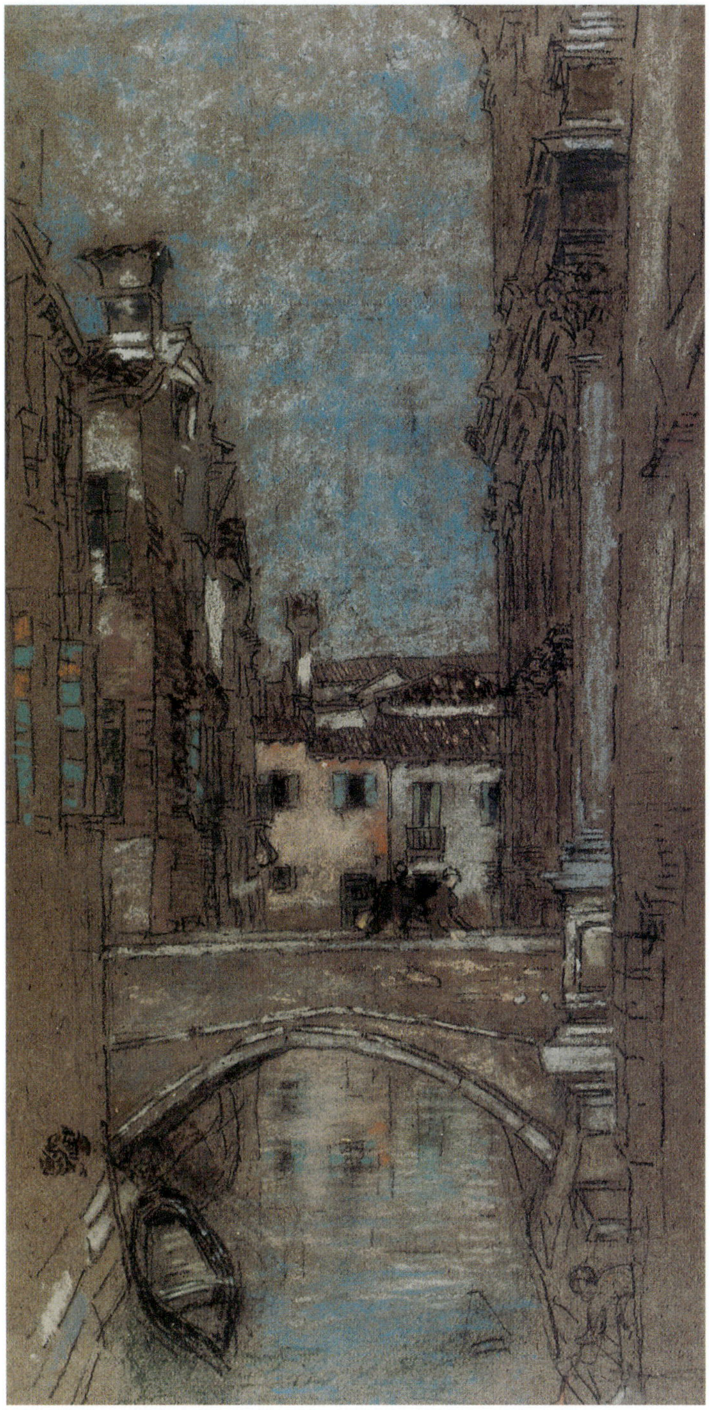

62
James McNeill Whistler
San Rocco
Pastel 300 x 155 mm
Boston Public Library, M.772

Format and framing

Whistler undoubtedly saw his pastels as a business proposition. He asked Huish to arrange for fifty frames to be made ready for his return. Fifty pastels were numbered and measured for framing. Twenty-five still have a neat inscription along the edge recording their number and giving the size of the mount or interior of the frame. For instance, *The Cemetery* (M.738) is inscribed 'No 2 – 10¾ x 6½' (width preceding height), although it measures 8 x 11⅞ in (203 x 301 mm).[34] It was intended that little margin should be left around the actual drawing, so that at least 1½ in (38 mm) was covered by the frame.

Some of these numbered pastels, like *Winter Evening* (M.755), date from the winter of 1879–80 and others, like *The Little Back Canal* (M.779), appear to date from the spring. Only a few, like *Sunset; red and gold – Salute* (M.810), may be associated with Whistler's stay at the Casa Jankowitz in the summer. Most were in the Fine Art Society's 1881 exhibition, but in no case does the number on the pastel correspond to the catalogue number. *The Cemetery*, for instance, was no.36, not no.2.[35] It seems certain that the numbering was done in Italy, when Whistler ordered the frames, and long before the pastels were packed for the return journey. A few of these pastels were never exhibited, including one which was probably given to Mrs Bronson as a parting gift.[36]

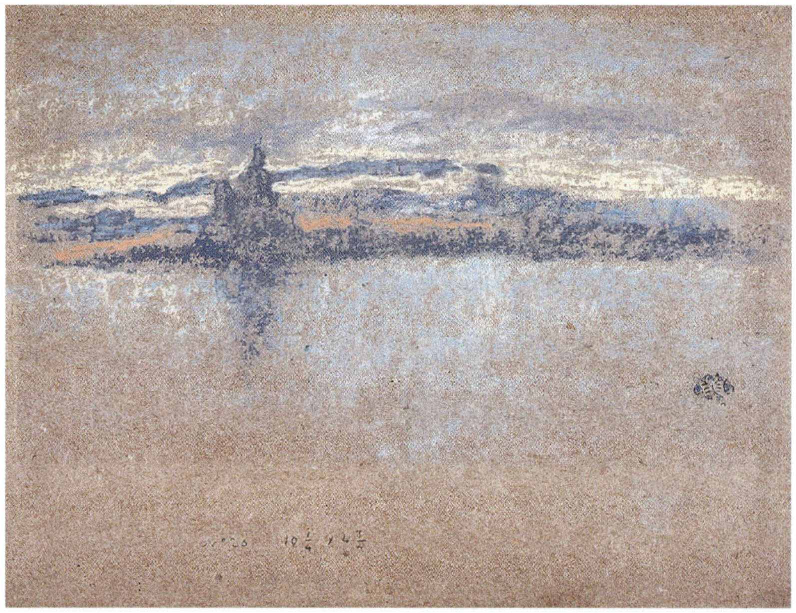

63
James McNeill Whistler
Salute – Sundown
Pastel 200 x 268 mm
Hunterian Art Gallery, M.809

64
James McNeill Whistler
Salute – Sundown, framed
Hunterian Art Gallery, M.809

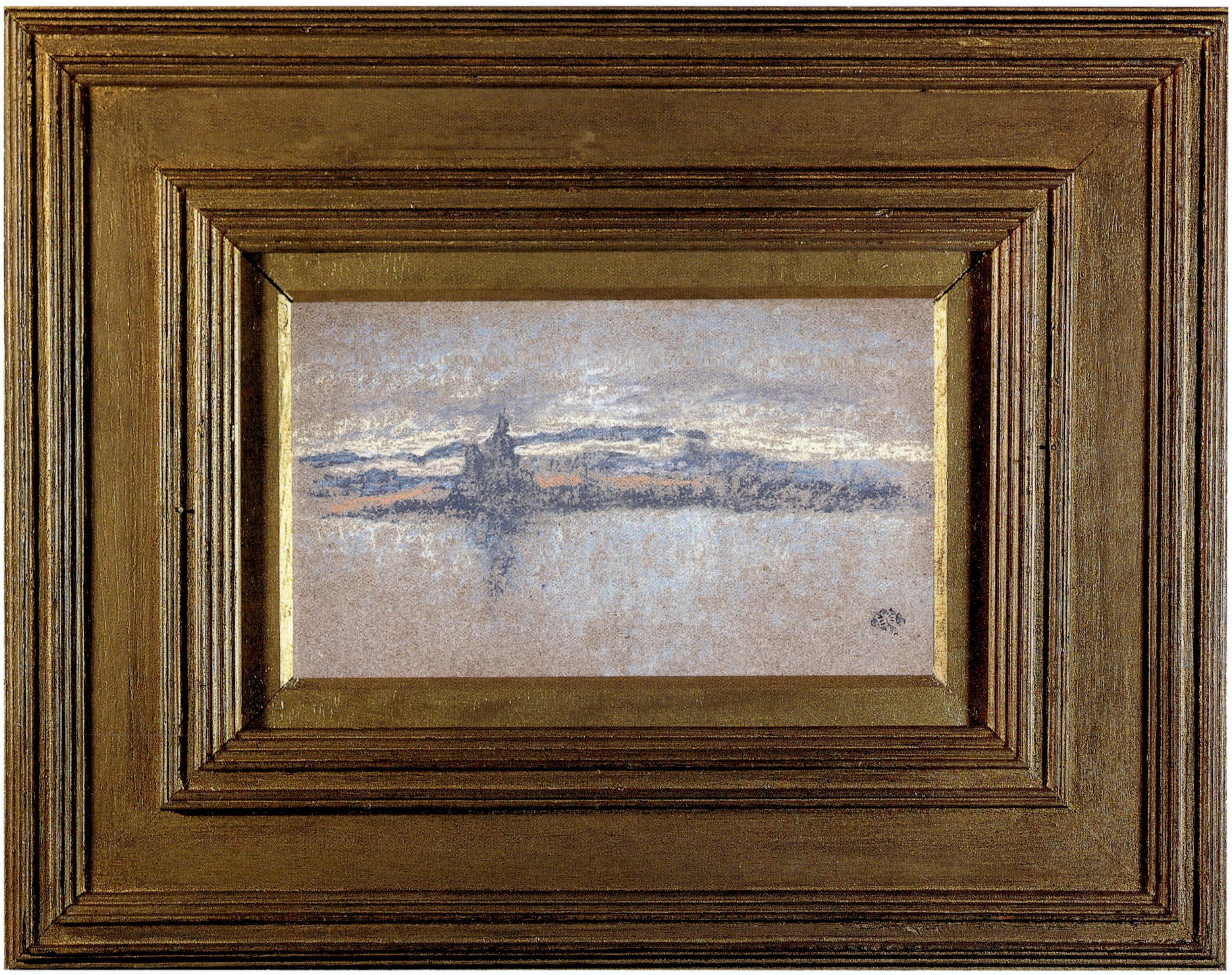

Whistler's compositions were always closely related to the shape and size of the paper. Most pastels were drawn well within the edges. Even extremely narrow pastels, like *Long Venice* (M.748), appear to have been conceived and drawn from the start on narrow envelope format paper, and vertical compositions, like *San Rocco* (fig.62), on similarly attenuated vertical sheets. Whistler drew the Rio de la Frescada with the Corinthian pillars of San Rocco on the right (the home of the greatest collection of Tintorettos in Venice) from the Ponte San Rocco, and from the same convenient bridge, looking the other way, he drew the bell tower of Santa Maria Gloriosa dei Frari in *Under the Frari* (M.771). In each case, the narrow vertical format accentuates the height of the churches.

Framing the pastels gave Whistler an opportunity to change both scale and emphasis. Big pastels like *The Tobacco Warehouse* (M.762) were reduced in size, and the narrow format of *Salute – Sundown* exaggerated.[37] (figs 63 and 64) Whistler was concerned to maximise the impact of the drawings. Careful framing was an essential part of their presentation. When it came to hanging the 1881 show, the variations in format and the alternation of vertical and horizontal pictures provided effective contrasts.

On 2 May Whistler wrote home to his son Charlie that he would bring back 'a perfect gallery of beautiful pastel drawings – about sixty in all – which I fancy will represent nearly a thousand pounds! – The frames are already ordered and by this time probably made in London – where the collection will doubtless be exhibited – probably at the Fine Arts Society.'[38]

Hearing that Whistler was planning to return, Thomas Way, who originally provided the pastel paper, advised him on how to pack them:

> I have been very anxious about the careful transit of these same for I know how soon they are injured. Can you have a dozen light deal boxes made the exact size of the paper each to hold a limited number of the pastels – with tissue between each – & no room for shaking & consequent rubbing – They should be packed – if possible – under the eye of someone from the consulate who should be asked to sign them to show that there is nothing contraband – Thus you would be saved the risk of their being over hauled on the homeward journey –.[39]

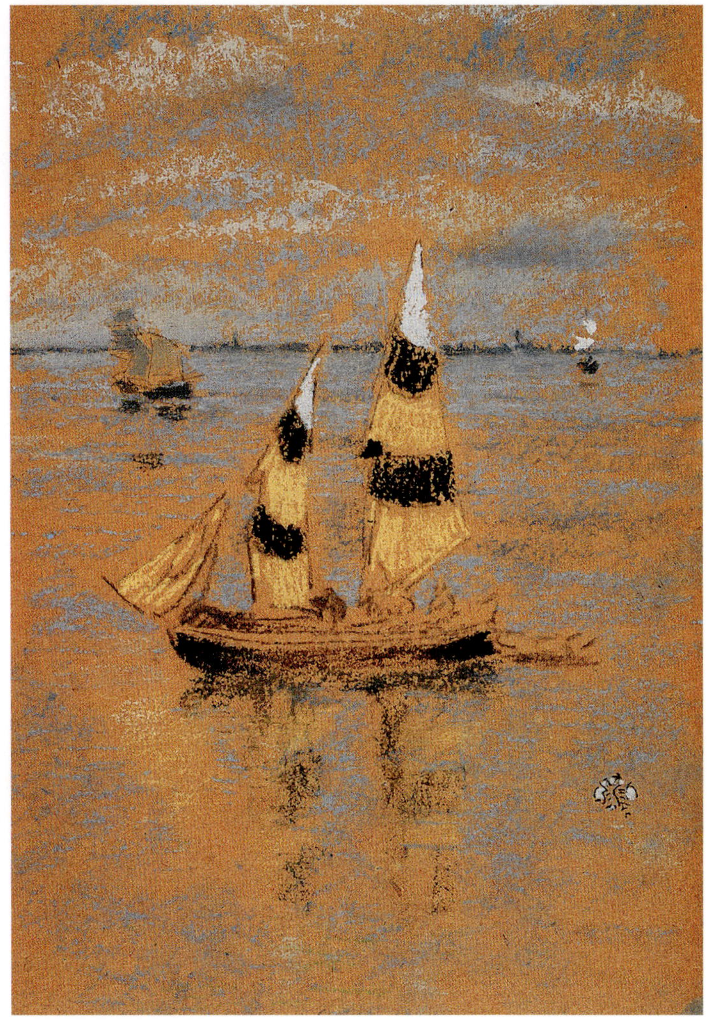

65
James McNeill Whistler
Fishing Boats
Pastel 290–6 x 200–2 mm
Cincinnati Art Museum, M.819

Preserving, storing and packing them was certainly a problem. Pastels are fragile, and the more thickly worked, the more liable to crumble and lose definition. Whistler kept them between leaves of varnished or silver-coated paper, rarely showing them. However, Way's concern was premature. Whistler settled down to work through the long summer days and ceased to communicate with London.

Summer pastels

In midwinter, he sought sheltered corners: in midsummer, shade and cooling breezes. *Fishing Boats* (fig.65) and the exquisitely detailed *Blue and silver – The Islands,*

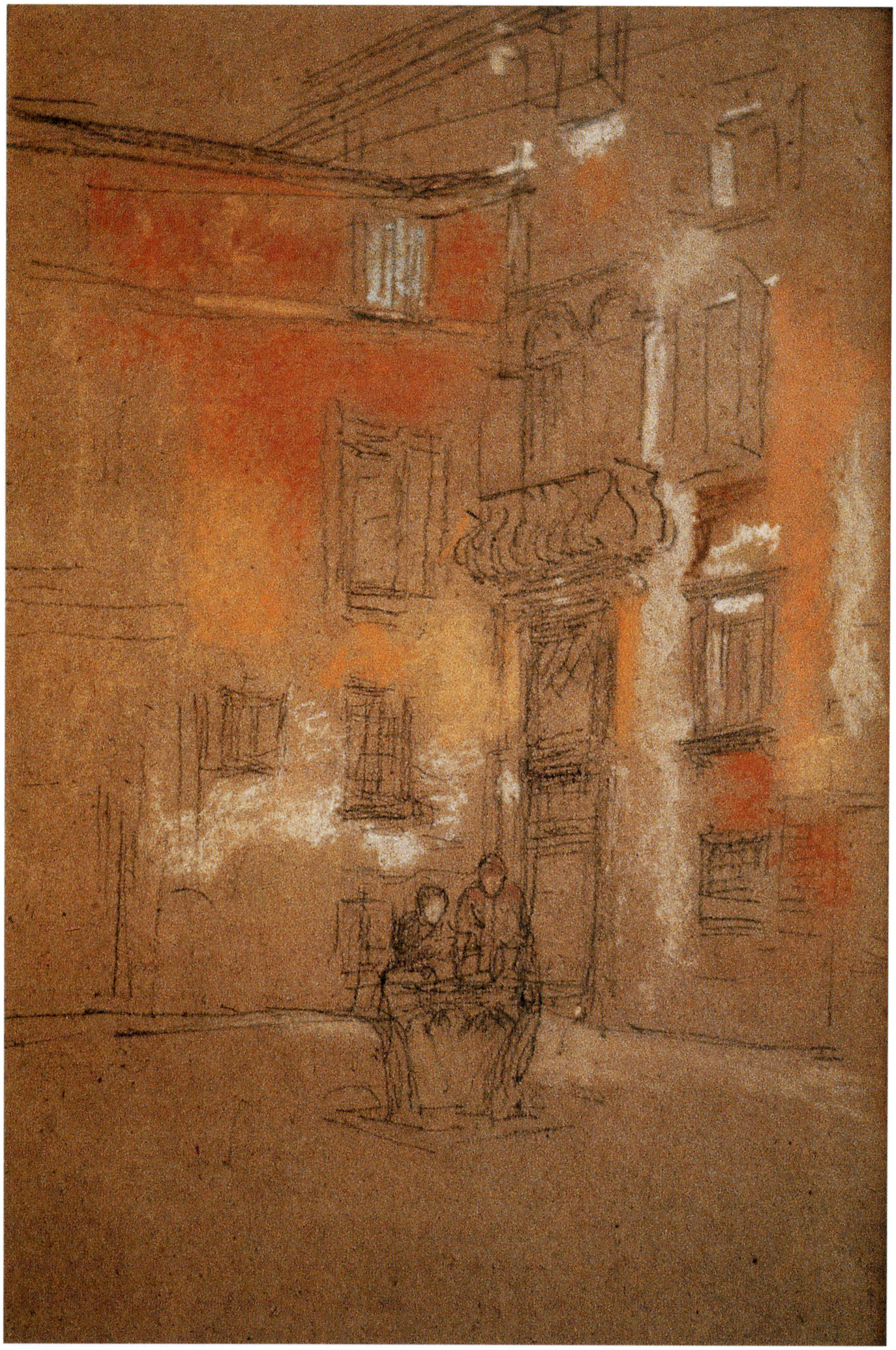

66
James McNeill Whistler
Venetian courtyard
Pastel 302 x 203 mm
Dr and Mrs John E. Larkin, Jr., M.793

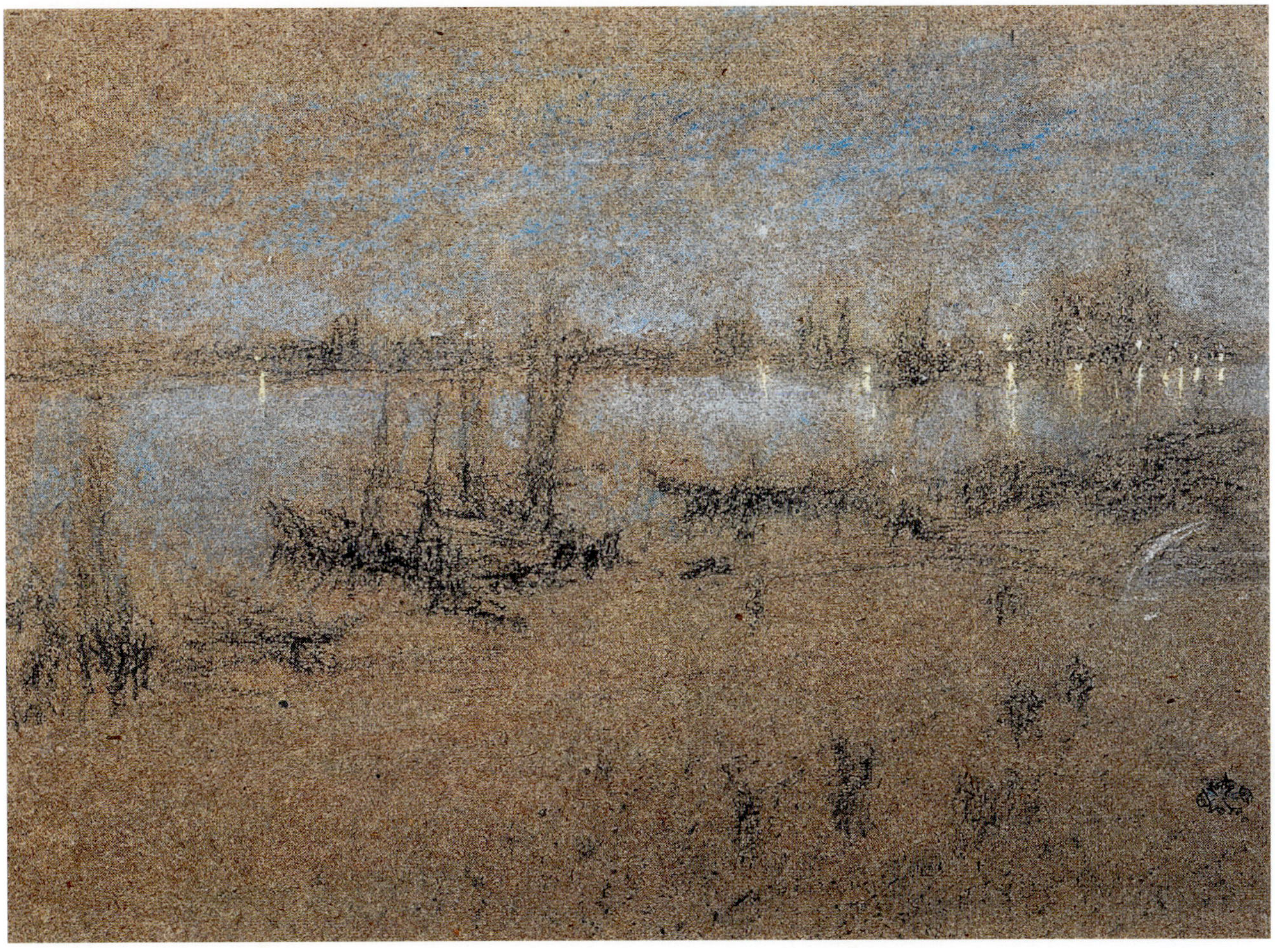

67
James McNeill Whistler
Nocturne – The Riva
Pastel
203 x 301 mm
The Frick Collection, M.799

Venice (M.822) were drawn out on the lagoons, which provided a welcome respite from the city's heat. In *Fishing Boats* (fig.65), the clouds and lagoon were drawn lightly, scumbled with grey and white, and some areas rubbed. By contrast, each stripe of the dramatic triangular sails was drawn firmly in yellow, black and white, making, as Godwin commented, 'a most powerful mosaic of black and gold'.[40]

Except at sunset, he preferred not to work facing straight into the sun. However, many an evening at sunset he drew the view from his rooms at the Casa Jankowitz, experimenting with colour combinations and a variety of linear effects. Although a couple of Whistler's glowing sunset studies – *Venice at Sunset* (M.741) and *Winter Evening* (M.755) – date from his first month in Venice, most probably date from the final weeks before his return to London, at the end of the autumn of 1880.

Within a short stroll there were tiny courtyards, sheltered and shady, like the Corte Bollani in Castello, just off the Riva degli Schiavoni and halfway between the Casa Jankowitz and the Piazza San Marco, where Whistler drew *Venetian courtyard* (fig.66). The gorgeous Venetian red of the wall is conveyed by a strictly controlled range of colour, from pale ivory and beige to orange, light red and sienna.

The pastels that he drew that summer show his total command of the medium. Bold, broken lines of clear colour – red and blue and green – and deftly rubbed and scumbled areas of softer shades of white, beige and light brick-red enrich the lean black outlines of *The Steps* (fig.68). Distinctive lines catch the individual character of the local women gossiping by the canal.

Increasing confidence in the use of line and coloured line distinguishes the late pastels, which show women at their work in the area around the Via Garibaldi. Broad strokes and dashes render the colour of their dress but not their features, so that the viewer is somewhat distanced from the subject (fig.70). By contrast, in an etching of a similar subject, a young woman threading beads, a mother with a baby and an older woman behind, are each clearly

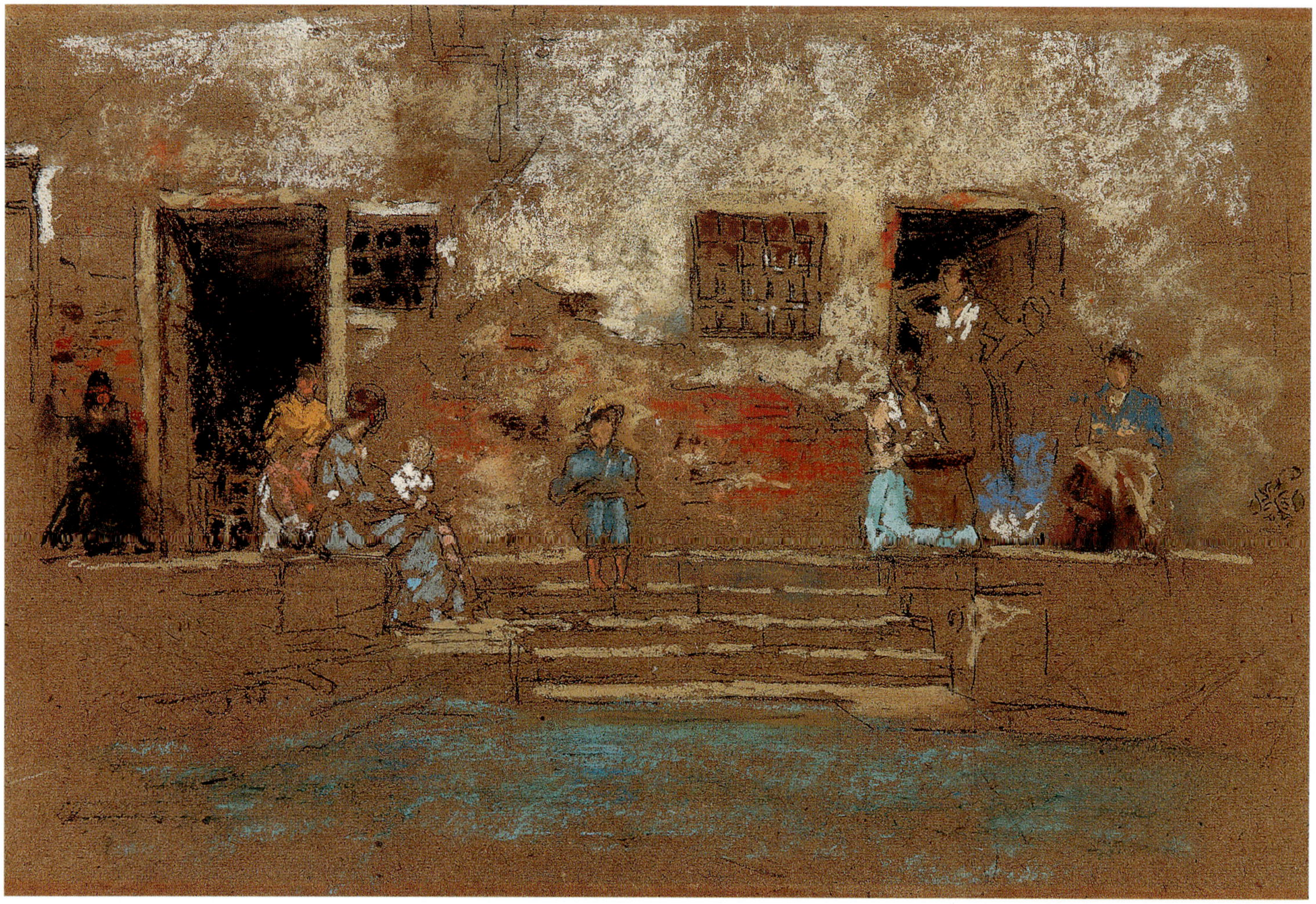

68
James McNeill Whistler
The Steps
Pastel 194 x 300 mm
Freer Gallery of Art, M.786

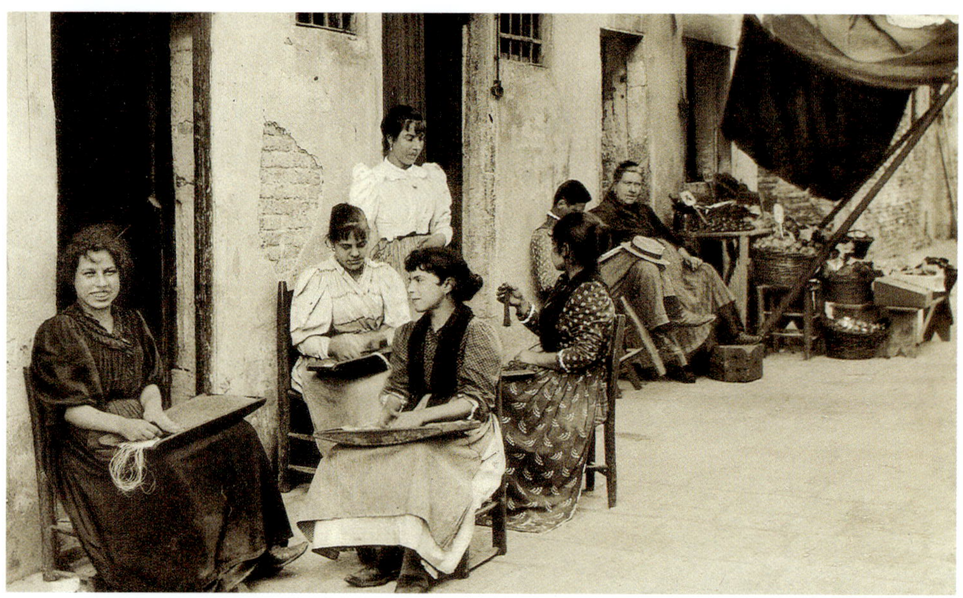

69
Bead-Stringers 1880s
Archivio Filippi
Photograph

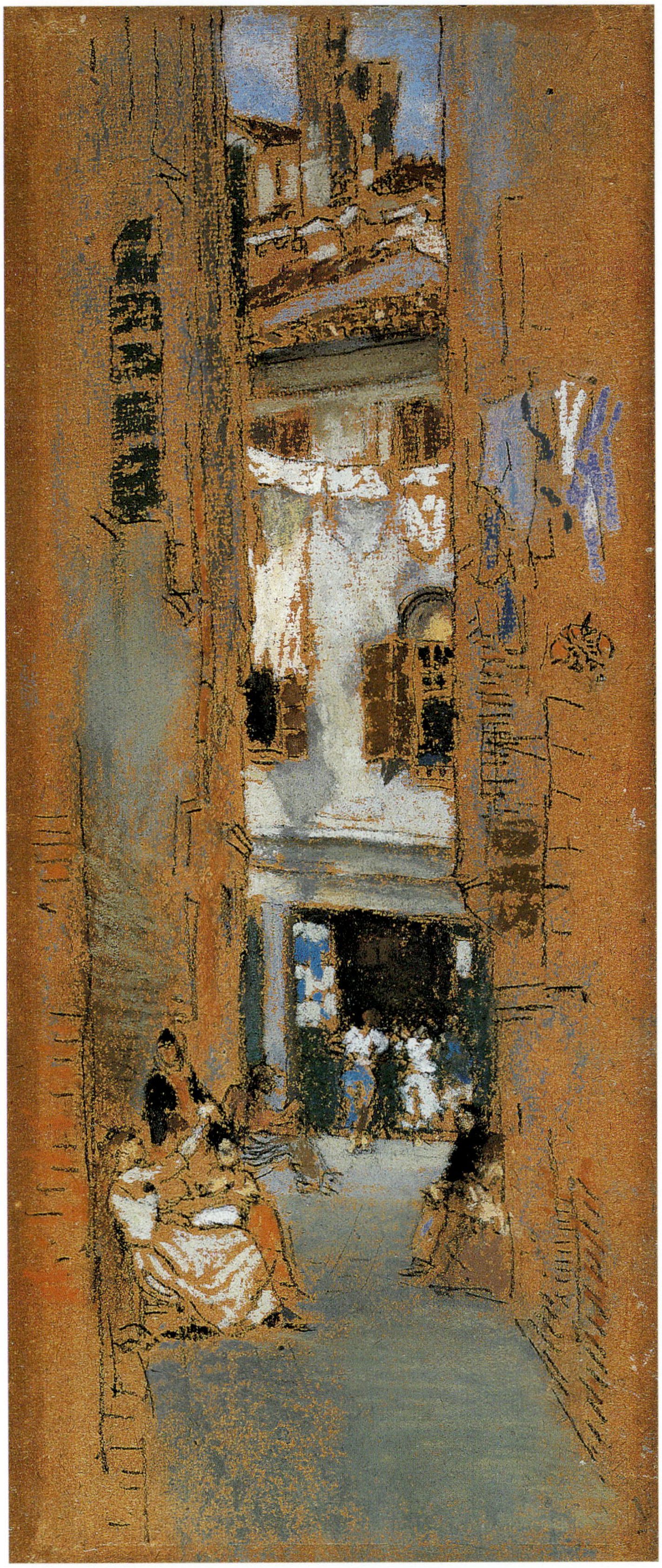

70
James McNeill Whistler
Bead-Stringers
Pastel 275 x 115 mm
Freer Gallery of Art, M.788

71
James McNeill Whistler
Bead-Stringers
Etching 227 x 152 mm
Fine Art Society, K.198 IV

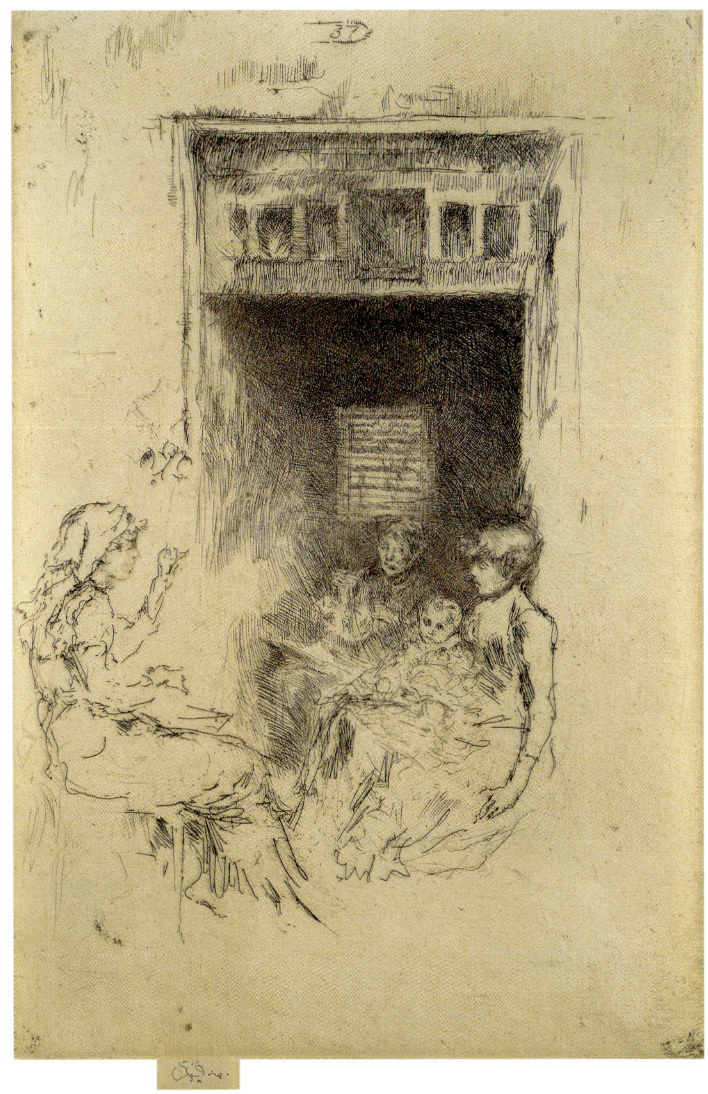

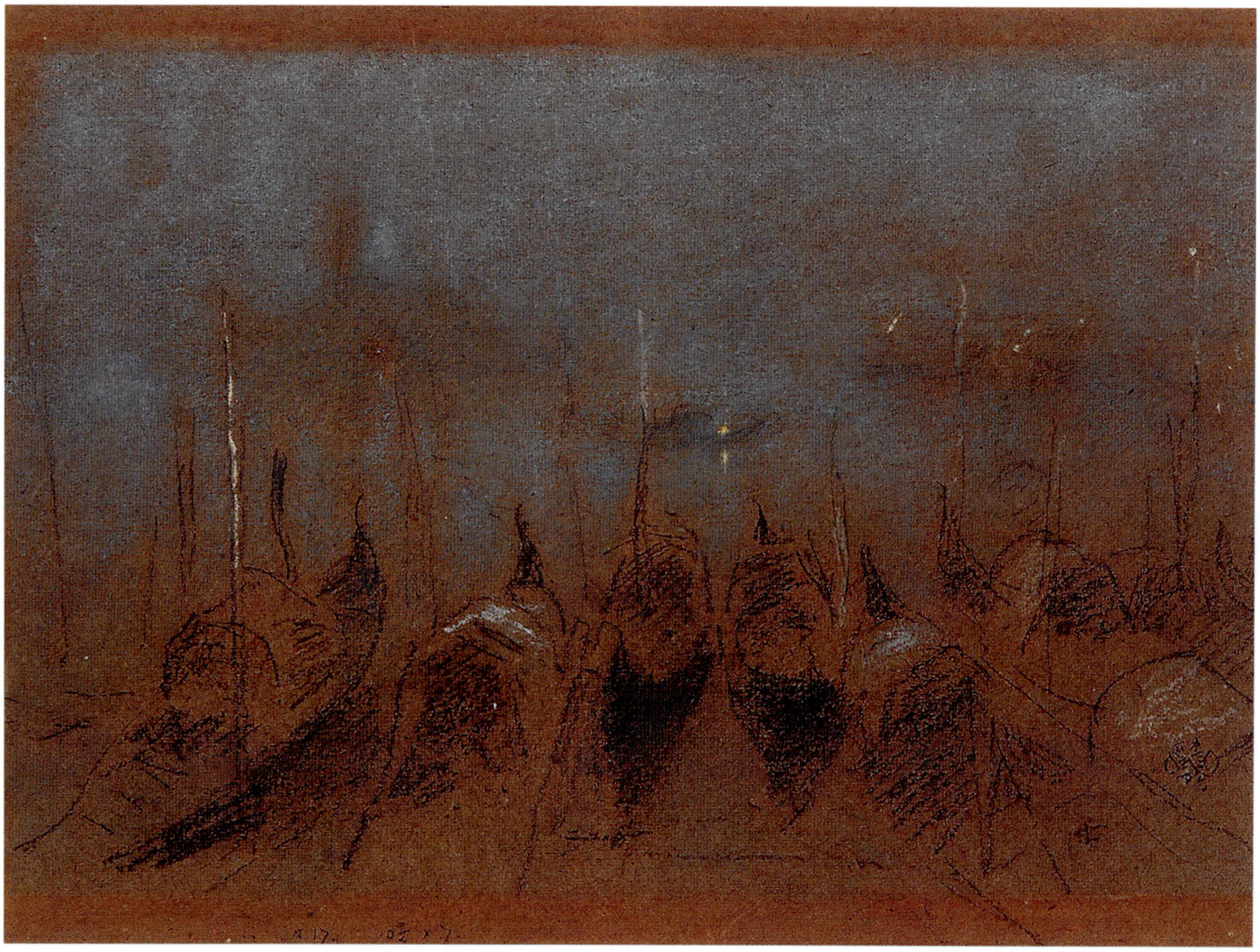

72
James McNeill Whistler
Nocturne – San Giorgio
Pastel 202 x 298 mm
Freer Gallery of Art, M.803

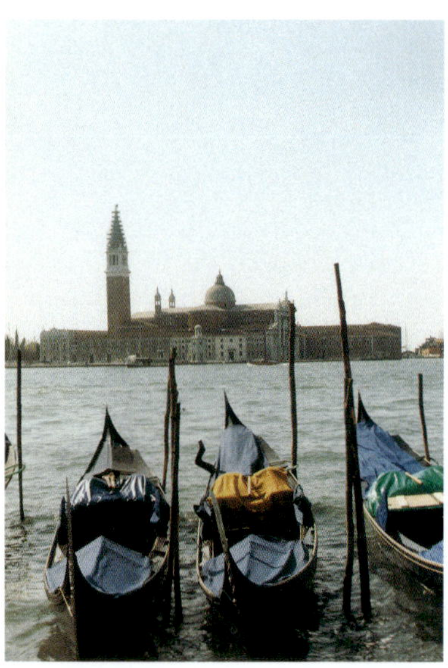

73
San Giorgio from the Molo
Photograph

delineated (fig.71). The interaction between the women, and the actual individuals represented, changed as this etching progressed. The costume, setting and work are 'typical' of Venice, but 'exotic' for a non-Italian audience. The close format and detail brings viewer and sitters together, and, as so often in Whistler's etchings, there is a sense in which the viewer is a voyeur, peeping into a picturesque and private world.[41]

Etching and pastel: the day's work

Throughout the summer and autumn, etchings and pastels alternated in his work, inspiring new developments in subject, composition and technique. 'He rose early, worked strenuously, and retired late', Bacher remembered:

> I have known him to begin an etching as early as seven o'clock in the morning [...] take up another until twelve-noon – get a bite of lunch, and commence on a third, sometimes an etching or perhaps a pastel – then take a fourth [...] and continue upon it until dusk, the subjects being wholly different. Whistler always had a half dozen under way, more or less complete.[42]

In this way he would have consistent direction and intensity of lighting on the subject. He tried to avoid the situation of having to alter the shadows on a building, for consistency of lighting made for harmony of effect. Inevitably the subjects of etchings and pastels overlap, and the sites chosen by Whistler fall into groups within easy walking or rowing distance of each other.

A pattern emerges of works done by day that show the lagoon or the working areas of the city, followed by sunset studies drawn from the Public Gardens and the Casa Jankowitz, and nocturnes from the Riva degli Schiavoni (fig.67) and on the Piazzetta. He continued to work after dark, drawing the half-visible forms of boats and the distant towers of San Giorgio across the lagoon. In *Nocturne – San Giorgio* (fig.72), he rubbed in the blue sky around the tower, leaving the brown paper to indicate the substance of the tower itself. In these late pastels, as in his better known etchings, he obsessively experimented with the medium to create subtle harmonies conveying his private vision of the life and light of Venice.

1 Nd. [15/30 April 1880], GUL E61.

2 He could also have seen work in private collections. The Goncourts owned a drawing of *Flora*, in red and white chalk on grey/brown paper, and *The Temple of Diana*, in red on cream paper; but Whistler may not have had access to their collection this early. Musée du Louvre, and Pierpont Morgan Library; M. M. Grasselli and P. Rosenberg, *Watteau 1684–1721*, exh.cat., National Gallery of Art, Washington, 1984, cat.nos 60, 71.

3 Ibid cat.no.100.

4 For example, *Draped model*, Art Institute of Chicago, M.332; *A nude binding up her hair*, Hunterian Art Gallery, M.352; D. P. Curry, 'Artist and Model' in Curry 1984, pp.35–9, 46–8, discusses Watteau's influence.

5 Freer Gallery of Art, M.468, 484.

6 Pastel, 152 x 400 mm, Museum of Fine Arts, Boston, in C. S. Stuckey, *Claude Monet 1840–1926*, Art Institute of Chicago, 1995, repr. p.189.

7 *Globe*, 16 Nov 1875; see M.566.

8 M.700–1; lithotints: N. B. Spink, H. K. Stratis and M. Tedeschi, *The Lithographs of James McNeill Whistler*, Art Institute of Chicago, 1998, cat.nos 11–12.

9 Way 1912, p.38.

10 M.727, 728, 739, 746, 753, 755.

11 'A Impressionist', unidentified press cutting, nd. [Feb 1881], GUL pc4.

12 Getscher 1991, p.128, no.45.

13 Oil, Private Collection, USA.

14 *World*, 9 and 16 Feb 1881, quoted in M.755.

15 Note of sales, 8 Aug 1882, GUL NB1, p.3. For a full description of the sites chosen by Whistler, see Grieve 2000.

16 M.728, 734, 741, 743, 749, 751, 755, 760–2, 765, 769, 772–5, 777, 783–4, 787, 790–4, 802–3, 806, 809, 810, 814; in addition M.737, 738, 739, 742, 746, 753, 754, 759, 763, 767, 770, 786, 807, 822 may be the same paper.

17 The paper used, ie for M.745, 747–8, 750, is unknown; brown papers include M.766, 782, 788, 805; orangey brown, M.744, 801, 764, 808.

18 Pennell 1908, I, pp.276–7.

19 Bacher 1908, p.75; M.752, 756, 758, 811–12, 817 and 820 are on grey, M.813 on beige, M.816 on a grey-green paper, and M.818 on dark grey paper.

20 *Pan*, 5 Feb 1881.

21 Godwin 1881, pp.98–9.

22 Bacher 1908, p.75.

23 Ruskin 1851–3, III, p.318.

24 M. M. Lovell, *Venice, The American View*, exh.cat., Fine Arts Museums of San Francisco, 1984–5, no.94. A contemporary inscription on the pastel reads 'Ponte Raspi = / o Sansoni – San Cassiano' (M.778).

25 Grieve 2000, repr. p.58.

26 Whistler to A. M. Whistler, nd. [March/May 1880], GUL W559; Getscher 1970, pp.117–18; Thorp 1994, pp.65–8, no.23.

27 Merrill 1992, p.148.

28 H. Woods to L. Fildes, quoted in Fildes 1968, p.57.

29 For example, *On the Venetian Lagoon*, 1879, oil, 180 x 450 mm, and *Venetian Backwaters*, 1888, six watercolours, each 248 x 115 mm, sale cats, Sotheby's, London, 26 April 1976 (65) and 24 Nov 1983 (78).

30 Bacher 1908, pp.201–6; see also Pennell 1908, I, p.269; Way 1912, p.53.

31 Martin Rico, *Recuerdos de mi vida*, Madrid, nd., p.113; quoted in M. F. MacDonald, 'Whistler as artist, master and friend' in *James McNeill Whistler: Walter Richard Sickert*, exh.cat., Fundación 'la Caixa', Madrid and Bilbao, 1998, p.22.

32 Maud Franklin to Bacher, nd. [Jan/Feb 1881], quoted in Bacher 1908, p.206; see also *Pan*, 5 Feb 1881.

33 Whistler to E. Brown, nd. [Nov 1883/Feb 1884], GUL LB9/16; see also Pennell 1908, I, p.269; Halsby 1990, p.87.

34 Whistler to H. Whistler, nd. [March 1880], GUL W683–4; Bacher 1908, p.76; Pennell 1908, I, p.278. The inscribed pastels are M.727, 737–9, 741, 748–9, 751, 753, 755, 762–4, 769, 771, 773–4, 779, 782–4, 803, 809–10, 816–17.

35 J. McNeill Whistler, *Venice Pastels*, exh.cat., Fine Art Society, London, 1881, cat.nos 36, 27, 49, 4, 50 or 35, 32, 18, 48, 29, 5, 13, 7, 8, 1, 17, 3, 52, 2, 51, 31, 12, respectively. Not all marginal inscriptions have survived. Two pastels bearing partial inscriptions may have been among the fifty listed (M.794, 818). Four pastels not exhibited were listed as nos 18, 22, 27 and 31 (M.748, M.816, M.741, and M.763).

36 *Venice* (M.816); see Bacher 1908, p.77, on sale of pastels.

37 *The Tobacco Warehouse* (M.762) 307 x 214 mm (12 1/16 x 8 7/16 in) was reduced to '11 x 5'; *Salute – Sundown* (M.809) on paper 200 x 268 mm (7 7/8 x 10 9/16 in) was to be framed as '10 1/4 x 4 3/4'.

38 Whistler to C. Hanson, 2 May 1880, GUL H55; Getscher 1970, pp.118–19, 147.

39 T. Way to Whistler, 1 May 1880, GUL W79.

40 *British Architect*, 4 Feb 1881, pp.59–64.

41 See Lovell 1989, p.72 and Grieve 2000, pp.132–3, 152–3. Grieve identifies the site of *Bead-Stringers* (M.788) as the Calle Drio Erizzo in Castello.

42 Bacher 1908, pp.23, 98.

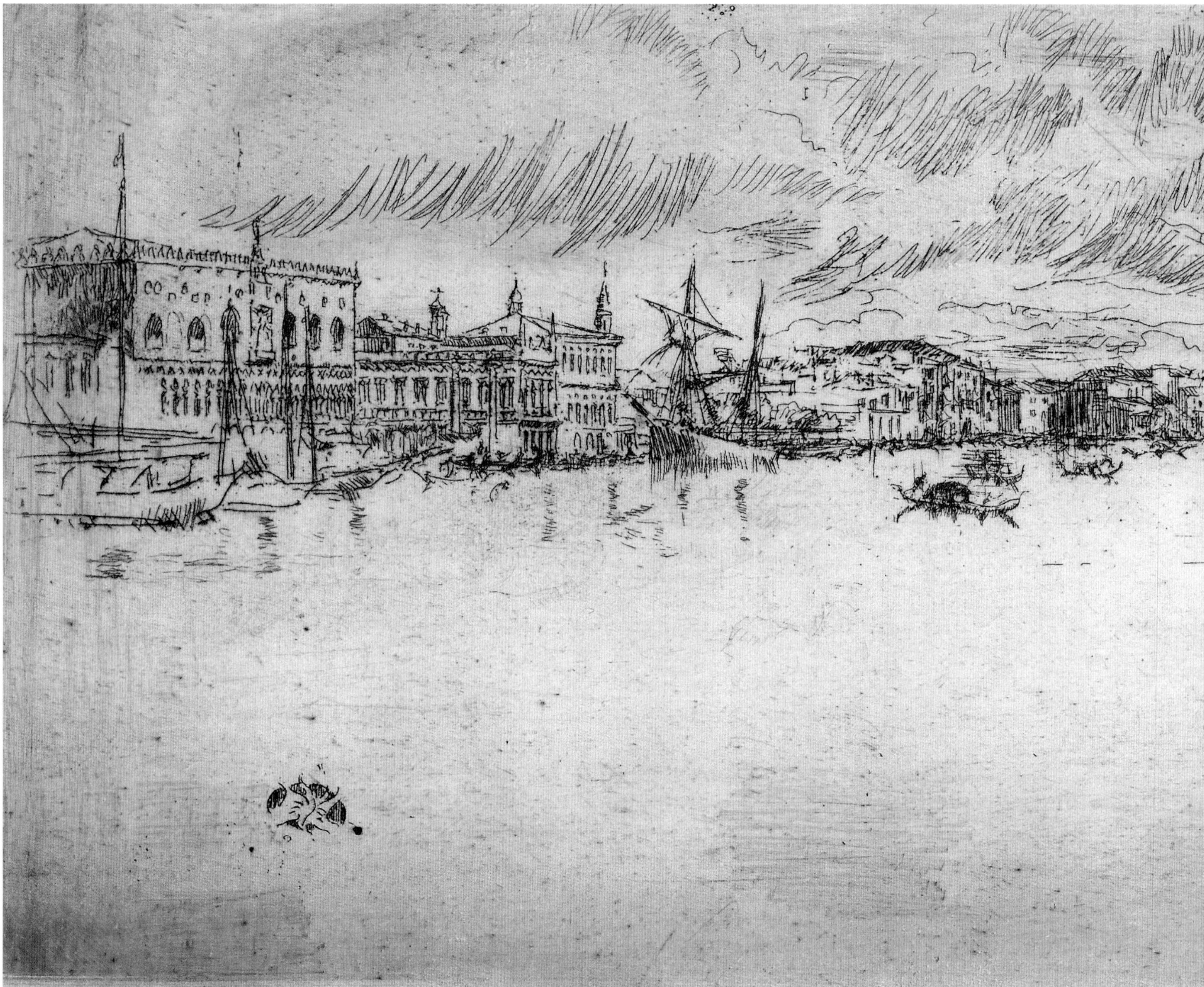

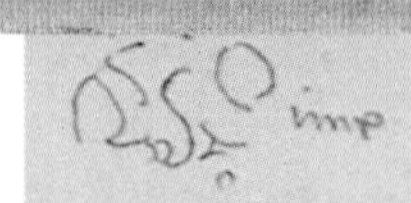
imp

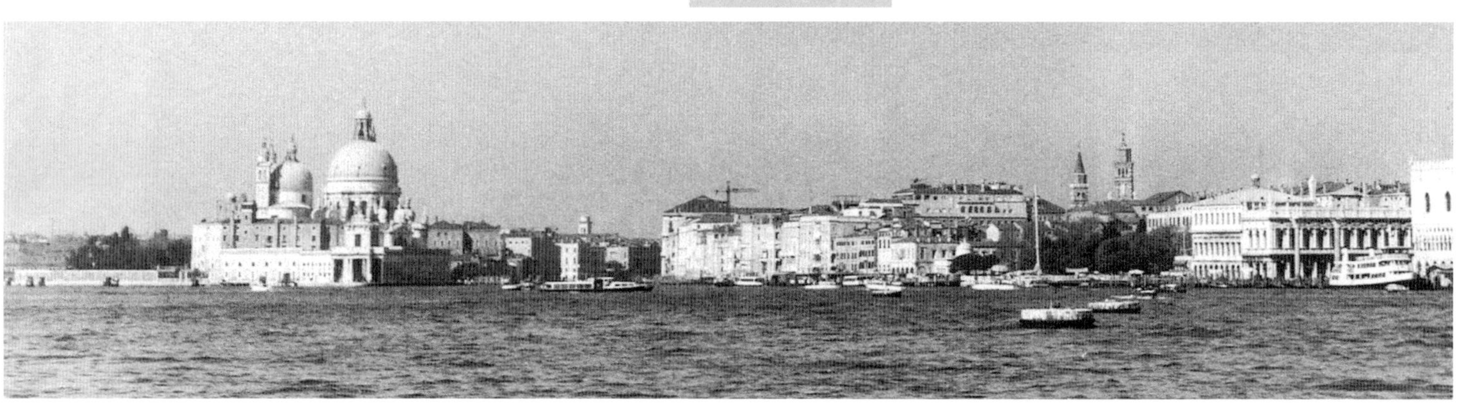

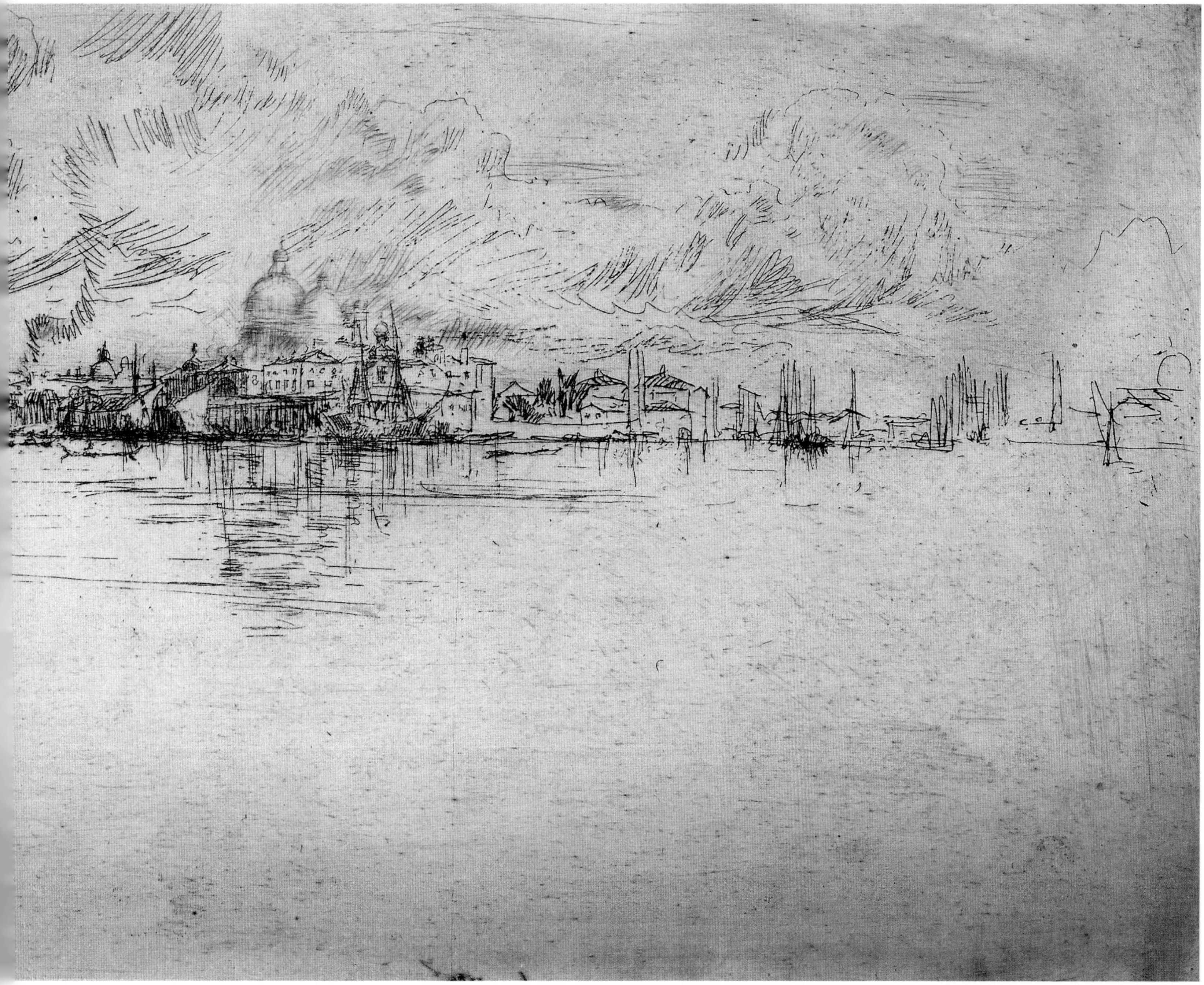

76
James McNeill Whistler
Long Venice
Etching 127 x 307 mm
Fine Art Society, K.212 v

77
Santa Maria della Salute from the Public Gardens
Photograph

Local craftsmen

Whistler was a perfectionist, and details were refined for weeks, both in Venice and back in London. Craftsman and technician, he appreciated tools and materials. He sought out shops selling artists' materials and workshops producing copperplates in Venice. Finding that the largest Hughes and Kimber plates suited his purpose best for the wide horizons and complex architecture of Venice, he ordered more large plates from local artisans. Almost immediately he tried out a handmade copperplate for *The Beggars* (K.194). Otto Bacher wrote: 'There was a simple artisan in Venice whose work upon copper was most beautiful. He could hammer out and grind down a plate to just the thinness which Whistler desired [...] reasonable in his prices, hence all of our plates were made by him.'[4]

In fact Whistler bought a number of hand-finished plates from two local craftsmen, whose work can be distinguished in the surviving copperplates. Similarities in craftsmanship and size suggest he ordered several at a time, buying others of various sizes when necessary. The backs of eight plates, including *The Piazzetta* (K.189) and *Fishing-Boat* (K.208) show the distinctive pebbled marks of a ball hammer. *Doorway and Vine* (K.196), being similar in size, may have been etched on one of these 'pebbled' copperplates, although the plate has not survived.[5]

Whistler usually carried small copperplates ready for etching and drypoint, which were easy to carry and hold. Many of the small Hughes and Kimber plates, such as *Old Women* (K.224), and 'pebbled' plates such as *Nocturne: Shipping* (K.223), are drypoints, which Whistler could draw and print quickly and send to patrons to raise money.[6]

Ten other plates, including *The Palaces* (K.187), are distinguished by small flakes or shavings of copper on the back. Four other plates now missing, including Whistler's smallest plate, *Little Venice* (K.183), may have come from this second shop.[7] Several of these subjects on 'flaked' plates are views of the lagoon with shipping done probably during the summer of 1880, and others are highly finished, elaborate subjects, intended to satisfy the Fine Art Society, and possibly made when Whistler considered returning late in 1880.

These 'flaked' plates may have been ordered with particular subjects in mind. For instance, extremely narrow plates emphasised the horizontal format of *Long Venice* (fig.76) and the vertical format of *The Mast* (K.195). None of the Hughes and Kimber plates were big enough for Whistler's largest etching, *The Palaces* (fig.78), so the big plate was acquired specially. It was so big that Whistler could not possibly have held it in his hand, but, instead, leant it on the coping of a bridge. From the Ponte de Pescaria, on the Riva de l'Ogio in San Polo, he looked straight across the Grand Canal to etch a *traghetto* station dwarfed by two Gothic palaces, the Palazzo Sagredo and the smaller Palazzo Pesaro.[8]

Large plates: 'landscapes like luncheon trays'

The scale of such plates presented problems of manipulation, both in drawing and printing. There was also a danger that Whistler would be unable to maintain the variety of line and intensity of detail in areas of repetitive detail. In *The Palaces* Whistler avoided this danger by vignetting and by completing details selectively.

Huish had heard a rumour that Whistler was etching large plates, rather than the Fine Art Society set. Whistler was indignant. The etcher, he told Huish, should avoid large plates, 'that he may not find himself worming his weary way across a waste of copper'. He attacked the 'Amateur' who etched 'landscapes like luncheon trays – while lines are bitten furiously until in the impression they stand out like the knotted veins on his own unthinking brow.'[9] The fact that Haden had established a reputation with his largest plate, *The Breaking up of the 'Agamemnon'*,[10] in 1870 may account for the ferocity of Whistler's attack. Whistler refined his statement and when the 'Second Venice Set' was published in 1886 he enclosed a list of 'Propositions' in the portfolio, stating: 'That in etching, the means used, or instrument employed being the finest possible point, the space to be covered should be small in proportion'.[11]

Etchings by Bacher and Duveneck

Frank Duveneck in his few etchings combined a large format with broad treatment. *The Riva, No.2* (fig.79) which he etched in 1880 is smaller than *The Palaces*, but a later etching, *Palazzo Ca d'Oro, Venice* is nearly twice as big. Used to working broadly with brushes in oil paint, Duveneck etched his lines deeply to create bold effects. Bacher claims that Duveneck's etching, with its strong

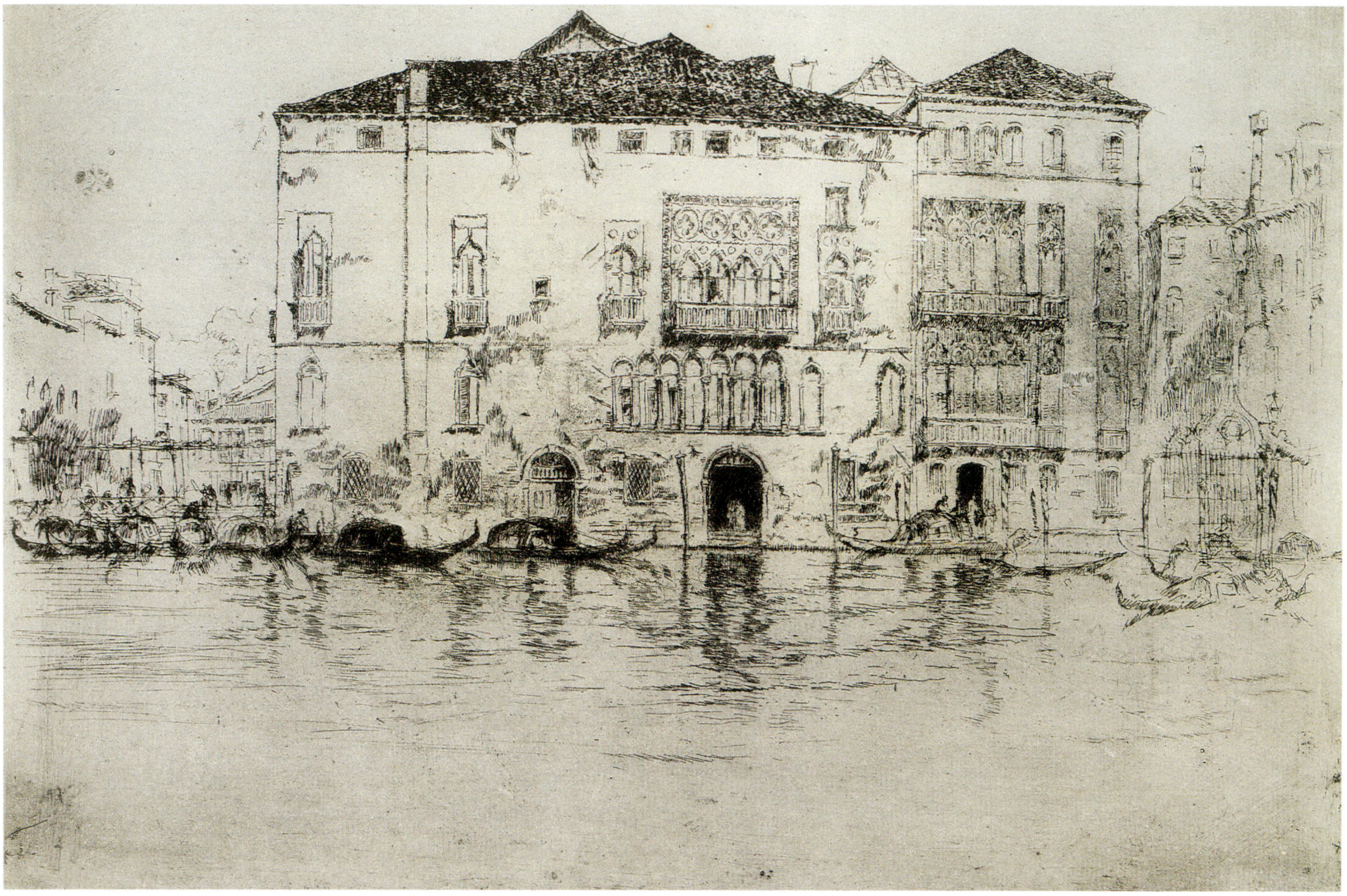

78
James McNeill Whistler
The Palaces
Etching 252 x 358 mm
The Frick Collection, K.187 II

composition dominated by the curve of the Riva and emphasised by the vertical plate, impressed Whistler, who etched two versions of the same view in horizontal format, (K.192, 206).[12] However, Canaletto's painting of the same panorama, *The Riva degli Schiavoni towards St Marks*, of 1736, in Sir John Soane's Museum in London, and several other versions of the scene, could have been known to Whistler before he left for Venice.[13]

Bacher's etchings show the influence of both Whistler and Duveneck. Whistler's influence is reflected in the small format: *Venice, Shipping and the Ducal Palace*, etched from Whistler's window, has an extremely narrow horizontal format, although some etchings, like *Lido, Venice*, (fig.80) are considerably larger. Duveneck's influence is seen in the strength of line and complex compositions.[14]

Bacher's collection

Whistler probably met Bacher in May, and used his printing press from June to August. As a reward for his help, Bacher acquired several etchings, presumably those proved and printed during that period. He had proofs of the first state of ten etchings including *Nocturne* (K.184) and later impressions of *The Traghetto, No.1* (K.190), *The Mast* (K.195) and *The Steamboat, Venice* (K.228). Of these, four appear to be Hughes and Kimber and five 'flaked'.[15] He had only one 'pebbled' plate, *Upright Venice* (K.205), which was started during the winter, or at latest by April. Bacher says it was completed 'six months' later when he was working with Whistler, so it may have been completed in October immediately before Whistler left Venice.[16]

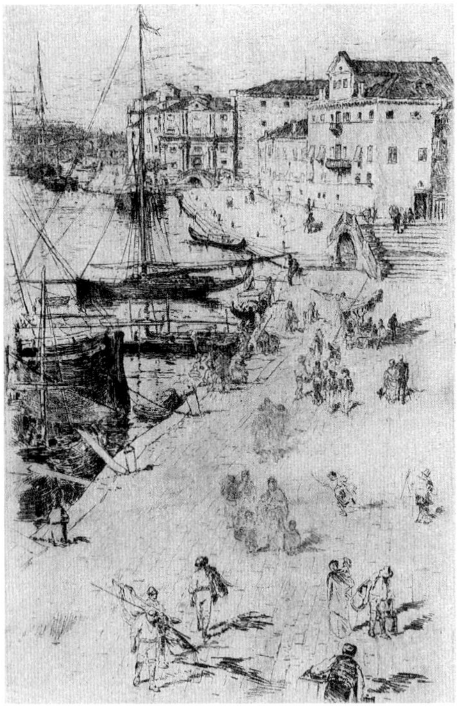

79
F. Duveneck,
The Riva, No.2 1880
Etching 337 x 220 mm
Cincinnati Art Museum

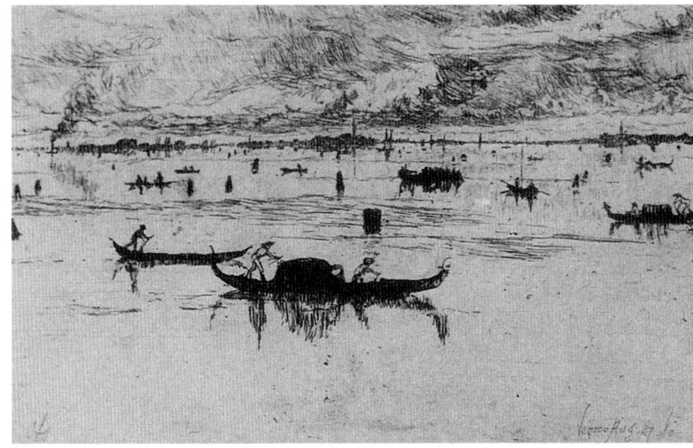

80
O. Bacher
Lido, Venice 1880
Etching 115 x 183 mm
New York Public Library

This suggests that there was some overlap in the use of the plates, but that both 'flaked' and Hughes and Kimber plates were primarily in use during that summer. This is confirmed by some of the subjects. *San Biagio*, for instance, is a 'flaked' plate, and it shows the watergate near the Casa Jankowitz where the American artists kept their boats (figs 81 and 82).

The plates that Bacher saw printed divide into two main groups. *The Doorway* (K.188), *The Traghetto, No.1* and *No.2* (K.190–1), *San Biagio* (K.197), *Ponte del Piovan* (K.209), *Garden* (K.210) and *The Mast* (K.195) are substantial plates which combine an intricate, detailed representation of buildings with small figures of people going about their business. *San Giorgio* (K.201) and three unfinished etchings, *The Steamboat, Venice* (K.228), *Shipping, Venice* (K.229) and *Venice* (K.231) are views of the distant city, drawn with minute detail. According to Bacher the last of these was cancelled, after only five proofs had been pulled, on 25 October 1880.[17] It must have been one of the last printed by Whistler in Venice, as Whistler used up his Hughes and Kimber plates.

These plates conveyed Whistler's mature view of Venice – a broad panorama of the glittering city far away across the lagoon, and intimate glimpses of life along the quiet backwaters. *Ponte del Piovan* (fig.83) was drawn from a gondola, looking north down the Rio de Ca' Widmann to the Ponte del Piovan detto del Volto, with the Palazzo Widmann beyond. The view from the bridge was popular, partly because a house on the left was said to be where Titian died. Nearby, from a gondola moored where the Rio de Ca' Widmann meets the Rio de la Panada, looking north, Whistler etched the Ponte de la Panada in *Gondola under a Bridge* (K.227). Nearer the bridge, he focussed on a single bay of the Sottoportico de la Panada in *Venetian Court* (K.230).[18]

These etchings demonstrate what Whistler called 'the secret of drawing' he had discovered in Venice:

> I began first of all by seizing upon the chief point of interest. Perhaps it might have been the extreme distance, – the little palaces and the shipping beneath the bridge. If so, I would begin drawing that distance in elaborately, and then would expand from it until I came to the bridge, which I would draw in one broad sweep. If by chance I did not see the whole of the bridge, I would not put it in. In this way the picture [would] necessarily be a perfect thing from start to finish.[19]

Whistler was closely bound to working on site, even during the winter: 'When "all outdoors" means lovely work of the most fascinating – with every possible joy thereto attached – golden guineas among others – then

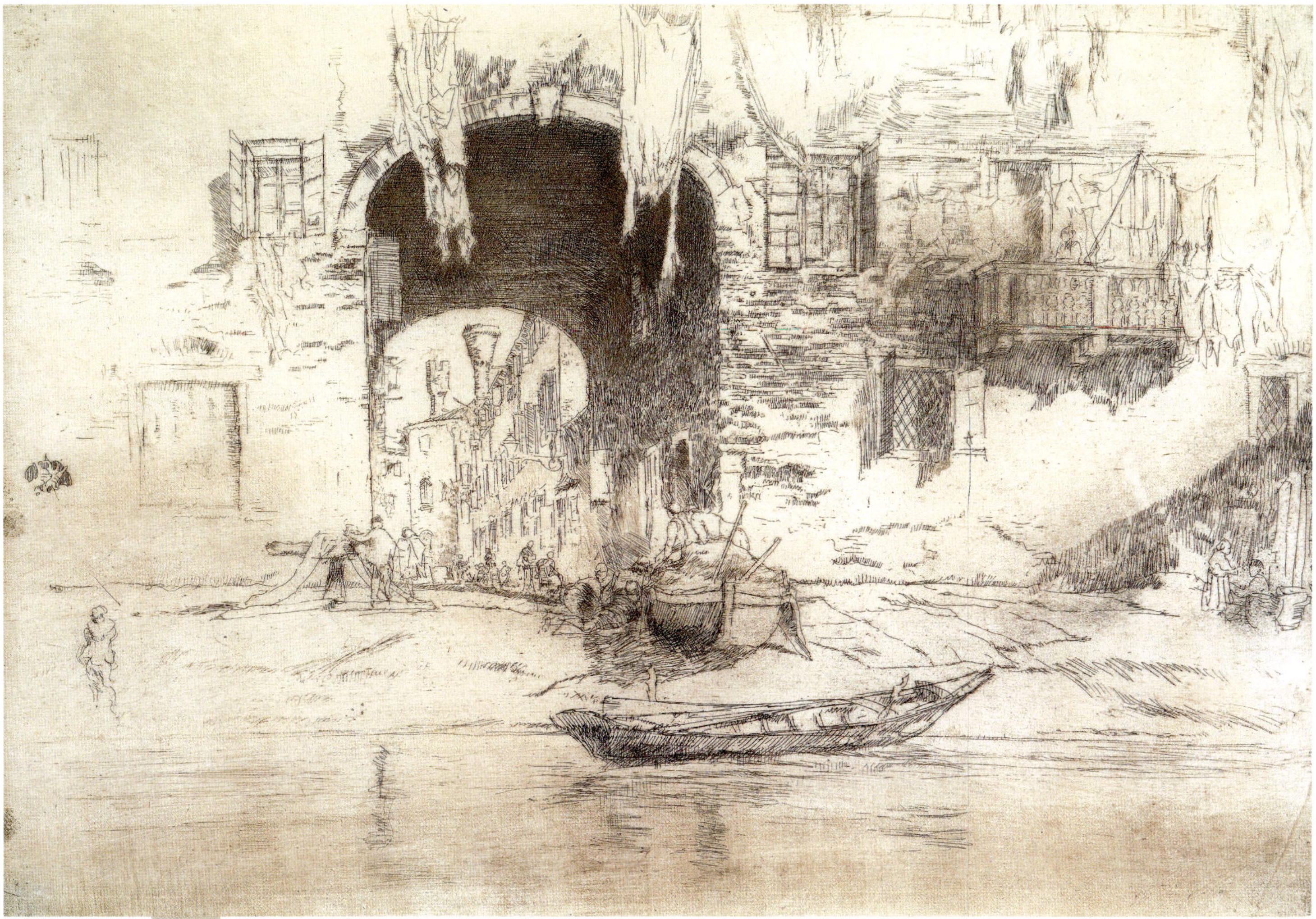

81
James McNeill Whistler
San Biagio
Etching 209 x 301 mm
Hunterian Art Gallery, K.197 IV

you can fancy the rage of the pent up painter! [...] suffering most acutely but unable to remain in my cage –'.[20] The subject dictated both technique and composition. These subjects were immediately recognisable as Venice yet characteristic of Whistler's point of view.

Bacher saw Whistler printing the most distinctive of his etchings, *Nocturne* (K.184). Three nocturnes are on Hughes and Kimber plates: *Nocturne, Nocturne: Palaces* (K.202) and *Nocturne: Salute* (K.226), while *Nocturne: Shipping* (K.223) and *Nocturne: Furnace* (K.213) are both 'pebbled' plates. Nocturnes were a recurrent theme in Whistler's work, a defiant assertion of his independence and aesthetic continuity. It was no small part of his aim to

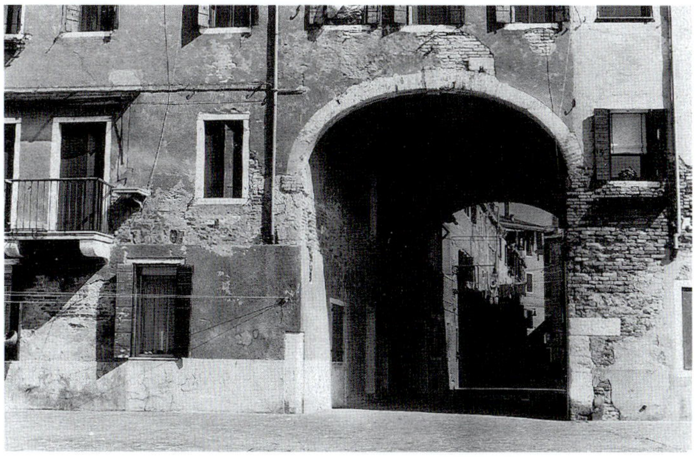

82
Sotoportego Secondo de le Colone, Castello
Photograph

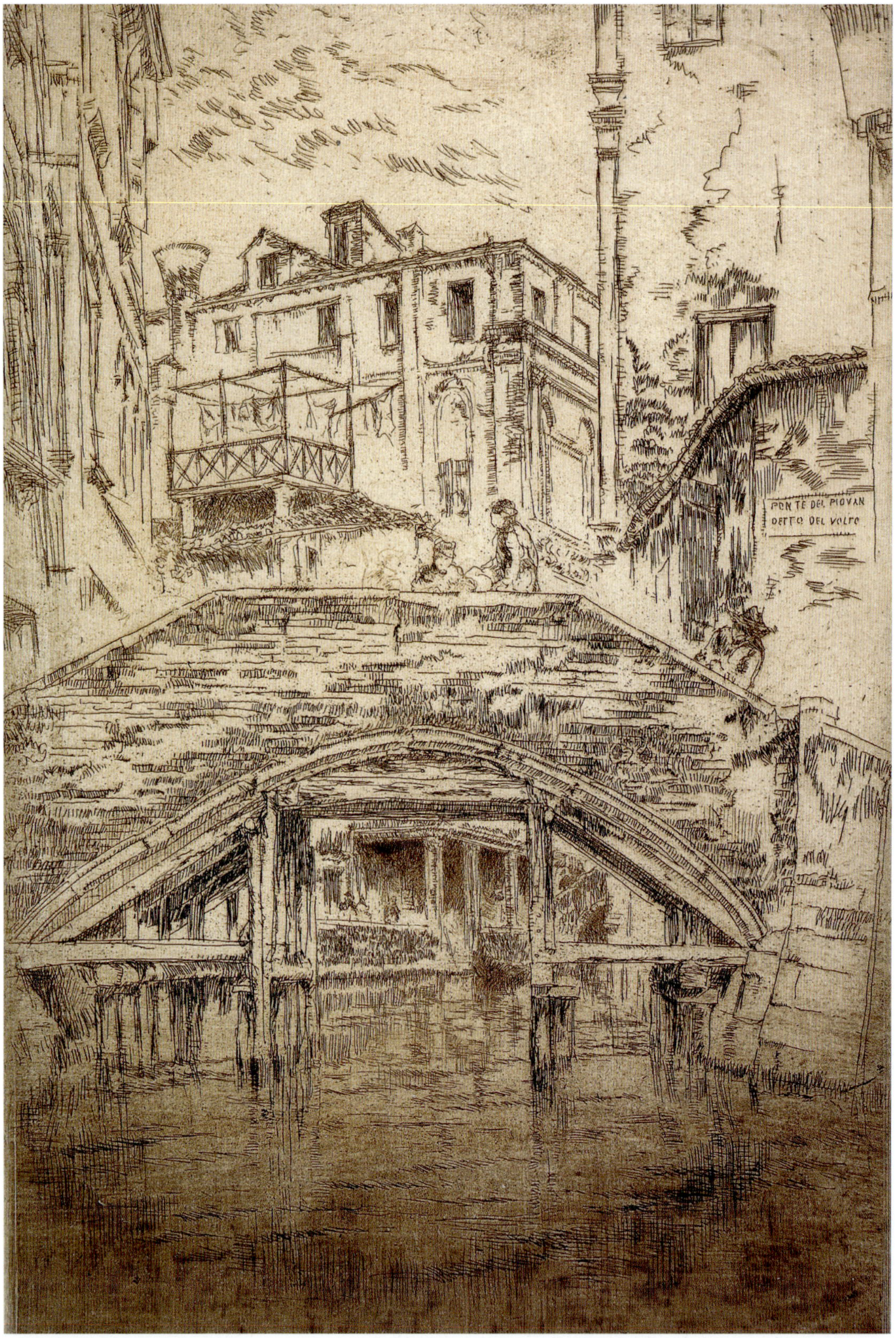

83
James McNeill Whistler
Ponte del Piovan
Etching 226 x 152 mm
Hunterian Art Gallery, K.209 IV

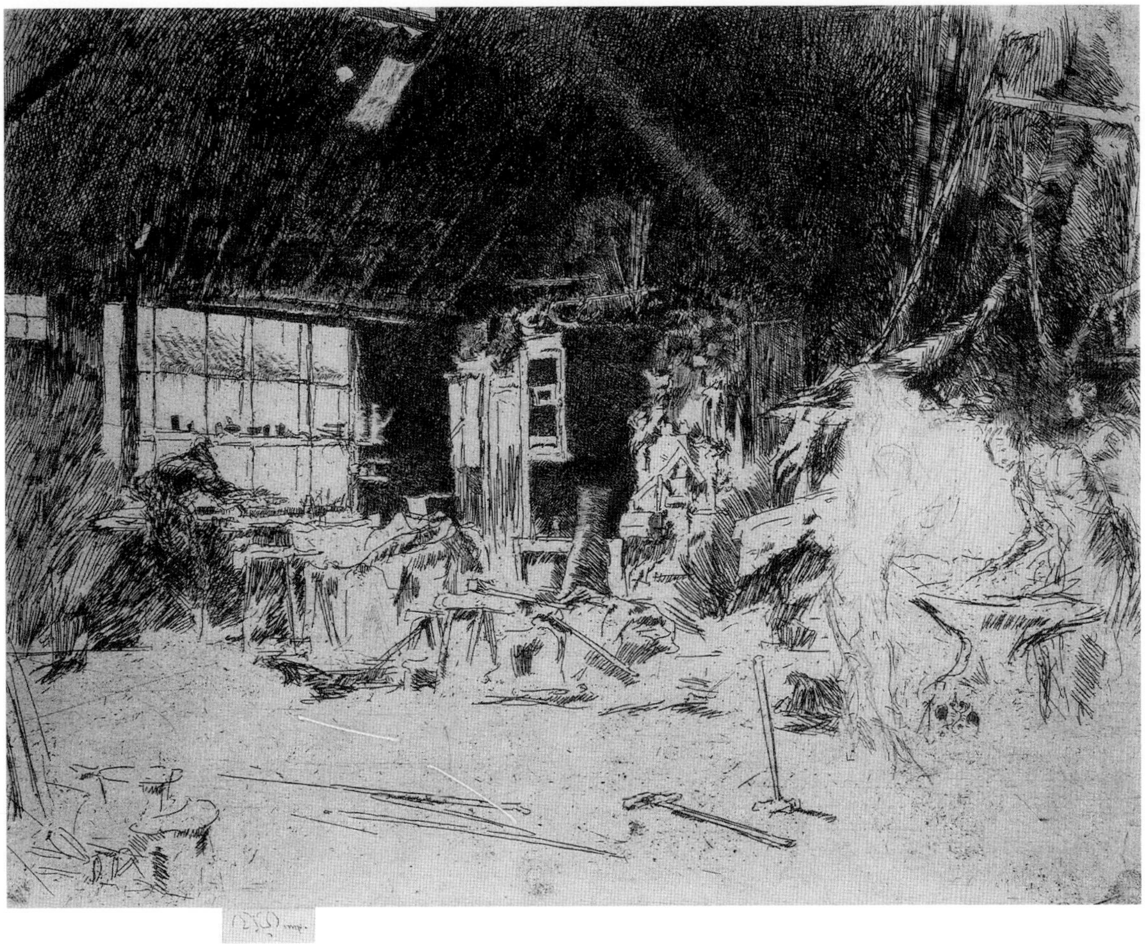

84
James McNeill Whistler
The Smithy
Etching and pencil 173 x 225 mm
Freer Gallery of Art, K.240 v

prove, by the unparalleled quality of his work, his choice of subject matter and distinctive technique, that he was right and Ruskin, Haden, Leyland and the critics – the 'Enemies' – were wrong. The plates of these nocturnes are of various types, the treatment different, and they must have been done at intervals throughout the year.

Having used the Hughes and Kimber plates, the 'pebbled' and 'flaked' plates, Whistler acquired a few more plates, presumably from local craftsmen, which appear to have been machine made. *The Smithy* (fig.84) may show the craftsman himself at work, but the figure was never completed, despite alterations suggested in pen and pencil on several proofs.[21]

A number of these plates remained unfinished, suggesting they were among the last done by Whistler in Venice. Although incomplete, one impression of *Wool-Carders* (fig.85) was beautifully reworked, becoming more watercolour than etching. These last plates depict the local people at work. *Turkeys* (K.199) and *Fruit-Stall* (K.200) were drawn in the working class area near the Via Garibaldi. *Venetian Water-Carrier* (K.232) was the only isolated single figure he etched in Venice, and only a couple of rough proofs survive, possibly pulled by Bacher after Whistler abandoned the plate.[22] These studies hark back to the realism of his first etchings, just as his compositions echo etchings like the *Marchande de Moutarde* (K.22) in the 'French Set'.

Whistler usually drew directly on the copperplate without preliminary studies, and then the copperplate was wrapped in paper to protect it from scratches. Occasionally he sketched subjects, such as *Venetian canal* (M.731) and *Bead-Stringers* (M.732), on this wrapping paper. One sketch was used in the preparation of an etching. From San Giacomo di Rialto in San Polo on the west bank he drew the Rialto bridge and the *campanile* of San Bartolomeo (fig.86). This view being obscured by people and awnings, he crossed the Grand Canal to etch *The Rialto* (fig.88) from a window over the Sottoportico Pirieta in the Campo San Bartolomeo. This provided a clear view of the bridge and the *campanile* of San Giovanni Elemosinario beyond, and was a variation on a popular

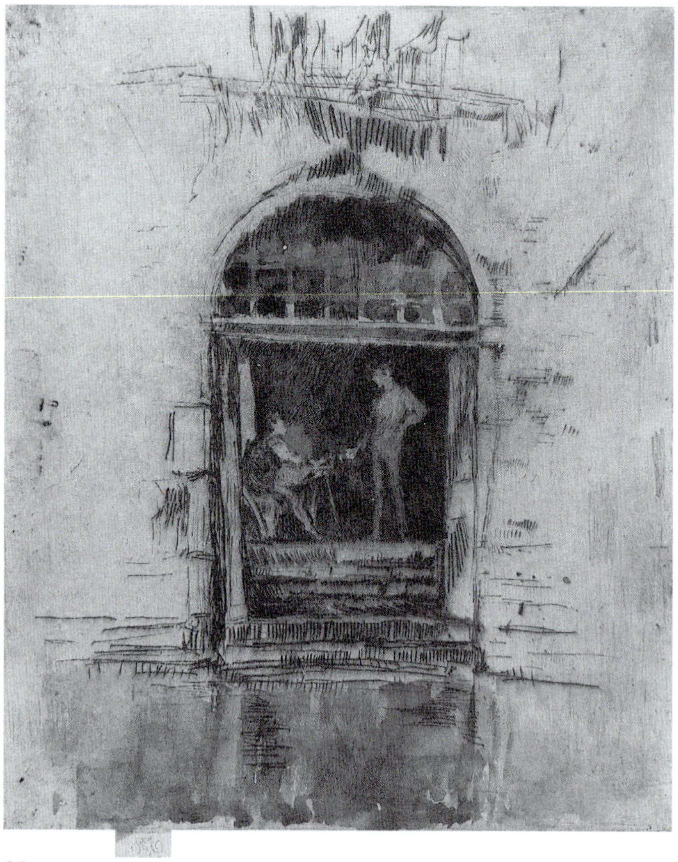

85
James McNeill Whistler
Wool-Carders
Etching and wash 270 x 185 mm
Hunterian Art Gallery, K.221 I

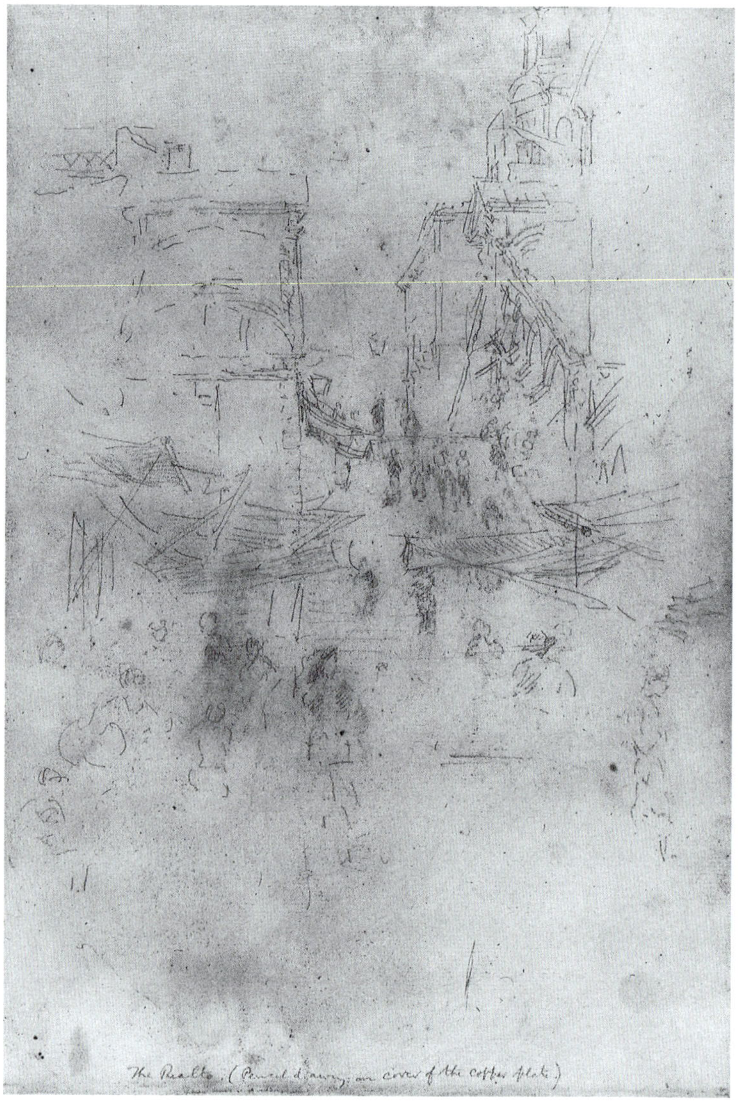

86
James McNeill Whistler
The Rialto
Pencil 384 x 335 mm
Hunterian Art Gallery, M.733

subject.[23] The nature of the city meant many sites were only accessible by water, but the advantage of working undisturbed from a window, supporting the plate on the windowsill or a table, are obvious.

Preparing the copperplate

A copperplate is about two millimetres thick, and is prepared with a thin acid-resistant shiny black coating. Whistler prepared the copperplates himself. In January he wrote asking Ernest Brown to send supplies, 'a couple of little balls of varnish ("etching ground" the proper name – and you get them at Hughes & Kimber, West Harding Street, Chancery Lane [...] While you are about it send 3 and a small bottle of "Stopping Out varnish"'.[24]

Later, Bacher saw him preparing his own etching ground:

> Whistler always used the old-fashioned ground composed of white wax, bitumen pitch, and resin.

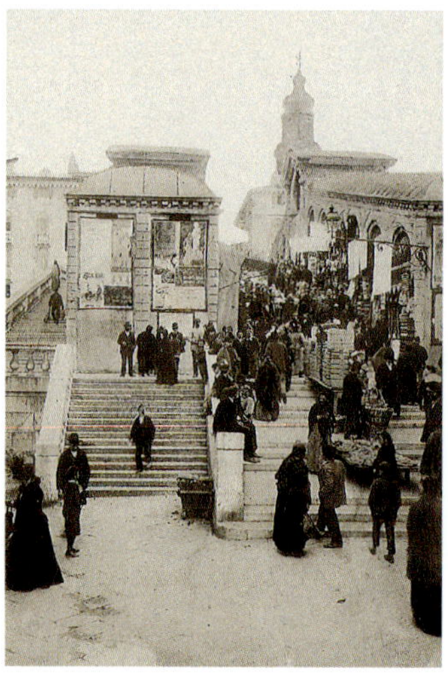

87
Rialto 1880s
Archivio Filippi
Photograph

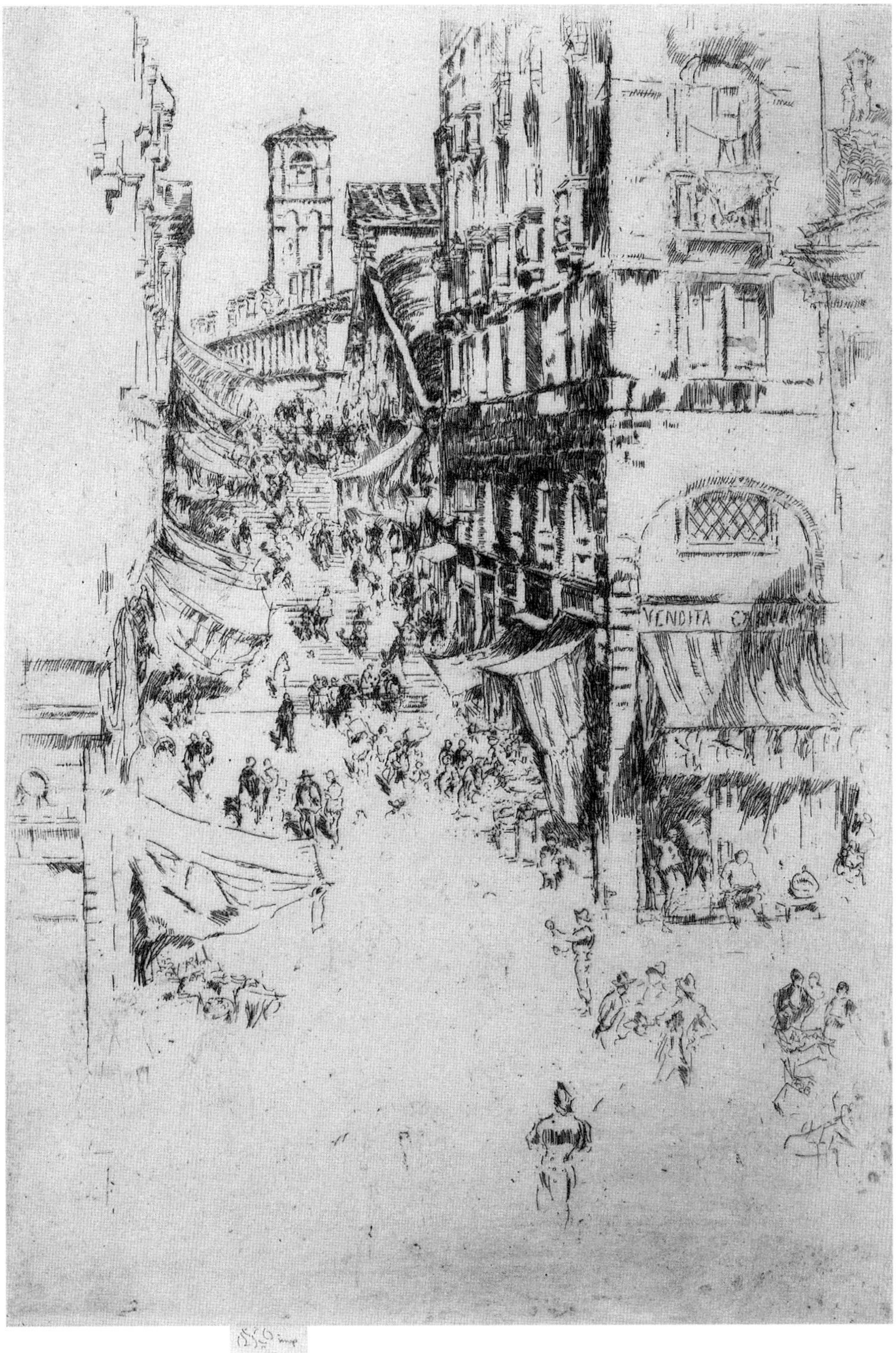

88
James McNeill Whistler
The Rialto
Etching 297 x 200 mm
National Gallery of Art, Washington, DC, K.211 II

He heated the plate with an ordinary alcohol flame, holding the copper in a small hand-vice brought with him from England. The silk-covered dabber that spreads the ground over the plate was fascinatingly managed by Whistler, who seemed to love every phase of etching. When he came to smoking the plate, he preferred the old wax taper made for that purpose.[25]

Bacher's assistance was welcome; he used what he called 'Rembrandt's preparation' to ground Whistler's plates: thirty grains of white wax melted in an open pot, fifteen of gum mastic and fifteen asphaltum or amber, ground separately. Smoking provided a shiny black surface through which the etched lines showed gold. Whistler always carried with him a grounded plate, and sometimes a clean one for drypoint.

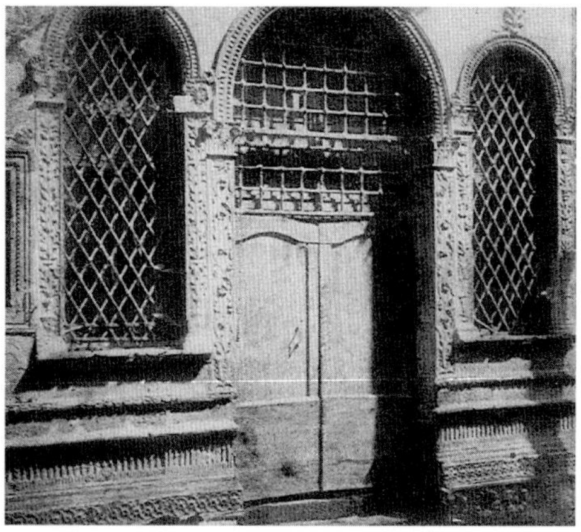

89
Otto Bacher
Palazzo Gussoni, Rio de la Fava 1880s
Photograph

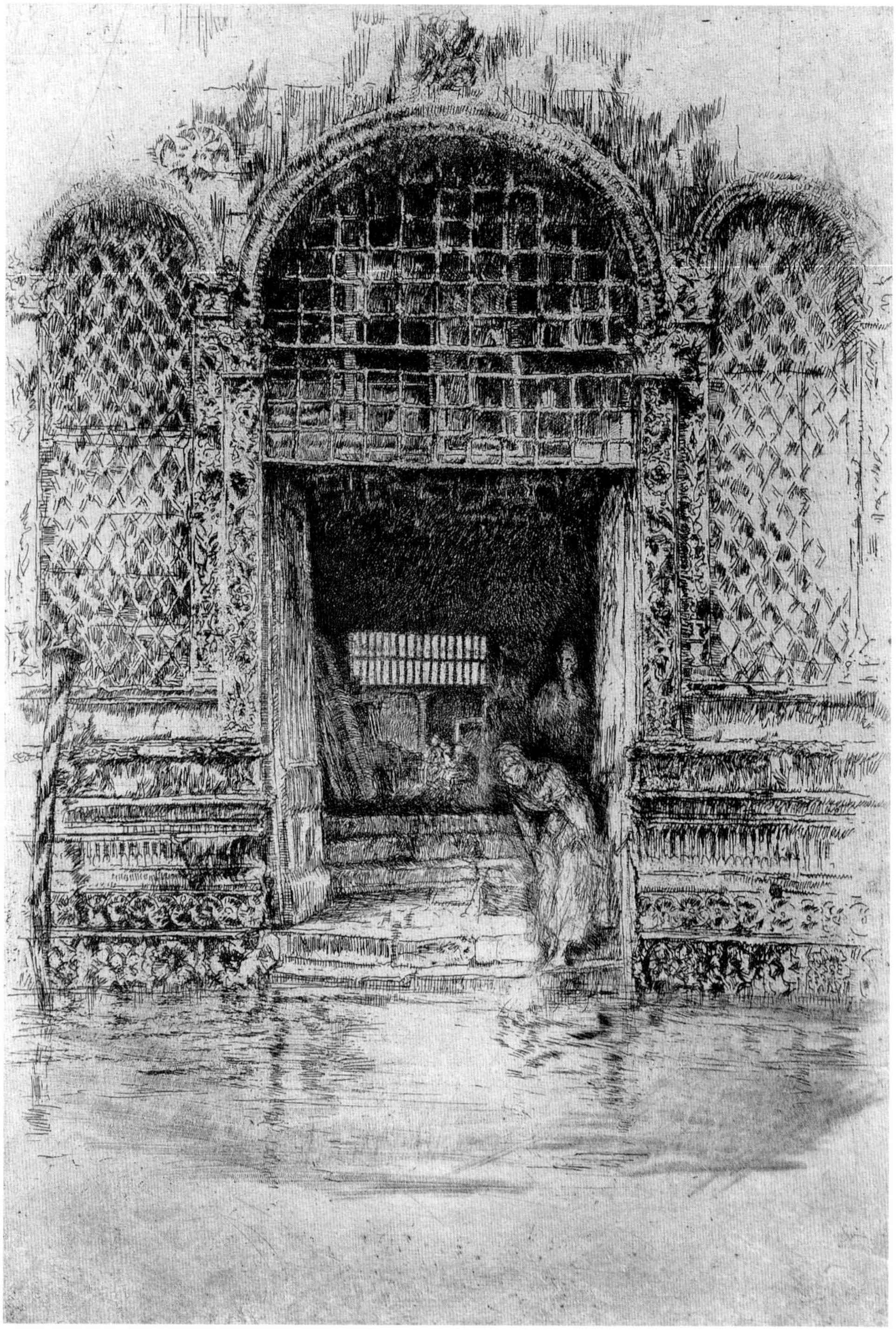

90
James McNeill Whistler
The Doorway
Etching 292 x 201 mm
Fine Art Society, K.188 IV

Etching and Drypoint

The etching needles were just dentist's tools, carried pushed into a cork and whetted on a small oilstone to the finest point. Whistler had excellent eyesight, but used an eyeglass to focus on areas of finest detail. Drawing with a needle on the copperplate throws up a fine ridge of copper that holds ink and, in the printing, produces a very fine, though soft and velvety, line. It can give very rich effects but wears down quickly. Whistler used drypoint for quick sketches like the gorgeous *Islands* (K.222), and also to modify etchings – for instance, to add, complete and replace details in *Nocturne* (figs 94 and 95). The ghosts of gondolas past are barely visible in late impressions; lines fade till they are fine as cobwebs, finally disappearing entirely. These fragmentary images, or layers of images, have something of the instantaneous, spontaneous effect of early photographs. The ephemeral nature of drypoint was no drawback to collectors, since it guaranteed rarity, nor to the artist, who could charge more for impressions. Whistler manipulated the market by elevating the value of ephemeral prints of 'unimportant' subjects: however, the fact that the wider subject was Venice, an accepted object of pilgrimage for generations of artists and patrons, reassured collectors of their 'importance'.[26]

Etching is a lengthier process, but an etched plate can produce dozens of impressions, where the drypoint can produce only half-a-dozen. Even an etched plate must be steeled before the full editions of a hundred and more, beloved of print dealers, can be produced. Whistler preferred to maintain the plate in its etched condition under his control and revise it as he went on.

Etching the plate

Bacher's first etchings were drawn directly with the waxed plate in an acid bath, by what was called Hamerton's positive method. It was fast, but he soon turned to Whistler's method as it allowed more time, 'drawing the subject leisurely in one to a dozen sittings and biting the plate indoors, away from the subject.' Bacher learnt:

> how to etch a deep, variegated door with a deeper figure somewhere in that darkness, all contrasted against something in the near opening that was much darker and which made the doorway effective. If he etched a doorway, he played with the lines and allowed them to jumble themselves into beautiful forms and contrasts, but was always very careful of the general direction they should run as a whole.[27]

The variations in line and shading in *The Doorway* (fig.90) are a good example of this method. *The Doorway* shows the Palazzo Gussoni, a small Renaissance palace dating from about 1500 and attributed to Pietro Lombardo. It faces west across the Rio de la Fava, south of the Ponte San Antonio. Whistler drew the doorway, with its fine carving and intricate ironwork, from his gondola moored opposite.[28] According to the critic Harry Quilter, he too spent several days that spring drawing 'a specially beautiful doorway', until Whistler asserted his prior right to the subject, saying he had had the grill put up over the door.[29] In a strongly symmetrical composition, the door frames a series of receding and interlocking parallel planes, a carpenter's workshop with doors and windows leading to an inner courtyard. Whistler was delighted that the chairs hanging from the ceiling were recognisable in his etching.[30] Successive states of the etching show that he made almost no alterations to the deeply etched detail of the iron and stonework, but never fully resolved the figure of a girl that forms an intermediary between the dark interior and the viewer.

The lines have a wiry three-dimensional quality that is mainly a product of Whistler's use of acid. He used the 'old negative process' for biting. With the tip of a feather he dripped and brushed nitric acid diluted with water on the plate. 'If he desired to make any change on some particular spot, he would blow away the acid, make the desired change, and re-cover with the feather.'[31] Thus he could vary the depth of biting. Then he drained off the acid and checked for accidental scratches or false biting. Lines sufficiently etched could be painted out with stopping out varnish, made of asphaltum varnish, old etching ground, white wax and ether, applied delicately with a brush.

When Whistler was etching the elegant P&O steamer for *San Giorgio*, (fig.91) Bacher was an interested observer:

> he painted out small parts of the general lines with the retouching varnish, varying them up and down, sometimes leaving them for several days, until the desired shape was obtained. The boat was left white

because it fitted the general scheme of the plate.
Working at irregular intervals, Whistler devoted a month or six weeks to this plate. It is the only Whistler plate that was bitten with Dutch mordant. He [...] always said that it was over-bitten.[32]

Inking the plate

When satisfied that the lines were properly bitten in, he would clean the plate with turpentine, and it was ready for printing. He spread ink with a dabber, moving the plate over the surface of a plate heater. The cooled plate was wiped 'in light, quick strokes – *pit-pat-pat* – that fairly cut away the stiff ink', said Bacher. Some 'lines are bitten so shallow that only with the greatest care and knowledge is it possible to retain the ink in them', he added, but Whistler could pull a rich proof from plates that 'would baffle an ordinary printer.'[33]

In several of his most evocative plates Whistler left a carefully graduated film of ink over the surface of the plate, which, when printed, conveyed something of the atmosphere and the warm glow of light across the still lagoons that no amount of etching in line or drypoint could convey. The most extreme example is *Nocturne*, (figs 94 and 95) in which the tower of San Giorgio Maggiore and the masts of sailing ships were suggested with delicate vertical lines, and a few lamps, by the finest of radiating lines. The first proof stayed in Whistler's estate; it was printed in black ink on off-white paper, wiped almost bare of ink, and it looks curiously bleak and naked. Later impressions were usually printed with tone, the artist '"wiping out" spots along the shore to represent gas-lights'. It was, Bacher said, 'the most meager in lines of any of his plates of Venice, yet, by the use of tone and few lines, he has expressed more than in any other plate which I can remember.'[34] It required careful and individual printing to produce effects ranging from sunset to black night. Each impression was virtually a monotype.

This was a method that greatly appealed to Bacher. In Florence the Duveneck 'boys' had drawn on plates with 'some pointed instrument or thumb, using burnt sienna or ivory black and a medium' and printed the results on Bacher's press. His fellow-students called each unique print a 'Bachertype'; and Bacher thought they influenced Whistler.[35]

All Whistler's Venetian nocturnes rely to some extent on the surface tone of ink to give depth and atmosphere to the web of lines. *Nocturne: Shipping* (K.223) and *Nocturne: Furnace* (K.213) are less dependent on variations in tone, but are usually quite heavily inked and always carefully wiped. In *Nocturne: Salute* (K.226) difficulties in printing the insubstantial spidery drypoint lines resulted in a paler treatment, reminiscent of a misty dawn. By contrast, a richer and more dramatic use of black plate-tone is seen in later impressions of *Nocturne*, where tall ships and the tall campanile of San Giorgio are lost in enveloping misty darkness.[36]

For Whistler the new subject – Venice – inspired a fresh approach to materials, both etching and pastel, and the materials, as he mastered them, suggested new approaches to the subject. Collaborating in printmaking and evolving new techniques, he produced some of his finest works. Whistler printed on Bacher's press, or, for the largest plates, helped an old Venetian printer to print on his wooden presses. He told the American printer, Joseph Pennell, that he worked with an old press said to have been used to print Canaletto's plates. It 'used to pull with difficulty up to a certain point, and then went with such a rush that it had to be stopped, for fear the bed would come out on the floor.'[37]

Making corrections: proofs and states

Whistler's proofs in Venice were usually printed on heavy wove paper. Seen against the light, wove paper is plain, whereas in laid paper the grid-like pattern of the wire paper-making frame shows up as light lines. Proofs printed in black ink, with the plate cleanly wiped, produced a clear proof that was then checked for omissions and mistakes. Corrections were sometimes drawn on the proof with diluted ink or watercolour, not necessarily from nature. Several were worked over with ink, and some of the suggested alterations were carried out, making a new state of the plate. An impression of *The Balcony* (K.207) in an intermediate state between I and II was touched up in pen, vividly suggesting alterations to the figures, but these were not carried out exactly.[38] Additions in dark brown ink to *Old Women* (fig.96) blend with the soft furry lines of fresh drypoint. Whistler apparently meant to complete the child on the left and shade the window and doorways behind the figures, but never returned to the copperplate.

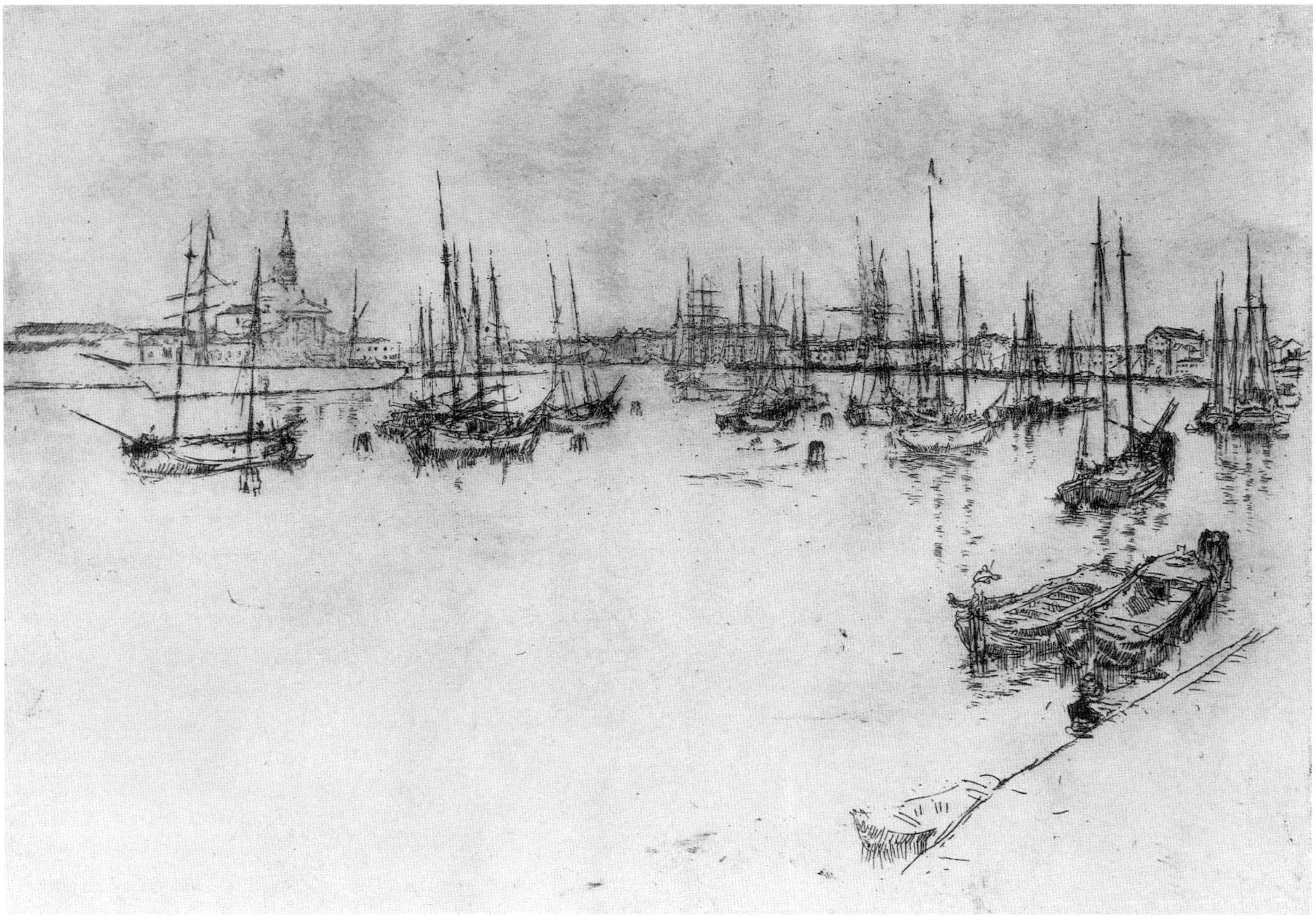

91
James McNeill Whistler
San Giorgio
Etching 208 x 302 mm
Hunterian Art Gallery, K.201 III

There were various ways of completing additions or alterations in the studio. He could add drypoint lines to modify and complete details or whole areas, as in *Nocturne* (K.184). He could also rub areas down with stone and charcoal, to soften or eliminate lines. Whistler could also recoat the plate, and rework it. Extensive rebiting was sometimes necessary, as in *The Beggars* (K.194 I–III) and *The Balcony* (K.207). In such cases the plate was placed face down on the anvil and hammered with the ball of a hammer over the area needed. The area could then be burnished, recoated, redrawn and rebitten.[39]

Dramatic alterations were made in *Upright Venice* (figs 92 and 93). The horizon, with the distant domes of Santa Maria della Salute and shipping, was etched in first, exquisitely clear and sharp.[40] A rough proof of the first state was printed in black ink on a heavyweight off-white laid paper, with broad margins. Another proof was printed on eighteenth-century Venetian paper, also in black ink.[41] In the second state Whistler created a strongly structured composition, with the diagonal line of the quayside cutting across the foreground, boats by the *riva* and groups of figures.

This was beautifully printed in brown ink, with a light film of ink wiped vertically to indicate water. The first state left much to the viewer's imagination, while the second state defines the boundaries of space.

The most radical revisions of all involved the etchings of *The Traghetto, No.1* and *No.2* (K.190–1). When Bacher first

92
James McNeill Whistler
Upright Venice
Etching 252 x 178 mm
National Gallery of Art,
Washington, DC, K.205 I

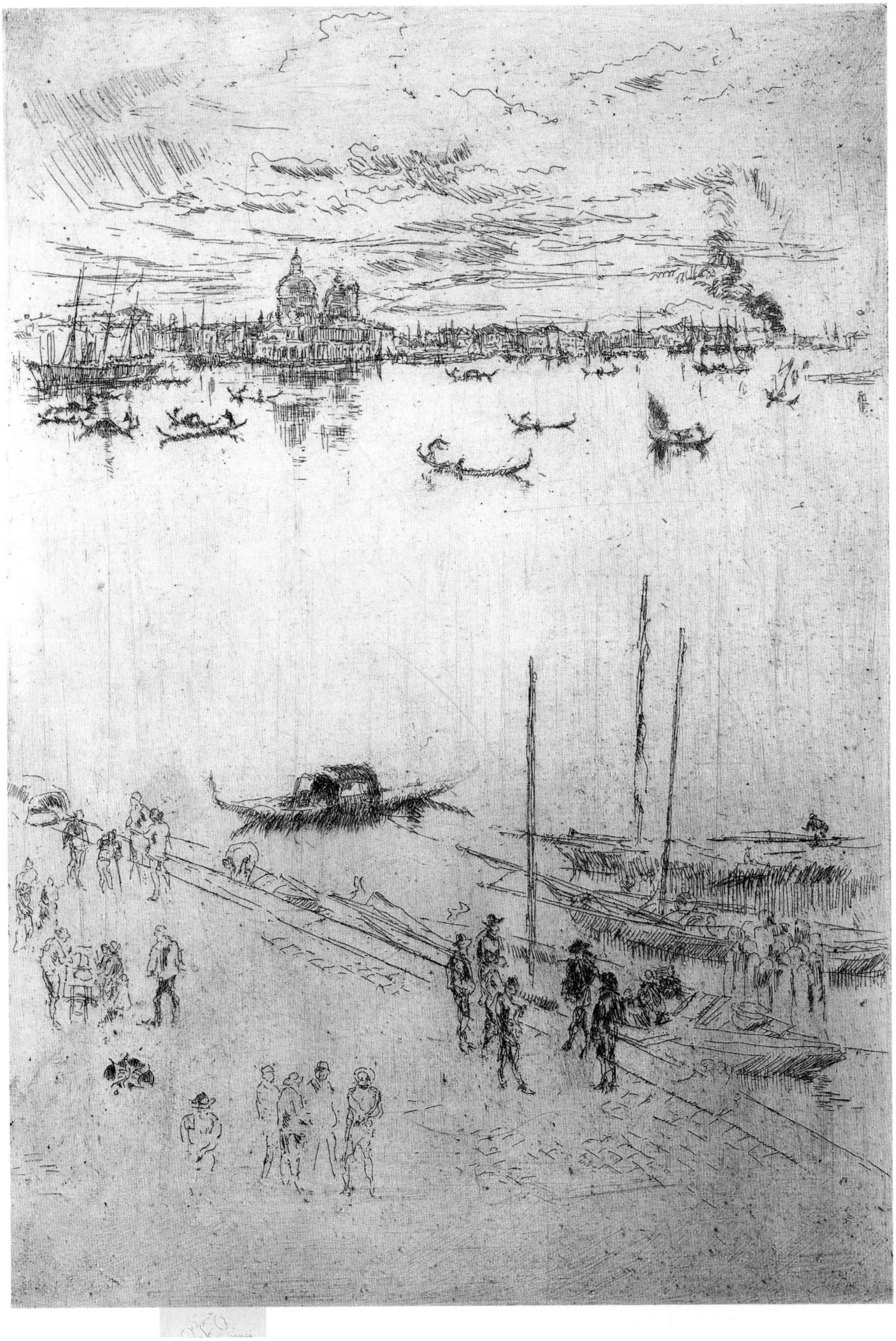

93
James McNeill Whistler
Upright Venice
Etching 252 x 178 mm
Private Collection, K.205 II

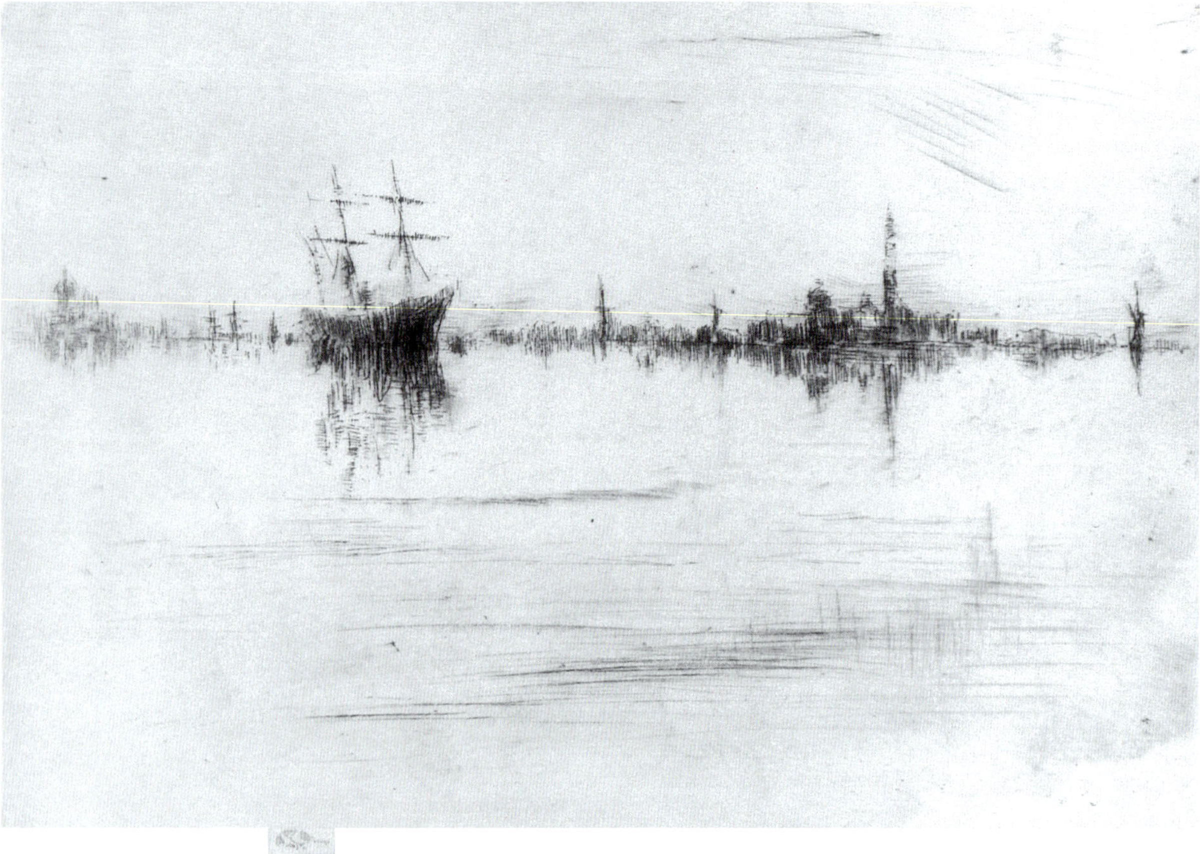

94
James McNeill Whistler
Nocturne
Etching 198 x 294 mm
Hunterian Art Gallery,
K.184 I

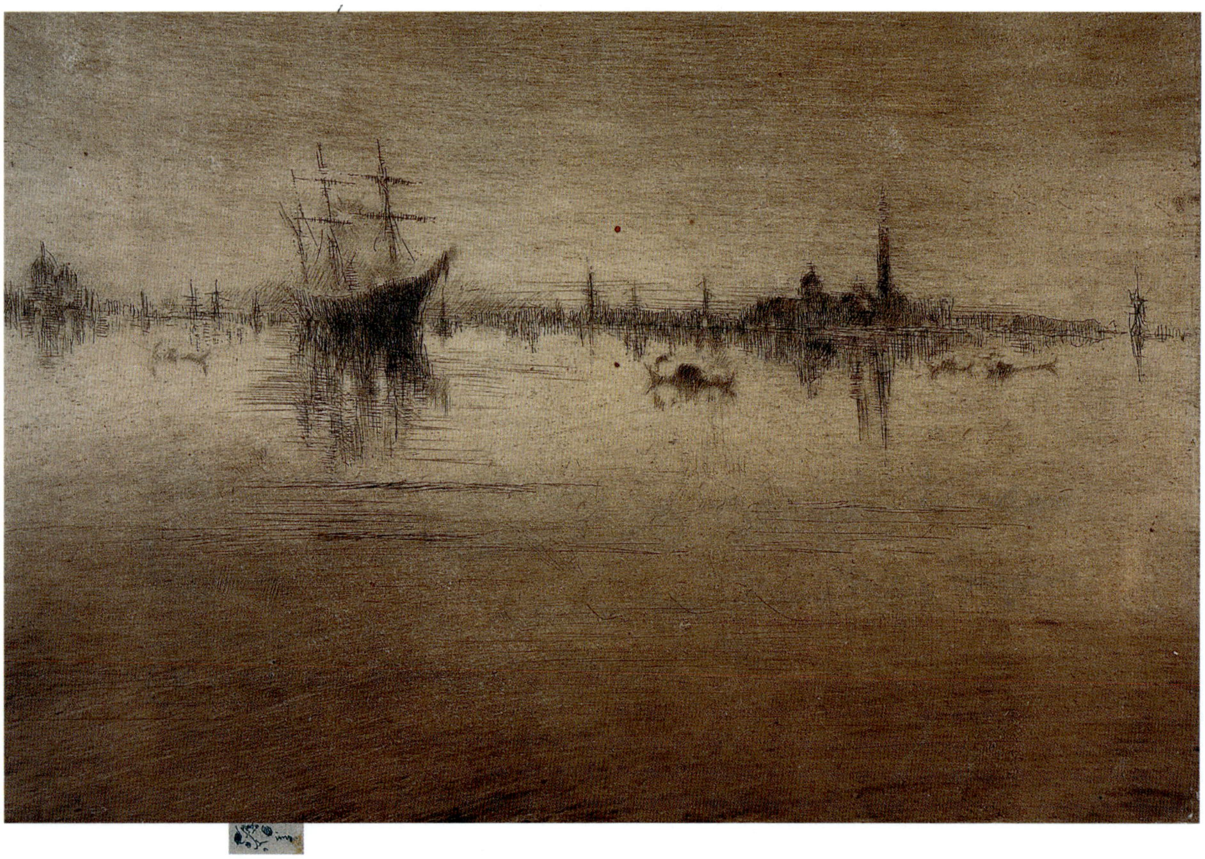

95
James McNeill Whistler
Nocturne
Etching 198 x 294 mm
Hunterian Art Gallery,
K.184 IV

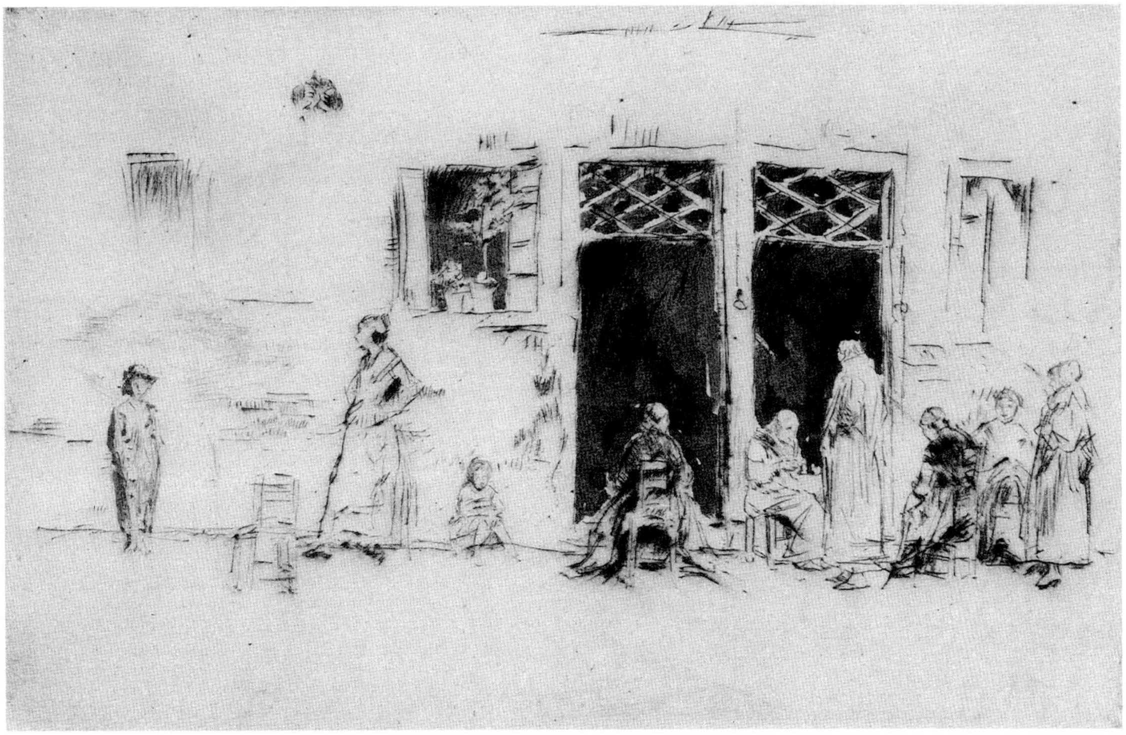

96
James McNeill Whistler
Old Women
Etching and watercolour 126 x 202 mm
Freer Gallery of Art, K.224 I

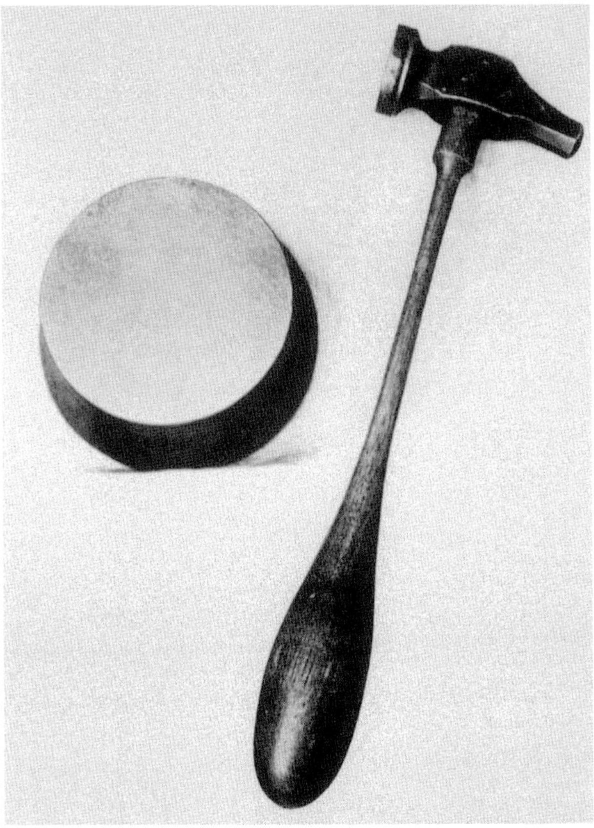

97
Whistler's hammer and anvil
Photograph by Bacher, from Bacher 1908

visited Whistler early in the summer he was shown the first proof of *The Traghetto, No.1*. He described it as 'the most remarkable of all', but he thought 'much of the life and charm' was lost in the second state, and by the third, 'The plate was ruined, irrevocably ruined!' Whistler pulled a few proofs of each state before abandoning the plate completely. Bitterly he admitted changing it because Jobbins, 'a – duffer – a painter – thought it was incomplete.'[42]

After moving to the Casa Jankowitz, Whistler planned to reproduce this damaged plate. The coppersmith made a plate identical in size, which was prepared with a black ground. An impression in white from the original plate was printed onto the new plate. Over the weeks, Whistler selectively etched the original lines of *The Traghetto*, checking them against the first proof. Finally *The Traghetto, No.2* (fig.99) was printed on the Venetian printer's press, and, as Bacher recorded, 'fortunately the new proof was exquisite [...] but it was not a duplicate of that marvellous first proof.'[43] Whistler compared the proofs, planning additional biting and drypoint. In the second state, figures were added to left of the arch, the butterfly was raised, the shadows deepened. A few proofs of the first three states preceded a radical reworking of the entire plate, and by its fourth state the artist was satisfied, and pulled a good number of impressions.

Selecting paper

Such complex proofs required good paper, but contemporary papers made from chemically processed wood pulp, bleached with chemicals, lacked the qualities needed for subtle printing effects. Like Rembrandt, Whistler sought special antique papers for his etchings. He asked Brown to 'send me some pieces of old Dutch paper for in Venice nothing can be had of any kind. You might see to this yourself, as you know what I like [...] Mr Way has sent me some Japanese paper and it arrived quite safely and in good condition.'[44]

Whistler scoured second-hand shops in Venice, as he had in Paris and Amsterdam, to find suitable endpapers and flyleaves torn from books. Judging from a remarkable early impression of *Nocturne: Shipping* (K.223 II) on laid paper, the search was moderately successful – for the inscriptions on the back show that the sheet was torn from some ancient Dutch manuscript.[45]

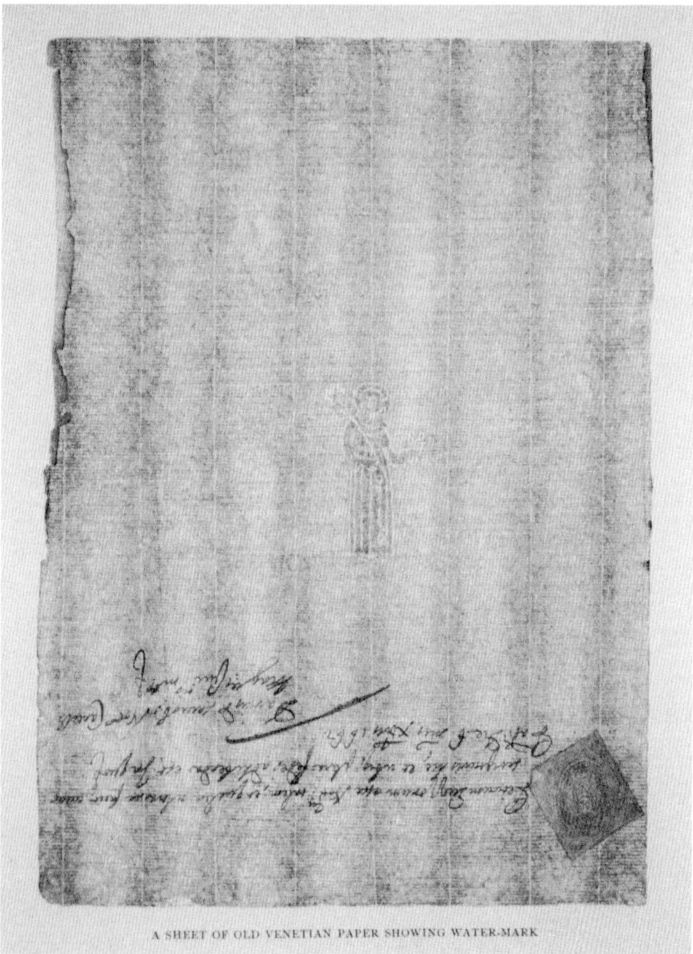

98
Venetian laid paper, from Bacher 1908, p.125

Bacher noted that 'Whistler printed many of his etchings on old Venetian paper which took the ink remarkably well because of its matured, glue sizing.'[46] When Bacher bought some old yellow Venetian paper, with 'rare old watermarks' (fig.98), Whistler offered to trade it for one of six proofs of 'a very beautiful etching'.[47] Some proofs printed in Bacher's company and acquired by Bacher are on old, thick, soft wove papers with broad margins. For example, a pristine first state of *The Doorway* (K.188) acquired by Bacher and now in the Art Institute of Chicago, was printed in black ink on an unusual off-white wove paper. Whistler very rarely used wove paper except for these early proofs, but by no means all proofs were on such paper. The same collection houses the first proofs of *La Salute: Dawn* (K.215 I) and *Islands* (K.222 I), both printed in black ink on warm, light beige coloured laid paper.[48] The Potter Palmers of Chicago acquired a rare proof of *Gondola under a bridge* (K.227) that shows similar characteristics, being printed in black ink, with no background tone, on heavy laid paper with wide margins.[49]

Whistler also used Japanese papers, both laid and wove, of varying thickness and colour. Although not always of good quality, they had a colour and glossy texture which he admired and which some collectors liked. The Detroit collector, Charles Lang Freer, sometimes asked specifically for impressions on Japanese paper, which accounts for the high proportion of these papers in his collection. Freer also focussed on the rare early proofs of Venice etchings, and even here it is clear that Whistler printed these proofs on a wide variety of papers.[50] *Nocturne* (K.184), for instance, is on a Van Gelder paper; *The Beggars* (K.194 I) on paper with a shield watermark; *Long Lagoon* (K.203 I) and *The Riva, No.2* (K.206 I) have 'posthorn' watermarks; *The Little Mast* (K.185 I), *The Palaces* (K.187 I), *The Mast* (K.195 I) and *Ponte del Piovan* (K.209 I) are all on Japanese paper. *Two Doorways* (K.193 I) and *Nocturne: Palaces* (K.202 I) are on almost identical paper with a fleur-de-lys 'VGL' watermark, suggesting that they were printed at the same time.

This shows that for the first proofs, pulled both in Venice and immediately after his return to London, Whistler had a variety of paper at his disposal, and that he pulled proofs on more than one sort of paper. He did not do this solely in order to see what was most suitable for a particular print. He wanted the paper to add colour and variety to each set.

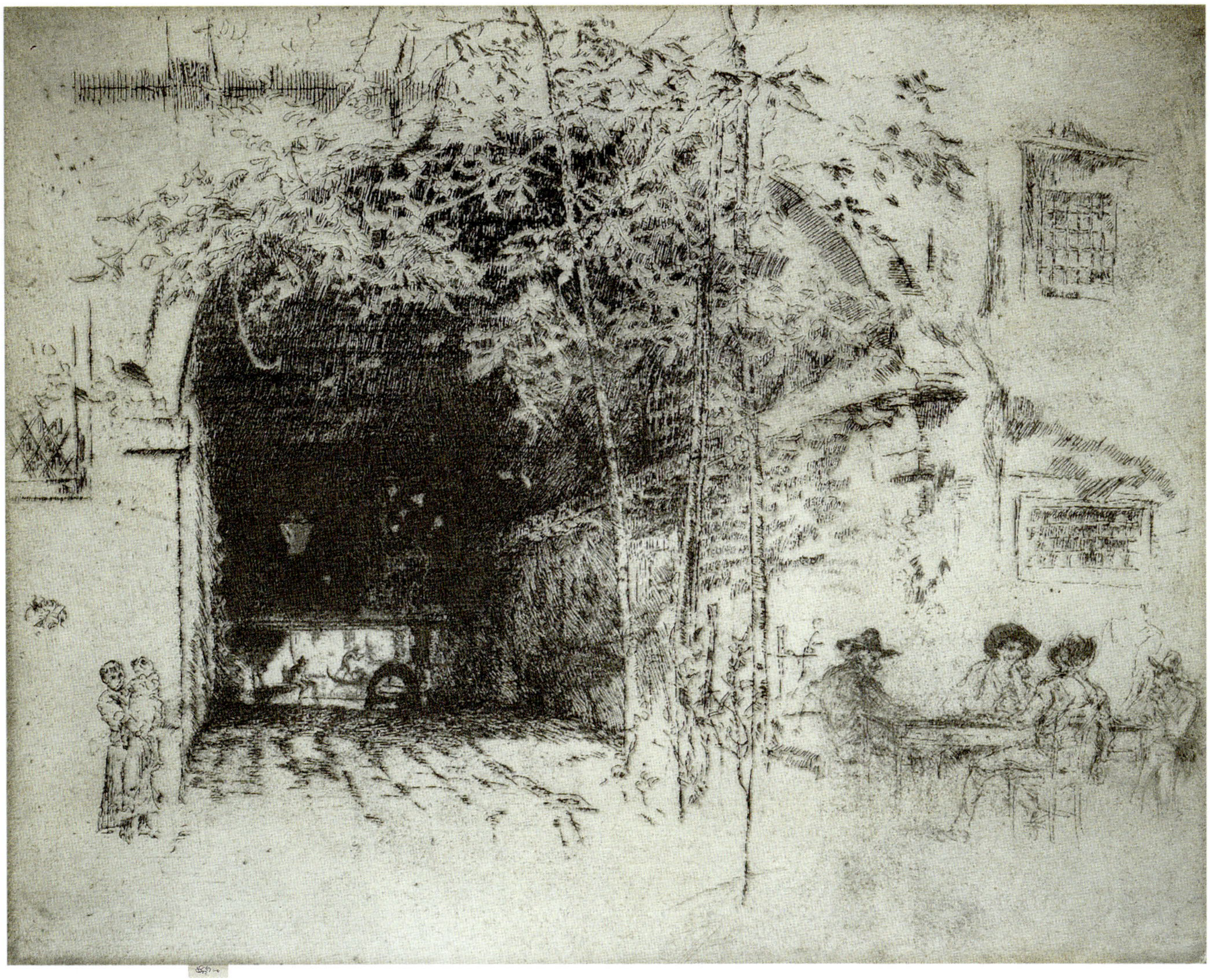

99
James McNeill Whistler
The Traghetto, No.2
Etching 240 x 304 mm
Fine Art Society, K.191 IV

The final touches

Each proof and each impression was carefully pressed and signed. The proofs printed in Venice were not trimmed, a broad and sometimes irregular margin being left around the print. Whistler's 'butterfly' (metamorphosed from his monogram 'JW') was usually etched on the plate itself, but he sometimes added a pencil butterfly as well. This butterfly was comparatively large and had three roughly horizontal veins on each wing.

In Venice, Whistler concentrated on finding suitable subjects and completing all the work that was necessary on site. After completing a satisfactory set of proofs, all subsequent work could be done in the studio, either in Venice or back in London. So the etching plates were wrapped up safely, ready for publication on his return.

1 Plates in Freer Gallery of Art, K.185, K.189, K.191, K.192; Hunterian Art Gallery, K.188, 193–5, 217–26, 240; Art Institute of Chicago, K.196–216, K.233. Getscher 1970, pp.33–6, and App.1, pp.277–84: his analysis of the plates is extremely helpful. Large plates were used for K.188, 192–3, 202, 204, 207, 211; similar size etchings, K.184, 227, 230, 231, middle size plates, K.198, 203, 209, 214, 226 and a similar sized etching, K.186, small plates, K.215, 216, 222, 224, and a similar sized etching, K.232.

2 Grieve 2000, p.43.

3 Mansfield 1909, cat.no.227 I (in Mansfield's collection); Getscher 1970, p.35.

4 Bacher 1908, pp.91–2. *The Beggars* measures 210 x 303 mm.

5 Pebbled plates are K.189, 191, 205, 208, 213, 217, 221, 223. K.208, 213, 217 and K.223 range from 155 x 233 mm to 170 x 233 mm. K.189 and K.205 are *c*.180 x 253 mm, K.221 is 286 x 229 mm and K.191, 240 x 303 mm; see Getscher 1970, pp.37–41, 47.

6 K.215–16, 222, 224, and K.217, 221, 223, 225, respectively; see Bacher 1908, p.35; Getscher 1970, p.47.

7 K.185, 187, 195, 197, 201, 206, 210, 212, 218, 219; see Getscher 1970, p.38. The plates vary in size but three (K.197, 201 and 206) are 208 x 303 mm, and a further two (K.210 and 219) are 237 x 302 mm (as is the etching K.190). K.218 is 130 x 222 mm, K.185, 186 x 266 mm, K.212, 126 x 308 mm, K.195, 162 x 340 mm, K.187, 251 x 359 mm. Missing plates are K.183, 190, 228, 229; Getscher 1970, pp.37–41.

8 Grieve 1996, p.28; see also Lovell 1989, pp.34–5.

9 Whistler to M. B. Huish, nd. [21/26 Jan 1880], GUL LB3/8, in Thorp 1994, pp.65–8, no.23. See Getscher 1970, pp.44–5.

10 197 x 418 mm; R. S. Schneiderman, *A Catalogue Raisonné of the Prints of Sir Francis Seymour Haden*, London, 1983, cat.no.133.

11 'Propositions', Whistler 1890, p.76.

12 Bacher 1908, p.144; *The Palaces* is 250 x 360 mm, Duveneck's *The Riva*, 337 x 220 mm, and *Palazzo Ca d'Oro, Venice*, 370 x 495 mm; E. Poole, 'The Etchings of Frank Duveneck', *Print Collector's Quarterly*, XXV, nos. 3 and 4, Oct and Dec 1938, pp.313-31, 447-63. See Getscher 1970, p.43.

13 Grieve 1996, repr. p.36.

14 105 x 342 mm and 177 x 278 mm, respectively. See Bacher 1908, repr. p.27 and *Illustrated Catalogue of Etchings and Engravings. Otto H. Bacher*, published by Frederick Keppel and Co., nd., cat.nos 15 and 17, repr. (New York Public Library Print Room).

15 Bacher also owned impressions of K.191, 197, 201, 209, 210, 229, 231: see Getscher 1970, p.39. He owned K.188 I, K.190 III, K.195 II, Art Institute of Chicago and K.228 II, K.232 (only state), Freer Gallery of Art, acq.nos 04.21, 04.20, Hughes and Kimber plates, K.184, 188, 209 and 231, 'flaked', K.195, 197, 201 210 and 228; Bacher 1908, p.121 (where he also described Whistler's work on K.193–4, 196, 207, 210 and 213).

16 Bacher 1908, p.270; Getscher 1970, p.40; Dorment and MacDonald 1994, cat.no.115.

17 K.231, Freer Gallery of Art, acq.no.04.294.

18 Yriarte 1878, p.182. For the history of bridges and canals, see G. Zucchetta, *I rii di Venezia, la storia degli ultimi tre secoli*, Venice, 1985, and *Venezia ponte per ponte*, two vols, Venice, 1992. See also Grieve 2000, pp.88–9.

19 Menpes 1904, pp.22–3.

20 Whistler to M. R. Elden, nd. [15/30 April 1880], GUL E61.

21 The dating of this etching is discussed by Fine 1984, p.117, cat.no.51. The butterfly and tiled roof, the copper-plate (Hunterian Art Gallery) and its inclusion in the second Venice show suggest it was etched in Venice.

22 Freer Gallery of Art, acq.nos 04.20 (stamped 'Otto') and 08.7, sold to Freer by E. Gottschalk (see M.781).

23 For example, *View of the Rialto bridge from San Giacomo di Rialto* by Samuel Prout; see J. Halsby, *Venice, The Artist's Vision, A Guide to British and American Painters*, London, 1990, p.27, and 1860 photograph in Filippi 1991, III, p.76, pl.85; Prints and photographs of the view from the opposite side, repr. in F. Ongania, *Raccolta delle vere da pozzo in Venezia*, Venice, 1889, II, pl.CXVIII, and Yriate 1878, p.95; Grieve 1996, p.29, fig.20; see also F. Ongania, *Calli e Canali in Venezia*, Venice, 1890–2; and *Calli, Canali e Isole della Lagune*, Venice, 1893–4.

24 Whistler to E. Brown, n.d. [26/29 Jan 1880], GUL F37.

25 Bacher 1908, pp.92–3.

26 See Lovell 1989, p.38.

27 Bacher 1908, pp.99–102.

28 Dorment and MacDonald 1994 (cat.no.104); for views of the door by M. Stone and C. H. Moore, see Grieve 1996, pp.33–4.

29 Pennell 1908, I, pp.267–8; Quilter's drawing has not been traced.

30 Bacher 1908, pp.193–4.

31 Ibid pp.108–10.

32 Ibid pp.198–9, repr. pp.222–3 as 'Wood Barges', see also p.110.

33 Ibid pp.112–13, 178.

34 Ibid pp.197–8, calling it 'Dawn'; See C. McNamara and J. Siewart, *Whistler, Prosaic Views, Poetic Visions*, exh.cat., University of Michigan Museum of Art, Ann Arbor, 1994.

35 Bacher 1908, pp.117–18. See Lochnan 1984, pp.198–9, repr., and pp.206–9.

36 K.184, K.201 III, National Gallery of Art, Washington, DC, acq.no.1942.15.18.

37 Pennell 1908, I, p.267; see also Bacher 1908, pp.113–15.

38 Freer Gallery of Art, acq.nos 05.189, 05.8; see also acq.no.05.197.

39 Bacher 1908, p.121, repr. p.120; see Dorment and MacDonald 1994, cat.no.103.

40 Lovell 1989, pp.53, 55, 58.

41 Signed by Whistler *c*.1886, inscribed '1st proof'; thanks to W. B. Kielsmeier, Covington Fine Arts Gallery, Tucson, for this information; other impressions, for example National Gallery of Art, Washington, DC, K.205 I, 1943.3.8539; K.205 II, 1942.15.22 and 1943.3.8540.

42 The first proof is in the National Gallery of Art, Washington, DC, 1949.5.548. Bacher 1908, pp.165–6, 169, 180, 183, first state repr. p.174. Grieve identified the site as the Ca' da Mosto in Canareggio (Grieve 2000, pp.84–5).

43 Bacher 1908, pp.169, 178–9, 183, repr. pp.175, 182.

44 Whistler to E. Brown, nd. [26/29 Jan 1880], GUL F37; Lochnan 1984, p.300. See also Menpes 1904, p.93.

45 Freer Gallery of Art, acq.no.07.365.

46 Bacher 1908, p.122.

47 Ibid pp.127–8, paper repr. pp.125, 141.

48 K.185 I, K.214 I, in black ink on laid paper; K.215 I and K.222 I, both trimmed to the platemark and later signed on the tab; Art Institute of Chicago, acq.nos 72.428, 1927.1671; for impressions of first states on off-white wove paper, for example National Gallery of Art, Washington, DC, K.204 I, 1943.3.8538; K.205 I, 1943.3.8539; K.212 I, 1943.3.8548; cream wove, K.190 I, 1949.5.548; K.211 I , black ink on laid paper, Metropolitan Museum of Art, New York, acq.no.17.3.112.

49 Estate of Pauline Potter Palmer, on deposit in the Art Institute of Chicago, platemark 297 x 204 mm, paper 333 x 223 mm.

50 For example in the Freer Gallery, Japanese paper, K.183 (two impressions), K.183 (two cancelled), K.184 III, 185 III, 186 II, 187 I, 188 VII, 193 III, 194 II, 195 I, 195 III, 195 V, 209 I (acq.nos 98.378, 05.179, 92.25, 94.40, 98.379, 94.24, 05.180, 98.382, 04.92, 98.390, 98.381, 98.393, 08.258, 98.394, 08.4). Freer's first proofs: K.184 I, K.185 I, K.187 I, K.193 I, K.194 I, K.195 I, K.202 I, K.203 I, K.206 I, K.209 I (acq.nos 04.17, 94.24, 98.382, 03.148, 03.149, 98.393, 06.39, 05.5, 05.6, 08.4); lists based on Bunting 1995, App.E.

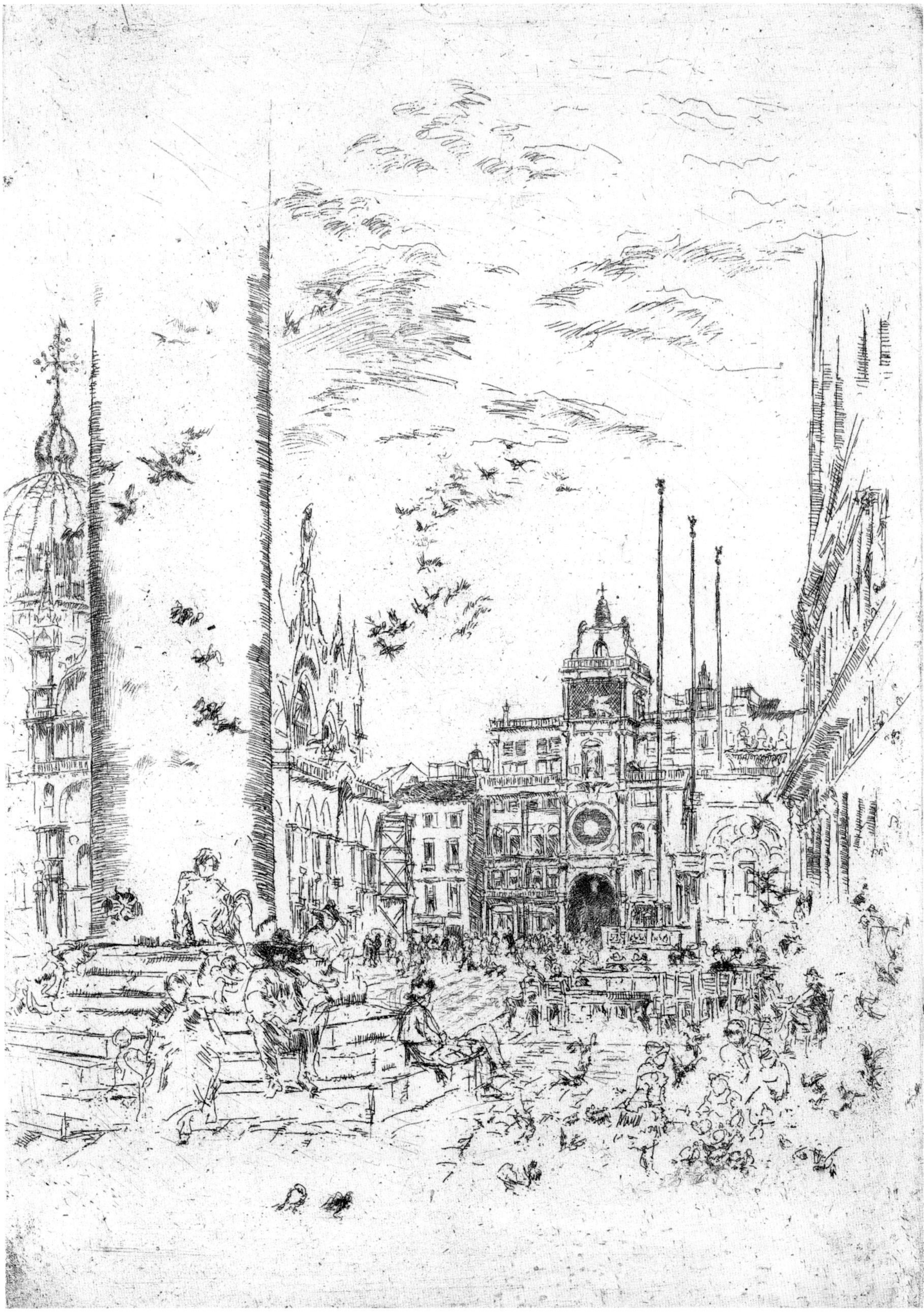

100
James McNeill Whistler
The Piazzetta
Etching 254 x 181 mm
Private Collection, K.189 IV

5 Mr Whistler's Etchings of Venice

It was November 1880. Cane in hand, Pomeranian dog at heel, Whistler walked into the Fine Art Society. The woodcuts of Thomas Bewick were being exhibited at the same time as *Twelve Great Etchers*, which included Whistler, Tissot and Bracquemond: 'the Twelve greatest living etchers!' commented Whistler, 'though as I said to him where [the] devil do they all come from'.[1] Goulding printed etchings at a press set up in the gallery. 'We are going in for no end of bunkum to get the people in', said Huish.[2] Whistler had mixed feelings about this circus: 'putting up my glass, I looked at the prints on the wall. "Dear me! dear me!" I said, "still the same old sad work!"' Haden was holding forth about Rembrandt, but hearing Whistler's strident laugh, 'he vanished'.[3]

Selecting the Fine Arts' set

Whistler went to stay with his brother William in Wimpole Street and immediately set to work, selecting and printing twelve etchings for the Fine Art Society. Bacher believed that Whistler had long planned a second set: 'As Whistler progressed with his contract, he would change an etching from the Fine Arts' set, as he called it, to his own, replacing it with a more recent plate.' The two sets, Bacher added, were 'fairly well defined' when Whistler left Venice.[4]

However, the exact shape of the first set was still under consideration as Whistler printed the etchings in London and the second set was not defined until 1886. A sketch of the first set shows three rows, one for each wall of the gallery.[5] The first contains *Little Venice* (K.183), *Two Doorways* (K.193), *The Little Lagoon* (K.186), *The Traghetto, No.2* (K.191), *The Piazzetta* (K.189), *The Mast* (K.195) and *The Palaces* (K.187). The next row had *The Riva, No.1* (K.192), *The Beggars* (K.194), *San Biagio* (K.197), *The Doorway* (K.188) and *Nocturne* (K.184). These two rows make up a total of twelve etchings. All were included in the 'First Venice Set', except *San Biagio* for which he substituted *The Little Mast* (fig.103).

At the bottom of the sheet he added two more contenders, *Upright Venice* (K.205) and *The Bridge* (K.204), and on the back, *The Dyer* (K.219). None of these were included: *The Bridge*, *San Biagio* and *Upright Venice* ended up in the 'Second Venice Set', and *The Dyer* was not published at all.

The set, as published by the Fine Art Society in 1880 under the title *Venice, a Series of Twelve Etchings*, was equally divided between horizontal and vertical formats, and included a variety of subjects and figures (beggars, bead-stringers and gondoliers). The views followed a well-worn route from St Mark's, in *The Piazzetta* (fig.100), along the Riva degli Schiavoni, to a distant view of the city, *Little Venice*. It included well-known sights, like *The Palaces*, and experimental plates, like the dramatic *Nocturne*. There was something to appeal to the discerning connoisseur and armchair traveller alike.

Printing the 'First Venice Set'

At first the Fine Art Society provided a printing press above the shop, but after a while the press was moved to two rooms on the first floor over a stationer's at the north-west corner of Air Street and Regent Street. A bay window provided inadequate light. Thomas R. Way, son of the lithographic printer, then studying at the South Kensington schools, came to help. 'It was little short of marvellous to see how he graduated and softened the ink with the palm of his hand,' wrote Way, 'he was accustomed to pull through his plates on the press himself, a feat requiring no little strength.'[6]

101
James McNeill Whistler
The Little Lagoon
Etching 225 x 151 mm
Hunterian Art Gallery, K.186 II

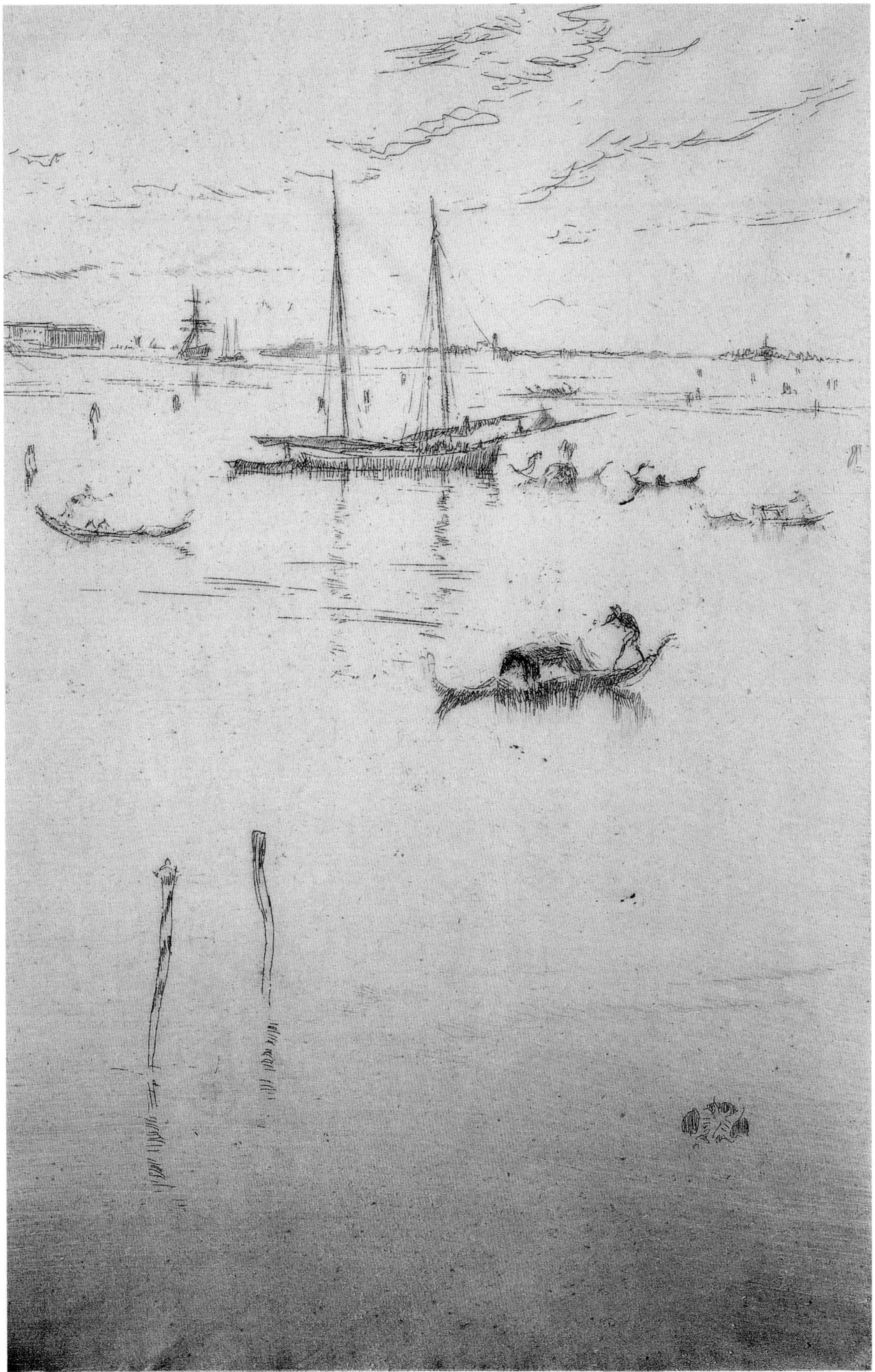

102
James McNeill Whistler
Little Venice
Etching 186 x 265 mm
Hunterian Art Gallery, K.183

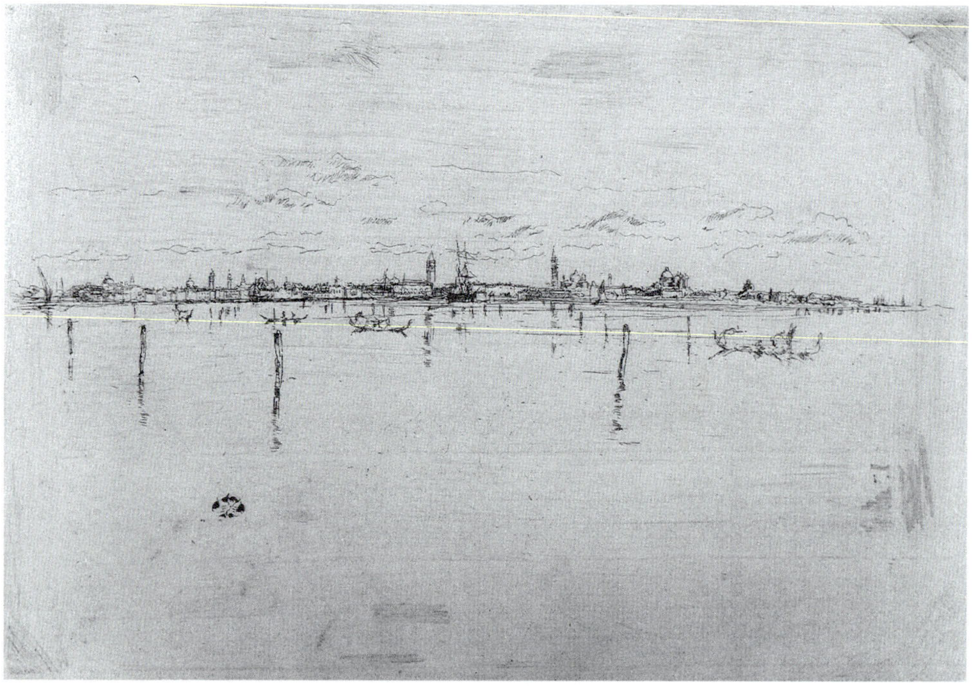

103
James McNeill Whistler
The Little Mast
Etching 266 x 187 mm
Fine Art Society, K.185 I

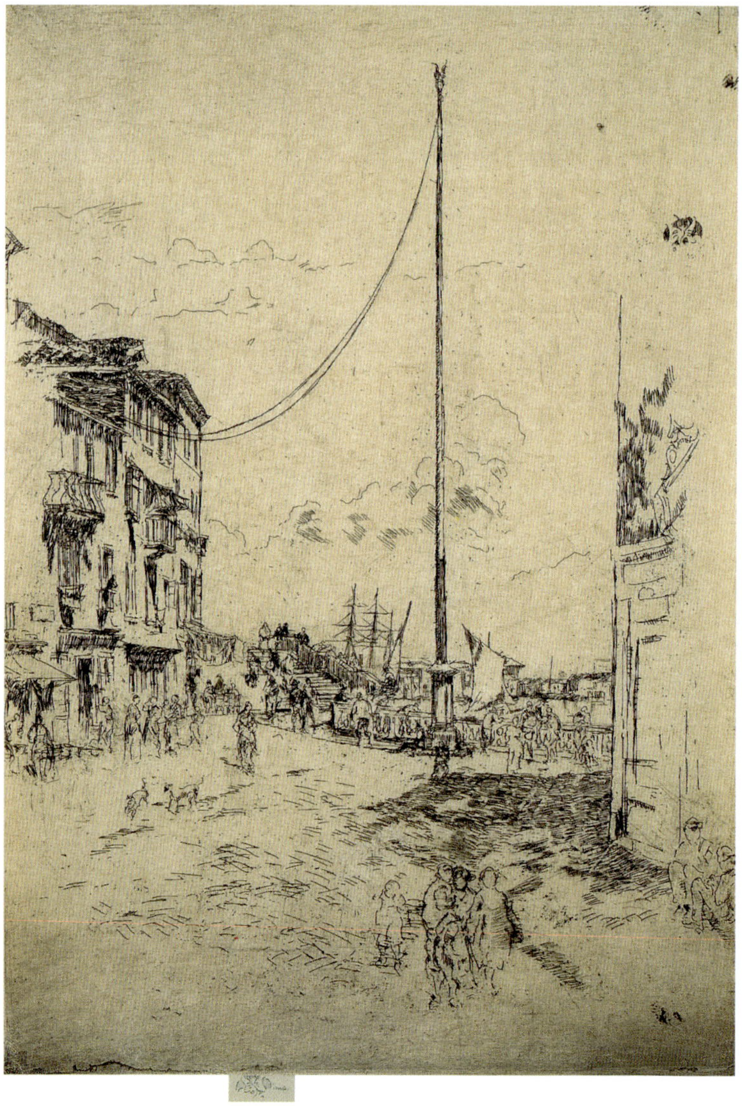

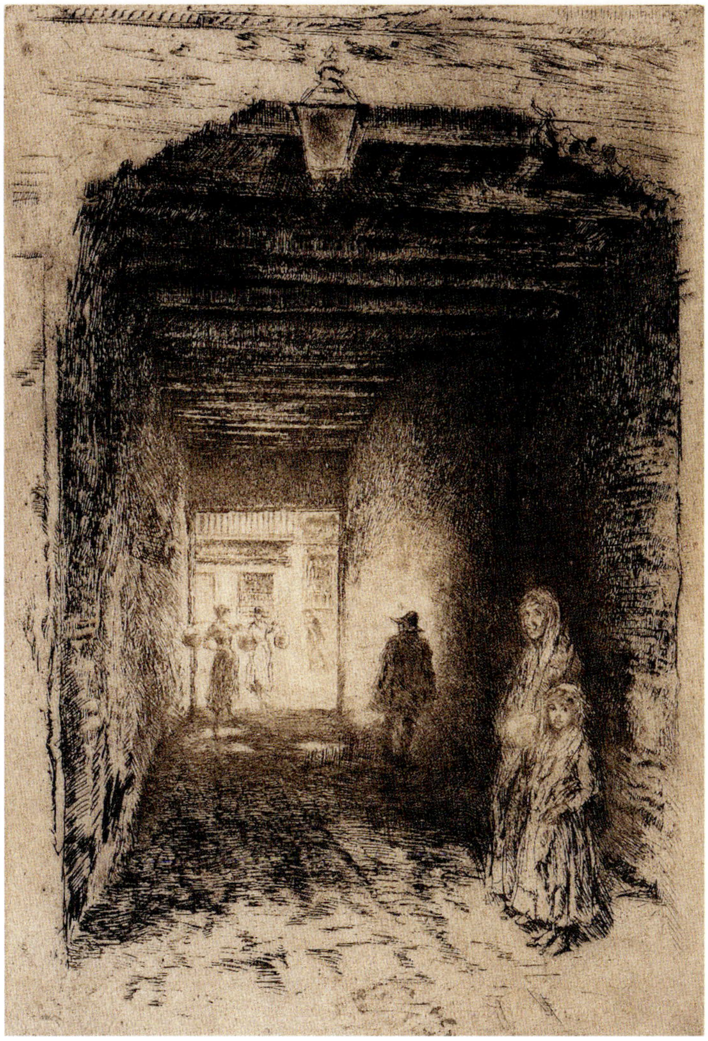

104
James McNeill Whistler
The Beggars
Etching 304 x 208 mm
Hunterian Art Gallery, K.194 VIII/IX

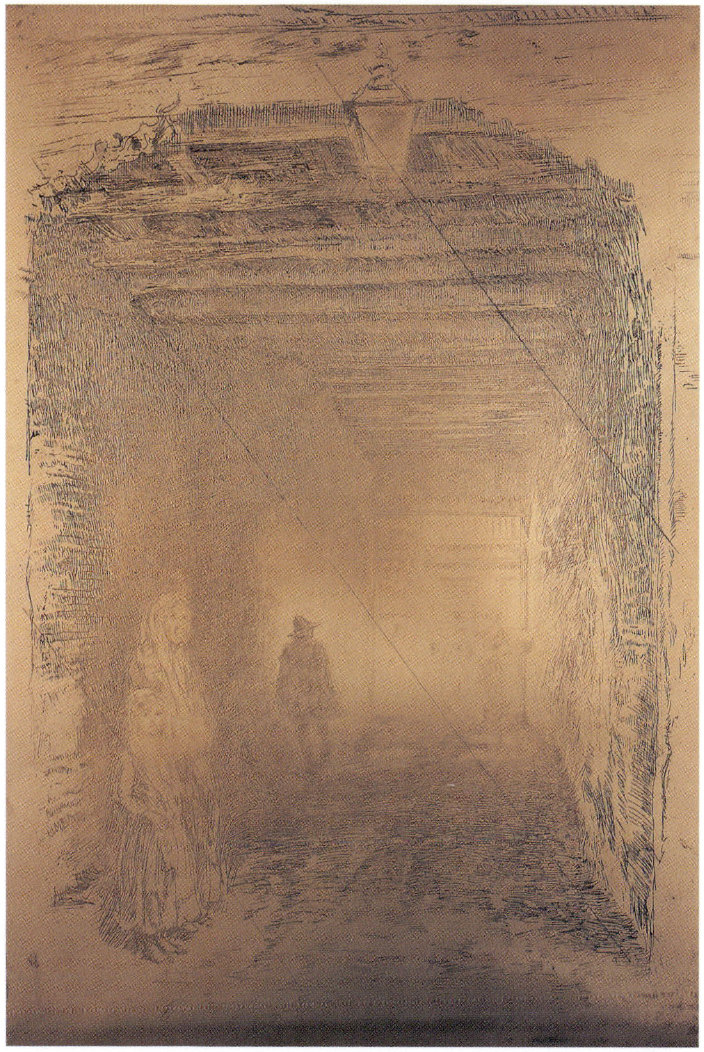

105
James McNeill Whistler
The Beggars
Etching 304 x 208 mm, copperplate
Hunterian Art Gallery, K.194

Some etchings were completed and printed with apparent ease. Most of the plates had been etched in Venice, but *Little Venice* (K.183) was drawn in Venice and etched back in London. Way watched Whistler 'holding it in one hand and moving the acid about with a feather, and without any stopping out. The first impression of it printed was quite satisfactory, and he did not need to rebite or reduce any part of it.'[7] It is a small plate, and despite the fine detail of the distant panorama, it stood up well to printing.

Whistler was almost satisfied with the first state of *The Little Lagoon* (fig.101). In the second state he only had to complete a gondola in the foreground before printing the full edition. With the minimum of wiry outlines and patches of vertical shading, bound together by carefully graduated plate-tone, he produced an atmospheric and elegant print. The use of tone in conveying space is strongly reminiscent of Japanese woodcuts.

Alterations made to *The Piazzetta* (fig.100) were minor and transitory, like the pigeons, and indeed the original pigeons were burnished out in later states (E.G. Kennedy lists eight states).[8] Most impressions of the etching were printed in its third state. When he went back to complete the edition, Whistler altered the appearance of the man on the steps – giving him a narrower brimmed, rakish hat – before printing the final state.

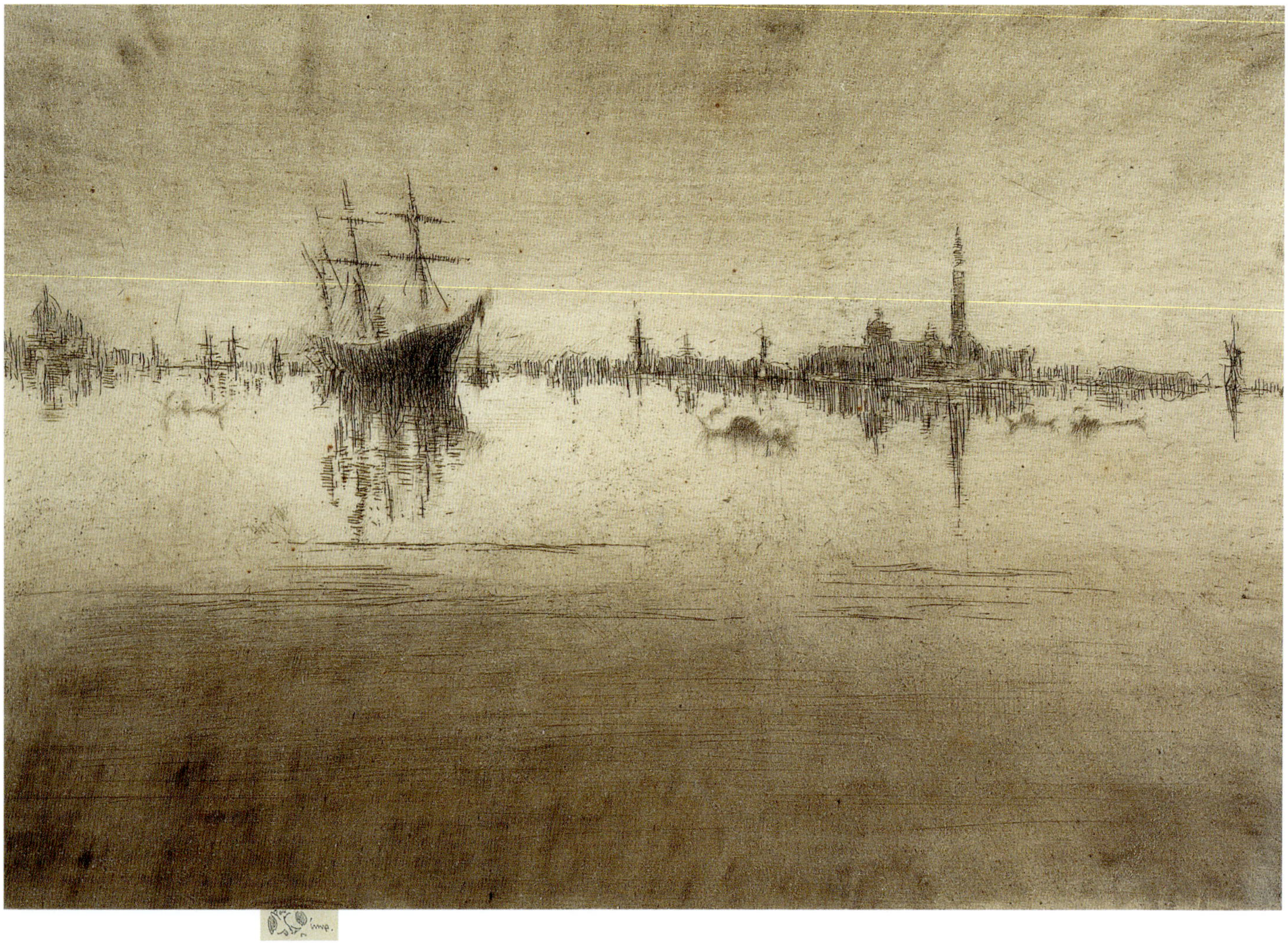

106
James McNeill Whistler
Nocturne
Etching 198 x 294 mm
Fine Art Society, K184 IV

Some new states reflect the need to keep the copperplate in a good condition and mark minor changes in emphasis. In the second state Whistler made a number of changes to the composition of *Nocturne* (K.184), drawing in the gondolas that give it a sense of space and scale. Otherwise in each state – and this etching went through at least seven states – he made delicate adjustments in drypoint. Thus while there were substantial editions of the third and fourth states, there were also smaller printings of intermediate states.

The Traghetto, No.2 (K.191) was brought to what appeared to be a satisfactory conclusion by the fourth state, but apparently it was not in a suitable condition for a large edition. After ten or twenty impressions the quality of the delicate lines deteriorated, particularly around the lamp in the shaded arch. When he got back to London, Whistler had trouble printing the plate. Way remembered:

> Again and again he took the charcoal and lightened it, only to rebite the whole again. It was the last of the set he had to prove, and as the invitations to the private view had already been sent out I was very anxious [...] but at last all came right; he obtained the silvery quality he wanted, and the lantern with its reflected light at the end of the dark archway, and the leaves falling from the little trees [...].[9]

After reworking that area Whistler would tinker with the figures, his attention divided between the carafe and the man on the left of the table, and the children. There are at least eight states in all, the largest edition being of the sixth state.

The Beggars went through substantial alterations in Venice, being changed completely in four early states. In the fifth state, K.194 IV, Whistler made minor modifications, shading the butterfly and enlarging the cloak and hat of the man in the alley, and printed this state in London to satisfy the first orders. One study for the etching is dated as late as 18 September 1881 (M.864).

The Beggars is the closest Whistler came to the genre tradition of his contemporaries, evoking exotic Italian characters and costume in a detailed and carefully observed setting to create a controlled illusion of authenticity. Back in London, some time later, the cloaked man was altered and then replaced, using T. R. Way as a model, looking rather dashing and mysterious in a broad hat and cloak (figs 104 and 105).

Contemporary critics found the figures 'picturesque and appropriate', and *The Globe* commented that, 'as regards beauty of tone and perfect balance of light and shade, [*The Beggars*] could hardly be surpassed'.[10] Mood and atmosphere were developed under studio conditions. In fact, the delicate task of turning areas of close cross-hatching into velvety shadows was best undertaken under such controlled conditions. In all there were at least twelve states of *The Beggars*, with many impressions pulled of the final state (K.194 IX). He never completed the edition and after his death the Fine Art Society called in Goulding to make up the numbers. The artist's changing intentions and high standards, as well as the copper-plates' idiosyncrasies and deterioration, infinitely prolonged the printing of the edition.

Preparing the sets

While preparing the first impressions for the Fine Art Society, Way's jobs included damping the old Dutch paper, brushing off loose fibres and pressing the proofs. The prints are on a variety of laid papers. For instance, the Venice sets acquired by Whistler's old friend George Lucas, and now in the Baltimore Museum of Art, include three on paper with the Arms of Amsterdam watermark. Other sheets bear a post-horn, 'Pro Patria', Fools-cap, fleur-de-lys, Van Gelder and many other watermarks; however, a Dutch watermark did not guarantee old paper since they were used by later papermakers as a guarantee of quality. Whistler also used early-nineteenth-century papers, and several sheets bear an 1814 watermark.[11]

The prints were finished off by being carefully trimmed down to the platemark and signed with an agitated little butterfly with veins on each wing (by 1882 the butterfly had evolved into an un-veined variety). Whistler placed his butterfly and the letters 'imp', indicating he had printed the impression, on a small rectangular tab at the bottom of the sheet, interrupting the rectangular format of the trimmed image. In later impressions, the tab and butterfly shrank until they were extremely small.

This was all part of Whistler's extreme care for the presentation of his work. A variety of papers and colours, of subjects and shapes, plus careful mounting and framing, combined to make each print unique. The whole 'First Venice Set' was a complex and rewarding visual experience.

The Exhibition

Carefully framed in white frames, the etchings hung in the small back room at the Fine Art Society in New Bond Street. Groups in vertical and horizontal format, lagoon and city subjects, alternated.[12] On Wednesday 1 December 1880 at 12 o'clock the exhibition of *Mr Whistler's Etchings of Venice* opened, one year late.[13]

'He has been frightfully occupied every day and every hour since we came home in bringing out the etchings and pastels – the etchings, of course, were exhibited first and were a great success [...] but of course all the other artists were furious', Maud told Bacher. Whistler added, 'You have no idea of the success of the etchings and pastels – but better still you have no idea of their real beauty – especially the etchings.'[14]

The show was extensively reviewed in established newspapers (*The Times*, *The World*, *Spectator*, *The Globe*, *Daily News* and *St James' Gazette*) and journals (*Art Journal*, *Artist* and *British Architect*), as well as in the more ephemeral specialist journals established during the etching revival (*Etcher* and *English Etchings*). Reviews were pasted into presscutting books, which Whistler showed to friends and used as ammunition for attacking his critics.[15]

'Artistic printing'

Etching was not generally accepted as a medium for creating works of art. Ruskin described it as a 'blundering art', suitable for amateurs, and considered the 'tricks of the etching trade' a 'waste of time'.[16] These statements coincided with Whistler's revived interest in etching in 1872–3. A spirit of conflict, taking up arms against the views of Ruskin and others, plays no small part in Whistler's art.

Many printers employed tone in printing, to give colour and variety to the etched line. Such 'artistic printing' was opposed by conservative critics like Ruskin and Hamerton and by purists like Haden. They upheld the supremacy of line and thought 'artistic printing' was intended to disguise bad drawing. Drawing, on the other hand, held an established position in the hierarchy of art and the association of etching and drawing helped validate the status of etching as an art.[17]

The controversy over 'artistic printing', which had divided English and French etchers since the sixties, was renewed in 1880. On the one hand, the *Etcher* supported 'artistic printing', emphasising the etcher's artistic and intellectual role. Frederick Wedmore and, later, Whistler's pupil, Mortimer Menpes, urged artists to print their own plates.[18]

On the other hand, the *Pall Mall Gazette* asserted 'Etching is Surface-Printing' and if etching required a printer for effects, it was not art but craft. Rembrandt was held up as an example; he often used line to create shadows with areas of white instead of the 'sooty blackness' of 'artistic printing'.[19] In 'artistic printing' no two prints would be exactly identical and this raised the question of reproduction, introducing questions of identity and price that were used by both sides.

On the whole, *The Times* thought Whistler's style a 'less legitimate and certain method' than pure line etching, but praised *Two Doorways* (K.193) for 'the effect scarcely at all dependent upon anything but actual work executed with the etching needle' and thought *The Riva, No.1* (K.192), which relied on line rather than tone, 'probably the most genuine and satisfactory piece of pure etching in the exhibition.'[20]

Several critics noted the 'artistic printing' of *Nocturne* (K.184). The *St James' Gazette* commented that it 'depends so entirely, not only for its effect but even for its substance, upon the printer, that an impression pulled by any hands other than those of its author would be without any sort of value.'[21] The *British Architect* agreed, adding that it was impossible to print in large numbers: 'the bones as it were of the picture have been etched' but it was merely 'brown smoke with clots of ink in diagonal lines', relying for effect on accident more than skill.[22] Whistler used this sentence, torn from context, as one of two comments on *Nocturne* in the catalogue when it was exhibited again in 1883; the other was Hamerton's unfortunate comment: 'The Nocturne is intended to convey an impression of night.'[23]

'Finish'

The next question was that of detail and finish. *The Daily News* claimed that in *Little Venice* (K.183) he 'attempted to convey impressions by lines far too few for his purpose', but the *St James' Gazette* praised his economical technique which 'in its simplicity and contempt for elaboration, reminds us more of the Spaniard Goya than any other acquafortiste'.[24] The comparison was unusual, Rembrandt being the artist most commonly compared with Whistler in the attempt to contextualise and validate his work.

Whistler's ability to convey light and mood with summary lines and tone rather than comprehensive detail found qualified appreciation. *The Doorway* (K.188) for instance, conveyed a 'striking [...] impression of a momentary effect.'[25]

Quilter saw the medium as suited to expressive 'jagged outline' rather than mathematical precision and grudgingly commended *The Palaces* (K.187) wherein 'Mr Whistler's drawing, which, though always masterly, is sometimes that of a very slovenly master, appears at its best'.[26] *The World*, while admitting the etchings were 'skilled' in conveying distance and atmosphere, dismissed them as 'of unimportant dimensions and of the slightest workmanship' which Whistler politely but firmly disputed: 'an etching does not depend, for its importance, upon its size' he wrote, storing up the reviews for later publication.[27]

In attacking 'the poor devil critics',[28] Whistler was taking a financial risk. The etchings were listed in the prospectus at fifty guineas for the set, which was comparatively high given that *Portfolio* sold etchings each month for half a crown.[29] The critics, relying on the criteria they applied to oil paintings, thought labour should be conspicuous and Whistler did not give value for money.

The 'Ideal' and the 'Picturesque'

The etching controversy coincided with the political and aesthetic controversy surrounding the restorations to St Mark's that provided, as the Fine Art Society had anticipated, useful publicity.[30] On the question of the restoration and representation of Venice two approaches divided the critics, the 'ideal' and the 'picturesque'. The 'picturesque' incorporated the contemporary world; the 'ideal' represented perfect beauty.[31]

In Venice Quilter, like Ruskin and Bunney, had carefully recorded historical architecture. In his reviews, he stressed Whistler's divergence from Ruskin. The Venice represented 'by a modern American', said Quilter, 'does not represent any Venice that we much care to remember: for who wants to remember the degradation of what has been noble, and the foulness of what has been fair?' He implied that an intellectual and emotional understanding of architecture was only attainable by those with a cultured European background:

> What has been done, and done with a cleverness so great as to be almost genius, is to sketch the passing, every-day aspect of canal, lagoon and quay; to give, in fact, to those who have not seen the city some notion of that outside aspect, in which wealth and poverty, grandeur and squalor, life and death, are so strangely mingled. And this outside aspect has, in the main, been truly given. It is not the Venice of a maiden's fancies or a poet's dreams, but the tangible Venice known to tourists.[32]

There were others who romanticised contemporary Venice and approved of what they interpreted as Whistler's 'picturesque' views. Whistler, said *The Globe*, avoided 'the stately edifices or comprehensive view that painting has made familiar' in favour of the 'picturesque beauty' of back streets and canals, 'full of local colour', such as the 'picturesque and appropriate figures' in *The Traghetto, No.2* (K.191).[33]

Whistler v the Press

Overall, the show was critically successful and received wider coverage than was usual for etching exhibitions. While the *Twelve Great Etchers* only received one brief review in *The Times*, lengthy discussions of Whistler's show tackled questions of style, content and technique.

Whistler hoarded reviews and in the catalogue for his second etchings exhibition at the Fine Art Society in 1883 he wryly annotated his works with a judicious selection of the earlier comments. Marginal 'Reflections' with tiny stinging butterflies further enlivened the pages. Each criticism was matched with an etching intended to illustrate and refute it. *Fish-Shop, Venice* (K.218), for instance, bore a dismissive note from the *Glasgow Herald*, 'Whistler is eminently vulgar'.[34]

The clippings were freely adapted to reinforce the message. Examples of his unscrupulous editing abound. The *St James' Gazette* wrote that the 'Venice Set' was as good as the 'Thames Set' which had established Whistler's reputation.[35] It specifically praised *The Doorway* (K.188): 'The architectural ornaments and the interlacing bars of the gratings which flank the doorway are skilfully and subtly suggested rather than absolutely drawn'. This was edited to read, 'The architectural ornaments and the interlacing bars of the gratings are suggested rather than drawn.' He probably made up some quotations which seem too good to be true, like one said to come from the Russian press, 'His colour is subversive'.[36]

Taking the etchings to America

The exhibition at the Fine Art Society in 1880 was followed up by exhibitions at Wunderlich's gallery in New York and Messrs Dowdeswell in London. Whistler assiduously sent groups of work to exhibitions abroad, to Paris and Munich, to New York, Pittsburgh and Philadelphia. Just before Christmas 1880 he spent a day with Ernest Brown printing a set for Brown to take to America. The first Venetian prints by Whistler exhibited in America, they hung in a small gallery specially decorated in white and gold at the Pennsylvania Academy of the Fine Arts early in 1881. Joseph Pennell, the future printmaker and Whistler's biographer, was among the visitors. Unfortunately, the exhibition was not a financial success and only eight sets of etchings were ordered.[37]

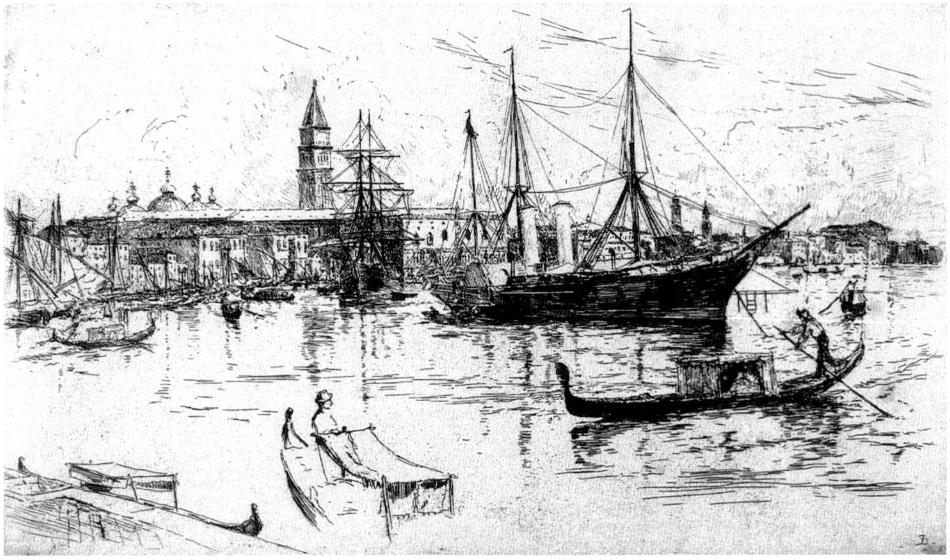

107
F. Duveneck
The Laguna or *View of Shipping from the Riva* 1880
Etching 306 x 340 mm
Hunterian Art Gallery, P.11

A 'storm in an aesthetic tea-pot'[38]

Meanwhile his fellow Americans, Bacher and Duveneck, exhibited their etchings in London with the Society of Painter-Etchers. Inspired by the French *Société des Aquafortistes*, the Society had been founded in 1880 to encourage original etching and included Haden among the founder members. Whistler disparagingly referred to Haden as a 'barber-surgeon' and President of 'Painter-etchers' – a jack of all trades and master of none.[39]

Early in 1881 the Society invited artists to contribute to their first exhibition, at Messrs Dowdeswell's gallery. Whistler attempted to dissuade Bacher from exhibiting: 'The Society of Painter-Etchers is already ridiculous and I intend that it shall die the death of the absurd. So just "wait a bit" – and send nothing to this Seymour Haden game, for I give you the straight tip – it can't possibly succeed.'[40] However, Bacher could not afford to ignore the invitation, and sent seventeen etchings. Whistler chided him for 'not following where I don't lead!!', calling it 'a thoroughly rotten scheme'. Then he relented and told Bacher, 'Your etchings were a success, and looked very pretty;' but, he added, 'you should not have gone over to the other kennel.'[41] In fact the exhibition met with favourable reviews and widened acceptance of the medium.[42] An American critic noted the influence of Whistler on the etchings not only of Duveneck and Bacher but of the other 'boys', Corwin, Wendel, Rosenberg and Hopkins.[43]

Duveneck sent etchings showing views similar to Whistler's: *The Riva, looking towards the Grand Ducal Palace*, *View of Shipping from the Riva* (fig.107) and *The Riva, looking towards the Caserna*.[44] Haden thought they were by Whistler and invited Brown to see them, implying that Whistler was evading his contract with the Fine Art Society. Brown had no problem distinguishing the artists' work. As Whistler explained, Duveneck was 'a great personal friend of his who was in Venice at the same time – who was with all his "boys" – was very much amongst all the etching business and consequently any similarity of style could only have occurred from that.'[45] Huish confronted Haden, who capitulated and apologised: 'We know all about Mr Frank Duveneck & are delighted to have his Etching'.[46] Whistler celebrated his small victory by publishing the correspondence privately as *The Piker Papers*.

Printing the sets

Having settled this dispute, the Fine Art Society still had a problem. It was not enough to have Whistler's plates and proofs. He had agreed to print at least twenty-five sets, 'for nothing save your own reputation'.[47] That meant Whistler was committed to printing 300 impressions in all. After the first big push to get sets ready for exhibition on his return it was like drawing teeth to get him to print a few impressions.

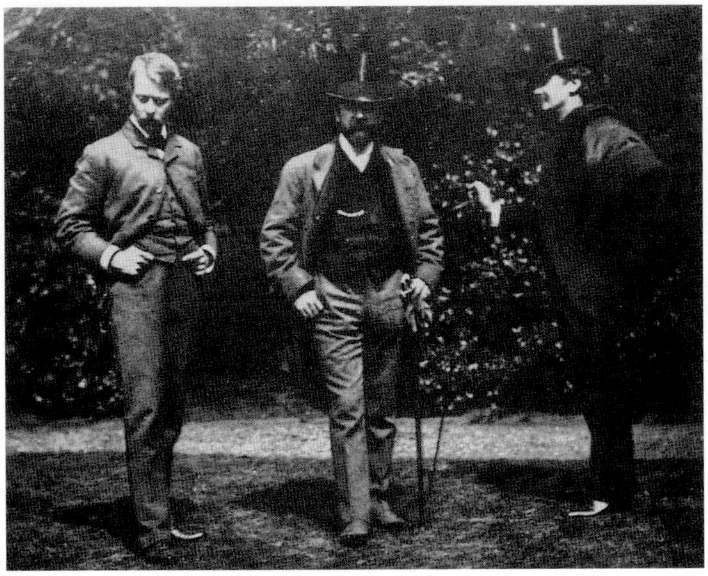

108
M.L. Menpes and W.M. Chase with Whistler
Photograph from Menpes 1904

In 1880, when the artist had finished printing a set of acceptable proofs, Huish wanted him to turn over the copperplates and proofs. In return, Huish would return the parcel of plates left with them in 1879, and, even more important, give him a cheque. By 20 December 1880, the Fine Art Society had paid Whistler the £150 of the original advance as well as instalments of £50 on 3 February, 20 October and 5 November, plus £43 7s 0d on 22 November. This left £336 13s 0d to make up the agreed total of £700 for the purchase of the copperplates. Whistler himself had to pay for frames.[48]

Two and a half months later, Huish suggested that Goulding could help Whistler: 'The Directors were asking what had been recouped of the £700 for these plates & I was obliged to say – nothing! As yet'.[49] He must have known this would be unacceptable and only meant to prod Whistler into action. Whistler disputed their figures: 'Your suggestion of the Directors having "met" me is ingenious my dear Huish – and shows a pleasant sense of humor and certain power of invention', he wrote, provocatively, 'The late lamented Czar by the way, "met" the bomb –'.[50] Whistler had only printed five sets, and these had cost the Fine Art Society seventy pounds to produce, which they could not possibly afford. He refused to print all one hundred sets without payment and proposed a price of two guineas a set, offering to print five sets that were immediately required if they would provide him with an assistant. A printer called Holgate was called in, but even then Huish calculated that Whistler was printing one impression a day at a pound or more a time. 'If the man has any capacity he ought by this time to be sufficiently indoctrinated to print them', said Huish, suggesting that it would be cheaper if Holgate did the whole job.[51]

Whistler was joined by several enthusiastic unpaid assistants. There was T. R. Way, and Menpes, who became an ardent pupil. Menpes sacrificed his own printing room, 'which I had specially arranged for the master', and in return received etching instruction.[52] An ex-Slade student, Walter Sickert, joined the team. As part of the learning process, he copied Whistler's *The Little Lagoon* (K.186).[53] Whistler was an admirable master, Sickert said later, 'Sunny, courageous, elegant, *soigné*. Entertaining, *serviable*, gracious, good-natured, easy-going. A *charmeur* and a dandy, with a passion for work. A heart that was ever lifted up by its courage and genius.'[54]

Even with assistance, printing was mortally slow: 115 etchings in February, 130 in April, fifty-six in August and twenty-four in December 1881, ten in January, four in February the following year.[55] The work finally came to a full stop. By February 1882 the Fine Art Society had sold 247 prints, just over twenty sets, for just under £700; these sets had cost £1000 to produce. To show a profit they needed forty sets and Huish agreed to pay eighty guineas to Whistler for printing these, but refused to cover the cost of another assistant and a room. Meanwhile he urgently begged Whistler to print some *Nocturnes*. Whistler had some 'scheme of laying these plates down like old wine' and making money years later, of which Huish heartily disapproved.[56] He wanted prints now and money now. It was all most unbusinesslike.

Huish complained that their printer was used to print other etchings. The artist categorically denied this, but Huish may have had some cause for complaint since Whistler's own notebooks record a suspicious number of sales of the other Venetian prints to dealers and collectors including Queen Victoria.[57] Prices started at four guineas and a first state of *The Rialto* (K.211) went for twelve guineas, a useful addition to Whistler's income. No wonder he was not tempted by Huish's tentative offer of more than two guineas per set if only he would print another ten sets. Whistler decided that attack was the best form of defence and loftily told them to collect the plates: 'you have only to send at once for the plates – and rely upon Mr Goulding or others for "Nocturnes" & "Doorways" "Beggars" & "Lagoons"', but in that case he refused to touch 'the degraded plate' again.[58]

Whistler did not seriously intend to hand over the plates, but it was not until August that Huish improved his offer: for twenty sets, they would pay the artist one hundred pounds (five pounds per set). Accusing the Society of 'apathy and indifference', Whistler complained, unjustly, that they did not want the sets when he offered to print them. He could not possibly 'lay aside other work to take up these plates at any moment their caprice might dictate', and tried to get the price raised to five guineas each for twenty-eight sets, plus three individual impressions, a total of £148 3s 9d. He also asked for half the payment in advance, a proposal that Huish firmly rejected.[59] Somehow the plates were being printed, but the business was to engage Whistler and the frustrated managers of the Fine Art Society for another decade.

1 Whistler to W. and H. Whistler, nd. [19/26 Oct 1880], GUL W988.

2 M. B. Huish to Whistler, 19 Oct 1880, GUL F41.

3 Pennell 1908, I, p.289.

4 Bacher 1908, pp.155–6; see Getscher 1970, pp.157–65.

5 *Sketch for the Selection and Arrangement of the First Venice Set*, Davison Art Centre, Wesleyan University, Middletown, Conn., pencil, 1880, M.836; another sketch (M.837) shows K.183, K.187, K.194, K.186 and possibly K.191 and K.193.

6 Way 1912, p.50, see also pp.42–3, repr. facing p.40.

7 Ibid p.45.

8 For example, Kennedy's catalogue number, ie K.189, is followed by the state in Roman numerals, thus the third state is K.189 III. An intermediate state is indicated ie K.189 III-IV. Kennedy's listing of states, though in general use, does not include all the actual states; see Chapter 7.

9 Way 1912, pp.46–7.

10 *Globe*, 3 Dec 1880.

11 For example, in the Freer Gallery of Art: 'Arms of Amsterdam', K.183, 210 VII (acq.nos 92.16, 02.121); 'Post-horn', K.183, 186, 196 III, 197 III, 203 I, 206 I, 209 V, (acq.nos 93.22. 94.41, 02.231, 06.238, 05.5, 05.6, 87.20); 'Pro Patria', K.188 III, K.205 II (acq.nos 98.385, 87.13); 'Foolscap', K.189 III (acq.no.02.133); 'fleur-de-lys', K.189 III, K.191 cancelled, K.193 I, K.202 I and VII, K.203 I, K.204 VIII, K.211 II (acq.nos 97.52, 02.277, 03.148, 06.39, 87.9, 87.10, 87.12, 87.22); 'Van Gjelder', K.184 I, 201 II (acq.nos 04.17, 04.18): see Bunting 1995, pp.18–19 and App.E. I am indebted to V. Bunting and Martha Smith, conservators, Freer Gallery of Art, for this information.

12 *British Architect*, 10 Dec 1880, shows them hung in the order: 1, 12, 9, 7, 11, 5, 4, 3, 2, 10, 6, 8; Getscher 1970, p.164; see Bendix 1995, pp.218–19.

13 Private view card, GUL LB12/34.

14 Maud Franklin and Whistler to Bacher, nd. [Feb 1881?], Bacher 1908, pp.156–8, 163.

15 See Bibliography of Reviews. Whistler's presscutting books are in GUL PC1–12, with most Venice reviews in PC4, 6 and 15. Major reviews were listed by Getscher and Marks 1986, pp.279–80. Bell 1987, pp.36–148, 361–89, provides a useful analysis and bibliography, including pp.37–8, 66, n.15 on specialist periodicals.

16 J. Ruskin, Oxford lecture, 1872, in Cook and Wedderburn 1903–12, XXII, p.421; J. Ruskin, *Athenaeum*, 27 Dec 1873, quoted by Bell 1987, pp.48–9.

17 Bell 1987, pp.45–9, 70, n.53–4; Lochnan 1984, p.197.

18 C. O. Murray, 'The Etcher Notes: Retroussage', *Etcher*, II, part xi, May 1880, n.p; R. S. Chattock, 'Practical Notes on Etching', *Etcher*, IV, part xxxii, Feb 1882, n.p.; F. Wedmore, 'Modern Etching', *Fortnightly Review*, XLI, no.ccxlv, May 1887, p.757; M. Menpes, 'On the Printing of Etchings', *Magazine of Art*, 1889, pp.328–31.

19 Anon., 'Etching vs Surface-Printing', *Pall Mall Gazette*, XXXI, no.4699, 15 March 1880, p.4; P. G. Hamerton, 'Etching and Surface Printing', *Pall Mall Gazette*, XXXI, no.4708, 25 March 1880, pp.2–3; see Bell 1987, pp.46–9, 71, n. 56.

20 *Times*, 25 Dec 1880.

21 *St James' Gazette*, 9 Jan 1880.

22 *British Architect*, 10 Dec 1880.

23 *World*, 8 Dec 1880; Hamerton is quoted in Whistler 1883, cat.no.95; Whistler 1890, p.95. See Dorment and MacDonald 1994, cat.no.122.

24 *Daily News*, 2 Dec 1880; *St James' Gazette*, 9 Dec 1880; the *Daily News* was quoted in Whistler 1883, cat.no.20 and *St James' Gazette* in cat.no.13, *The Doorway* (K.188); Whistler 1890, pp.96–7.

25 *St James' Gazette*, 9 Dec 1880.

26 *Spectator*, 11 Dec 1880, used in Whistler 1883, cat.no.41, *The Rialto* (K.211); Whistler 1890, p.101.

27 *World*, 8 and 29 Dec 1880, the latter having a letter from Whistler to 'Atlas' (Quilter); Whistler 1890, pp.50–1.

28 M. Franklin and Whistler to Bacher, nd. [1881], Bacher 1908, pp.156–8, 163.

29 FAS sales are recorded in GUL LB12/33; see Lochnan 1984, p.216, and Bell 1987, pp.53–4, 72, n.70.

30 E. Brown to Whistler, 31 Jan 1880, GUL F38.

31 Bell 1987, p.58.

32 *Times*, 25 Dec 1880; *Spectator*, 11 Dec 1880. See also Quilter's review, 'The Society of Painter-Etchers', *Times*, 2 April 1881, p.4; Bell 1987, p.58, n.91, pp.59, 61–2.

33 *Globe*, 3 Dec 1880.

34 Whistler 1883, cat.no.13, Whistler 1890, p.94.

35 *St James' Gazette*, 9 Dec 1880.

36 Ibid quoted in Whistler 1883, cat.no.13, and the 'Russian press' in cat.no.32, *The Balcony* (K.207); Whistler 1890, pp.96, 100. See Ruth Fine, 'James Abbott McNeill Whistler: Venice. Second Series ...', in *Visions of a Collector: The Lessing J. Rosenwald Collection in the Library of Congress Rare Book and Special Collections Division*, Washington, 1991, pp.15–18.

37 Pennell 1908, I, pp.291–2

38 Ibid, pp.295–6.

39 Bacher 1908, p.135; Lochnan 1984, pp.217–18; Bell 1987, p.38.

40 Whistler to Bacher, nd. [1881], in Bacher 1908, repr., pp.136–7.

41 Whistler and M. Franklin to Bacher, nd. [1881], Bacher 1908, pp.136–7, 140.

42 For example, *Times*, 12 April 1881.

43 R. Koehler, *American Art Review*, XI, 1881, p.231, quoted in W. W. Andrew, *Otto Bacher*, Madison, Wisconsin, 1973 (reprint of 1935 ed.), n.p.n.

44 Exh.cat., Society of Painter-Etcher's First Exhibition, London, 1881, cat.nos 28–30; see Lochnan 1984, p.217, repr., p.219.

45 M. Franklin to Bacher, nd. [1881], Bacher 1908, pp.138–9.

46 Huish to Whistler, 18 March 1881, GUL F63; F. S. Haden to Huish, 19 and 21 March 1881, GUL H44–5.

47 Huish to Whistler, 13 Feb 1882, GUL F73.

48 FAS account, 20 Dec 1880; Huish to Whistler, 21 Dec 1880, GUL F50–1.

49 Huish to Whistler, 8 March 1881, GUL F57.

50 Draft letter, Whistler to Huish, nd. [March] 1881, GUL F58.

51 Huish to Whistler, 15 and 16 March (enclosing a £300 cheque), 30 Aug 1881, GUL F61–2, 67.

52 Menpes 1904, pp.89–90.

53 Ruth Bromberg, *Walter Sickert: Prints. A Catalogue Raisonné*, New Haven and London, 2000, cat.no.47.

54 W. Sickert, 'The New Life of Whistler', *The Fortnightly Review*, Dec 1908, pp.1017–28, reprinted in Sitwell 1947, p.19.

55 FAS receipts for 16 Feb, 6 April, 25 Aug, 31 Dec 1881; 24 Jan and 7 Feb 1882, GUL F72.

56 Huish to Whistler, 13 and 15 Feb 1882, GUL F73–4.

57 K.196–7, 199–200, 202–13, later published in the 'Second Venice Set' and unpublished etchings K.218, 219, 222, 225, sales on 8 and 28 Aug, 12 Sept 1882, GUL NB1, pp.1, 3, 101.

58 Huish to Whistler and reply, 22–3 Feb 1882, GUL F75–6; M. F. MacDonald, *Whistler in Venice*, exh.cat., Hunterian Art Gallery, Glasgow, 1971, cat.no.84.

59 Huish to Whistler, 9 Aug 1882; E. Brown to Whistler, 31 Aug 1882; (draft) Whistler to Huish, 1 Sept 1882; reply, 15 Sept 1882; GUL F79–82.

6 The Pastel Show

The exhibition of Venice pastels was the second in a series of one-man exhibitions intended to re-establish Whistler's position in the London art world. The Fine Art Society's original decision to exhibit them was speculative since they had not seen them, but they would have agreed to almost anything to get Whistler back to London. They minimised the risk by choosing the quiet season at the end of January. As the New Year dawned, Whistler was preparing for the exhibition. On 2 January 1881 he called on A. S. Cole, 'as self-reliant and sure as ever, full of confidence in the superlative merit of his pastels'.[1]

He selected fifty-three pastels. Some were given site-specific names like *Fondamenta dei Mori* (M.760) and others misleading ones, such as 'Campo Sta. Martin – Winter Evening' (M.753). *Corte del Paradiso* (fig.109) was exhibited as 'Courtyard': if the name was ironic this was due to the inhabitants, for a small dark courtyard of that name lies off the busy Ruga Ciuffa, east of Campo Santa Maria Formosa. Titles like *The Riva – Sunset; red and gold* (M.807) and *Blue and silver – The Islands, Venice* (fig.111) have a value-added content of 'silver' and 'gold'. Titles like *The Red Doorway* (M.795) stressed colour alone. Contemporary drawings, including *Punch* cartoons (fig.114) and thumbnail sketches by T. R. Way (fig.110), help to identify them.[2]

Designing the show

Whistler designed and Thomas Way (senior) printed a modest catalogue in brown paper covers. The gallery was decorated in brown and gold. Godwin described, 'a low skirting of yellow gold [...] a high dado of dull yellow green cloth, then a moulding of green gold, and then a frieze and ceiling of pale reddish brown.'[3] T. R. Way remembered a skirting of red gold, the dado covered with 'rather dark, warm, green stuff' topped by wooden beading 'gilt with rich gold' under a frieze of Venetian red.[4] It was a sympathetic setting, the fabric providing a soft non-reflective background for the pastels in their gilt frames.[5] Whistler designed the frames, with slim bands of reeding either side of a flat fillet, in three shades of gold (yellow, pink and green): 'now "old gold" and now gold of almost a silvery complexion, to suit the scheme of colour adopted in his pictures'.[6] *The Palace; white and pink* (fig.112), for instance, suited a warm gold frame, while a yellow gold frame set off the cooler yellow of *Fishing Boats* (M.819). *Corte del Paradiso* was reframed in the nineties in a Whistler-designed frame, which was deep, with broad bands of fine reeding, and heavier than the original.

'The test-stone of this cabinet of jewelled art-work is *The Giudecca; note in flesh colour*, which holds the crowning place of honour, on the south wall of the gallery', wrote the *Daily Telegraph*: 'The decorative plan of placing the slender, curved black hull across the picture, on a straight line, is consummately successful in its avoidance of stiffness.'[7] (fig.113)

The pictures were hung mostly 'on the line', with some double hung, for variety.[8] *The Beggars – Winter* (M.727) was hung next to *The Palace in Rags* (M.770), the titles hinting at present poverty and former glory. Throughout the show, each pastel was framed to bring out its individual quality. It was placed beside complementary works and contributed to an overall coherent scheme. The careful decor and presentation of Whistler's work affirmed pastel's aesthetic status.

For years there had been growing concern about the inadequacies of contemporary galleries. In 1857, Ruskin had recommended non-intrusive decor, with each artist's works hung together, and paintings hung in two rows, lit from above.[9] In the late seventies, the Grosvenor Gallery developed effective hanging and lighting. A growing concern for domestic, as well as gallery, design was reflected in a fashion for architect designed houses, such

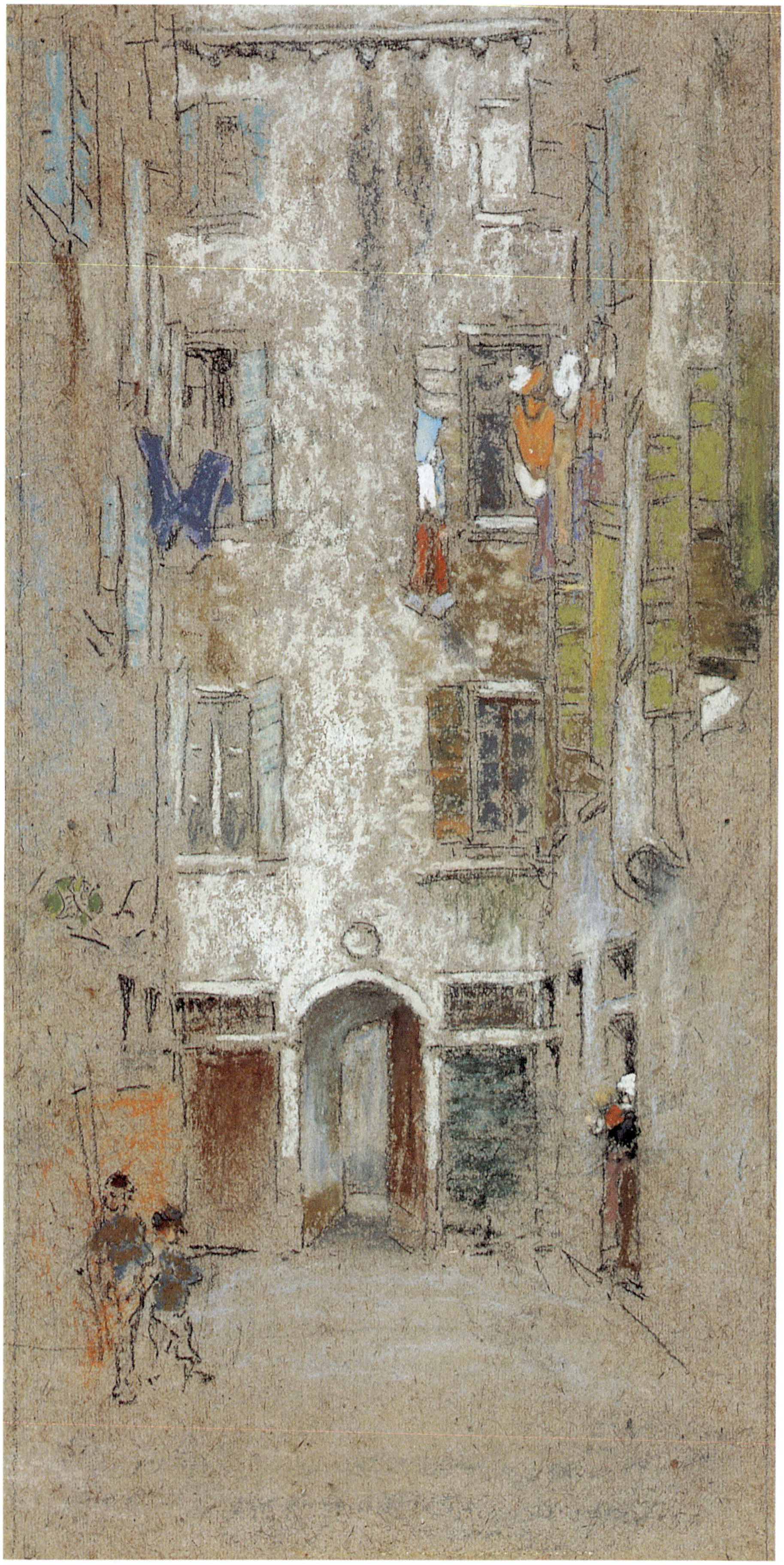

109
James McNeill Whistler
Corte del Paradiso
Pastel 192 x 288 mm
Fine Art Society, M.784

as the White House designed by Godwin for Whistler. Godwin was almost certainly consulted by both Whistler and the Fine Art Society during the designing of the rooms for the pastel exhibition and was involved in designing the new entrance on Bond Street in July 1881: a façade (fig.115) very like Whistler's etching *The Doorway* (K.188).[10]

The private view

The intimate decor surrounding the pastels was designed to appeal to a cultural and social elite, like the clientele of the Grosvenor Gallery, without bankrupting the Fine Art Society. Its success was demonstrated at the private view from 11 am to 6 pm on Saturday 29 January, which was a terrific crush. Whistler's guest list included many leaders of fashion and Society. Some visitors thought Whistler, being a wit, meant them to be amused. He laughed with them: 'I always did with people of that kind, and then they said I was not serious.'[11] The popular artist J. E. Millais, whose pictures were in the adjoining room, is reported to have said 'Magnificent, fine – very cheeky – but fine!' and wrote generously: 'I was so charmed with your Venice work that I cannot resist writing you a line to say so. They gave me real pleasure. The gradations, tenderness, lovely tints of sunset, & sea quite delighted me.'[12]

At prices ranging from twenty to sixty guineas, £400 of pastels were sold on the first day, and total receipts reached £1800. Godwin reported, 'Mr Whistler fears his pastels are not so good as he supposed – for they are selling.'[13]

Their celebrations were cut short when, on 31 January 1881, Whistler's mother died. He had rarely written from Venice during her illness and felt guilty and grief-stricken, but her death brought the two brothers, James and William, closer together. Returning from the funeral in Hastings Whistler found the show busy and press reaction encouraging.

The press

Neither Whistler nor the Fine Art Society left anything to chance, liaising openly with the press. Brown contacted two major critics, Burnand of *Punch* and Sala of the *Daily Telegraph*. Sala in his turn asked Godfrey Turner to write it up and when the review was cut he apologised. Huish asked T. R. Way to review the show for the *Art Journal*.[14]

The critics concentrated on the medium, the representation of Venice and the decor. They were slightly out of their depth, unsure of the vocabulary or the criteria to adopt in evaluating the medium. In the seventies, the words 'chalk' and 'pastel' and even 'crayon' had been used interchangeably. Ruskin thought the medium only suitable for studies: 'No pencil or chalk drawing is ever to be made for its own sake, as if pencil or chalk were beautiful materials. They are very imperfect and bad materials and are only to be used for study.'[15]

Likewise, Quilter in 1881 thought the drawings were 'more correctly described as sketches in black chalk touched with colour in crayons'. In a true pastel, said Quilter, the ground of the picture was covered with coloured chalk and so, by definition, Whistler's drawings, where the brown paper provided the background, were 'precisely the reverse of pastel'. Although they were 'perfect works – suggestive little pictures' they were only preliminary studies.[16]

Just as critics had queried the status of etching, they queried the status of pastel. 'Coloured crayons have not hitherto been judged a very desirable means of artistic expression,' said *The World*.[17] The *Athenaeum* was unusual in appreciating the subtle mid-tone effects gained from pastel on various shades of paper, writing that *San Biagio; flesh colour and grey* (fig.117) was 'first rate and extremely delicate, being a fine study of silvery, harmonious white with local colours, as in the choice tint of the purplish grey vapours floating past the deep, dull clouds behind them. This atmospheric effect is wonderfully well given.'[18]

The Palace; white and pink (fig.112), which shows the Ca' da Mosto on the Grand Canal from the Fabriche Nove in San Polo, was drawn with precise and expressive lines, in fifteen or more colours. However, the *St James' Gazette* thought it suffered 'in force and truth' from the combination of pale colours on pale grey.[19] Other critics disapproved of blank areas of brown paper, and of the brown paper *per se*. *Punch* called *The Brown Morning – Winter* (M.746) the 'Brown-Paper Morning' and implied that Whistler with his chalks was a pavement artist.[20]

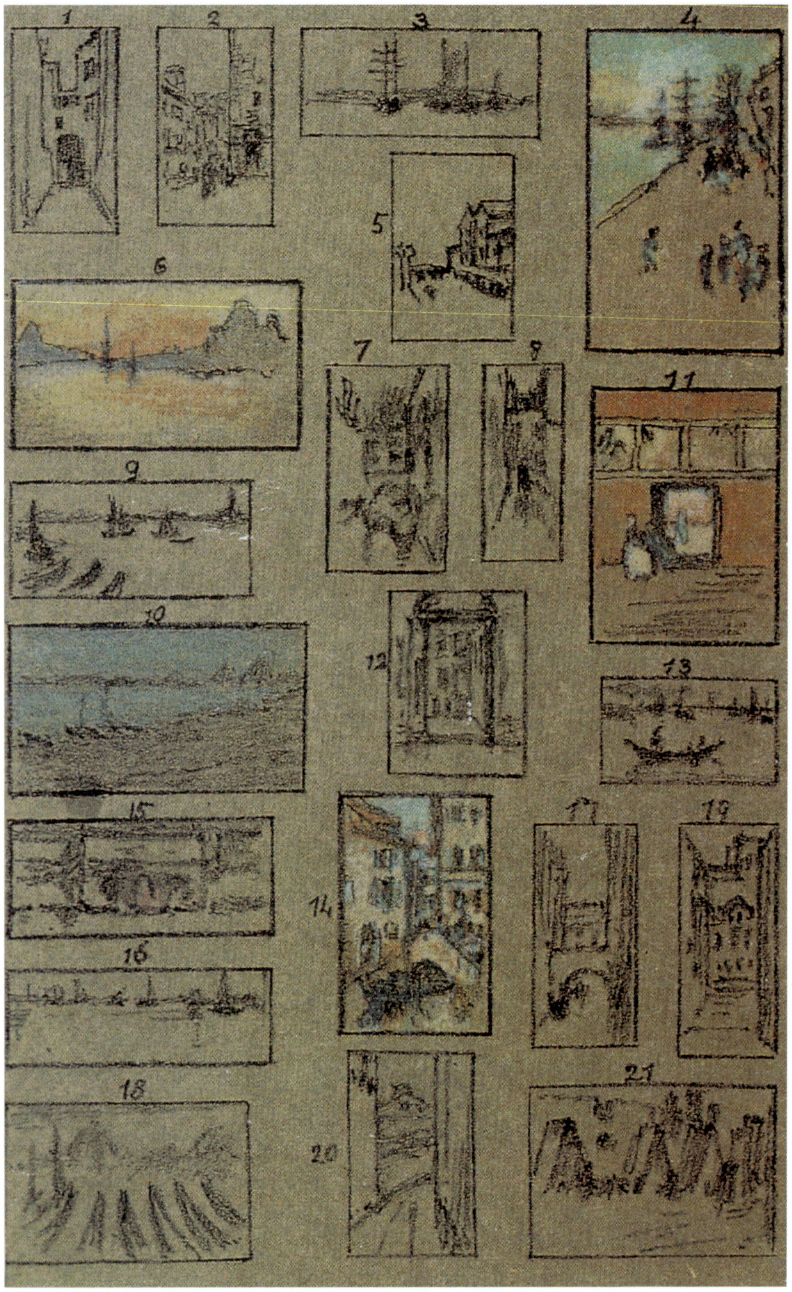

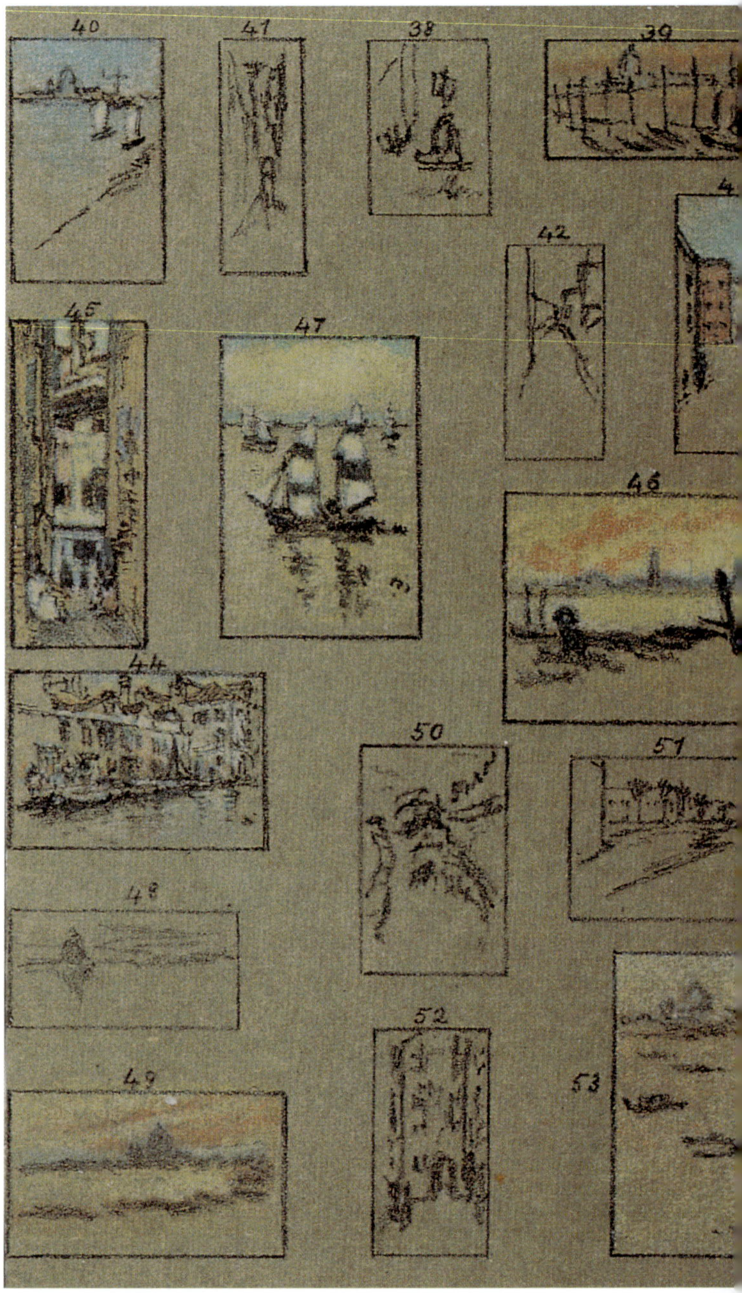

Impressions, studies and 'finished' pictures

Critics echoed the etching reviews in complaining of lack of 'finish'. The pastels had 'neither drawing, composition, working out of detail, nor scarcely any other requisite of a finished study or picture' complained one critic, while another grudgingly praised a 'success which would be completely satisfactory were it only pushed a little further'.[21]

The directness of the medium, as employed by Whistler, did not go unnoticed. The *Pictorial World* asserted that despite 'swiftness and dash that precludes anything like care and finish [...] every line has its full value.'[22] Wedmore thought the pastels confirmed Whistler's 'imperilled' reputation, being unified by his ability 'to see most sensitively' and 'record most summarily'.[23] As Lynne Bell writes in her sharp analysis of these reviews, 'The lack of a set of laws that prescribed or prohibited what could not be tolerated or rejected gave the critics an unprecedented latitude in their evaluation of the pastels.'[24]

Few critics were able to find antecedents except in Turner's watercolours. This was a matter for both praise

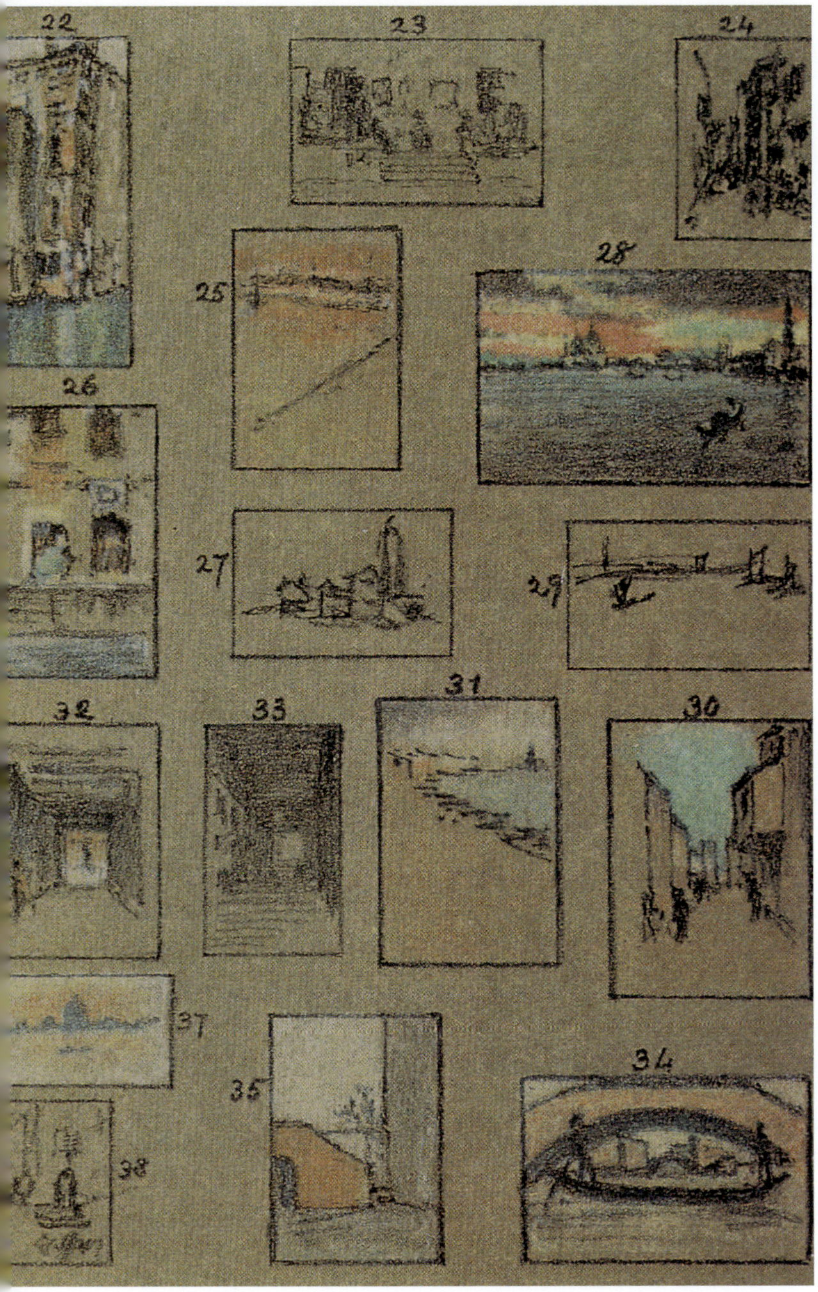

110
T. R. Way
Thumbnail sketches of Whistler's Venice Pastels, 1881
from Way 1912

and criticism. Both the *St James' Gazette* and *The Times* called *The Cemetery* (M.738) worthy of Turner and it was noted that, coincidentally, Turner's Venice drawings had been exhibited in the very same room in 1878. The more knowledgeable found plenty of respectable comparisons, with Hogarth for instance, and the pastels of George Morland.[25]

Some critics sought new standards of assessment. Quilter called Whistler 'impressionist' in 'the feeling and perception of transient beauties'. Pastel could be continued without difficulty after interruptions, ideal for impressions of a particular place and time. *Pan* also called Whistler an 'Impressionist Master', explaining, 'colour is the soul and secret of Mr Whistler's work. By its means, by his special knowledge of it, he claims to be able to present a certain moment of feeling – a peculiar sentiment that occurred to him when under certain passing colour-influences.'[26] An Italian paper, however, disagreed, saying he was an '*originale*'.[27]

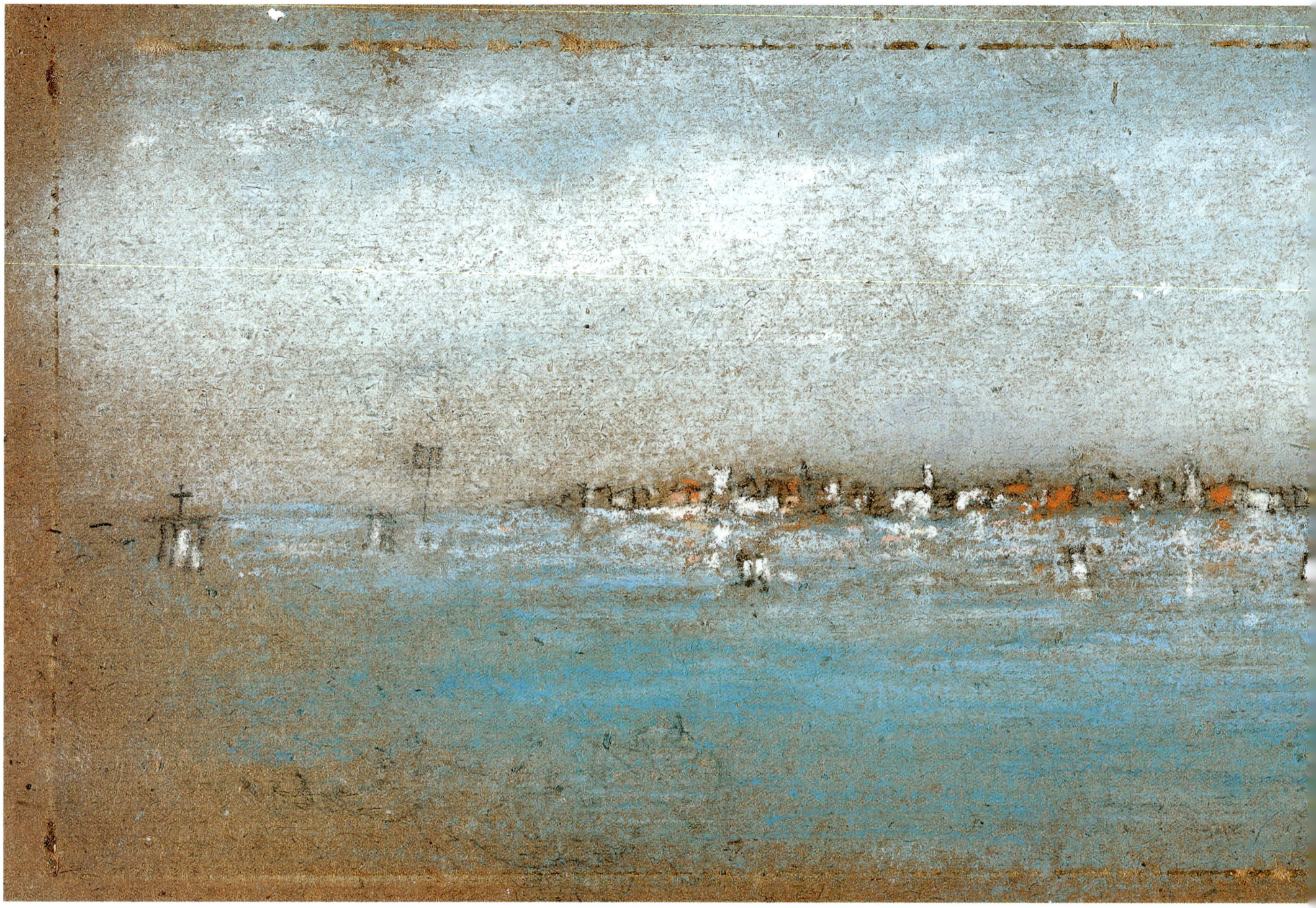

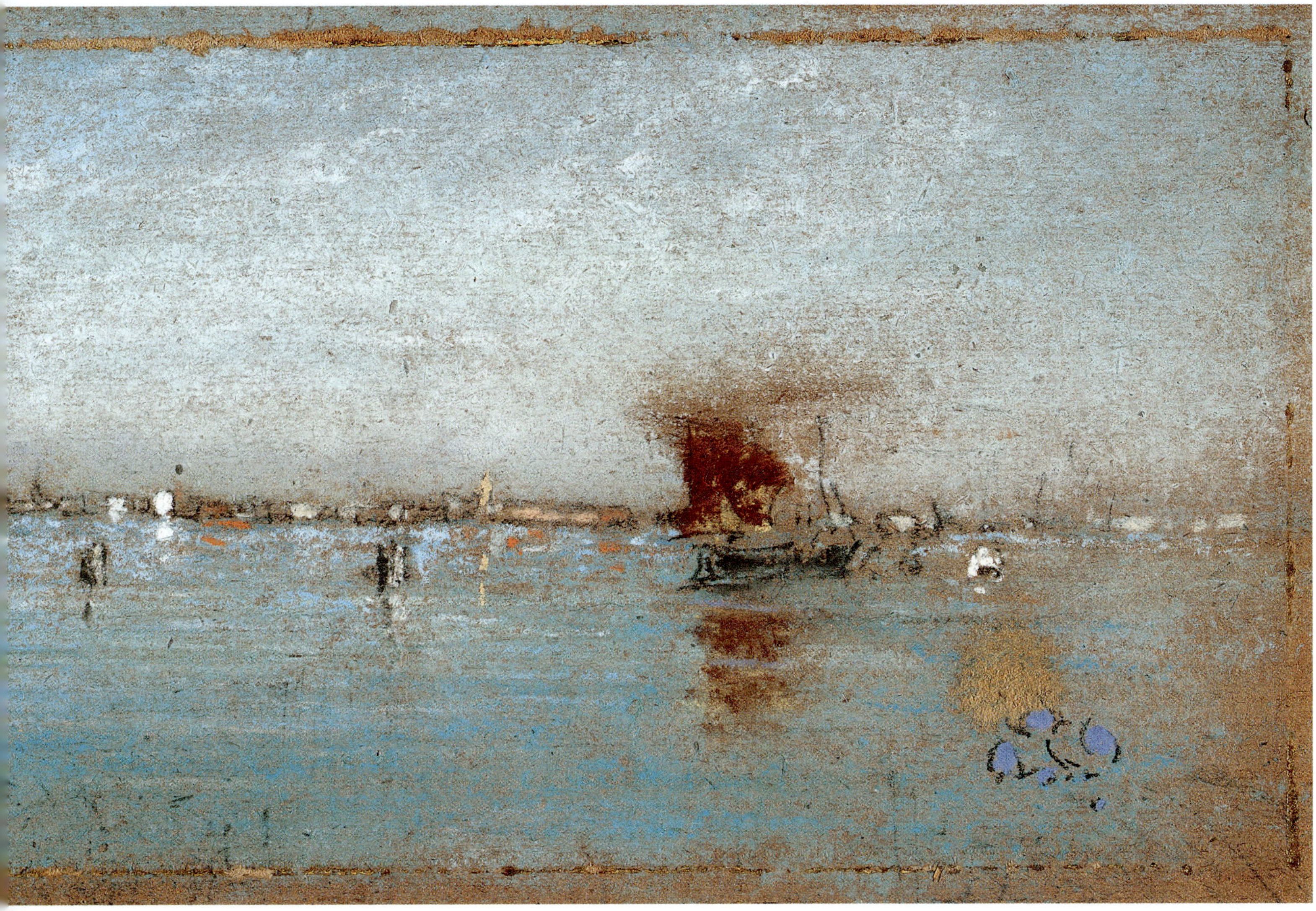

111
James McNeill Whistler
Blue and silver – The Islands, Venice
Pastel 91–3 x 284 mm
Freer Gallery of Art, M.822

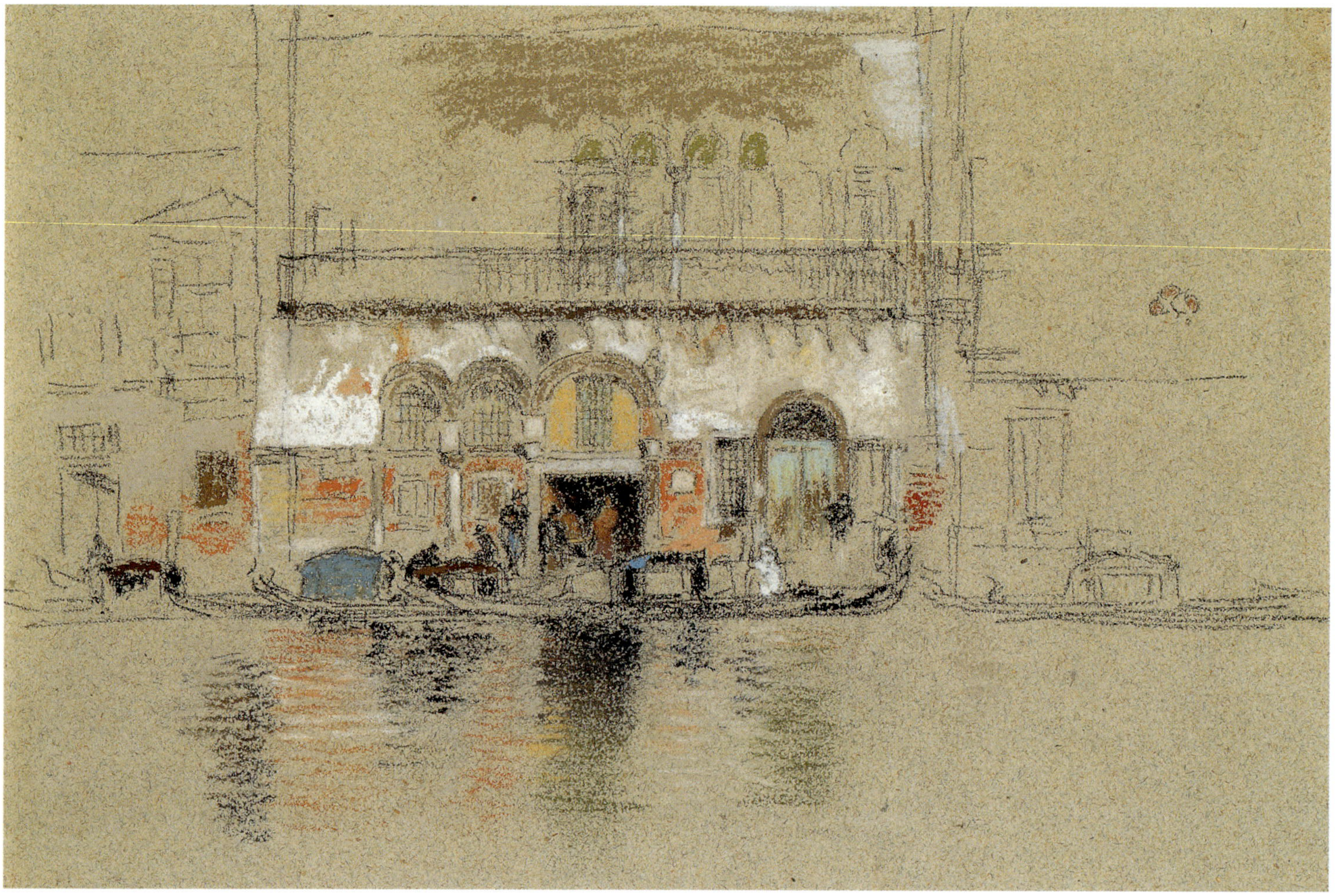

112
James McNeill Whistler
The Palace; white and pink
Pastel 182 x 284 mm
Private Collection, M.758

Views of Venice

Punch gave Whistler several 'puffs' including a whole page to himself, rivalling the coverage for the whole Royal Academy.[28] (fig.114) The first picture in the catalogue was *Sotto Portico, San Giacomo* (fig.116), a narrow drawing of a courtyard off the Campo Giacomo dell'Orto. 'A sort o' portico. Pretty clear so far', said *Punch*.[29] The pastel shows a shrine in a dark passage, and beyond, women at a well, picked out with exquisite detail. Touches of startling red and turquoise illuminate the drawing. Underneath is another drawing, barely visible and upside down – which accounts for the butterfly, which is hurtling downwards, its barbed tail waving defiantly.

Although Burnand found Whistler's images 'discouraging', many approved. The *Artist* recognised truth in his rendition of Venice, 'second-hand, dirty and everlastingly lovely.' It praised 'the artist who has the eye to see and skill to preserve these beautiful realities, and who does not go about to evolve [...] an ideal Venice from his inner consciousness'.[30] T. R. Way said Whistler showed 'notes full of life and vigorous colour of the present living Venice.'[31]

Godwin's review reflects the 'new criticism' of D. S. MacColl and R. A. M. Stevenson and also, since he undoubtedly discussed it with Whistler, the artist's views. He stressed the formal qualities of the pastels, praised Whistler's technique and described his working process.

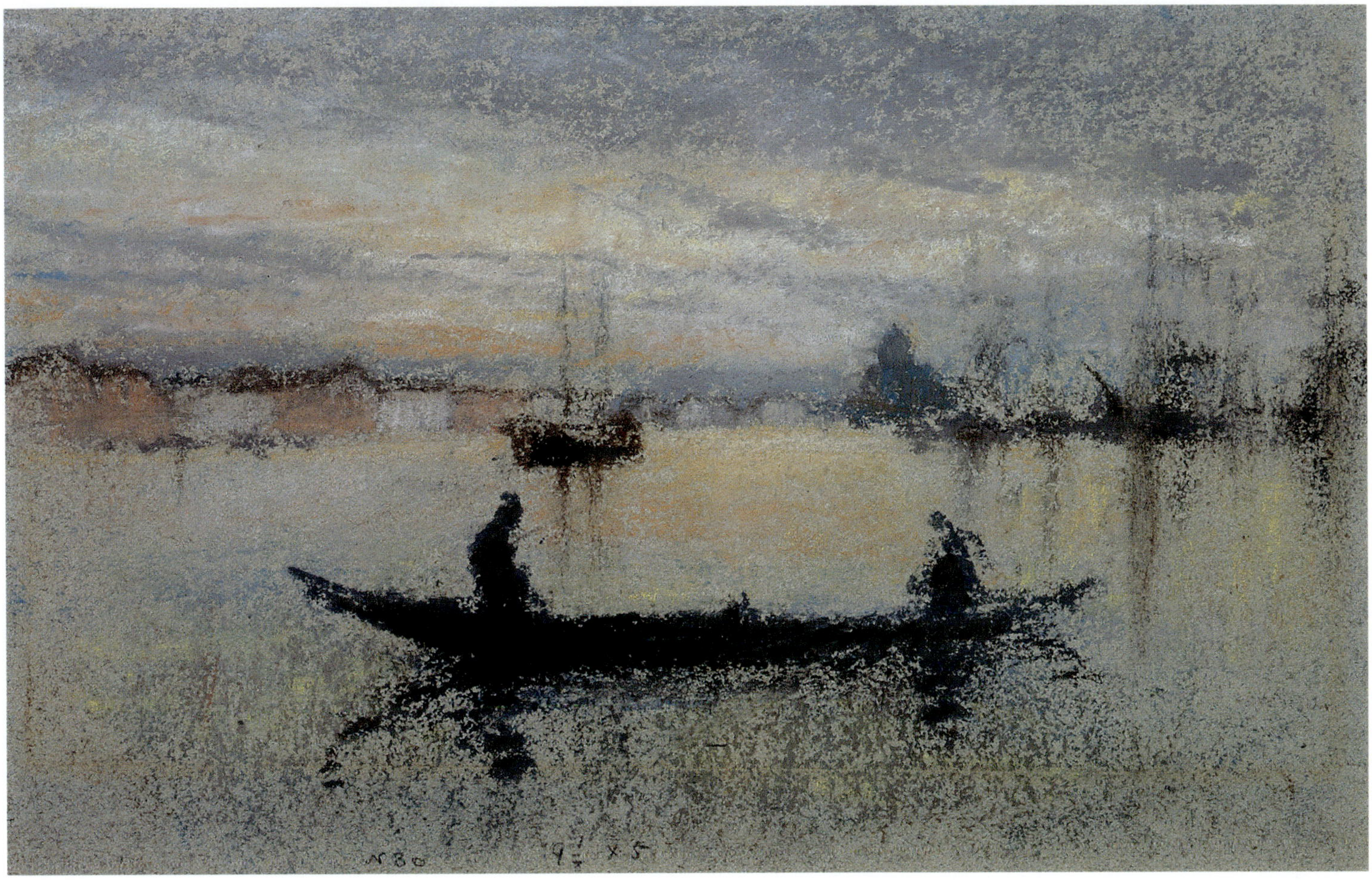

113
James McNeill Whistler
The Giudecca; note in flesh colour
Pastel 159 x 252 mm
Mead Art Museum, Amherst College, M.817

He blamed old-fashioned reproductions of Venetian views for the public's resistance to Whistler's 'new music', inspired as it was by the 'strength of his admiration' for Venetian architecture.[32]

Creating an image

Both Godwin and Way promoted an image of Whistler as separate and misunderstood, and as a threat to the critical establishment. They argued that Whistler was an artist of creative power and originality, serious, conscientious and hard-working: Way called him a genius. Echoing Whistler's words at the Ruskin trial, Godwin said that his work was 'the result and development of his past and vast experience'. Whistler's admirers exaggerated the opposition and implied that his work was too revolutionary for the public.[33] This approach was psychologically quite effective, flattering those who attended the show that they too were separate from the common herd.

The public certainly flocked to Millais' exhibition in the adjoining room, where his seventeen oils hung against crimson flock wallpaper. Despite the decor, 42,830 visitors admired Millais' paintings, his fees came to £2141, and his press coverage exceeded that for Whistler's pastels.[34] Whistler's exhibition was more modest but it too was critically and financially effective and established him at the forefront of the pastel revival.

WHISTLER'S WENICE; OR, PASTELS BY PASTELTHWAITE.

MR. WHISTLER is the artful Doger of Venice. TURNER made "studies" from which he subsequently developed his pictures: but Mr. WHISTLER is the "Chiel amang ye taking notes"—in colour, and, unable to keep them to himself, he exhibits them in the most generous and self-effacing way to the public generally. It is very kind of him; perhaps it is very deep of him. Does he want to discourage his brother artists from going to Venice? He may have conceived a violent animosity to Mr. COOK, and has hit upon this method of deterring intending tourists from visiting the "Pride of the Sea."

Whatever the motive for the exhibition, the artist seems to speak for himself, and say—"Well, Sir, I'm Master JIMMY WHISTLER I am, and if I can do this sort o' thing with a shilling box o' paints from the Lowther Arcade, a few sheets of blotting paper, and some brown-paper covers off the family jam-pots, I could do bigger work with improved materials, you bet!"

This address evidently conveys the suggestion that he should be forthwith presented by his friends and admirers with a real colour-box and the entire artistic paraphernalia. In furtherance of this design, we place before our readers our own "Notes" in black and white, suggested by those of Master WHISTLER.

N.B.—Visitors are requested to observe the principal figures, on which we only allow ourselves to touch lightly, and compare them with those in the brown-paper Catalogue. These notes being intended for practical guidance, every visitor should take them to the Gallery as a suggestive commentary which will be of the greatest assistance to him in appreciating the collection in detail.

No. 1. *Sotto Portico, San Giacomo.* A sort o' portico. Pretty clear so far.

No. 7. *The Little Back Canal.* Subject from the celebrated Triumviretta, *Coxio e Boxio.*

Sergento Bouncero. Don't be angry, Gentlemen. There used to be a Little Back Canal here.

Boxio e Coxio (*together*). Then put it up! [*Exit* BOUNCERO.

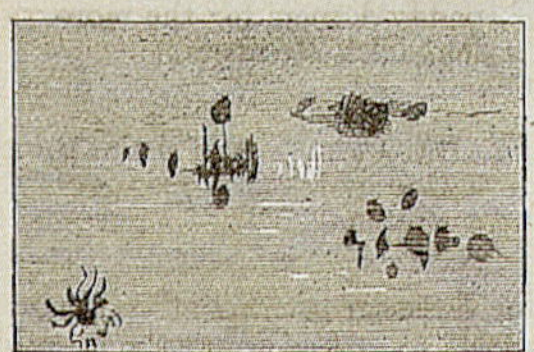

No. 10.

No. 10. *Nocturne—The Riva.* A Mud-bank note. "First Impression of Venice on a piece of Blotting-Paper."

No. 13. *The Giudecca: note in flesh-colour.* Suggestion for a Picture to represent Mr. IRVING as *Shylock* on a river—somewhere. Note for Jewdecca-rative Art.

No. 14. *The Bridge—flesh-colour and brown.* Suggestion for Sir WILLIAM TITE's pantaloons—say a pair of Tite's.

No. 18. *Nocturne at a Hotel.* Curious specimens of shoes left outside the bedroom doors to be cleaned. Suggestion for the Boots.

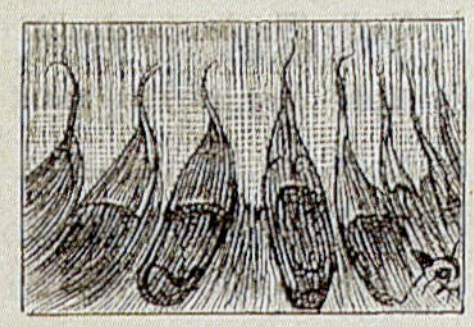

No. 18.

No. 21. *Fish Market, San Barnabo.* Suggestion of trade being very dull.

No. 22. *The Old Marble Palace.* We "dreamt that we dwelt in marble halls," and awoke with a severe cold. About this period we came to the conclusion, that if we wisited Wenice—WHISTLER's Wenice—we should soon become what Mr. MANTALINI described as a "demm'd moist uncomfortable body."

No. 27. *Campanile at Lido.* Suggestion for a camp in ile—this isn't in ile. *Note*—it's out in the desolate country, a truly-rural-Lido sort of place.

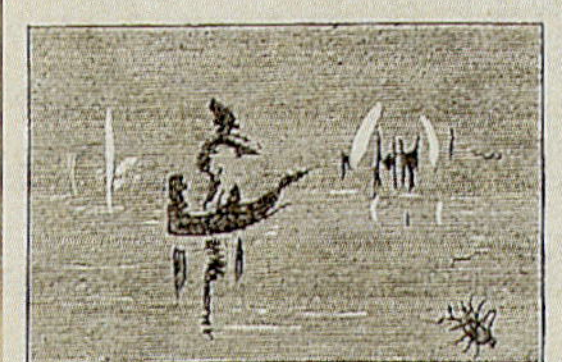

No. 29.

No. 28. "*Boat Ahoy!*" Suggestion for a picture of "there were three sailors of Bristol City, Who took a boat and went to sea."

No. 29. *The Giudecca—Winter: grey and blue.* Uncomfortably suggestive of a nervous man bent on taking a header.

No. 35. *The Staircase: note in red.* Suggestion that this note "should be taken as red."

No. 36. *The Cemetery.* This is what Master JAMES calls it. We prefer to consider it as suggestion for a dark scene in some Pantomime of *Gulliver*, representing *Gulliver's* cocked-hat adrift off Lilliput or Water-Lilliput.

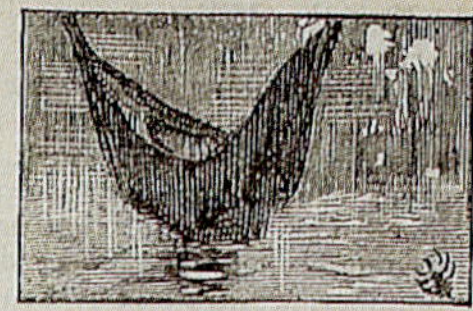

No. 36.

No. 37. *Swamped Buttercups.*

No. 38. *The Red Doorway.* Suggestion for the Home of SMUDGE, R.A.

No. 39. Suggestion for a view of the Polar Regions "from the steps of the Piazetta."

No. 43. *A Red Note.* Suggestive that bearer waits answer.

No. 47. *Awfully Cowl'd!* Suggestion for a picture representing three unfortunate Pierrots who, returning from a fancy ball in the country, have lost their way and stuck in a peat-bog.

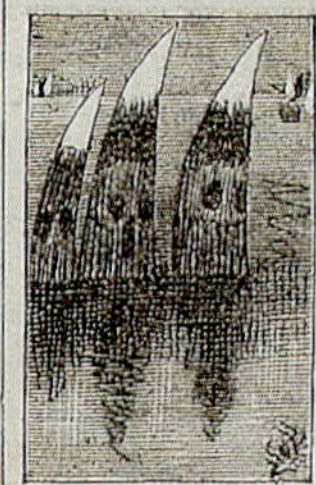

No. 47. ---

No. 51. *Campo Sta. Martin—Winter Evening.* Note in Real Jam, or "Venice Preserved."

No. 53. *The Brown Morning—Winter.* Master JAMES means the Brown-paper Morning.

And lastly, what in nature is this curious specimen that appears in every picture? It's not a Gnat: it's not a Mosquito. Can it be a—but this suggestion of Venice is unpleasant for travellers. Did Master JAMES stay in the Palace of the Doges, and at midnight was he aroused from his harmony in snores, and compelled to rise from the ancient bed, light a candle, and—but we will not pursue the subject further.

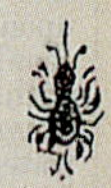

[Beautiful Venice! "When found make a note of." *Mem.* by J.W.]

IO TRIOMPHE!

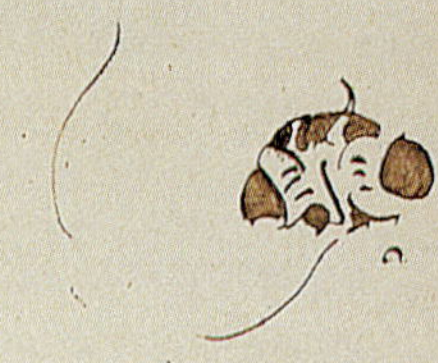

114
'*Whistler's Wenice; or, Pastels by Pasteltthwaite*'
Punch, 12 February 1881
Glasgow University Library

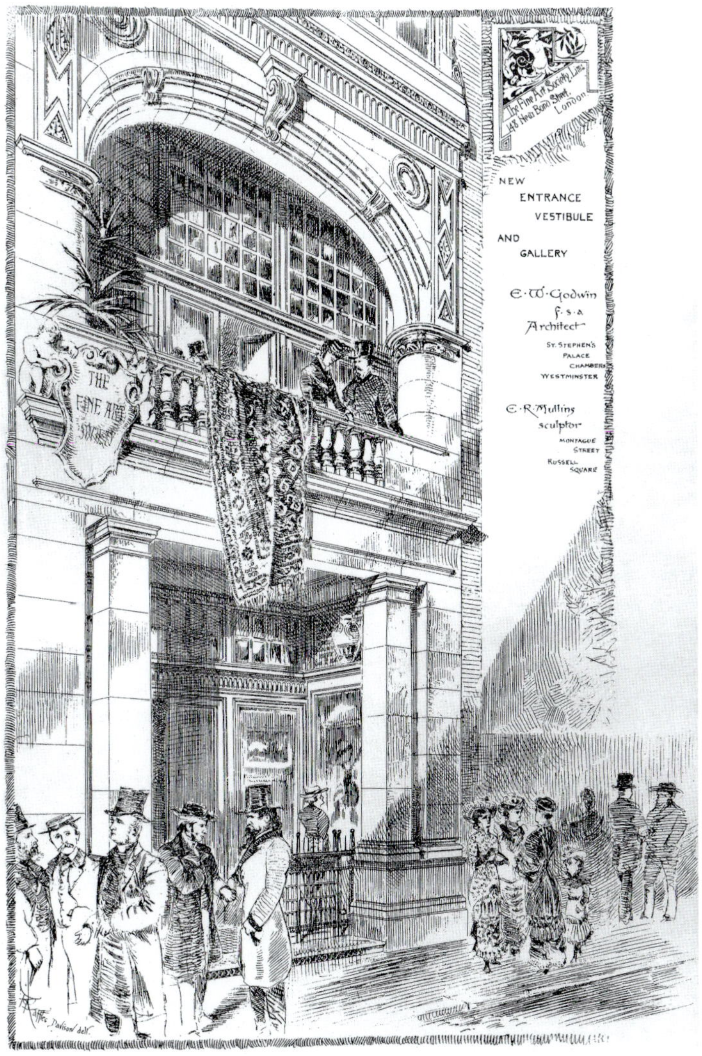

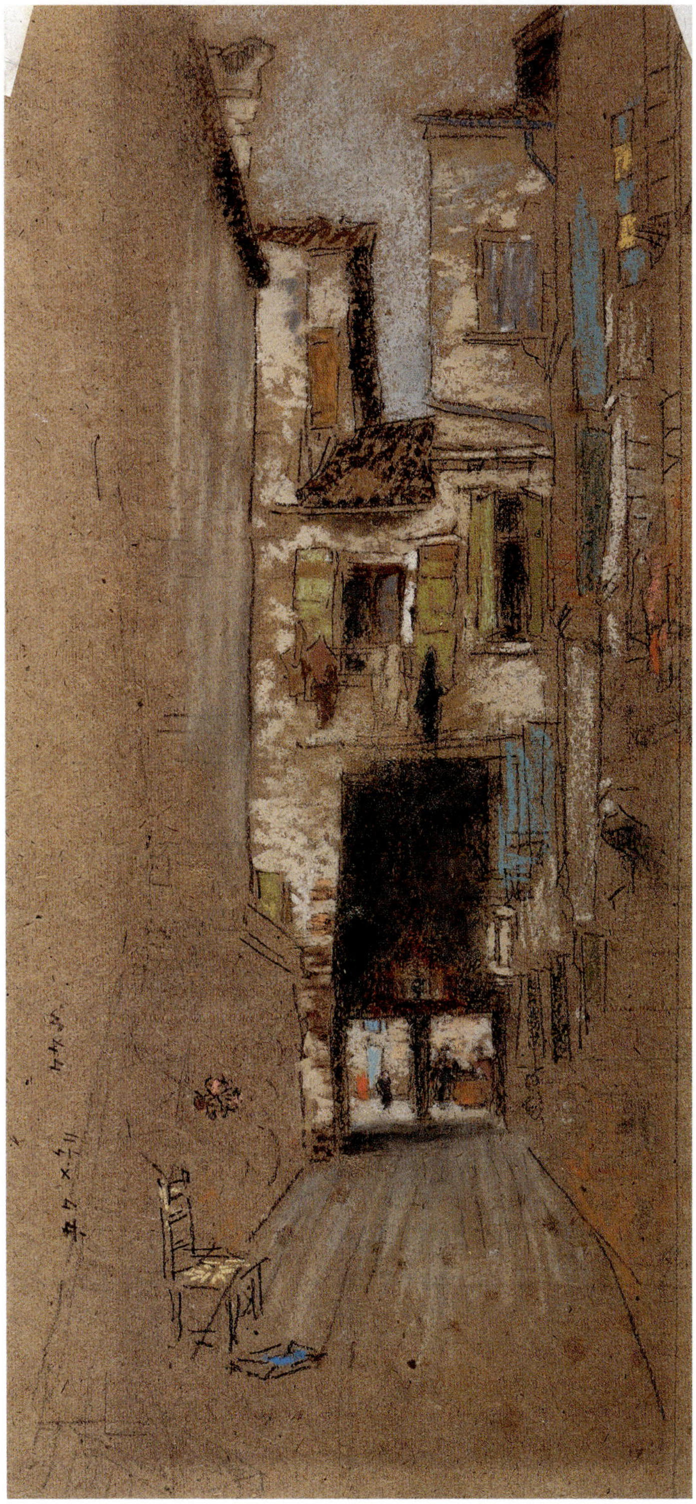

115
E. W. Godwin
Façade of the Fine Art Society
Drawing by T. R. Davison, from *British Architect*, XVI, 16 Dec 1881, p.632
RIBA Library Photographs Collection

116
James McNeill Whistler
Sotto Portico, San Giacomo
Pastel 305 x 140 mm
Private Collection, M.769

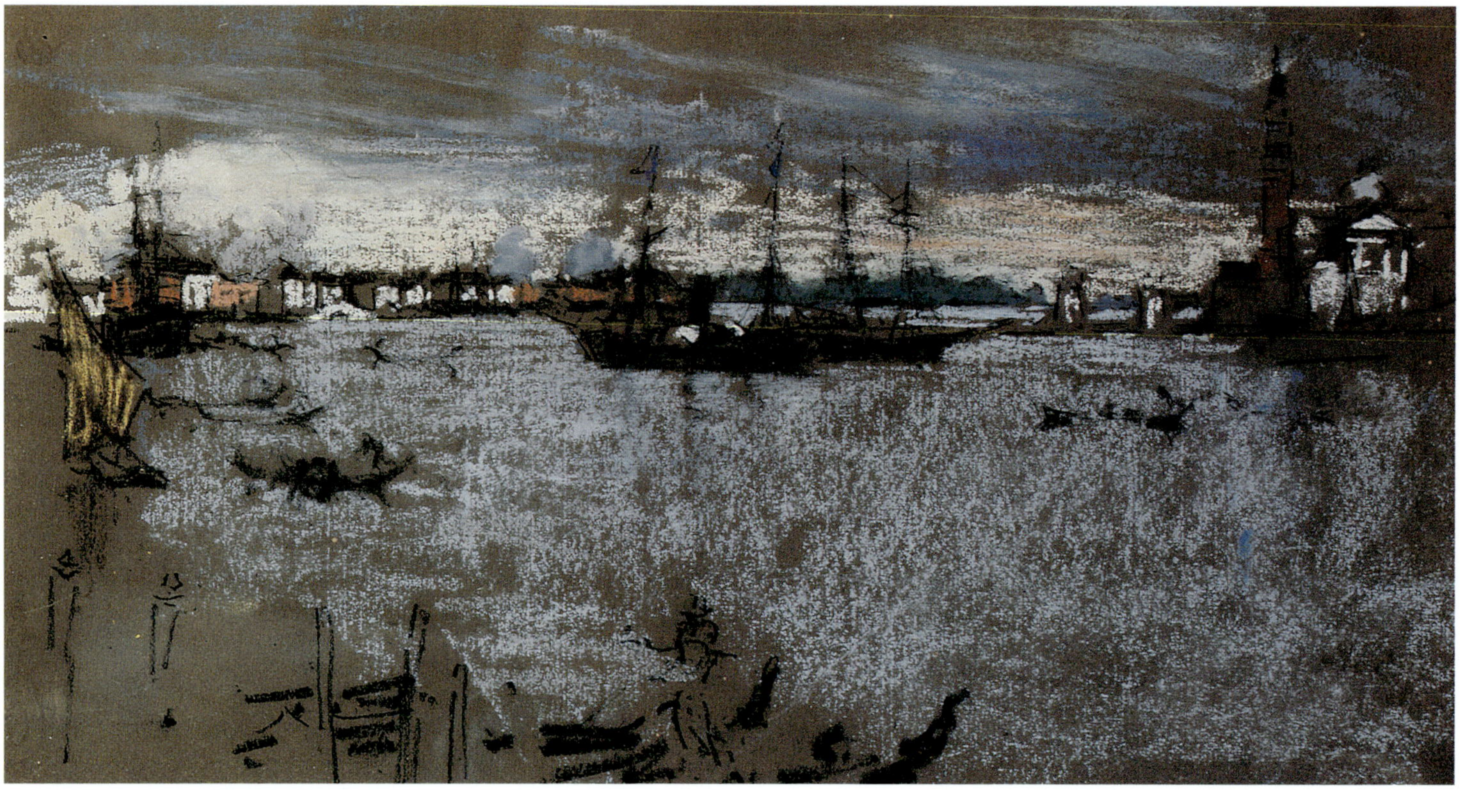

117
James McNeill Whistler
San Biagio; flesh colour and grey
Pastel 192 x 288 mm
Private Collection, M.818

1 A. S. Cole's diary, from Pennell 1908, I, p.292.
2 Way 1912, repr. facing p.52.
3 *British Architect*, 4 Feb 1881.
4 Way 1912, p.54; see descriptions in *Country Gentleman*, 5 Feb 1881, *Observer*, 6 Feb 1881, in letters from Huish to Whistler, 8 Dec 1880 (GUL F49) and M. Franklin to Bacher, nd. [21 March 1881?], (FGA 177); Bendix 1995, pp.220–3.
5 D. P. Curry, 'Total Control: Whistler at an Exhibition' in R. E. Fine (ed.), *James McNeill Whistler A Reexamination, Studies in the History of Art*, XIX, Center for Advanced Study in the Visual Arts Symposium Papers VI, National Gallery of Art, Washington, DC, 1987, p.77.
6 *World*, 2 Feb 1881.
7 *Daily Telegraph*, 5 Feb 1881, GUL pc4, p.48, quoted in M.817.
8 *British Architect*, 4 Feb 1881. E. W. Godwin, drawing of walls in exh.cat., GUL EC1881; Bendix 1995, repr. p.222
9 Cook and Wedderburn 1903–12, XIII, pp.81–8 and 176–7.
10 *British Architect*, XVI, Dec 1881, repr. p.632; J. O'Callaghan, 'The Fine Art Society and E. W. Godwin,' *FAS 100*, exh.cat., Fine Art Society, London, 1976, pp.4–9; A. Reid, 'The Architectural career of E. W. Godwin' in S. W. Soros (ed.), *E. W. Godwin. Aesthetic Movement Architect and Designer*, New Haven and London, 1999, repr. figs 61–2, p.171.
11 Pennell 1908, I, pp.292–3. Private view card, GUL pc15, p.23.
12 J. E. Millais to Whistler, 17 Feb 1881, GUL M348; Dorment and MacDonald 1994, cat.no.120.
13 *British Architect*, 4 Feb 1881; Pennell 1908, I, p.294.
14 G. Turner to Huish, 1 Feb 1881, GUL T215; *Daily Telegraph*, 5 Feb 1881. T. R. Way to Whistler, 2 Feb 1881, GUL W80; *Art Journal*, 1881, p.93.
15 J. Ruskin, 'The Laws of Fésole' and 'Catalogue of the Rudimentary series', 1872, in Cook and Wedderburn 1903–12, XV, p.369, XXI, pp.258–9; Bell 1987, pp.83–4, n.31.
16 *Times*, 9 Feb 1881.
17 *World*, 2 Feb 1881.
18 *Athenaeum*, 5 Feb 1881, p.206; M.818.
19 *St James' Gazette*, 9 Feb 1881; M.758.
20 *Punch*, 12 Feb and 19 March 1881.
21 *Queen*, 12 Feb 1881; *Artist*, 1 March 1881, p.72; *St James' Gazette*, 9 Feb 1881, p.13; Bell 1987, p.85.
22 *Pictorial World*, 5 Feb 1881.
23 *Academy*, 19 Feb 1881.
24 Bell 1987, pp.90–3.
25 For example, *St James' Gazette*, 9 Feb 1881; *Times*, 9 Feb 1881; *Observer*, 6 Feb 1881; *Academy*, 19 Feb 1881; *Country Gentleman*, 5 Feb 1881. See Bell 1987, pp.88–91, p.111, n.50.
26 *Times*, 25 Dec 1880; *Pan*, 5 Feb 1881.
27 *Fanfulla Sabato*, 26 Feb 1881.
28 *Punch* 1881, LXXX, 22 Jan, 12 Feb and 26 March 1881; 'Our Guide to the Academy', 7 May, pp.208–9, 14 May, p.217, and 21 May, p.237. See Getscher and Marks 1986, pp.280–4, L.3a–t, for bibliography, and Bell 1987, pp.80–1, 108, n.18, n.21 for analysis of reviews.
29 *Punch*, 12 Feb 1881, p.69; M.769.
30 Way in *Art Journal*, 1881, p.93; *Artist*, 1 March 1881; Bell 1987, pp.95–7.
31 *Art Journal*, 1881, p.93.
32 *British Architect*, 4 Feb 1881, p.62.
33 *British Architect*, 4 Feb 1881; *Art Journal*, 1881, p.93; Pennell 1908, I, pp.292–4; Bell 1987, pp.103–6.
34 For example, anon. [Quilter], 'Mr. Millais' Paintings', *Spectator*, 26 Feb 1881, p.284.

7 'Arrangement in White and Yellow': The Second Exhibition of Etchings

Despite problems with the 'First Venice Set', Whistler and the Fine Art Society planned a new exhibition for February 1883. Warily, Huish tried to arrange the details. He suggested that any costs of redecoration over twenty-five pounds would be borne from the first sales of etchings. There would be a twenty-five per cent discount plus fifteen per cent to trade. The etchings would be delivered within a month and the artist would be paid a month later. Huish hoped that the admission fee and catalogue sales at one shilling a time would also generate money.[1]

The private view

Whistler wrote to the sculptor, Waldo Story, a fellow American expatriate, announcing:

> Well great Shebang on Saturday 17. Feb – Opening of Show and Private View – "Arrangement in White & Yellow". I do the Gallery in Bond Street – where I have won my battle and am on good terms with the Fine Art Society – having it all my own way of course – hurrah! – All the World there – Lady Archie – the Prince – [...] great glorification – and the Butterfly rampant all over the place! I can't tell you how perfect – though you would instinctively know that there isn't a detail forgotten – Sparkling and dainty – dainty to a degree my dear Waldino – and all so sharp – White walls – of different whites – with yellow painted mouldings – not gilded! – yellow velvet curtains – pale yellow matting – yellow sofas and little chairs – lovely little table yellow – own design – with yellow pot and Tiger lilly [sic]! Forty odd superb etchings round the white walls in their exquisite white frames – with the little butterflies – large white butterfly on yellow curtain – and yellow butterfly on white wall – and finally servant in yellow livery (!) handing Catalogue in brown paper cover same size as Ruskin pamphlet!!! And such a catalogue! – The last inspiration! – Sublime simply – Never such a thing thought of – I take my dear Waldo, all this I have collected of the silly drivel of the wise fools who write, and I pepper and salt it about the catalogue under the different etching I exhibit! – in short I put their nose to the grindstone and turn the wheel with a whirr! [...] The whole thing is a joy – and indeed a masterpiece of Mischief![2]

The Fine Art Society echoed Whistler in targeting patrons, using advance publicity and concentrating hype on the decor and catalogue (fig.118). *The World*, for instance, announced that the invitation card was 'a little gem of daintiness'.[3] (fig.119) Whistler himself was newsworthy, a dandy, a wit and eccentric, and his status as an American outsider gave him social mobility. The private view on Saturday 17 February 1883 was a crush of breathtaking proportions, a social triumph crowned by the presence of the Prince and Princess of Wales.[4]

Yellow cravats were worn by 'Mr Whistler's more devoted friends' and he suggested the ladies wore black or white to complement the decor.[5] Pots of tiger lilies alternated with daffodils, jonquils, broom and any other available yellow flowers. Whistler designed butterflies with a sting in the tail, to be worn 'defiantly' (as he told Mrs Huish) by 'the brave and beautiful on the great day!'[6] He wrote triumphantly to his brother:

> you should have seen the faces when the Princess appeared with my little yellow butterfly on her shoulder!!! [...] I really had some 80 or 100 little butterflies made of white and yellow satin – most exquisite – wonderful little bodies of plush – with the crisp silk wings and the silver barbed sting!

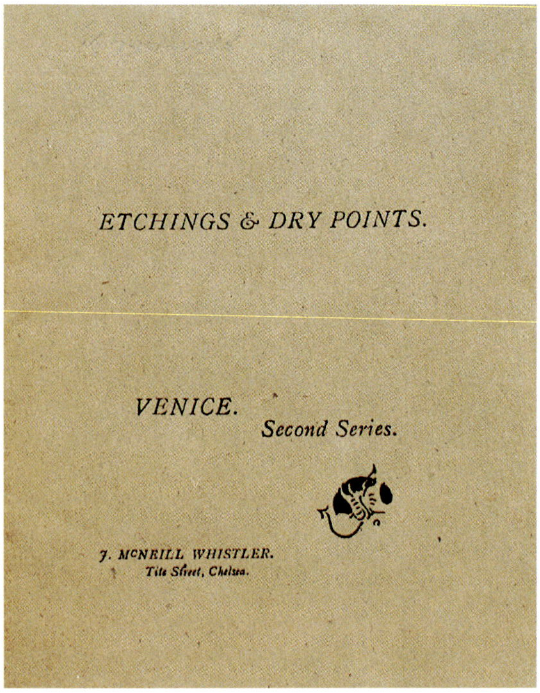
ETCHINGS & DRY POINTS.

VENICE.
Second Series.

J. MCNEILL WHISTLER.
Tite Street, Chelsea.

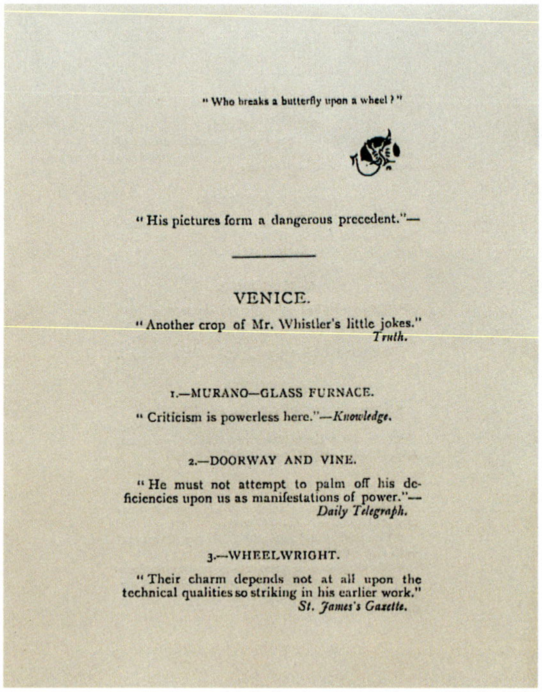
"Who breaks a butterfly upon a wheel?"

"His pictures form a dangerous precedent."—

VENICE.

"Another crop of Mr. Whistler's little jokes."
Truth.

1.—MURANO—GLASS FURNACE.

"Criticism is powerless here."—*Knowledge.*

2.—DOORWAY AND VINE.

"He must not attempt to palm off his deficiencies upon us as manifestations of power."—
Daily Telegraph.

3.—WHEELWRIGHT.

"Their charm depends not at all upon the technical qualities so striking in his earlier work."
St. James's Gazette.

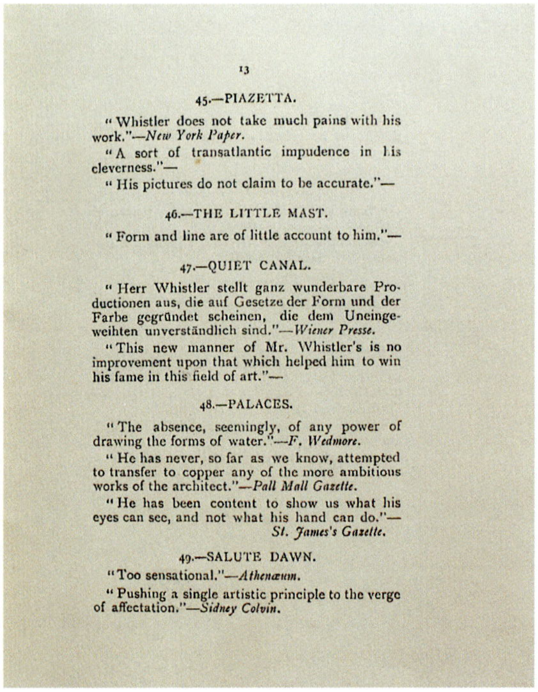
13

45.—PIAZETTA.

"Whistler does not take much pains with his work."—*New York Paper.*

"A sort of transatlantic impudence in his cleverness."—

"His pictures do not claim to be accurate."—

46.—THE LITTLE MAST.

"Form and line are of little account to him."—

47.—QUIET CANAL.

"Herr Whistler stellt ganz wunderbare Productionen aus, die auf Gesetze der Form und der Farbe gegründet scheinen, die dem Uneingeweihten unverständlich sind."—*Wiener Presse.*

"This new manner of Mr. Whistler's is no improvement upon that which helped him to win his fame in this field of art."—

48.—PALACES.

"The absence, seemingly, of any power of drawing the forms of water."—*F. Wedmore.*

"He has never, so far as we know, attempted to transfer to copper any of the more ambitious works of the architect."—*Pall Mall Gazette.*

"He has been content to show us what his eyes can see, and not what his hand can do."—
St. James's Gazette.

49.—SALUTE DAWN.

"Too sensational."—*Athenæum.*

"Pushing a single artistic principle to the verge of affectation."—*Sidney Colvin.*

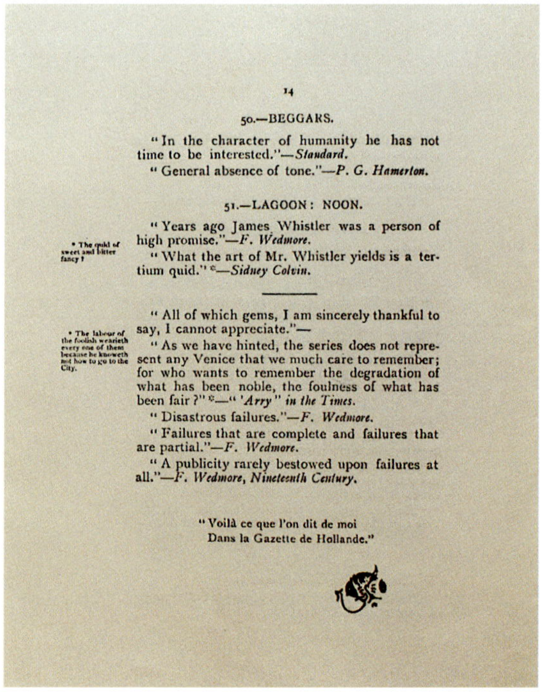
14

50.—BEGGARS.

"In the character of humanity he has not time to be interested."—*Standard.*

"General absence of tone."—*P. G. Hamerton.*

51.—LAGOON: NOON.

"Years ago James Whistler was a person of high promise."—*F. Wedmore.*

"What the art of Mr. Whistler yields is a tertium quid."*—*Sidney Colvin.*

* The quid of sweet and bitter fancy?

"All of which gems, I am sincerely thankful to say, I cannot appreciate."—

"As we have hinted, the series does not represent any Venice that we much care to remember; for who wants to remember the degradation of what has been noble, the foulness of what has been fair?"*—"*'Arry" in the Times.*

* The labour of the foolish wearieth every one of them because he knoweth not how to go to the City.

"Disastrous failures."—*F. Wedmore.*

"Failures that are complete and failures that are partial."—*F. Wedmore.*

"A publicity rarely bestowed upon failures at all."—*F. Wedmore, Nineteenth Century.*

"Voilà ce que l'on dit de moi
Dans la Gazette de Hollande."

118
J. McN. Whistler, Catalogue, Fine Art Society, 1883
Glasgow University Library

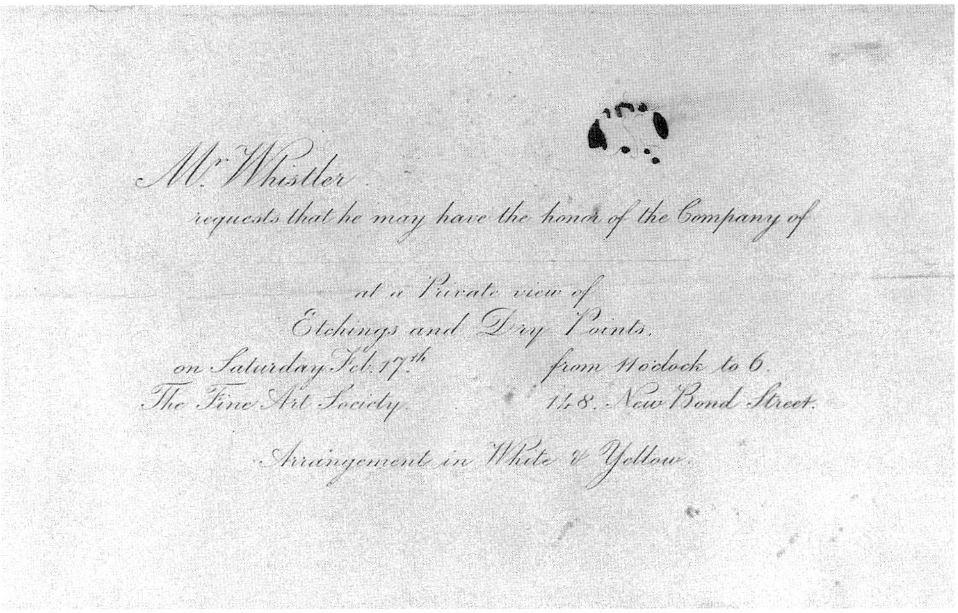
Mr Whistler
requests that he may have the honor of the Company of

at a Private view of
Etchings and Dry Points,
on Saturday Feb. 17th from 11 o'clock to 6.
The Fine Art Society 148, New Bond Street.

Arrangement in White & Yellow.

119
Private view card
Fine Art Society 1883
Glasgow University Library

These were worn by all that was lovely and distinguished in England![7]

By the first Saturday in March, 600 had paid for admission (at a shilling each, that came to thirty pounds). By 5 April, 2000 catalogues had been sold (also at a shilling each) or given away, and the Fine Art Society sent Whistler £91 14s 0d out of the £100 due to him. The man who sold the catalogues wore white and yellow to match the decor. Huish, therefore, kept back five pounds for what he called 'the poached egg "business"' – the attendant's uniform. It probably did not come as a surprise when Whistler disputed their sums. The Society had agreed to pay 'the yellow man's wages' as he was 'one of the elements of the exhibition – like the hangings and various arrangements in Canary', wrote Whistler, 'and I shall neither pay for the man – nor his socks, nor his hose, nor anything that is his.'[8]

The critics and the catalogue

The show attracted wide attention and press coverage. Reviews appeared in the dailies, including the *Daily News* and *The Times*, in journals such as the *The Academy*, *Building News* and *Artist*, and in Society papers like *Society* and *Country Gentleman*.[9] Discussion of the installation and catalogue far exceeded that of the etchings. Favourable accounts of the decor appeared in several papers and there was an impression that this care for presentation elevated the status of the exhibition. For example *The Times* said, 'many of us have seen the same kind of idca carried out in the houses of the nobility, but it is something quite new for a public art gallery.'[10] However, praise was punctuated by jokes about the colour scheme, jaundice and yellow fever. News of the show spread abroad, where Pissarro, hearing it described, thought the colour scheme a 'charming combination'.[11]

Although any discussion of the decor and catalogue brought welcome publicity, Whistler continued to harass the critics. In *Art and Art Critics* in 1878 Whistler had questioned Ruskin's credentials, suggesting criticism should be based on scientific laws and not personal taste. On the other hand, in 1879 he unashamedly incorporated favourable reviews in his prospectus for a print after the portrait of Rosa Corder.[12] Then, in 1881, he hung a *Punch* caricature in the Fine Art Society during his show. Finally, in 1883 he challenged the power of the press by his use of earlier presscuttings, editing them freely and publishing excerpts out of context.

There were distinguished precedents for this: Théophile Gautier, for instance, in 1835 suggested using quotations to ridicule critics and Thomas Carlyle printed a letter of rejection from his literary adviser in *Sartor Resartus*.[13] It was part of a growing examination of the role and function of critics. Some responded with indignation,

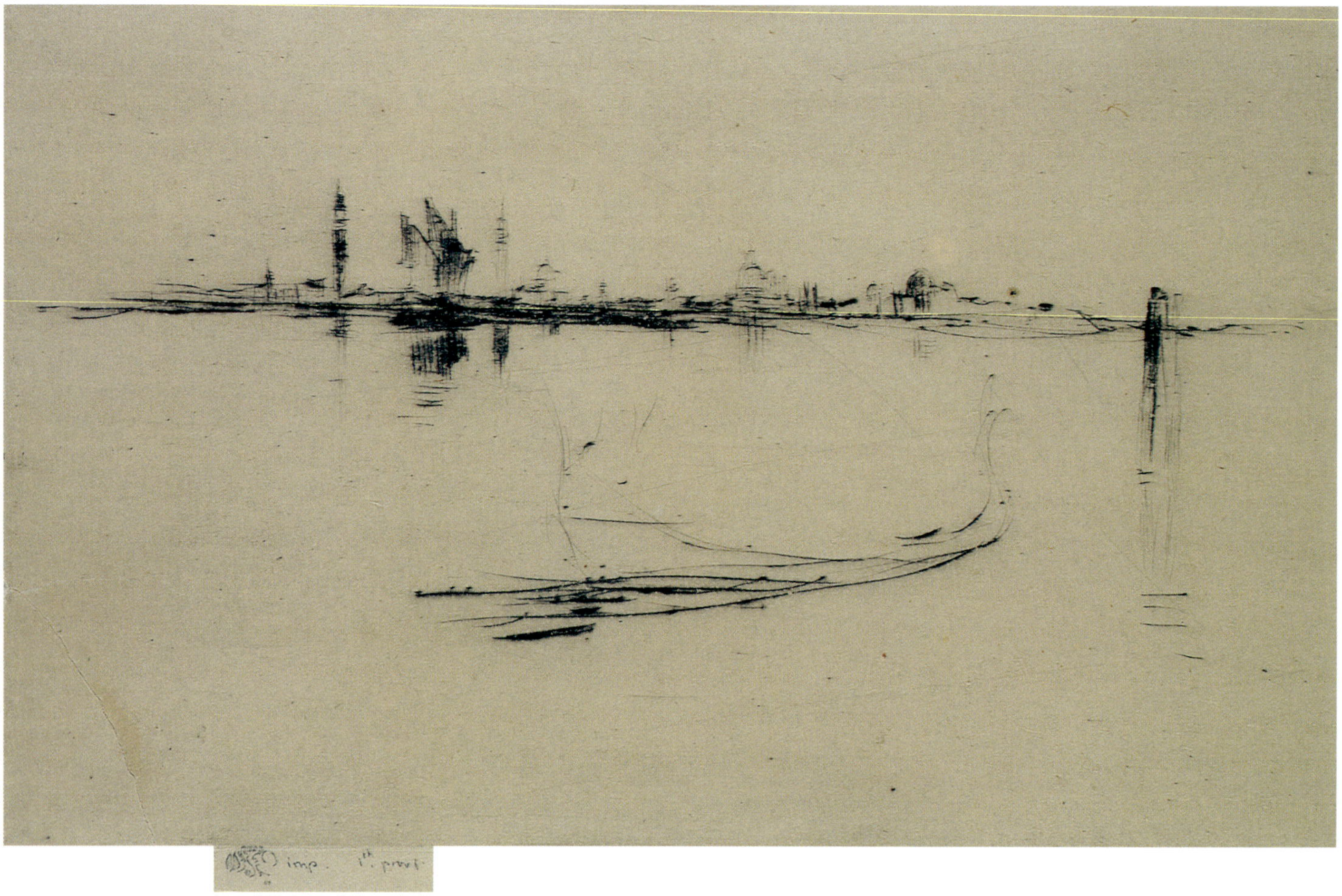

120
James McNeill Whistler
Islands
Etching 127 x 201 mm
Art Institute of Chicago, K.222 I

Wedmore in particular complaining about Whistler's cut and paste methods.[14] Not all were offended, 'It is an Exhibition of Etchings and Dry Points', wrote *Society*, 'but the points made in the Catalogue are still dryer'.[15] But many critics were defensive, hurriedly deploying their columns to counter the attack. They responded by questioning the etiquette of such a publication, implying that Whistler was no gentleman.[16]

There was some underlying anti-Americanism (*Punch* mocked Whistler for his 'American gall') and criticism of a classless mercantile society buying culture with dollars. J. S. Sargent was to experience something of the same prejudice, diluted by his membership of the Academy.[17] Whistler was aware both of the advantages and disadvantages of his nationality. He illustrated the catalogue entry for *The Piazzetta* (K.189) with an earlier review, 'A sort of transatlantic impudence in his cleverness'; the artist believed that nationality had nothing to do with artistic skill.

The critics also countered by seeing Whistler as a showman, a reaction which entered folklore.[18] It was probably more accurate, as some contemporary critics discerned, to say that both the Fine Art Society and Whistler found it paid to have publicity at any price.[19] Whistler wrote,

> It has been the most brilliant campaign! …
> The Critics simply slaughtered and lying round in masses – The people divided into opposite bodies, for and against – but all violent! – and the Gallery full! – and above all the Catalogue selling like mad!
> The papers have been full of the affair – and in short it is Amazing![20]

Whistler's friends – artists like Louise Jopling – approved, 'Whistler had adroitly turned the laugh on his critics', she wrote later.[21]

Views and reviews

The catalogue and decor deflected comments on the etchings. Few remarked on the actual views. By 1883 Whistler's view of Venice was more or less accepted. Sweny, for instance, approved the inclusion of 'the Venice of every day life'.[22]

Individual etchings inspired a variety of comments and interpretations. *The Little Lagoon* (K.186), *Islands* (fig.120) and *Nocturne: Shipping* (K.223), which were hung in the prime site over the mantelpiece, were judged by one critic 'very slight in execution', while another admired the economy of 'a few telling strokes'.[23] Several critics admired the use of tone in *The Dyer* (K.219) but opinions of the figure were divided.[24] Comments on *The Doorway* (K.188) vary so much that one wonders if they were talking about the same etching. 'Admirable', said the *Daily News*, 'but the woman in the foreground is unpleasantly like one of those poor wretches, with faces eaten away by disease, now not uncommon in Italy.'[25] Another critic found it 'remarkable for the care bestowed, and successfully bestowed, upon the figure, which is certainly graceful, and which [...] bears close inspection.' This suggests that the impression exhibited was in an early state, possibly the third state, before radical revisions of the figure.[26]

Wedmore suggested that the poor reception of the 'First Venice Set' was partly due to 'wrong expectation'. They should not expect 'elaborate record' from Whistler, he said, but 'the turn of a canal, the movement of passing folk in the crowded byways, the effect of sunlight on the greenery of a garden, and of shadow in the depth of a doorway'. He compared the second set to the Thames etchings, praising them for carrying the artistic qualities of 'abstraction and selection' as 'far as they can go'.[27]

'Artistic printing', which had caused such a furore several years earlier, went almost without comment. Indeed, the use of tone in *Nocturne: Palaces* (K.202) was repeatedly commended, 'it is charged with poetical appreciation and feeling, and is [...] full of suggestion', wrote one critic.[28] J. Forbes Robertson defended the artist's economy in creating effects and explained the 'skill and finesse' of Whistler's printing.[29] However, uneven 'finish' was occasionally questioned: the *Daily News* thought the etchings 'incomplete as drawings, yet have a certain charm of indistinctness, dash and colour.'[30] Possibly Whistler himself focussed debate on this subject, through the catalogue and by his selection of an incomplete etching like *Wool-Carders* (K.221), in order to question existing conventions. The word 'impressionist' was used in some cases as an insult and in others as an explanation for Whistler's technique.[31] Generally, by 1883, critics, influenced by French painting and the 'new criticism', were demanding less conscientious and conspicuous detail.

The show goes to New York

Later in the year, Edward Guthrie Kennedy and Hermann Wunderlich recreated the exhibition in Wunderlich's galleries at 808 Broadway. Some New York papers compared Whistler to the Impressionists, as having their 'love of episode, and the knack of expressing life to the core by a mere suggestion [...] but he is far away above them in purity and in feeling for the beautiful.'[32] Some assumed he was English, but most embraced him as a fellow-American, his expatriate status making him especially newsworthy: 'Among American artists abroad none have achieved more prominence than Mr James McNeill Whistler', announced the *New York World* on 11 October 1883, in a review entitled 'Whistler's Queer Conceit. A Novel Arrangement in White and Yellow'.

The decor was an enthusiastic interpretation of the Bond Street show. Invitation cards to the private view, signed with 'an intoxicated butterfly', imitated the London ones.[33] The decor dominated reviews: the *Daily News* devoted most of its column to the subject, presenting Whistler as aesthete and showman:

> The gallery of 51 etchings here is 'arranged' in a manner that would delight Mr Oscar Wilde. It is in white and yellow – that is, the walls of the rooms are hung with white flannel [...] the woodwork and the furniture are painted a bright chrome yellow. The mantel is olive, with a lambrequin of yellow velvet. The hearth and fireplace are of brown and yellow tiles. Standing near the yellow door is an attendant in a cream-coloured livery, with gold

> buttons and yellow frogs, collar and epaulettes and yellow stripes running down the pantaloons.[34]

The *New York Mail and Express* extolled its 'bizarrerie':

> The walls covered with white felt, the white frames of the etchings, the yellow base and moulding, the yellow plush seats and the little yellow and white chairs and tables and other furniture [...] the yellow tiled fireplace and the yellow Chinese vases [...] and finally the strip of yellow material stuck up under the ceiling with the artist's queer mark upon it [...] quite throw the etchings themselves into the shade.[35]

The critic added that this scheme echoed the light colours fashionable thirty or forty years earlier. Perhaps it was the decor admired in Whistler's own milieu before he left America. The critic thought it was 'nothing but an amusing and not very refined advertisement for a number of works which hardly need showing, as they are not new.' Admitting that 'the critics have dealt badly with Mr Whistler', he discussed questions raised in London: 'the alleged want of feeling in Mr Whistler for the nobility of Venice [...] his lack of poetry and his unresponsiveness to the "character of humanity".' He argued that Whistler was a poet, able to find 'nobility even amidst squalor, to see the glories of the past even in ruins, not only to feel, but to be able to make others feel, the melancholy and the mournfulness caused by the debasement of that which remains beautiful in spite of its debasement.'[36]

The *New York World* mentioned only three etchings, two with approval, and one without (the critic thought *Lobster Pots* (K.235) cast doubts on the artist's sanity).

The *Daily News* combined incomprehension of Whistler's paintings with admiration of his etchings, 'probably the most delicate and beautiful ever done by any English artist', but this enthusiasm was of doubtful value since the critic apparently had no idea what an etching was.[37]

The exhibition formed the foundations for a long and occasionally stormy friendship between E. G. Kennedy and the artist. Kennedy ("O'K" to Whistler) was visiting Whistler regularly from at least 1885 and posed for his portrait between 1893 and 1895. His catalogue of Whistler's etchings, published in 1910, is generally regarded as definitive and where possible all etchings are given the number and state given by Kennedy.[38] Thus, *San Biagio* is K.197 and there are nine states described by Kennedy, listed as K.197 I to K.197 IX. Kennedy had access to many important print collections but not to Whistler's records. Furthermore, his catalogue is not comprehensive. For example, the Hunterian Art Gallery has impressions of ten distinctly different states of *San Biagio*, including two not recorded by Kennedy and three different cancelled states.

Kennedy also made little attempt to identify subjects, date etchings, establish the size of editions or discover how many prints were printed when, where, or by whom. He did not realise, for instance, that *The Smithy* (K.240) might be a Venetian subject.

The publisher, the press, and the printers

Throughout 1883 printing proceeded slowly. Huish assumed that Whistler would hire a press and provide materials, receiving five guineas for printing each set of twelve. On 11 January 1883, he sent a hundred pounds for printing to date, forgetting that Whistler insisted on being paid in guineas, not the pounds of the tradesman. Again and again Whistler demanded the extra shillings and eventually Huish sent the missing five pounds. The artist also refused to take responsibility for the press, unless he could buy it himself. He offered to pay half price: Huish refused.[39]

Whistler was undoubtedly bloody-minded, but the Fine Art Society was not entirely blameless. Over a year later, in June 1884, they sent twenty pounds for four sets plus three extra impressions (that is, fifty-one prints in all). Whistler as usual demanded the extra pound, and Huish, as usual, complied, under protest: 'You forget that you took three months to print these etchings for us – and now grumble because the coin isn't sent in three days.'[40]

Another printer joined the succession of Whistler's assistants. In 1885 Whistler saw an etching by Frank Short at the Hogarth Club, and took some of his plates down to Short's studio in Wentworth Yard. There, he cancelled some of the Venice plates, pulling a couple of impressions from the cancelled plates before Short lacquered them. In return, Short chose from stock what he considered 'one of the best proofs of *The Traghetto* I know!'[41] Whistler printed *The Traghetto, No.2* (K.191) intermittently for years: the first eight prints on 16 February 1881, a dozen on 6 April, two on 25 August, and seven on 31 December. He may have printed as many as nine, with Short's assistance, in 1885. Records suggest that by 1889 he had printed about sixty impressions, leaving forty to go.[42] This was typical of progress.

Originally twenty-five sets were to be printed by Whistler and seventy-five by another, but in the end most were printed by Whistler and assistants. Although Whistler had printed twenty-five sets in 1881, from 1882 to 1886 he only printed six sets, that is, some seventy impressions. Sporadic outbursts of border warfare between the Fine Art Society and Whistler continued for some years, until he shifted camp a few doors up to Messrs Dowdeswell at 133 New Bond Street. They held two exhibitions of his '*Notes*' – '*Harmonies*' –'*Nocturnes*' in 1884 and 1886 and scooped up the 'Second Venice Set' of etchings in 1886.

1 M. B. Huish to Whistler, 13 Dec 1882, GUL F83. Whistler received £80 6s 6d: that is, £107 2s 0d less 25%, on 16 July 1883.

2 5 Feb 1883, Pierpont Morgan Library, Heinemann MSS. 244; in Thorp 1994, pp.74–6, no.28. See Bendix 1995, pp.224–8. Descriptions appeared in *Daily News*, 20 Feb 1883; *Building News*, 23 Feb 1883; *Advertiser*, 24 Feb 1883; *Society*, 24 Feb 1883; *People*, 25 Feb 1883; *Daily Chronicle*, 26 Feb 1883; *Bazaar*, 28 Feb 1883; *Times*, 1 March 1883.

3 *World*, 7 Feb 1883.

4 *People*, 25 Feb 1883; Bell 1987, pp.118–19. A private view card is in GUL F88. *Echo*, 2 March 1883, and *Times*, 1 March 1883; see *Lady's Pictorial*, 24 Feb 1883, in Spencer 1989, pp.199–200.

5 *Weekly Register*, 24 Feb 1883.

6 Whistler to Mrs Huish, nd. [Feb 1883], GUL LB3/18.

7 Nd. [Feb 1883], New York Public Library; M.879.

8 P. Mugford, for Huish, to Whistler, 31 March 1883, Whistler to Huish, nd. [March/April 1883] (quoted) and Huish to Whistler, 5 April 1883, GUL F89–91. Partial sales records, April–Aug 1883, GUL NB1/4.

9 Whistler's press cuttings, in GUL pc6 and 8 (see Bibliography of Reviews). Getscher 1970, pp.223–36, records reviews in the 1883 catalogue; Getscher and Marks 1986, pp.284–7, L4a–p; Bell 1987, p.121.

10 *Times*, 1 March 1883; see also *Daily News*, 20 Feb 1883; *Weekly Register*, 24 Feb 1883; *Society*, 24 Feb 1883; *Punch*, 3 March 1883; *Pictorial World*, 31 March 1883: Bell 1987, pp.121–3.

11 C. Pissarro to L. Pissarro, 28 Feb 1883, J. Rewald (ed.), *Camille Pissarro. Letters to his son Lucien*, London, 1943, p.22; see also Spencer 1989, p.198.

12 Pamphlet on Corder, GUL LB11/71; see YMSM 203.

13 Théophile Gautier, *Mlle. de Maupin*, 1835, preface; T. Carlyle, *Sartor Resartus: The Life and Opinions of Herr Teufelsdröckh*, 1833–4, rp. 1981, pp.50–1; see Bell 1987, pp.126–7.

14 Hollingshead used reviews similarly, see *Punch*, 24 March 1883; *Academy*, 24 Feb 1883; *World*, 21 Feb 1883 and 'What the World Says' in Whistler 1883; Whistler's letter to *World*, no.452, XVIII, p.13, reprinted as a pamphlet, 'Caviare to the Critics' in 1883. See Getscher and Marks 1986, p.6, A.6, and p.32, B.21.

15 *Society*, 24 Feb 1883; in Bell 1987, p.134.

16 Whistler's nickname for Harry Quilter, 'Arry, offended *Daily News*, 26 Feb 1883, and *Artist*, 1 March 1881.

17 *Punch*, 3 March 1883. Whistler 1883, cat.no.45, reprinted in Whistler 1890, p.102.

18 *Ashton Standard*, 24 Feb 1883; *Weekly Register*, 24 Feb 1883; *Coventry Standard*, 23 Feb 1883; *Bazaar*, 28 Feb 1883; *Architect*, 10 March 1883; *Magazine of Art*, 1883.

19 *Country Gentleman*, 24 Feb 1883; *Punch*, 3 March 1883; *Architect*, 10 March 1883; see Bell 1987, pp.131–2.

20 Whistler to W. Story, nd. [Feb 1883], LC PC.

21 L. Jopling, *Twenty Years of My Life, 1867–1889*, London 1925, p.226.

22 *People*, 25 Feb 1883; in Bell 1987, p.134.

23 *Daily Chronicle*, 26 Feb 1883; *Building News*, 23 Feb 1883.

24 For example, criticism in *Bazaar*, 28 Feb 1883, approval in *Daily Chronicle*, 26 Feb 1883.

25 *Daily News*, 20 Feb 1883.

26 Unidentified presscutting, [Feb/March 1883], GUL pc 6/51.

27 *Academy*, 24 Feb 1883; 'Mr. Whistler's New Series of Etchings', *Academy*, XXXI, no.782, 30 April 1887, pp.313–14, in Bell 1987, p.135.

28 *Magazine of Art*, 1883; *North London Advertiser*, nd. [c.23 Feb 1883] GUL pc6/44; and *Coventry Standard*, 23 Feb 1883; *Building News*, 23 Feb 1883; unidentified press-cutting, nd. [Feb/March 1883], GUL pc6/51.

29 *Pictorial World*, 1 March 1883; see Bell 1987, pp.135, 137–9 and Getscher 1970, p.226.

30 *Daily News*, 23 Feb 1883; 'Finish', censured in, for example, *Artist*, 1 March 1883; *Times*, 1 March 1883; *Echo*, 2 March 1883; favourably reviewed in *Coventry Standard*, 23 Feb 1883; *Building News*, 23 Feb 1883.

31 *Building News*, 23 Feb 1883; *Rochdale Observer*, 24 Feb 1883; *Artist*, 1 March 1883.

32 *Daily News*, 15 Nov 1883. American cuttings kept by Whistler, GUL pc3/59 & pc4/12.

33 *James McNeill Whistler. Arrangement in White and Yellow: A Centennial Celebration*, exh.cat., Wunderlich & Co., Inc., New York, 1983, cat.no.44, repr.; another card is in GUL pc3/61.

34 *Daily News*, 15 Nov 1883.

35 *New York Mail and Express*, 24 Oct 1883.

36 Ibid.

37 *New York World*, 11 Oct 1883; *Daily News*, 15 Nov 1883.

38 Thomas 1874, listed 86 etchings; see also P. G. Hamerton, 'Mr. Whistler's Catalogue of Mr. Whistler's Etchings', *The Portfolio*, XVIII, March 1887, pp.61–2; F. Wedmore, *Whistler's Etchings. A Study and a Catalogue*, London, 1886, listed 214 etchings (2nd ed. 1899, listed 268); Mansfield 1909, listed 445 etchings; Kennedy (K) listed 450. See also Lochnan 1984, Appendix A, pp.277–85; and Getscher and Marks 1986, pp.83–6, D.1–6. Four unpublished etchings and 20 unpublished plates are in Glasgow University and 1 unpublished etching in the Freer Gallery of Art.

39 Huish to Whistler, 11 and 15 Jan 1883, Whistler to Huish, 12 Jan 1883, GUL F85–7; a pound (£1 0s 0d) was 20 shillings, and a guinea, 21 shillings (£1 1s 0d).

40 C. Lungley sent Whistler £20, 6 June 1884; Whistler to Huish, nd. [June 1884]; Huish to Whistler, 19 June 1884 (quoted); and reply, nd. [19/20 June 1884]; GUL F103–6.

41 Pennell 1908, I, p.283.

42 Lists by Whistler and receipts from FAS, dated 16 Feb, 6 April, 25 Aug, 31 Dec 1881 and nd. [1881]; 24 Jan, 7 Feb 1882, nd. [1882]; 25 Jan, 24 Feb, 21 March, 7, 9 and 18 April, 18 June, 13, 16 and 20 July, 1 and 8 Aug, 1883; 15 Feb, 6 March, 16, 20 and 29 July 1885, nd. [after Feb 1885], nd. [1885]; 13 Jan and 25 June 1887; 13 Mar, 2 and 11 April 1889, GUL F69, F72, F107, F110, F117, F123–4, F149, F150. Some lists duplicate others, the most detailed listing being GUL F117.

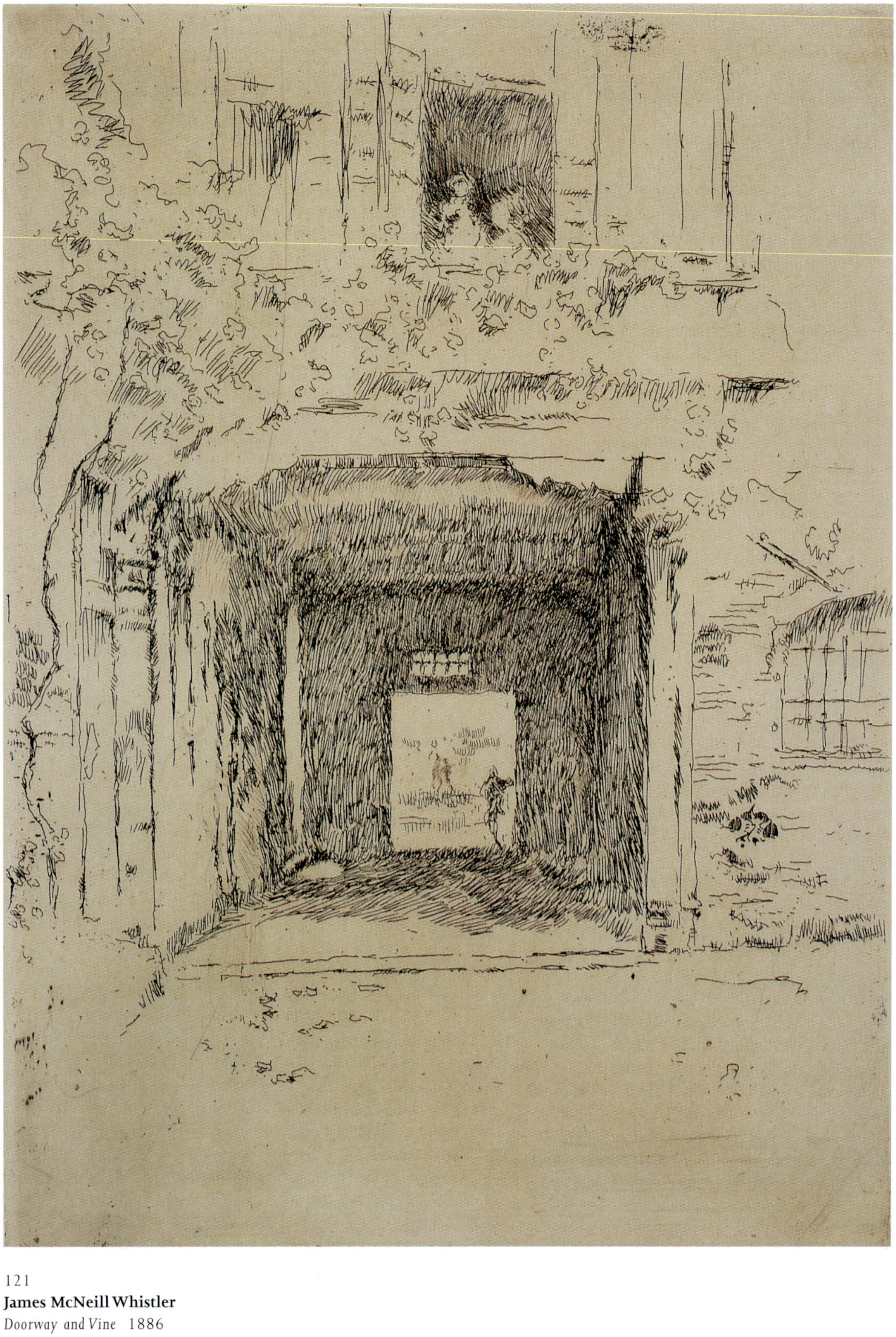

121
James McNeill Whistler
Doorway and Vine 1886
Etching printed by Salmon 234 x 170 mm
National Gallery of Scotland, K.196 III

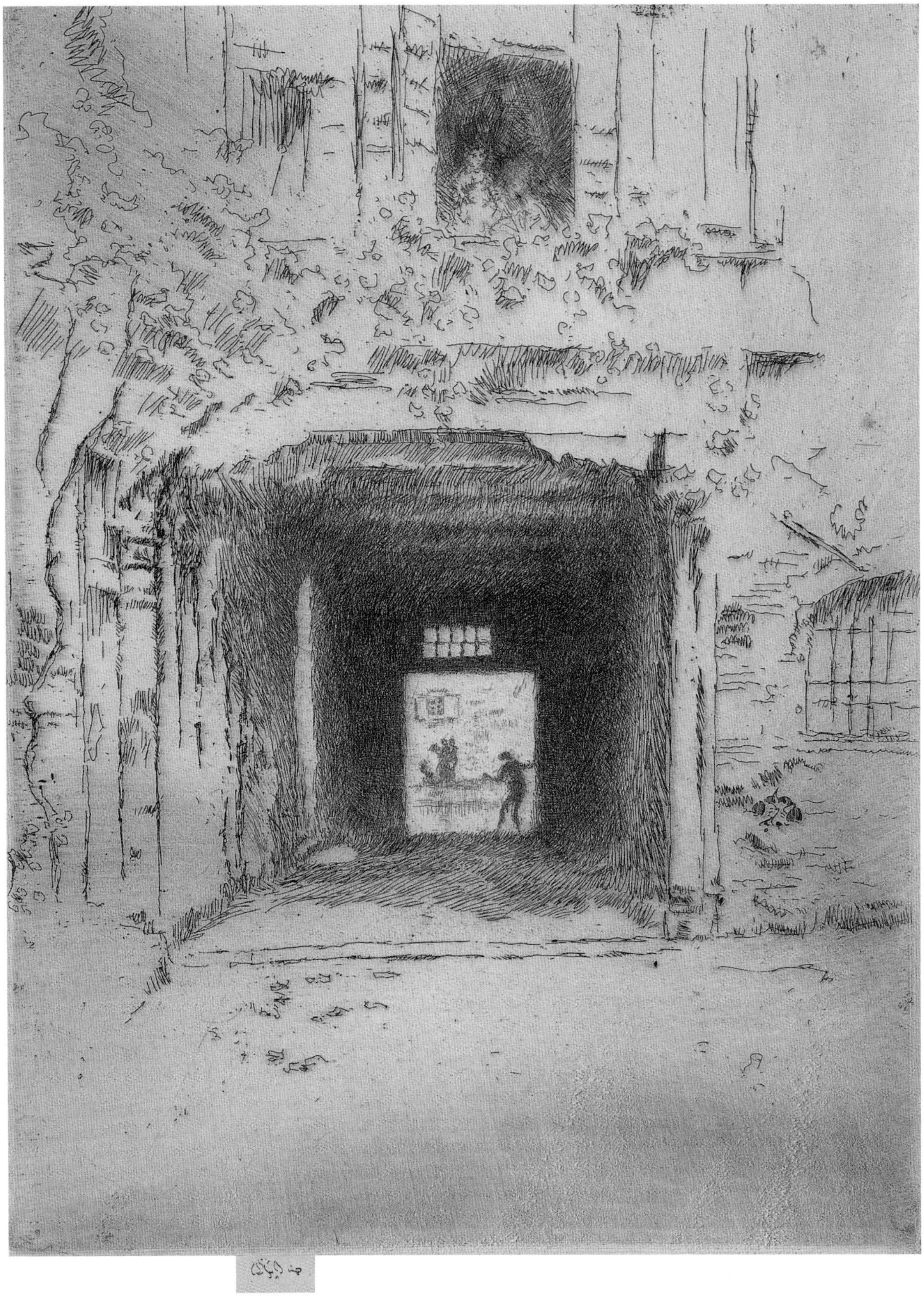

122
James McNeill Whistler
Doorway and Vine 1886
Etching printed by Whistler 234 x 170 mm
Hunterian Art Gallery, K.196 VI

8 The 'Second Venice Set'

In February 1886 Messrs Dowdeswell offered to act as middlemen in a speculative venture, the publication of a second set of Venice etchings. They suggested £400 or £500 for the plates plus an unspecified number of sets printed by Whistler. Although he needed the money, he objected, 'it is absurd that lovely plates like these should be thrown on the streets at about 20 guineas apiece!' They had been exhibited in 1883 but otherwise, Whistler claimed, 'The plates are all fresh as far as the public are concerned – they [...] haven't been "run" at all because they have remained in my hands and I have not occupied myself with them – Whatever proofs I have pulled can go to the buyer'.[1] In fact Whistler retained the proofs and sold them later.

He selected twenty-six impressions of his etchings (mostly of Venice) as a sample:

> Some of them are not by any means the finest impressions of the plates – indeed in one or two cases they do not quite represent the plates in their completed condition – notably – in the plate No.24 where the figure had not yet been introduced – also No.5 is an impression before the figure outside the door was finished.[2]

Dowdeswells' joined with another dealer, Alphonse W. Thibadeau, for this project and agreed on £600 for a set of twenty-two Venice plates and four other subjects. *A Set of Twenty-six Etchings* (the 'Second Venice Set') was published in 1886. The Venice subjects were *Doorway and Vine, San Biagio, Bead-Stringers, Turkeys, Fruit-Stall, San Giorgio, Nocturne: Palaces, Long Lagoon, The Bridge, Upright Venice, The Riva, No.2, The Balcony, Fishing-Boat, Ponte del Piovan, Garden, The Rialto, Long Venice, Nocturne: Furnace, Quiet Canal, La Salute: Dawn* and *Lagoon: Noon* (K.196–216). Four later subjects were included, three of London (K.234, 236–7) and one, *Lobster Pots* (K.235), of Hastings. It was to be a limited edition of thirty sets (plus twelve additional prints of each of fifteen subjects). Whistler was enthusiastic about this second set, which comprised many of his most beautiful etchings.

To make up the set, Whistler included some prints which matched ones in the first set: *Long Venice* for instance was the equivalent of *Little Venice* (K.183). There was another nocturne, *Nocturne: Palaces*, another bridge, *Ponte del Piovan*. Whistler's largest plate, *The Palaces* (K.187) in the first set, was comparable to *The Bridge*, while *The Riva, No.1* (K.192) in the 'First Venice Set', was matched by *The Riva, No.2* in the second.

The Rialto was done on one of the copperplates brought to Venice specifically to prepare the Fine Art Society set and was probably etched fairly early on. However, in the end *The Rialto* went into the 'Second Venice Set'. A variety of sizes, subjects and treatment were required for each set. It may be that having selected the immediately recognisable view of St Mark's, *The Piazzetta* (K.189), for the first set, Whistler felt it necessary to reserve this well-known site for the second set.

There were also disparities between the two sets. It appears contradictory, but the second included Whistler's earliest Venetian etchings, some of which were his most innovative and progressive works. Two of his most minimal and experimental etchings, *Nocturne: Palaces* and *La Salute – Dawn*, were included in the second set.

The Salmon run

Messrs Dowdeswell and Thibadeau were taking a considerable risk. With the example of the Fine Art Society before them, they were afraid that if Whistler printed the 'Second Venice Set' for them it would never be completed,

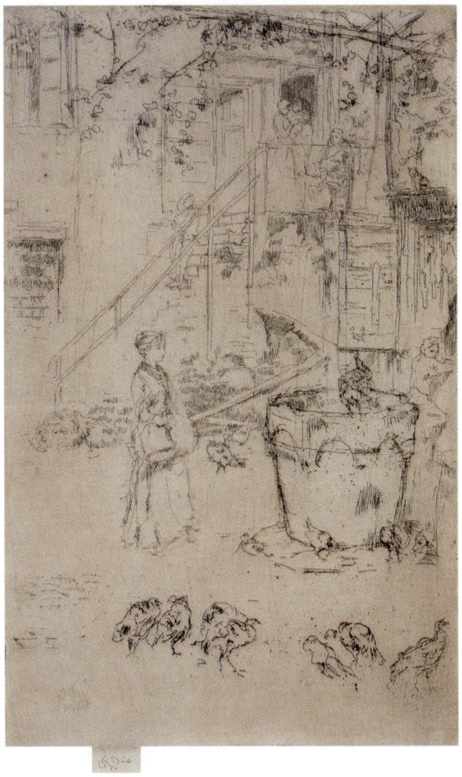

123
James McNeill Whistler
Turkeys
Etching
208 x 132 mm
Ewan Mundy
Fine Art, K.199 II

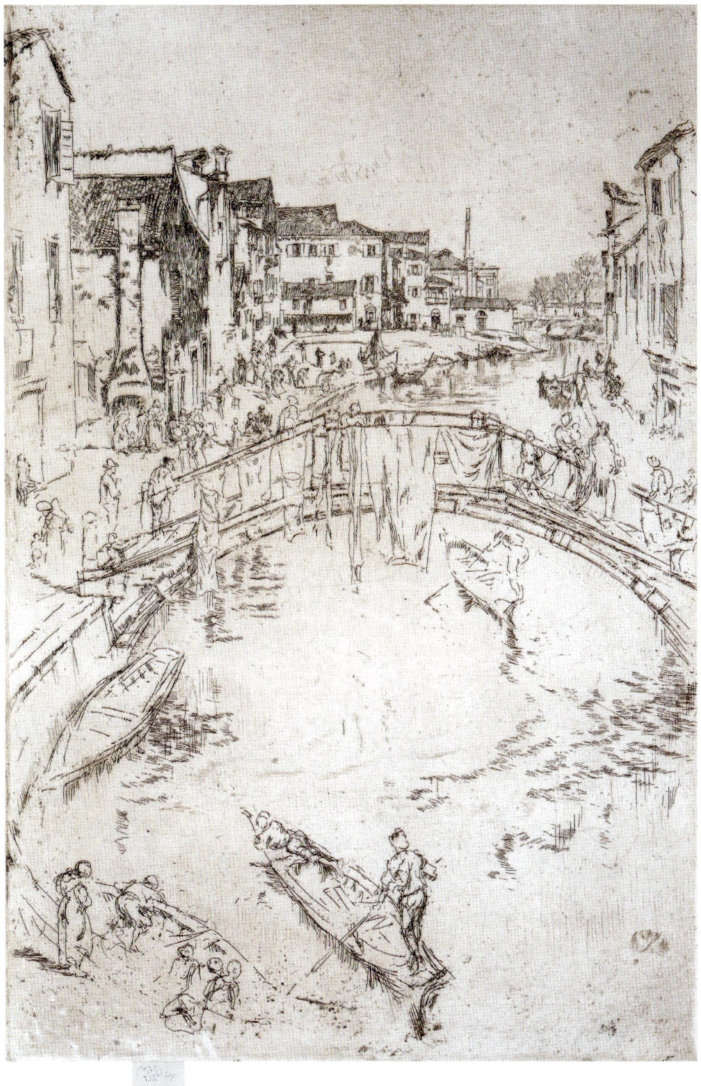

124
James McNeill Whistler
The Bridge
Etching
293 x 201 mm
Private Collection, K.204 III

so, with Whistler's approval, the French sculptor and printmaker Emile Frédéric Salmon was asked to print a set. Salmon, trained under Barye, Hédouin and Gaucherell, exhibited at the Salon from 1859. He became well-known as a printmaker, illustrating the works of Victor Hugo and making engravings after works of art.

In March 1886 Whistler handed over his precious copper-plates to Thibadeau: 'A few impressions were printed in Paris on a paper chosen by Thibadeau which Whistler liked. There had been some talk of the plates being printed in Paris but before the end of the negotiations with Dowdeswell Whistler decided to print himself.'[3]

Salmon's set was acquired by the printer E. S. Lumsden, and was bought by the Scottish National Gallery in 1949.[4] It provides a unique example of a set of Whistler's Venice etchings printed by another printer. The etchings are printed in black ink on a lightweight, laid paper (with a fine brick-like grain on the surface) with margins. There is a light even plate-tone overall, but no manipulation of the ink. The etched lines are extremely sharp and the effect is light and bright. It shows the state and quality of the etching plates at the time that Whistler was prepared to sell them to Messrs Dowdeswell.[5] For instance, *The Riva, No.2* (K.206) was sold in its first state, *Doorway and Vine* (figs 121 and 122) in its third and *The Bridge* (fig.124) in its eighth state. The states of the Edinburgh etchings coincide closely with those of the earliest sets bought by collectors like G. A. Lucas or Isabella Stewart Gardner. Lucas owned practically two complete sets, now in Baltimore Museum of Art, including impressions of states predating the Edinburgh sets.[6]

The 'Second Venice Set' was finally printed entirely by Whistler (with some assistance), for which he received a further £238 17s 6d. His ledgers and receipts record the progress of the edition from 1886 to 1887. Perhaps surprising even himself, he managed to complete the edition within a year. The first proofs were delivered in April 1886 when he sent two dozen impressions of fourteen etchings.[7]

He seems to have printed a few plates at a time, sometimes sending Dowdeswells' only one or two impressions. For instance he sent single impressions of *San Biagio* (K.197) on 2 April, 28 July, 31 July and 20 August, two on 21 September and six on 29 October. More usually he sent a mixed bag of two to three dozen or even more at a time. Occasionally he would concentrate on a single plate, for instance, sending nine impressions of *Long Lagoon* (K.203) on 28 July, sixteen on 29 September and seventeen on 2 October.[8]

The first plates completed and cancelled were *The Rialto* (K.211) and the London etching, *Little Court* (K.236), on 6 October 1886. The edition was completed by July, the last plates being *The Balcony* (K.207) and *Garden* (K.210) on 16 July 1887.[9] The copperplates were cancelled (some with a huge decorative butterfly deeply etched into the plate) and cancelled prints were exhibited when the set was published to prove that the edition was limited. The plates themselves were turned over to Messrs Dowdeswell as the printing ended. They are now housed at the Art Institute of Chicago.

Since Whistler decided to print the edition for Dowdeswell himself, it would seem that he wanted to achieve a different effect from that seen in Salmon's set. Menpes mentions that, on Whistler's instructions, he destroyed some mechanically wiped, professionally printed impressions[10], possibly ones printed by Salmon.

Ink colour, plate-tone and paper made a considerable difference to their appearance. Walter Dowdeswell sent Whistler samples of paper, and more as the printing progressed. At one point he complained, 'I don't think much of this cheap looking paper you send – nothing seems as yet to compare with the first specimens you found.'[11] In some cases Whistler made substantial changes before printing the edition for Dowdeswells', suggesting that when he saw the plates printed by Salmon he recognised deficiencies in them which he took pains to remedy.

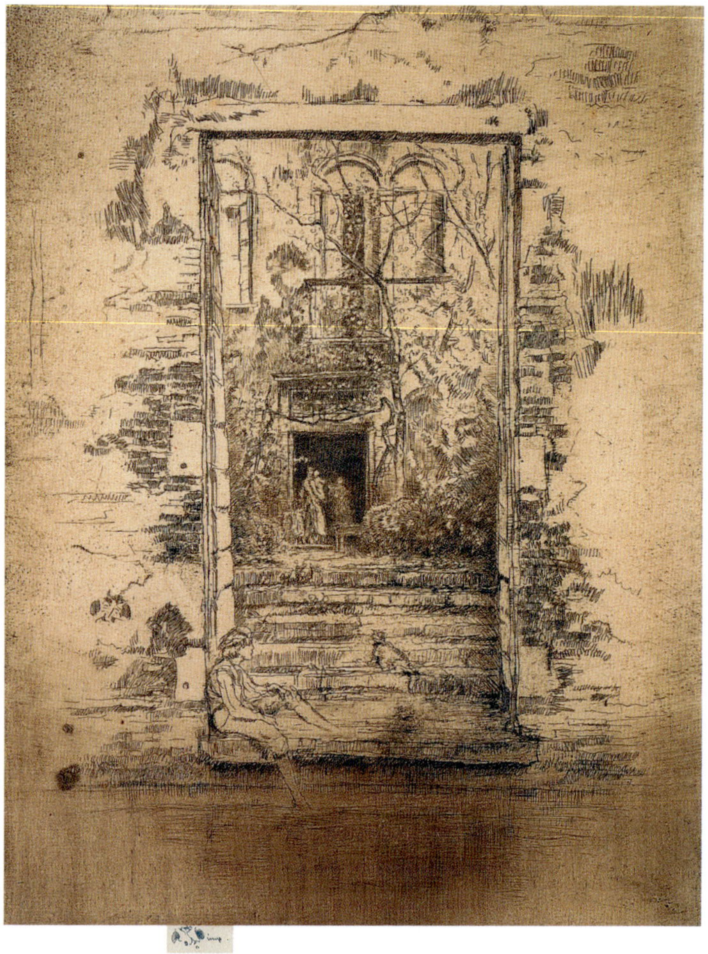

125
James McNeill Whistler
Garden
Etching 302 x 238 mm
Fine Art Society, K.210 III

Preparing the plates: proofs and states

Occasionally Whistler was quickly satisfied with an etching and prepared to let the Dowdeswells have it in an early state. So when it came to printing the plate himself he made little or no alterations. This is certainly the case with *Turkeys* (fig.123). A good number of prints were made of the first state, even before the butterfly signature was added. This is the more surprising because there was a gritty roughness in the surface of the etched plate, which could have been polished off but was left, and adds a darker tone to the pleasant intimacy of the scene.

Sometimes major revisions had been carried out before Whistler left Venice, as in *San Giorgio* (K.201), or *Upright Venice* (K.205). This plate was one of the first to be completed for the 'Second Venice Set', in April 1886.

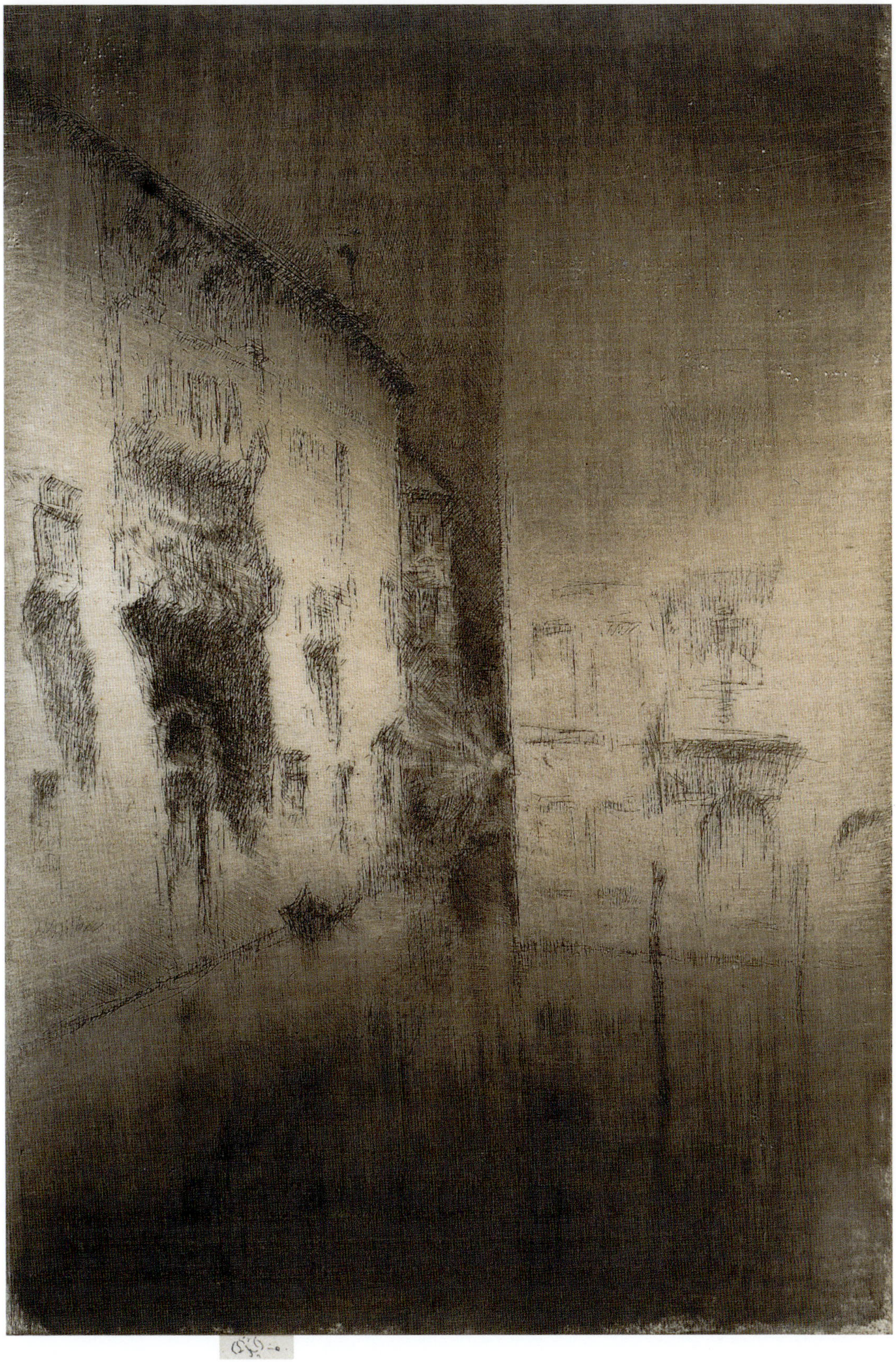

126
James McNeill Whistler
Nocturne: Palaces
Etching 293–6 x 200 mm
Private Collection, K.202 VIII

The Bridge is a highly complex composition with a great variety of detail; eight preliminary states precede the main edition (K.204 VII) and it may be that many of these were done in Venice. However, it is one of several etchings that Whistler continued to print and sell after 1882 and the states may reflect the need to maintain the plate.[12] By 1886 some of the drypoint lines which had added an area of interest in the sky had worn down. Whistler did not bother to replace them – indeed it was probably preferable to have two quieter areas in the plate (the sky and the water below the bridge) in what was otherwise a rather busy plate.

He made many preliminary and many subsequent states of some etchings, with variable numbers of prints pulled from each. He was basically satisfied with *San Biagio* (K.197) in its third state. But when he came to print it for the 1886 edition, he was moved to make further alterations in a further five states. These alterations were not mere doodling; perhaps Salmon's print had showed up the thinness of the distant figures. Whistler reworked them and each time he pulled a few more impressions he touched up the figures and strengthened the shadows.

The printer (in this case Whistler) was allowed by custom to keep one or two proofs of each new state. Now Kennedy noted nine states of *San Biagio*, and there are at least two more, so Whistler could quite legitimately have kept, say, twenty-two proof impressions. When he had sold the plate it was in its fifth state, so the subsequent six states were produced during the year he was printing it for Dowdeswells'. The bonus of twelve proofs were, again by common consent, not supposed to be sold for a year or so after the official publication of the set. During that year Messrs Dowdeswell had sole rights. It is almost certain that Whistler retained more proofs than this, possibly having it in mind to lay them down, like wine, for future sales, for a large number remained in his estate at his death.

There were considerable alterations to figures in *Bead-Stringers* (K.198) and in the *Fruit-Stall* (K.200) in eight preliminary states before the main editions were pulled in the ninth state (K.198 VIII and K.200 VII). Another plate that went through at least nine states was *Garden* (fig.125), which was printed by Salmon in the sixth state. The figures were altered, lines added, lines rubbed down, by Whistler during subsequent states, without radically altering the total effect, which had been perfectly acceptable when printed by Salmon. 'How do you like the proofs?' wrote Whistler to Walter Dowdeswell in September 1886, 'Isn't "the Garden" lovely?'[13]

'I have seen him print twelve proofs', said Menpes, 'and every proof a state. He would continually keep adding drypoint and scraping, and as he himself would say, caressing the plate into form.'[14] *Nocturne: Palaces* (fig.126) was a daring plate: difficult to print, relying heavily on the quality of the ephemeral drypoint lines. Areas of shading were replaced or altered in each of the ten states and yet in the best impressions of the principal states (K.202 VII, VIII and IX), it is the inking of the plate that coordinates and unifies the widely dispersed lines of shading. The linear pattern of marks is unusual and the inking makes each print unique.[15] One of the first of Whistler's etchings bought by C. L. Freer was an impression of K.202 VII, which was wiped with sweeping horizontal strokes, opening out like a half-open fan. Another of Freer's purchases, an impression of the eighth state, with beautiful soft vertical wiping, bears on the back the two tiny circles °° that mark proofs of particular quality.[16] Not all impressions were actually printed by Whistler, for according to Menpes, the 'Master', having 'educated and trained' him, permitted him to take over at times.[17]

Another night scene, *Nocturne: Furnace* (figs 127 and 128) relies almost equally on line and plate-tone. Salmon's print of *Nocturne: Furnace* showed the sharp brightness conveyed by the fine broken outlines: what was added in Whistler's impressions was a contrasting warmth of colour and velvety depth of shadows. The square door opening on the water was wiped clean to emphasise the glow of light from the furnace. The ink was wiped with repeated vertical and horizontal strokes to suggest darkness and reflections. Achieving the balance between line and tone took time and concentration. 'Did you see what a lovely state I have put your Nocturne Furnace in?', Whistler asked Walter Dowdeswell.[18] It was among the last of the plates to be printed, completed and cancelled on 26 February 1887.

No record of the sales of the 'Second Venice Set' has survived so it is impossible to know if it was an economic success from the point of view of Thibadeau and Messrs Dowdeswell. Thibadeau, who had been actively selling the Venetian etchings in Europe, went bankrupt a couple of years later and departed abruptly for America, but this is

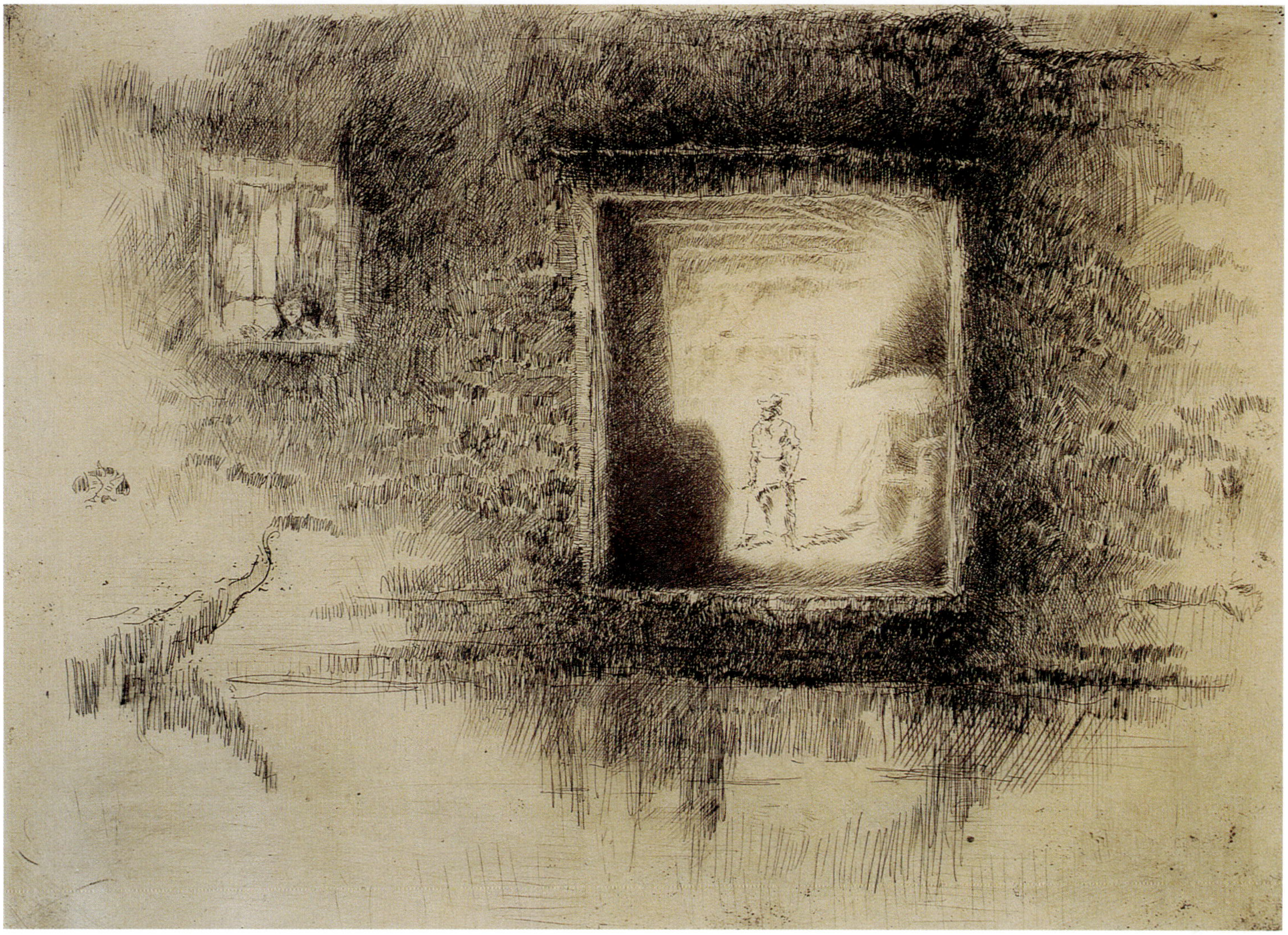

127
James McNeill Whistler
Nocturne: Furnace 1886
Etching printed by Salmon 168 x 231 mm
National Gallery of Scotland, K.213 III

unlikely to have been entirely Whistler's fault.[19] However, from the artist's point of view, the venture was entirely satisfactory. Whistler felt that Messrs Dowdeswell had been more than reasonable in their dealings:

> I wish to acknowledge the delicate discretion on your part in the matter of the printing of the promised proofs – You have not nagged and worried about them – for which considering the great pressure of work, I am grateful – and in return I have great pleasure in telling you that I forgot not my promise, and that the proofs are all printed – on exquisite old Dutch paper – and very beautiful they look.[20]

1 Dowdeswell to Whistler, 16 Feb 1886, GUL D65; reply, nd. [Feb 1886], LJR; MacDonald 1976, p.39.
2 Whistler to Dowdeswell, nd. [Feb/March 1886], LJR.
3 Annotation signed 'E. D.' on *La Salute: Dawn* (K.215 IV), Scottish National Gallery, Edinburgh. *The Bridge* (K.204 VIII) is annotated 'Early trial impression of final (8th) state'. Whistler to Dowdeswell, 28 March 1886, noted leaving 12 plates with Thibadeau; Dowdeswell noted Salmon printing plates, note, nd. [1886]; LJR.
4 Acq.nos P1734–46 and 2650–60E; see E. S. Lumsden, *The Art of Etching*, London, 1925.
5 Etchings printed by Salmon, followed by the total number of states listed by Kennedy: K.196 III/X, K.197 V/IX, K.198 VI/VIII, K.199 I/II, K.200 VII/VII, K.201 III-IV/IV, K.202 IX/IX, K.203 I/II; K.204 VIII/VIII, K.205 II/IV, K.206 I/II, K.207 V/XI, K.208 III/V, K.209 V/VI, K.210 VI/VIII, K.211 I/II, K.212 I/V, K.213 III/VII, K.214 III?/V,

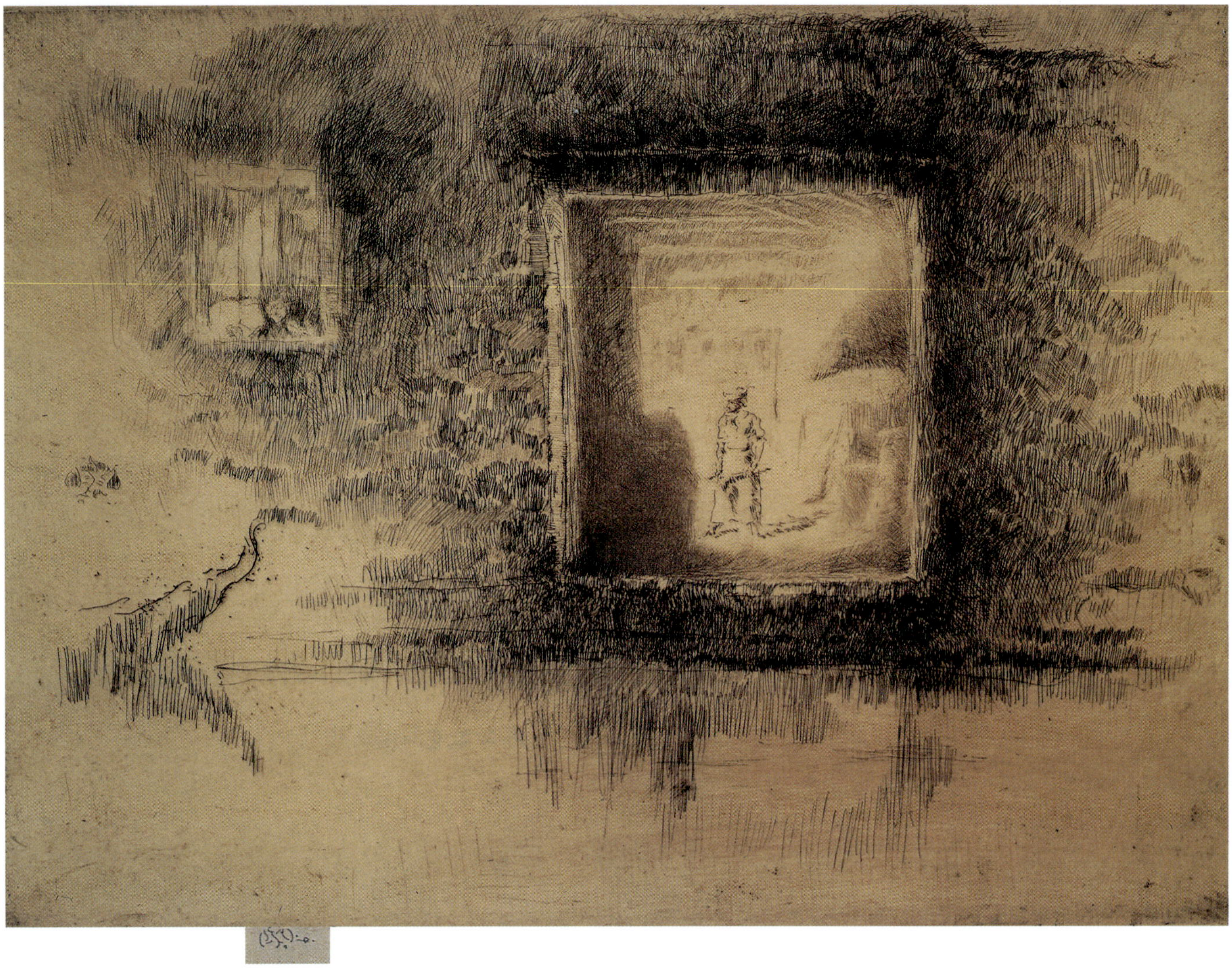

128
James McNeill Whistler
Nocturne: Furnace
Etching printed by Whistler 1886
168 x 231 mm
Hunterian Art Gallery, K.213 v

K.215 iv/iv, K.216 iii/iii, K.233 v/v.

6 Lucas owned K.196 v and vi, K.197 i K.198 V, K.199 i, K.200 vi and vii, K.201 iv, K.202 vi, K.203 i, K.204 ii and viii, K.205 ii, K.206 i, K.207 vi, K.208 iv, K.209 ii and iv, K.210 vii, K.211 ii, K.212 ?, K.213 iv, K.214 v, K.215 iv, K.216 iii, K.233 v. I am indebted to Jay Fisher for this list. Another early set, in the I. S. Gardner Museum, Boston, includes later states, ie K.198 viii, K.199 ii, K.202 vii, K.203 ii, K.207 iii, K.209 vi, K.213 vi.

7 Receipt, 2 April 1886, GUL D69; see MacDonald 1976, p.39.

8 The receipts are incomplete and overlap: 2, 3, 4, 18 April; 2, 18, 20, 28, 31 July; 20, 25 Aug; 21, 25, 29 Sept; 2, 6, 21, 26, 29 Oct; 15 Dec 1886; 5 and 15 Jan 1887, Dowdeswells' receipts, GUL D69, 70, 74–83, 86–90, 92–3, 95.

9 Destroyed plates delivered: K.211 and K.236, 6 Oct; K.209, K.216 and K.235, 21 Oct; K.208, 5 Dec 1886; K.205 and K.215(?), 15 Jan 1887; K.212, 17 Jan 1887; K.202 and K.204, 27 Jan 1887; K.200, 8 Feb 1887; K.213, 26 Feb 1887; K.207 and K.210, 16 July 1887; Whistler recorded receipts, GUL D69–95, GUL NB1, pp.32–9 (cancellations recorded, pp.33–5); receipts kept by Dowdeswells', LJR.

10 Menpes 1904, p.92.

11 Whistler to W. Dowdeswell, nd. [1886/1887], LJR.

12 Sales of K.196–7, 199–200, 202–13, 8 and 28 Aug, 12 Sept 1882, GUL NB1, pp.1, 3, 101.

13 Whistler to W. Dowdeswell, 27 Sept [1886], LJR.

14 Menpes 1904, p.91. See MacDonald 1976, cat.no.83, on printing problems.

15 Freer Gallery of Art, acq.nos 87.9, 93.23. Kennedy bought impressions of the final and cancelled states of *Nocturne: Palaces*, see Kennedy to Whistler, 12 April 1893, GUL W1202.

16 See Heijbroek and MacDonald 1997, pp.35, 88.

17 Menpes 1904, p.100.

18 Whistler to W. Dowdeswell, nd. [Feb 1887], LJR; MacDonald 1976, cat.no.95.

19 The National Gallery in Berlin has etchings bought directly from Thibadeau; I am grateful to Martin Hopkinson for pointing this out to me. Thibadeau's effects were auctioned at Sotheby's, London, 9 Dec 1889; see M.423.

20 Whistler to Messrs Dowdeswell, nd. [July 1887], LJR; MacDonald 1976, p.39.

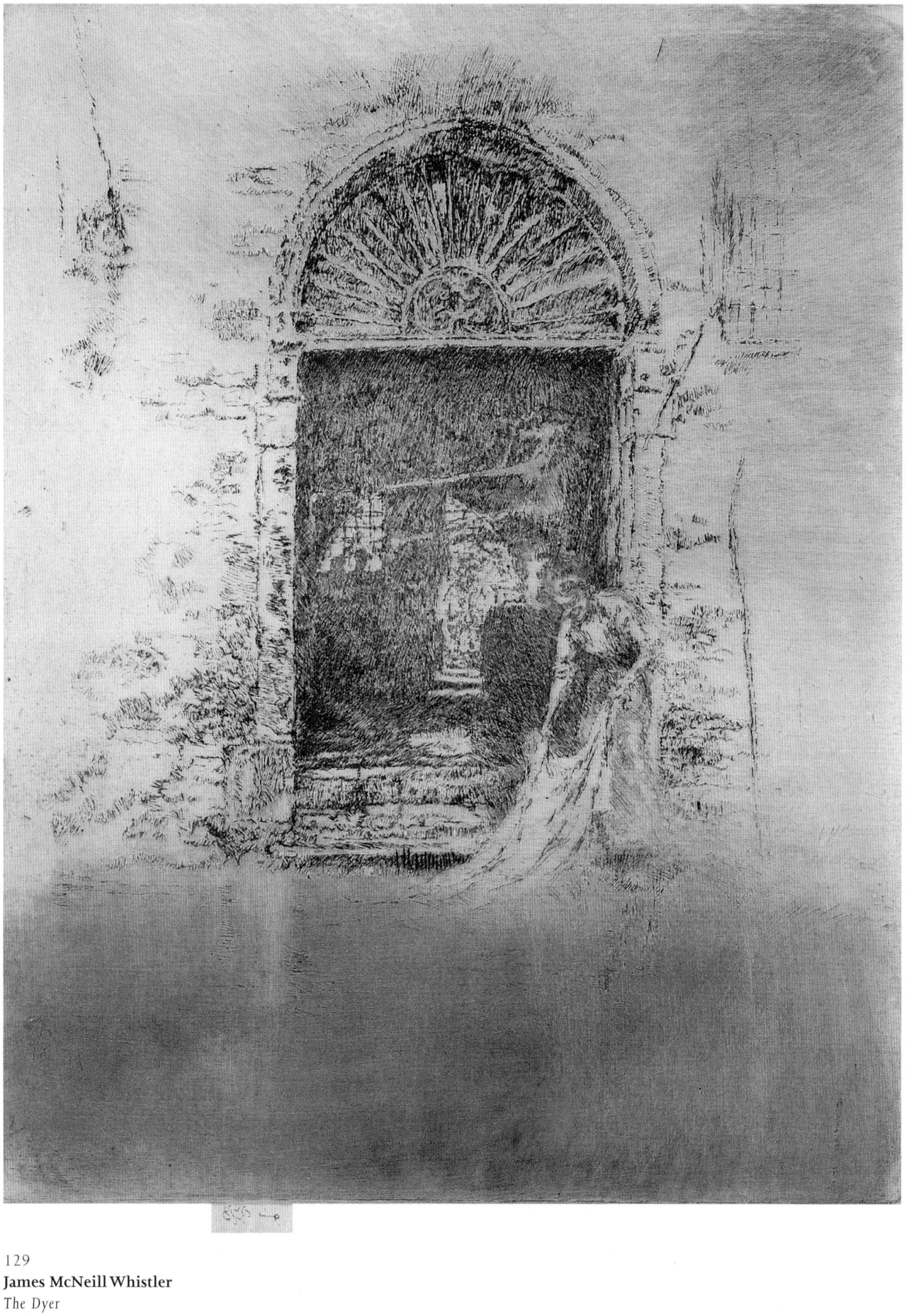

129
James McNeill Whistler
The Dyer
Etching 302 x 235 mm
Fine Art Society, K.219

9 Nocturne: The Last Years

Despite his commitments to the Fine Art Society and Messrs Dowdeswell, Whistler was under no obligation to restrict sales of unpublished etchings. Having selected two sets, he was left with a number of other Venice etchings. *The Dyer* (fig.129) and *Fish-Shop, Venice* (K.218) must have been serious contenders for inclusion in the published sets.[1] However, the figure of *The Dyer* caused Whistler enormous problems, which he attempted to resolve with repeated proofs, counter-proofs, rubbing down and rebiting, to no avail. Kennedy liked it and was pressing Whistler to complete the plate and send him more proofs in 1888, but instead, Whistler abandoned it.[2]

This and the other unpublished etchings and drypoints are rare, but Whistler capitalised on their rarity, tempting dealers and collectors with rare proofs. For instance, sales to Thomas McLean in 1882 included impressions of *Fish-Shop, Venice*, and two drypoints, *Little Salute* (K.220) and *Islands* (K.222), for four guineas, plus *The Dyer* for eight guineas. Between 1886 and 1887 McLean bought impressions of *Nocturne: Salute* (fig.130) for six guineas and the first proof for ten guineas, as well as one of only two cancelled proofs of *The Traghetto, No.1* (K.190) for twenty guineas. Whistler also capitalised on his proofs of the 'First Venice Set'. For instance, he sold a 'unique state' of *The Beggars* (K.194) to McLean for twenty-one pounds in October 1887, noting 'I believe only proof pulled of that state'.[3]

At the same time he managed to get the larger plates of the 'First Venice Set' in order and printed twelve full sets for the Fine Art Society. The butterfly signature on many impressions dates from 1887 (it is distinguished by one or two dots or slightly slanting lines, like quizzical eyebrows, at the top of the butterfly). Thus the printing of the two sets overlapped. The experience of printing the plates inspired new etchings, including sets of 'East London' and the 'Naval Review',[4] and 1887 became the most important year in Whistler's etching career.

Completing the Fine Art Society sets

In January 1889, in response to a request for more sets, Whistler started work on new states of the 'First Venice Set', hoping, he said, that these would be better than ever, and Brown sent some paper.[5] Whistler found that five of the plates were cracked, but he managed to complete editions of several etchings – *Little Venice* (K.183), *Nocturne* (K.184) and *The Little Lagoon* (K.186) and, shortly afterwards, *The Riva, No.1* (K.192). But at that point he still had an enormous number to print: sixty-eight of *Two Doorways* (K.193) for instance, and eighty-seven of *The Piazzetta* (K.189).[6]

He had made radical changes to *Two Doorways* in Venice and in four subsequent states. Young women and men in a gondola were replaced with a bent old man on the steps. By the seventh state, the old man, not surprisingly, had grown a long white beard and behind him stood a girl with a basket. At this point, the plate was cancelled with an enormous, deeply etched butterfly (fig.131). These states display the changing views of the artist. The forbidding façade framed figures of unprepossessing realism, similar to those in *The Beggars* (K.194), perhaps reflect the frustration of the ageing artist committed to completing old plates when he preferred new challenges.

In Amsterdam in 1889 he created some of his finest prints, drawing on the experience gained over the previous two years. He extolled these new plates for 'combining a minuteness of detail always referred to with sadness by the critics who hark back to the Thames Set etchings, with greater freedom and more beauty of execution than even the Venice set'.[7] He wanted to sell the new set to the Fine Art Society and threatened to destroy his earlier plates because of the promise of this new work. However, the Fine Art Society was not prepared to enter into yet another contract. Whistler wanted too much money and the scheme died. Nevertheless, the printing of

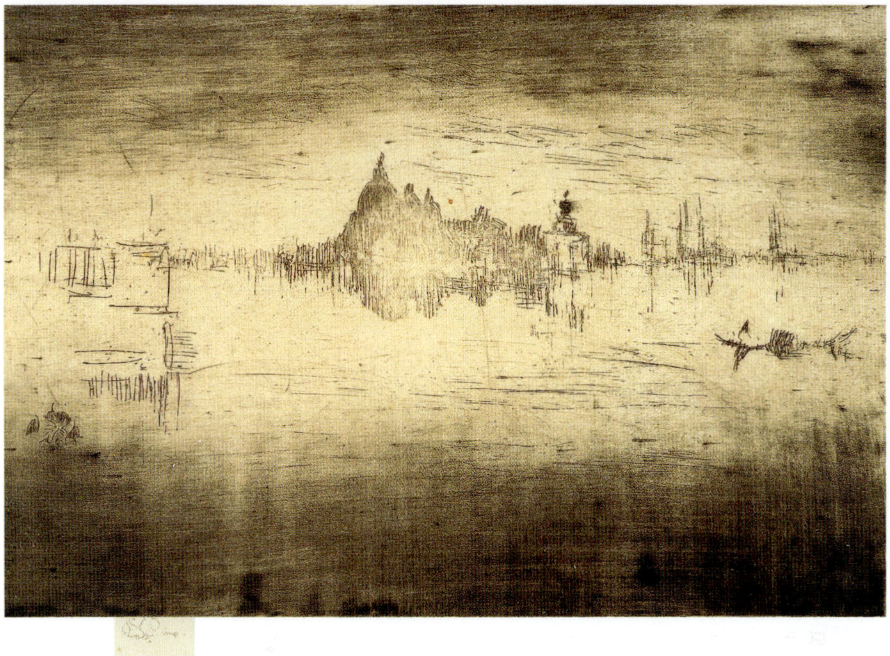

130
James McNeill Whistler
Nocturne: Salute
Drypoint 153 x 225 mm
Fine Art Society, K.226 v

the Venetian plates influenced, and in its turn was influenced by, that of the Dutch plates. 'The work continually develops new interests and these last etchings of mine have opened up a future beside which the past is mere child's play', he told Huish.[8] As for the Venice etchings, 'I believe they will come out far more beautifully than ever!' he assured Brown, 'I am making of them wonderful new states!'[9]

Three years later, in May 1892, having read in the papers that the artist had completed printing some of the Venice etchings and was moving to Paris, Huish wrote to Whistler asking him to leave the etchings behind. Whistler ironically thanked him for his belated interest. Brown even offered to collect etchings from Paris, if he could be sure there was something for him to collect. They were eight months too late, Whistler said, and went on at some length about their neglect, 'insolence, meanness, and crass stupidity' and the demand from American collectors like H. O. Havemeyer, Howard Mansfield, Charles Lang Freer and his colleague, Colonel Hecker, for his latest prints. 'I will really have given you a fortune –', he assured Huish, 'All collectors will be obliged to have these proofs'.[10]

Huish explained, not particularly tactfully, that they only tried to stop him printing plates that were not in demand. By then Huish had received five of the completed copper-plates, but not the proofs of them. Whistler promptly sent five packages of prints by post and one with the dealer D. C. Thomson, demanding payment of £112 17s 6d. To their dismay, one of the packages, containing thirteen impressions of *The Doorway* and *The Beggars*, was pierced right through by customs officials. Fortunately the Fine Art Society was able to get them repaired, or so they reassured Whistler, but this confirmed his abiding distrust of officialdom. After several reminders, he promised to try and complete the editions:

> even were I able to begin again at once, it would take endless trouble & much time to get those two plates again into the condition in which they will give proofs of the same beauty as those harmed [...] when great labour & much thought has been expended in getting a plate into perfect condition for the press, it is wise that such plate should be printed right out – in spite of the momentary want of popularity.[11]

After at least three preliminary states of *The Palaces* (K.187), he printed many impressions of the fourth state and completed the edition with impressions of a final, fifth state. Despite the fact that he was making only minor

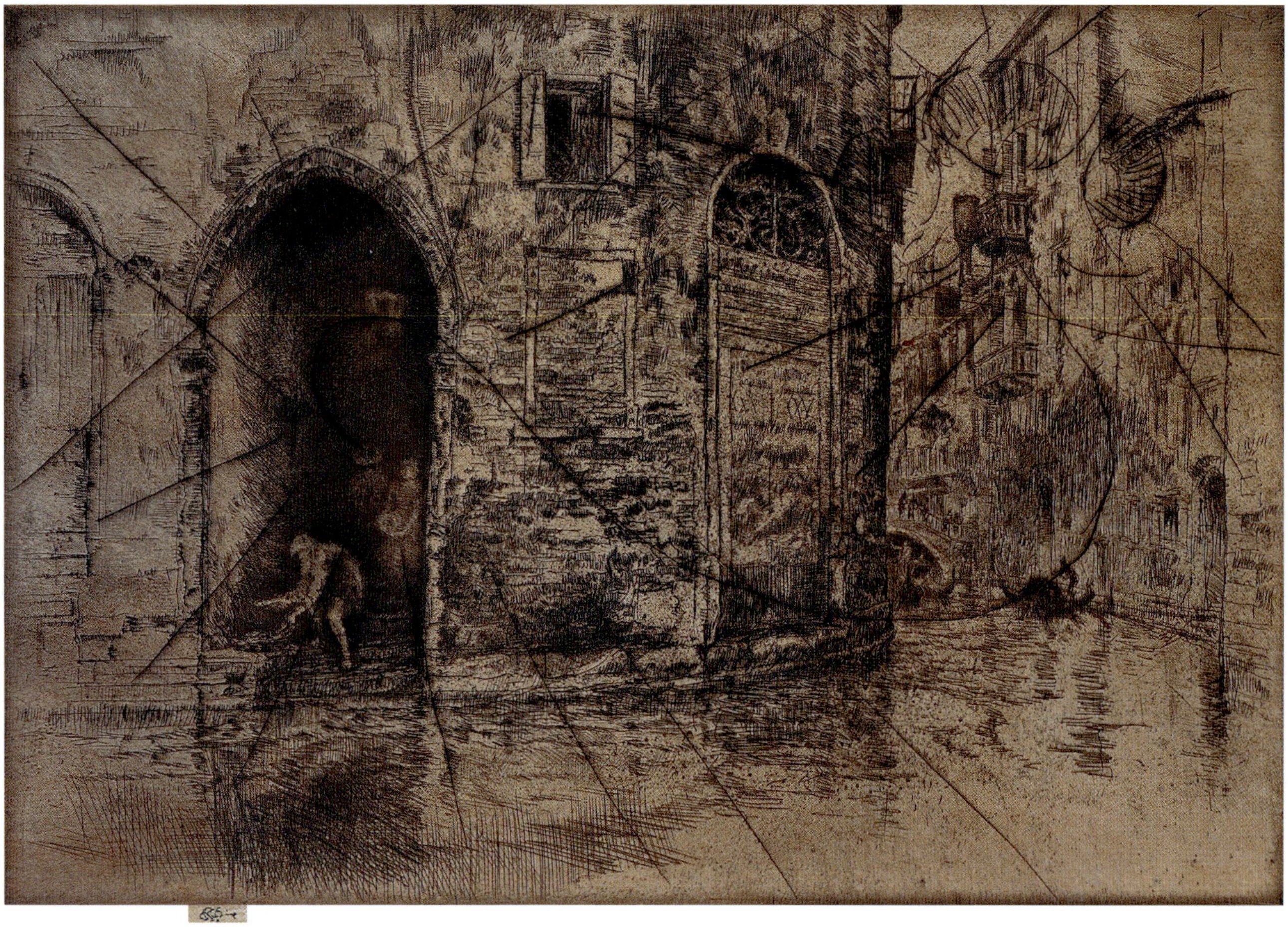

131
James McNeill Whistler
Two Doorways 1886
Cancelled etching 202 x 292 mm
Hunterian Art Gallery, K.193

revisions, the printing of the plate took a very long time, perhaps just because it was large and unwieldy. *The Doorway* (K.188) went through at least ten states, not seven as listed by Kennedy; Whistler pulled a few proofs of the first three states and then of three intermediate states. Substantial changes were made to the figures in the third and the final states and to the interior in every state.

Three months later, in October 1892, Brown was asking for more impressions of *The Doorway* and *The Beggars* for an exhibition, and cancelled impressions of *The Palaces*. Whistler perked up and suggested exhibiting a selection of the etchings in the old frames, 'the narrow white one with the brown lines', a set of the early proofs with wider margins, proofs from the destroyed plates and the plates. This, he thought, would make 'a peculiar and interesting little exhibition – where all the Diletanti and connoissuers [sic] could have wagged their heads to their hearts content.'[12] He sent several impressions, marking the back of some 'ex' for exhibition, and proofs selected for Mansfield and Kennedy.[13]

The Fine Art Society would only consider a show when and if they got the remaining etchings. They outlined a new set of prices dependent both on demand and on the scale and detail in the print, with some etchings costing twice as much as others. One small, supremely elegant etching, *The Little Lagoon* (K.186) was priced at six guineas, and a large, gloomy print, *Two Doorways* (K.193) at eight guineas. Two magnificent etchings, *The Doorway* and *The Beggars* (when the Fine Art Society could get them), were priced at fifteen guineas. They still had fifty-

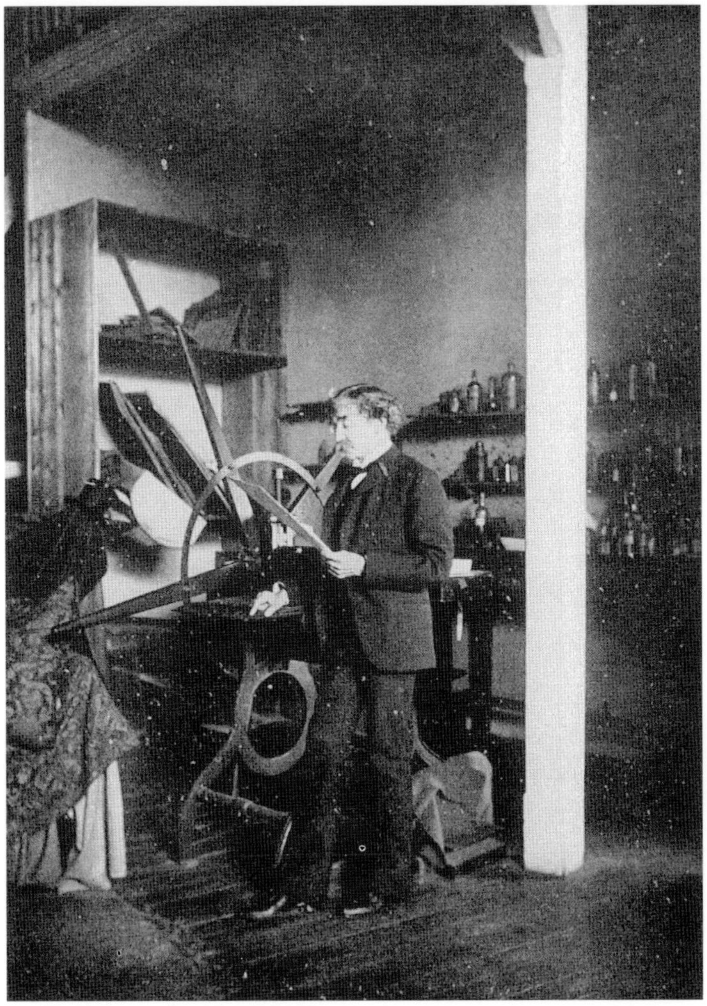

132
Whistler at his printing press in the rue Notre Dame des Champs, Paris
1898
Photograph by Dornac, from Pennell 1908, II, repr. facing p.136

two proofs of *The Traghetto, No.2* (K.191), which was apparently not popular, and were keeping the price low at eight guineas.

The idea of an exhibition lapsed – perhaps it was no more than a ploy to entice more prints out of Whistler. Brown sent samples of Japanese paper, hoping to encourage Whistler to complete the sets of *The Doorway* and *The Beggars*. Out of the hundred required, they had received seventy-eight prints of the former and fifty-five of the latter.[14] Whistler thanked him for the paper, but said he was too busy to print: 'All this great over refinement and anxiety for the perfection of quantity is dead loss & vexation –' he said, 'for my own reputation, the complete beauty of <u>one</u> proof is enough – & the production of scores of the same plate is really a madness!'[15]

This was contrary to the whole principle of publishing sets of etchings, upon which Whistler's reputation had originally been based. Brown was placatory, praising Whistler's perfectionism, and was rewarded with another packet of trial proofs within the month. At this point, Whistler actually had the grace to acknowledge their patience.[16] Another year, and Whistler reported on the progress of the remaining plates:

> These four are certainly beauties [...] plates are as whimsical and as difficult to deal with as horses! And when I do take up these two or three remaining ones the Lord knows how they may jib and shy and buck and bolt with me – the trouble they will give I know well – and the amount of coaxing & light handling required before I get them back into anything like training again![17]

Clients wanted impressions of *The Doorway* and *The Beggars* so Whistler sent off a single proof of *The Beggars* and then, on 10 August, two of each on Japanese paper. These were particularly choice impressions, set aside, the artist said, for '"Crowned Heads" or Museums!'[18] Thereafter, occasional cheques record Whistler's intermittent engagement with the sets for the Fine Art Society.

The end of a saga

With the help of his wife, who organised his studio, listed his etchings and kept track of those printed, Whistler might have completed the edition, but progress came crashing to a halt when she was diagnosed with cancer in 1894. For two years Whistler's main concern was her health. No sustained work on the etchings was possible, though collectors and dealers were pressing him to select the 'richest impressions' for their collections.[19]

He turned instead to lithography, which had the advantage of requiring less involvement from the artist – the lithographs were printed by Way in London – and in 1895 an exhibition was held at the Fine Art Society. When Beatrice died in 1896, Whistler was distraught. He quarrelled with Way and virtually abandoned printmaking. In 1901 he visited Corsica for his health and made a few etchings which he printed on his return, but these were his last etchings.

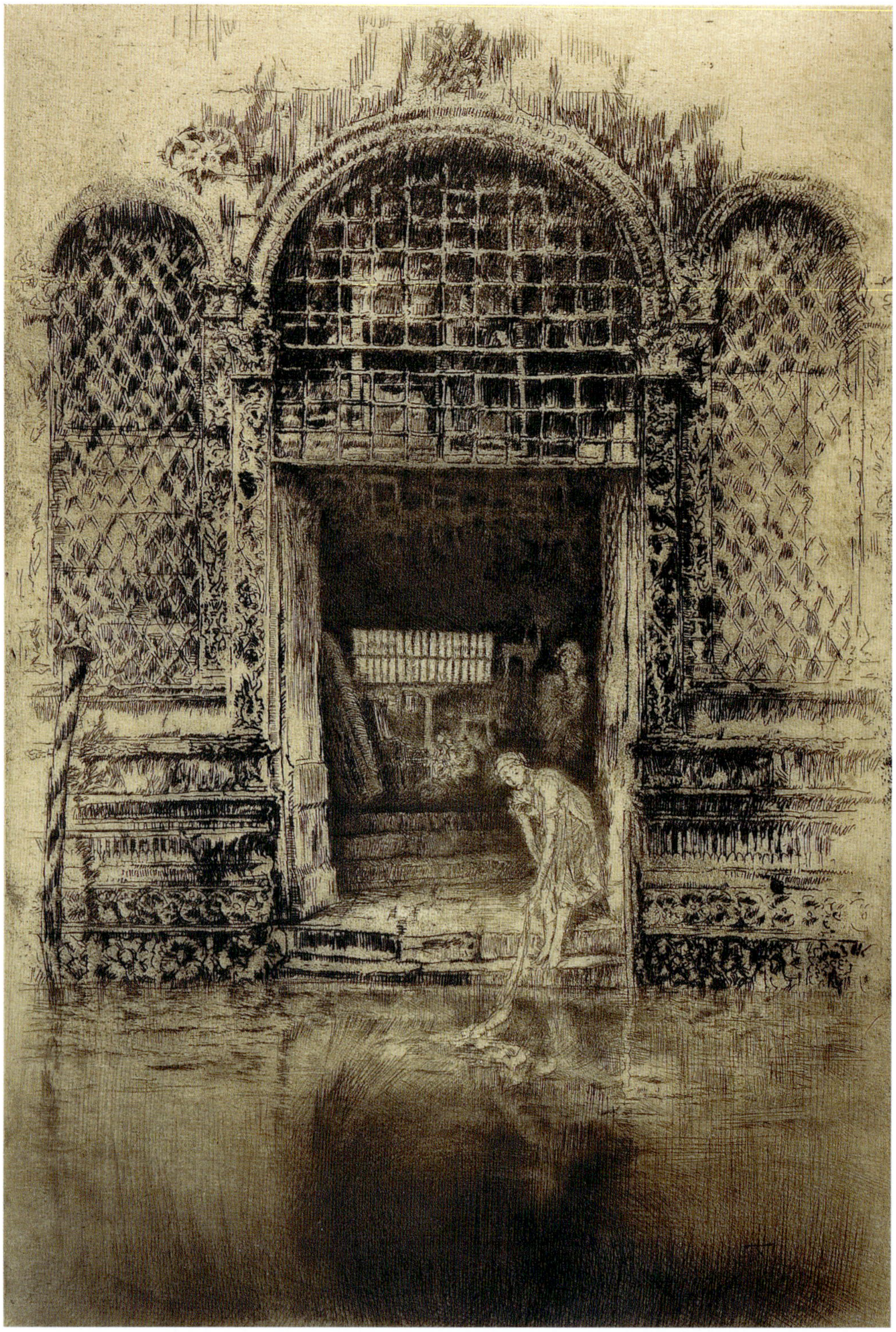

133
James McNeill Whistler
The Doorway c.1903
Etching printed by F. Goulding
292 x 202 mm
Hunterian Art Gallery, K.188 final state

The Fine Art Society had left him alone after begging in vain for more proofs of the two remaining etchings. Whistler's declining health made it increasingly unlikely that he would complete the editions and although Brown suggested sending a printer to work under his supervision, nothing came of this.[20] The artist died in July 1903. Huish, with an unusual want of tact, immediately wrote to Whistler's sister-in-law, Rosalind Birnie Philip, asking for the Venetian copperplates. Eventually, Huish arranged that Frederick Goulding should print the few remaining prints, sixteen of *The Doorway* (fig.133) and twenty-two of *The Beggars*, and Goulding completed the edition under Rosalind's supervision by December 1903.

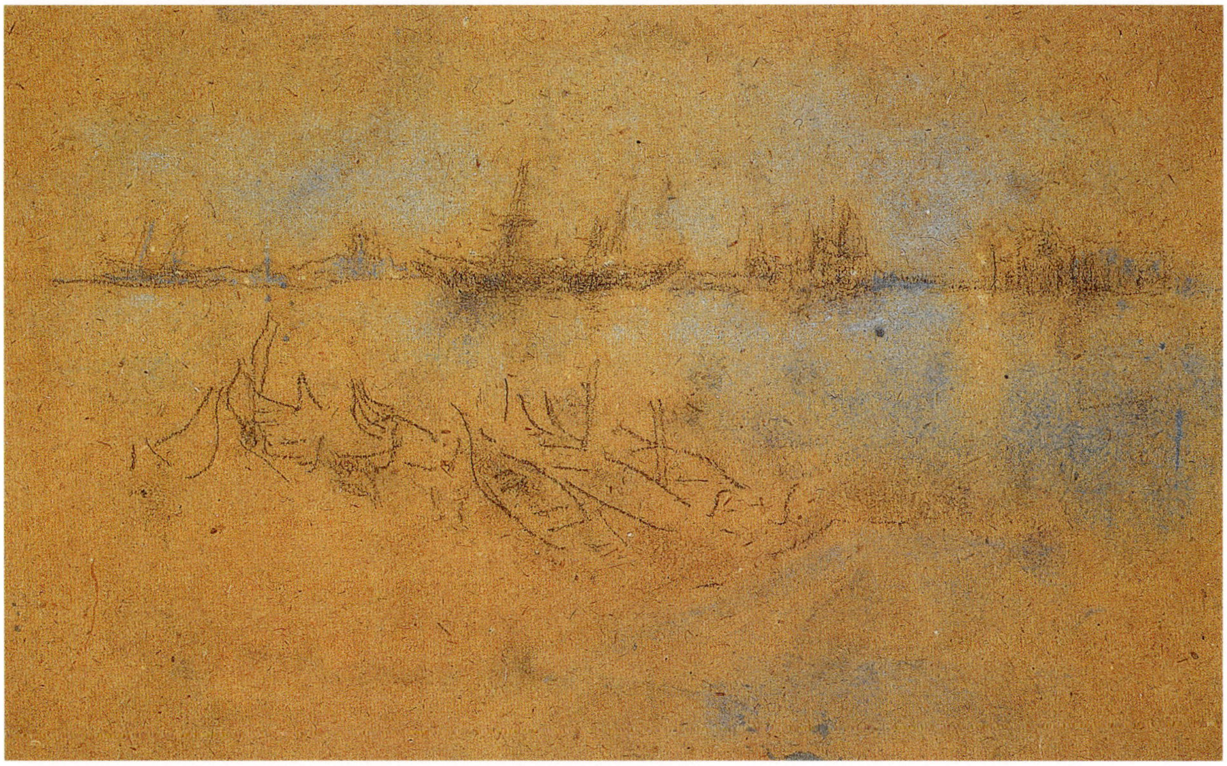

134
James McNeill Whistler
Nocturne: ships and gondolas, Venice
Pastel 200 x 299 mm
Hunterian Art Gallery, M.801

These last proofs, closely modelled on Whistler's, are fine examples of Goulding's work, dramatic in their use of ink tone to enhance the etched lines. They show that the plates had survived in fine condition and they conclude the epic history of Whistler's Venice sets.[21]

1 *Fish-Shop, Venice* underwent numerous alterations; some indicated in a proof with pen and wash, Freer Gallery of Art, acq.no.03.38.

2 E. G. Kennedy to Whistler, 20 April 1888, GUL W1145.

3 Whistler's ledger, 8 and 28 Aug 1882, 1 Nov 1886, 5 Oct, [Oct/Nov], 21 Dec 1887, GUL NB1/3, 25–7.

4 1887, K.242–331 including sets, K.252–301, 310–15 and K.316–31.

5 Whistler to E. Brown, nd. [April] 1889, GUL LB9/8; Brown to Whistler, 17 Jan 1889, GUL F131; Huish to Whistler, 30 Jan 1889, GUL F137, sending 100 guineas.

6 Whistler to E. Brown, nd. [March 1889], GUL LB9/7; receipts from FAS to Whistler, 15 April, 26 April, 2 May 1889 and nd. [after April 1889], GUL F150–3. Lists record 63 of K.185, 75 of K.187, 59 of K.188, 87 of K.189, 82 of K.190, 68 of K.193, 75 of K.194, 64 of K.195, FAS, list, nd. [after April 1889], GUL F150.

7 Whistler to Huish, nd. [3 Sept 1889], GUL F164, and [27/29 Nov 1889], GUL LB7/102–3. Heijbroek and MacDonald 1997, pp.137–8.

8 Nd. [27/29 Nov 1889], GUL LB7/102–3.

9 Nd. [Dec 1889], GUL LB9/8.

10 Huish to Whistler, 26 May 1892 and reply, nd. [after 26 May 1892], GUL F172–3; E. Brown to Whistler, 9 and 14 June 1892, GUL LB1/6, 9; Whistler to FAS, 15 and 22 June 1892, GUL F176, 178, and nd., GUL LB1/7.

11 Whistler to Huish, nd. [3 July 1892], GUL LB3/32, in MacDonald 1971, cat.no.96; see also Huish to Whistler, 18 June 1892, GUL LB12/15; and replies, nd. [22 June 1892], GUL F178, LB3/14: Brown to Whistler, 1 July 1892, and Huish to Whistler, 2, 4 and 29 July 1892, GUL F180–1, 183; Huish to Whistler, 14 July 1892, GUL F142; reply, nd. [July/Aug] 1892, GUL LB3/33.

12 Whistler to Huish, nd. [Sept/Oct] 1892, GUL LB3/31.

13 Brown to Whistler, 17 Sept 1892 and 7 Oct 1892, GUL F187–8.

14 Trial proofs of K.188, 190 and 193 were sold; Brown to Whistler, 21 Oct 1892, GUL F189; 7 and 8 April 1893, GUL F190–1; in GUL F191 Brown lists sales; Brown to Whistler, 4–5 May 1893, GUL F193–4.

15 Whistler to Brown, nd. [May 1893] GUL LB9/20.

16 Brown to Whistler, 20 May 1893, GUL F197; Brown sent £7, 19 June 1893, GUL F198; Whistler to Brown, 22 June 1893, GUL LB9/23; nd. [Jan 1894], GUL LB9/18; Whistler to Huish, nd. [1893], GUL LB3/28.

17 Copy, Whistler to Huish, nd. [Aug 1894], GUL F209 (original in private collection); in MacDonald 1971, cat.no.100.

18 Ibid; see also Huish to Whistler, 8 June 1894, GUL F202; Whistler to Huish, nd. [1894], LB3/27, 10–31 July 1894, 7 Aug 1894, GUL F204–5; receipt for final states by L. U. Earle, 11 Aug 1894, GUL F206–7, GUL NB1/10. Cheques for £31 and £10 10s 6d, see Whistler to Brown, nd. [Sept 1894], GUL LB9/25/2, 3 Oct 1894, GUL LB9/24, nd. [1894], LB9/40 and Huish to Whistler, 7 May 1895, GUL F223.

19 E. G. Kennedy asked Whistler for *The Doorway*, 29 Jan 1895, GUL W1234.

20 Huish to Whistler, 7 Dec 1898; FAS to Whistler, nd. [1901] and E. Brown to Whistler, 8 Nov 1902, GUL F290, 303, 311.

21 Huish to R. B. Philip, 1 Aug, 14 Sept, 22 Oct 1903, GUL F323–4, 326; reply, 15 Sept and 26 Oct 1903, GUL P485, F327; Huish to Philip, 29 Oct and 13 Nov 1903, GUL F328–9. Huish asked for the cancelled proof and arranged to cancel plates, offering to present them to a museum. He received proofs on 14 Dec 1903 and paid the final £19 for printing on 17 Dec: Huish to Philip, 3, 12, 14 and 17 Dec 1903, GUL F330–1, 333–4; reply, 18 Dec 1903, GUL F335.

10 Palaces in the Night

Whistler looked back on Venice as a 'marvellous City – the Sapphire of the Seas!'[1] He saw himself as changing people's perceptions of Venice by his vision and imagination, just as he had altered their feelings for Thames-side London. In 1885, in his famous 'Ten O'Clock' Lecture, he used Venice as a symbol of this transformation:

> And when the evening mist clothes the riverside with poetry, as with a veil, and the poor buildings lose themselves in the dim sky, and the tall chimneys become campanili, and the warehouses are palaces in the night, and the whole city hangs in the heavens, and fairy-land is before us – then the wayfarer hastens home; the working man and the cultured one, the wise man and the one of pleasure, cease to understand, as they have ceased to see, and Nature who, for once, has sung in tune, sings her exquisite song to the artist alone [...][2]

Whistler's pastels of 'palaces in the night' are indeed exquisite, but they were his last. On his return from Venice he continued to exhibit and to draw in pastel, not the streets of London, but nude and draped women. Throughout his career Whistler changed direction after he had explored a particular theme or technique to his satisfaction. Thus his immersion in the subject of Venice and his exploration of the medium of pastel between 1879 and 1880, with the subsequent exhibition, was an unrepeatable experience. Over the following years, the decorative and symbolic element in his work gained in importance, building on methods developed in Venice.

The remarkable effort required to print the Venetian etchings for over twenty years was sustained by his own perfectionism and by continual changes to the copperplates and the technique required to print them. His etchings of Holland in 1889 paralleled and extended the technical expertise gained in printing the Venice plates. In etching he continued to explore certain subjects, themes and compositions: glimpses through dark doorways, the geometrical façades of old buildings, working men and women in narrow streets, shopfronts, details of wrought iron, sculptured stone and crumbling brick.

Whistler's influence

The Venetian etchings and pastels had a profound effect on the development of Whistler's career, and a wider influence on his pupils, colleagues and other artists. The harmonious presentation of his work was widely reported and radically affected exhibiting practices. In pastel, his emphasis on the importance of the medium itself, working on a small scale on brown paper, had considerable impact on the Pastel Revival. Although not personally involved in the establishment of pastel societies, such as the *Société des Pastellistes français*, he continued regularly to exhibit groups of pastels in Europe and America. Some of Whistler's pastels remained in his possession and were shown privately to fellow artists and prospective patrons, others went into private collections.

There were various opportunities for artists to examine Whistler's work. For instance, a little known artist, C. E. Holloway, who visited Venice in 1875 and 1895, drew a street scene that shows the influence of Whistler's compositions. It was published in the *Studio* after Holloway's death (fig.136). A restrained drawing, it is comparable to Whistler's *Bead-Stringers* (M.788), which Holloway could have seen in the collection of their mutual friend, Thomas Way, and which was published in a special *Studio* album after Whistler's death. High quality lithographic reproductions by Way's son, T. R. Way, published in the *Studio* (fig.135), spread Whistler's

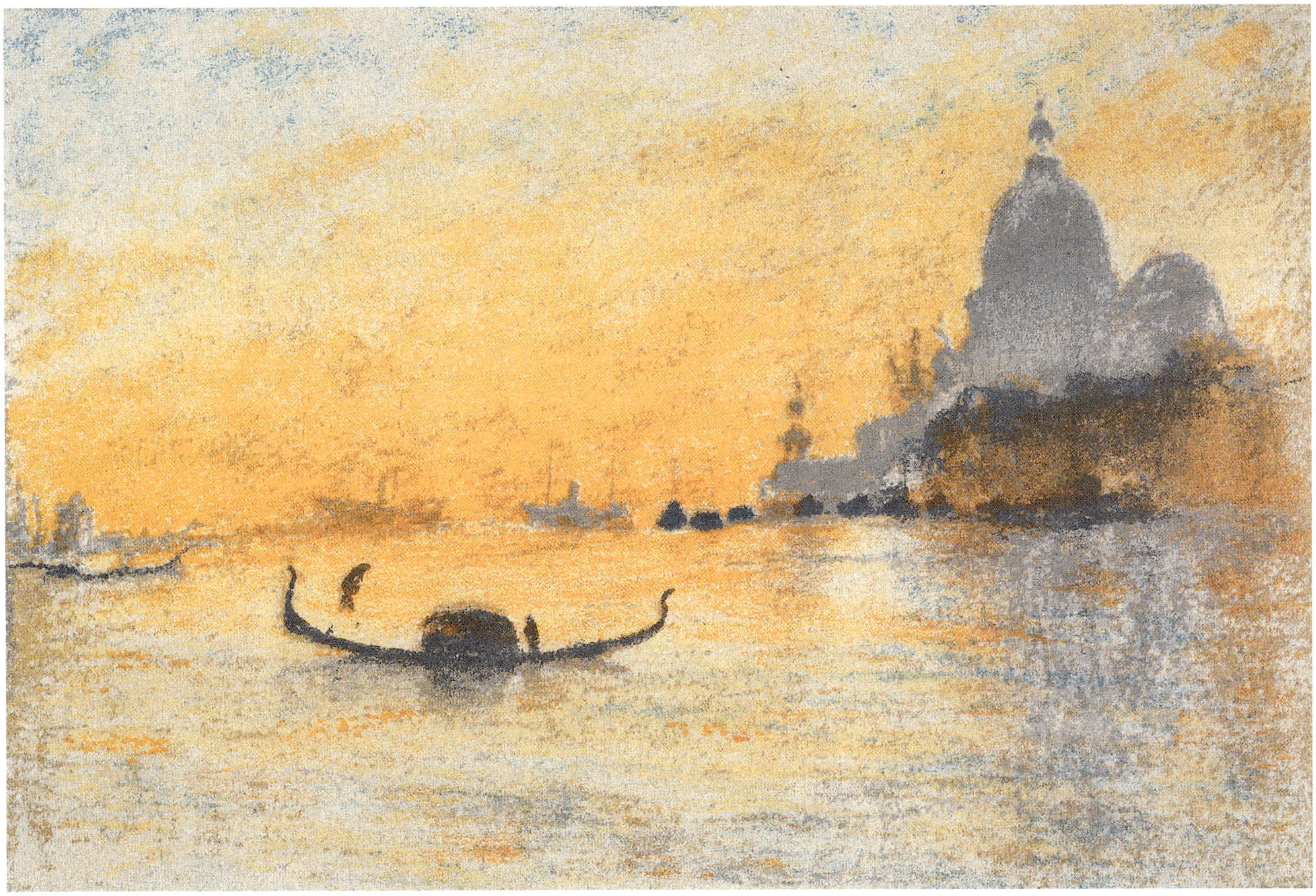

135
Thomas R. Way after James McNeill Whistler
Santa Maria della Salute
Pastel, 146 x 222 mm, whereabouts unknown, M.815
lithograph by T. R. Way after Whistler, from *Studio*, XXIX, Jan 1907, p.144

influence widely, long after the pastels had been dispersed. Most of Way's collection was bought by C. L. Freer, and bequeathed to the Freer Gallery of Art in Washington.

Both Way and Freer lent their pastels to one or other of the memorial exhibitions after Whistler's death.[3] The first, in Boston in 1904, mined several of the great American collections of etchings and pastels – there were 315 etchings in all. The second was held in London in 1905 by the International Society of Sculptors, Painters and Gravers, of which Whistler had been the first president. It was organised in part by Joseph Pennell, who had helped Whistler print some of the last Venice plates in Paris, collected Whistler's etchings and was working on the definitive biography of Whistler's life. He was a fine draughtsman and his etchings make effective use of the descriptive facility of etched lines in strikingly simple compositions (fig.137). Whistler's sister-in-law and executrix, Rosalind Birnie Philip, lent her support to two other memorial exhibitions, in Paris in 1905 and in Rotterdam in 1906. Having inherited the artist's estate, she eventually passed it to the University of Glasgow – rare Venice pastels, copperplates, artist's proofs, etchings and all.

Pupils and colleagues

The extraordinary variety and visual power of Whistler's etchings had both an immediate and a lasting influence.

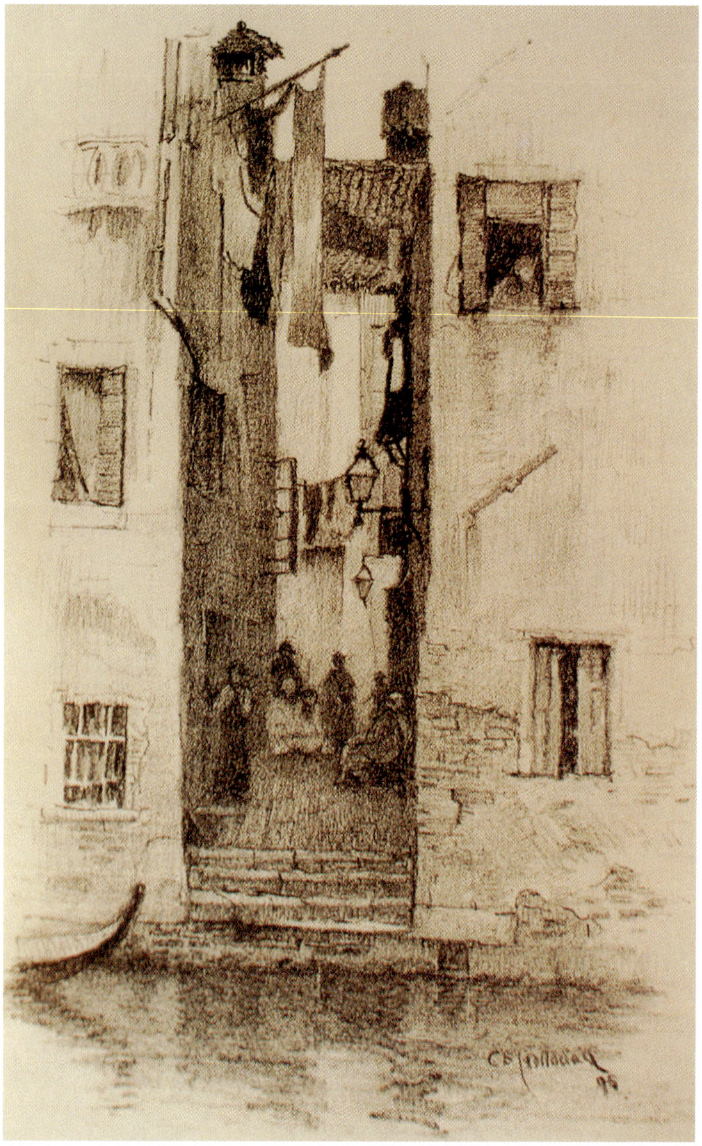

136
Charles E. Holloway
A Street in Venice 1895
Auto-lithograph, from *Studio*, XI, 1897, f.p.126

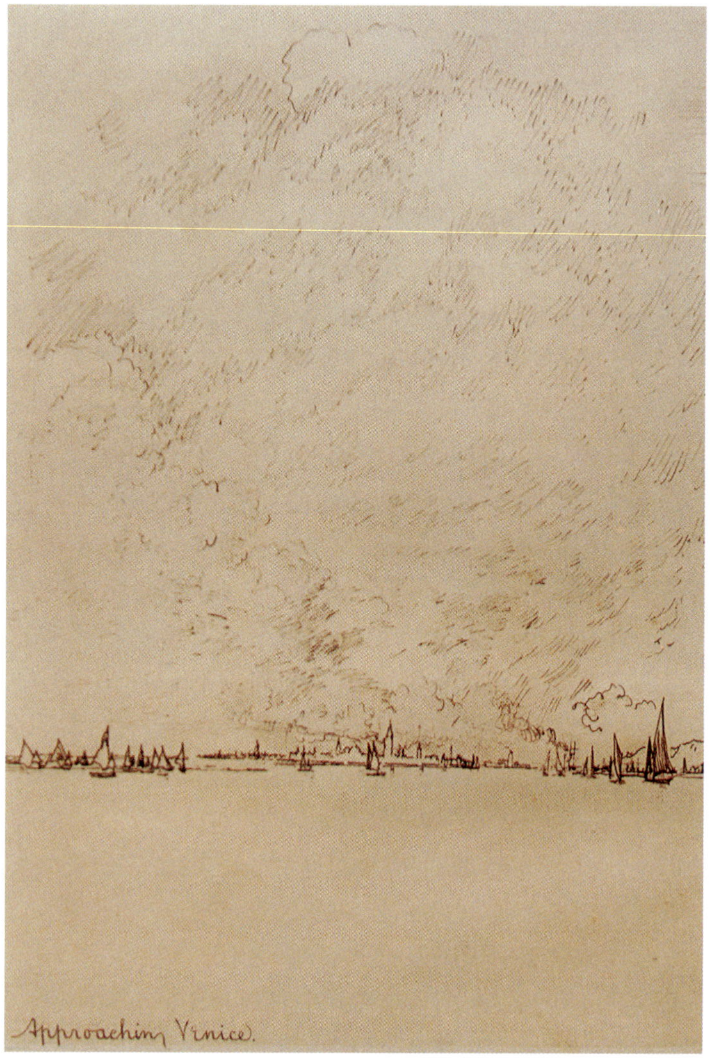

137
Joseph Pennell
Approaching Venice
Etching 122 x 88 mm
Frontispiece, from H. James, *Italian Journeys*, London, 1901

The collaboration between the expatriate Americans in Venice in 1880 – including Whistler, Duveneck, Bacher, Pennington, Elwell and Blum – was stimulating to all involved. The younger artists were most influenced by Whistler and some, like Bacher and Pennington, renewed the relationship in London a few years later. Pennington's nocturnes and pastels and his monogram (fig.138), like Elwell's, have been mistaken for Whistler's. Blum and Bacher were drawn to the same subjects as Whistler and employed Whistlerian techniques.[4] Blum used expressive broken lines in etching and tone in printing compositions strongly reminiscent of Whistler's (fig.139). While Whistler's influence spread throughout Europe, particularly in Eastern Europe[5], it was strongest in Britain where his assistants and pupils in London, Sickert and Menpes, learnt to etch under Whistler's supervision. At first they carried his precepts to extremes, etching with spidery lines on tiny plates, but the basic training stood them in good stead as they each developed individual styles. They continued to work on a small scale and their use of expressive, thinly etched lines and vertical shading is ultimately derived from Whistler.

The vertical lines in Sickert's etchings at first glance appear regular and mechanical (fig.140). Close-up they reveal a descriptive unevenness that effectively conveys the

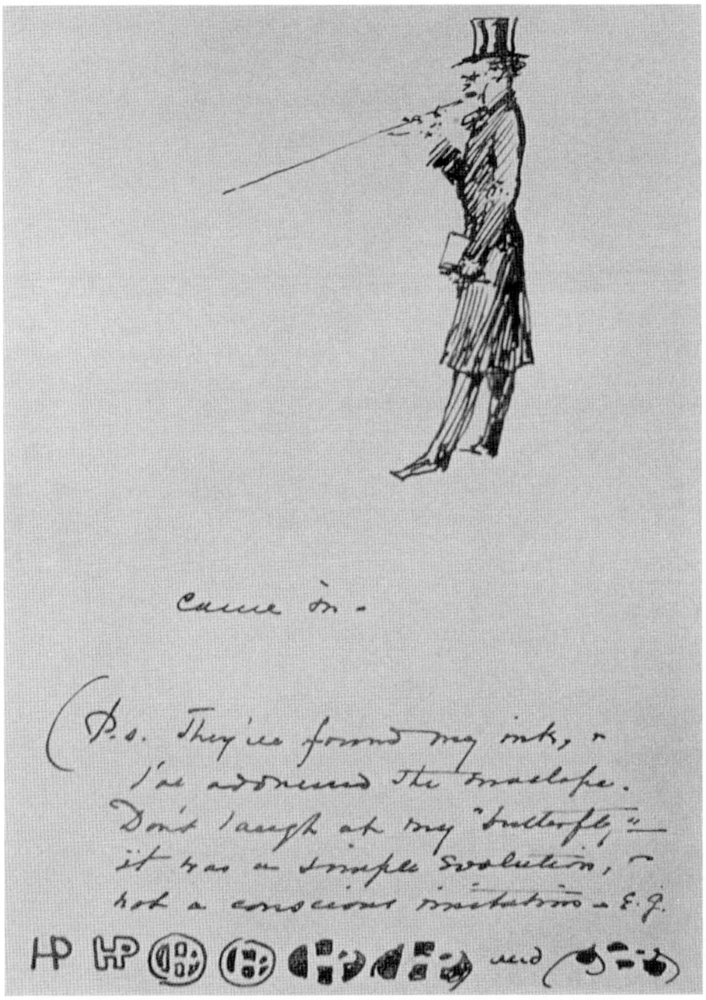

138
Harper Pennington
Sketch of Whistler
Pen and ink, 1880s, from Pennell 1921, repr. facing p.202

play of light and reflections, comparable to an etching such as Whistler's *Nocturne: Salute* (K.226). *Nocturne, Palaces* (K.202), which Menpes had helped to print, had a profound effect on his work. He experimented with a combination of vertical lines, wiry outline and 'artistic printing', including the use of colour in printing (fig.141). In retrospect, the issue of 'artistic printing' appears an irrelevance; the result justifies the means. Some twenty years later, a great admirer of Whistler's work, the self-taught Scottish etcher, James McBey, etched a *Venetian Night* (fig.143) that employs a similar combination of loose vertical lines and ink tone to convey mysterious palaces half lost in darkness.[6]

Sickert believed that the professional printer, and not the artist, was best equipped to print etchings. Although he had employed 'artistic printing' when working with Whistler's plates, he rejected it for his own. He was a sharp commentator on Whistler's inconsistencies in word and deed. In the Venice etchings he thought that 'only the portions done on the spot are fresh and right' and these 'rose to the height of exquisite and facile etching'.[7] Sickert's choice of well-known subjects, like St Marks, for prints and paintings may have been a market-driven decision or a reaction against Whistler's side street subjects. When etching, Sickert reversed the view on the copperplate, so that it appeared the right way round when printed. He complained that Whistler's etchings, which were so realistic and site-specific, showed Venice back-to-front. He suggested reproducing them in reverse: 'Let us enjoy [...] without having to reverse them in a looking-glass, the witty comments of the hand that flew like a swallow over the surface of the copper in lyrical appreciation of the loveliest city in the world.'[8]

In the footsteps of Whistler

Whistler's own achievement stands not just on the Venetian work but on the sustained achievement of printmaking over fifty years. Late in his career – indeed, at the time he more or less gave up etching in 1894 – two Scottish artists, the young etcher D. Y. Cameron and the photographer James Craig Annan, visited Venice. Annan named Japanese art, Velasquez and Whistler as the chief influences on his work.[9] He and Cameron could have seen Whistler's Venetian etchings in London or Glasgow, since his father, Thomas Annan, bought them direct from the artist for sale to Glasgow collectors.

By chance or design they followed in Whistler's footsteps; Annan, for instance, photographed an alley off the Campo Santa Margarita and Cameron etched Tintoretto's house on the Fondamenta dei Mori.[10] Annan's atmospheric twilight view of the *Riva degli Schiavoni* (fig.142) is comparable to Whistler's pastel *Nocturne – The Riva* (M.799). Two years later, in 1896, Annan published his folio of eleven photogravures (etched and printed from copperplates) entitled *Venice and Lombardy*. An edition of seventy-five, it shows his assimilation of Whistler's printmaking, selection and presentation of subjects.

Cameron's *Etchings of North Italy* were published in 1895 by W. B. Paterson, another Glasgow dealer who stocked Whistler's work. A set of twenty-six etchings, like Whistler's 'Second Venice Set', it was both a tribute and

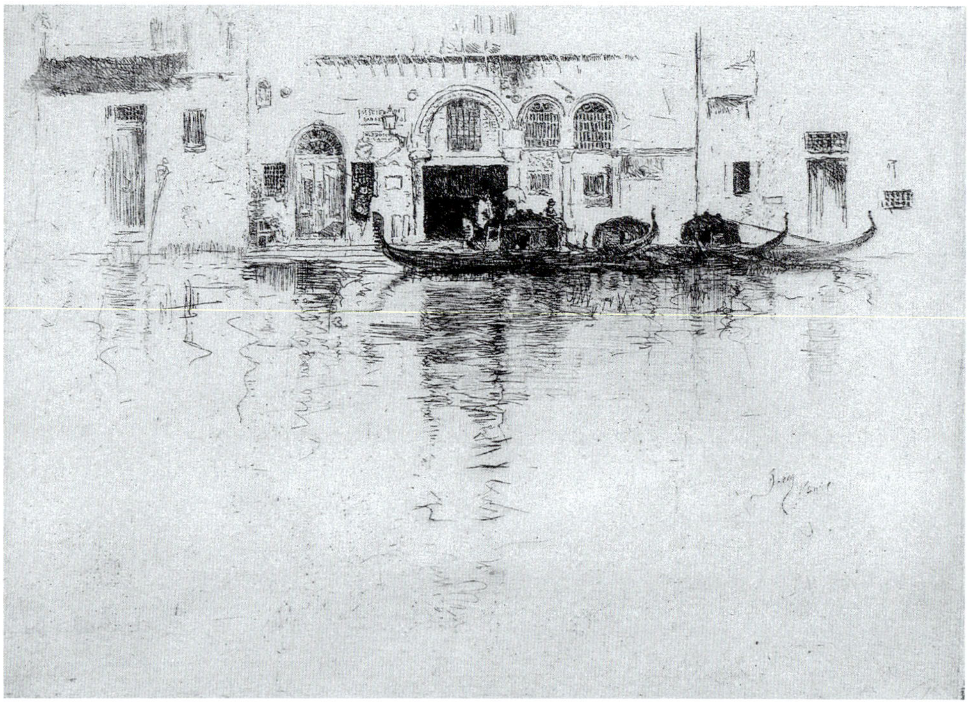

139
Robert F. Blum
Venetian Doorway and Gondolas c.1880
Etching 130 x 180 mm
British Museum

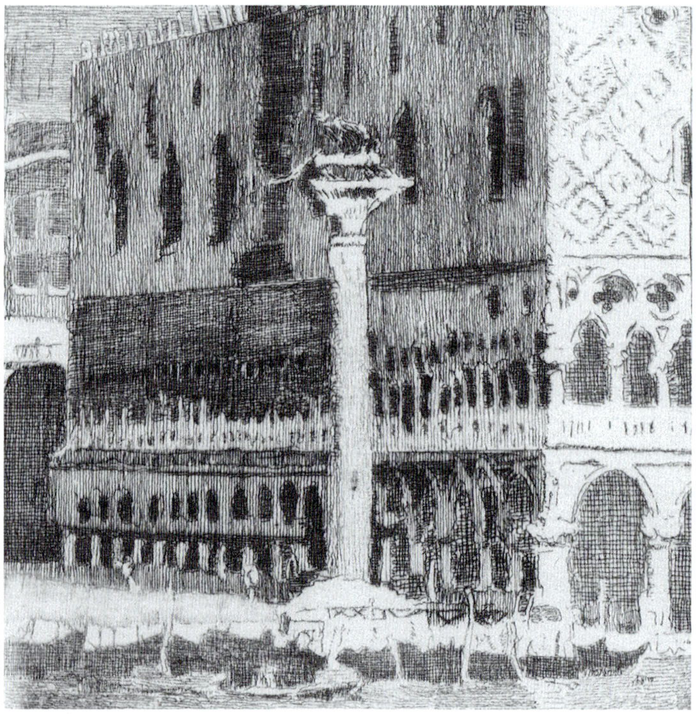

140
Walter R. Sickert
Venice, The Lion of St Mark 1915
Etching 140 x 120 mm
Private Collection, B.172 I

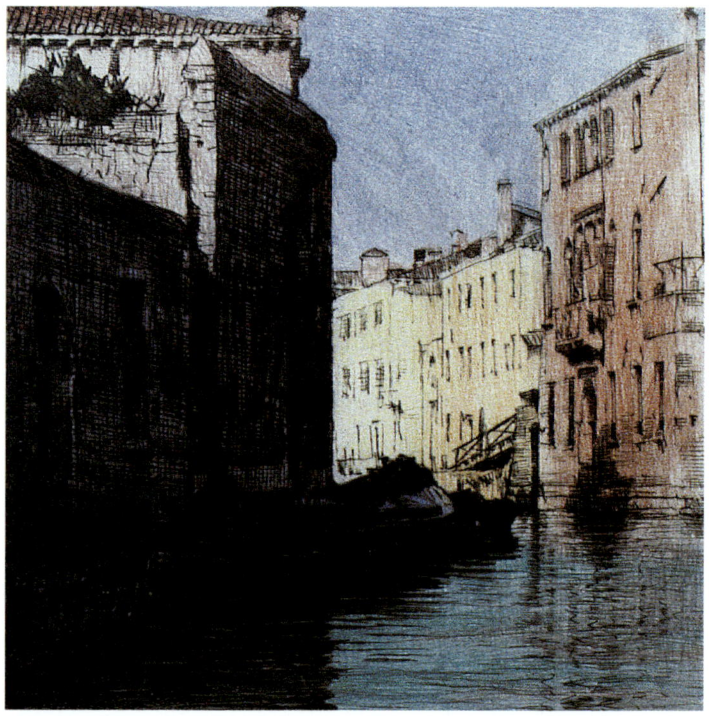

141
Mortimer L. Menpes
Palaces c.1904
Etching 120 x 110 mm, printed in colours
Private Collection

142
James Craig Annan
Riva degli Schiavoni 1894
Photogravure 107 x 147 mm
Scottish National Portrait Gallery

a challenge to Whistler. It contained portraits and detailed studies of architectural details which showed his skill as a draughtsman and printmaker, as well as prints which deliberately paralleled Whistler's. Cameron's etching *Church Interior, Venice* (R.219), for instance, is comparable in composition to Whistler's *The Beggars* (K.194) and his *Venice from the Lido* (fig.144), like Annan's photogravure of the same title (fig.145), echoes Whistler's *Little Venice* (K.183).

These prints, published in sets, carefully presented and exhibited, do not reproduce Whistler's work but build on its foundation. Through Annan, the influence of Whistler was transmitted to other photographers, including Stieglitz and Alvin Langdon Coburn. The prints of Cameron and Annan are the finest homage paid by two great printmakers to Whistler, a great master of the nineteenth century.

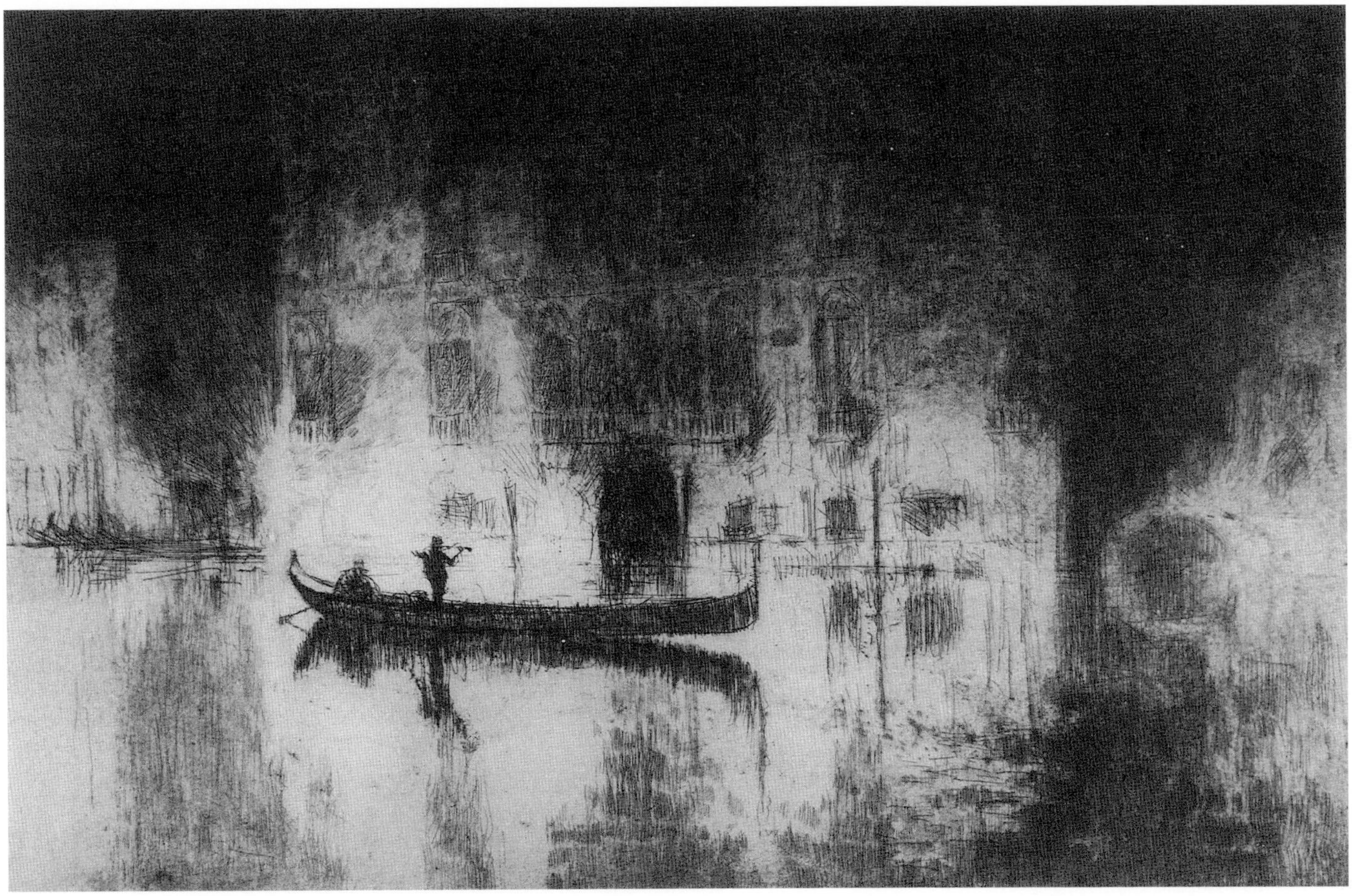

143
James McBey
Venetian Night 1925
Etching 273 x 445 mm
Aberdeen Art Gallery

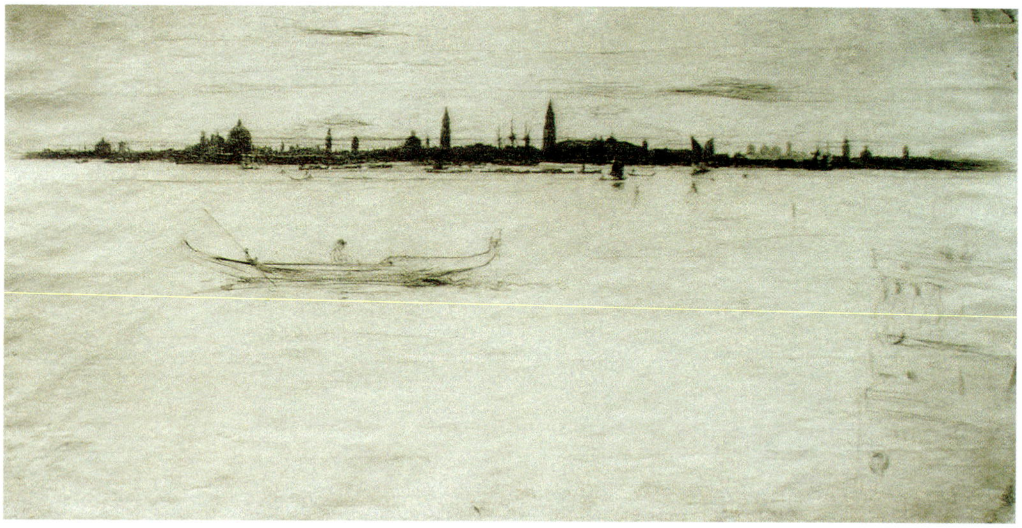

144
David Y. Cameron
Venice from the Lido 1894
Etching 176 x 350 mm
Private Collection, R.220

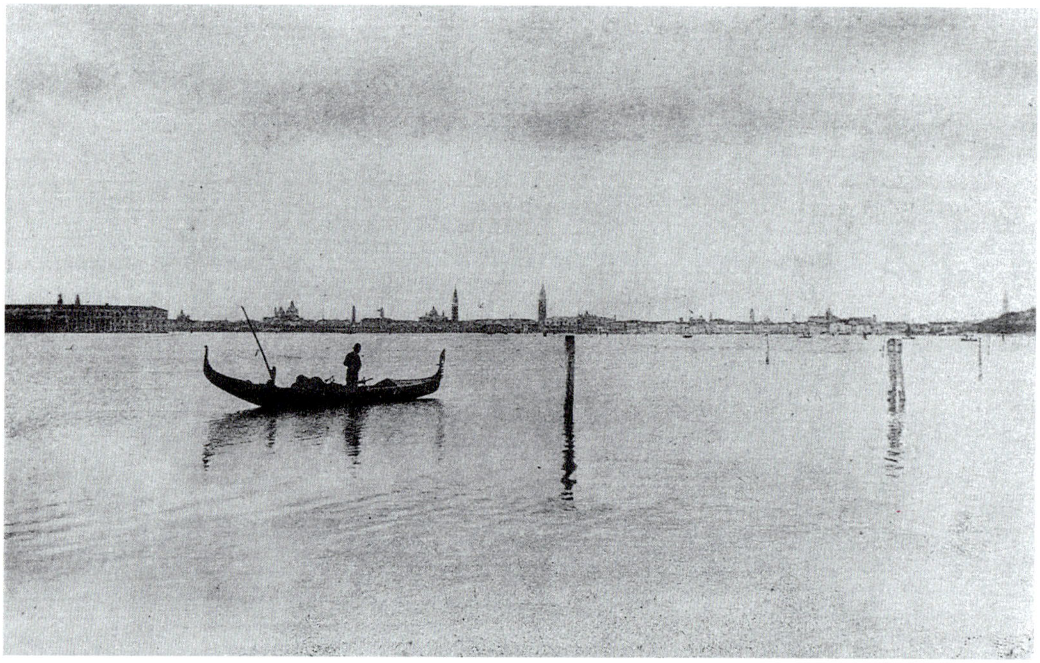

145
James Craig Annan
Venice from the Lido 1894
Photogravure 97 x 150 mm
Scottish National Portrait Gallery

1 Whistler to Grimani, Mayor of Venice, nd. [1898?], Archivio Biennale, Venice.
2 Whistler 1890, p.144.
3 *Oil Paintings, Water Colors, Pastels and Drawings: Memorial Exhibition of the Works of Mr J. McNeill Whistler*, Copley Society, Copley Hall, Boston, Feb 1904; *Memorial Exhibition of the Works of the late James McNeill Whistler*, New Gallery, London, Feb–April 1905; *Oeuvres de James McNeill Whistler*, Palais de l'Ecole des Beaux-Arts, Paris, May 1905; *Aquarellen, Pastels, Teekeningen, Etsen, Lithographieën en eene Schilderij door James MacNeill [sic] Whistler*, Kundstkring, Rotterdam, Oct–Nov 1906.
4 Blum's etching, *Venetian Canal and Bridges*, British Museum (1906-2-28-11), shows the same scene as Whistler's pastel, *The Bridge; flesh colour and brown* (M.759); Bacher's etching *Bead-Stringers*, New York Public Library, shows the square seen in Whistler's *Old Women* (K.224). See Grieve 2000, pp.47, 132–3.
5 The work of Joseph Pankiewicz and other etchers is discussed by Irena Kossowska, 'Whistlerian Inspirations in Graphic Works of Polish Modernists', in *Ars Longa: prace dedykowane pramieci profesora Jana Biadostockiego: materialy Sesji Stowazyszenia Historyków Sztuki*, Warsaw, 1999, pp.442–66. I am grateful to M. Hopkinson for this reference.
6 Getscher 1977–8, pp.275–6.
7 'The New Life of Whistler', *Fortnightly Review*, XC, 1 Dec 1908, pp.1017–28; in Sitwell 1947, pp.12–13.
8 'Abjuro', *The Art News*, 3 Feb 1910; in Sitwell 1947, pp.12–13.
9 Annan interviewed in 1896, see W. Buchanan, *The Art of the Photographer J. Craig Annan 1864–1946*, Edinburgh, National Galleries of Scotland, 1992, pp.14–18.
10 Alfred Maskell, 'The new photograph', *Studio*, IV, Oct 1894, p.33, repr.; F. Rinder, *D.Y. Cameron, An illustrated catalogue of his etched work*, Glasgow, 1912, cat.no.209.

11 Letters from Venice

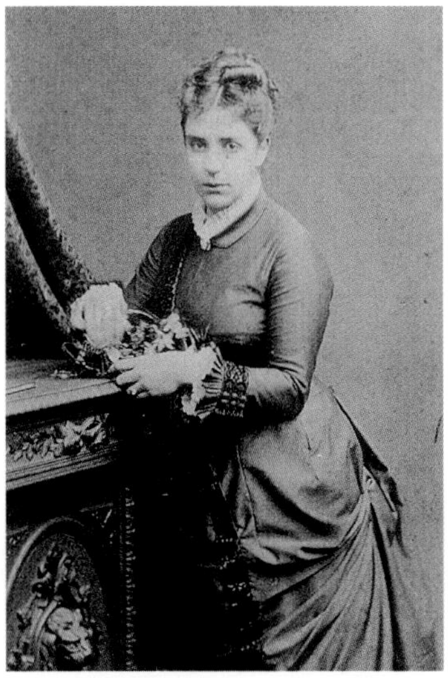

146
Helen Whistler
Photograph 1880s
Glasgow University Library

Whistler's letters home reveal his feelings, record his progress, and show his response to Venice as a city and subject.

1. Soon after his arrival he wrote to Helen, wife of his brother, Dr William Whistler:[1]

> I meant to have answered your wee little note my dear Nellie long ago – directly it reached me in short – which is long ago I am sorry to say – mea culpa! mea culpa Nellie ! – but dont think on the other hand that it is quite all the way you suggest –
>
> You propose to be shocked at my silence and withold the choice scraps from the newspapers until I write – while really it was you who owed me a letter – for surely you must have had my two notes of adieu before I left England – I certainly wrote to bid you both Goodbye – and certainly expected to find here at the Poste Restante an answer or rather a jolly letter full of amiable things and little tit bits of scandal about Godwin – or Holland Park – "various" –[2] I went and asked for one whether or no, and was quite disappointed when the man said there was nothing of the kind for me – Italian my dear Nellie is a poor language – We have not been brought up to believe so but it is – so – and for that reason only – I shall not come back speaking it fluently – Beside Spanish it is mean – and strangely enough it appeals to me not at all – and now that it has taken to snowing I begin rather to wish myself back in my own lovely London fogs! They are lovely those fogs – and I am their painter! – Of course you know Venice is superb and if I hadn't dined horribly today – and yesterday too – and the day before for the matter of that, nothing could induce me to speak the truth and acknowledge that I am bored to death after a certain time away from Piccadilly! – I pine for Pall Mall and I long for a hansom! – The fact is the food of this country is fowl! – Chickens I have had roast and chickens I have had boiled – chickens in the pot many days old until neither the birds themselves nor their eggs are any longer tolerable. I went out the other night and bought for gold some tea – and tried to make a certain curious fat do for the bacon Mrs Cossins used to send up on the silver dish now ...... well well never mind where it is – dear funny old Mrs Cossins! little Watts used to say he always liked her when she was very drunk![3] and I scarcely thought I should ever look back myself with affection for her! [...] Dr Reid I saw for a moment on his way to Egypt.[4] Do you write Nellie and tell us a lot of everything – I shall be so delighted to get back! – The etchings are of course very swell – but one is frozen out and so I am still behind hand with them! It is of a cold you have no idea – cold way beyond anything I know in London – ice and snow all over the place – lovely though – but upon the whole I think it is more beautiful in the rain! however I will tell you all that when I get back – don't expect me yet though – Willie might look in at the Fine Art Society and pick up any gossip – I have never written them a line and doubt not they are very anxious – Now Goodbye – and much love to both – I suppose you will write to the Mummie directly – and so tell her how glad I was to have the woollen cuffs, which I popped on then and there – [...]
>
> Again with love to all
> Your affectionate brother
> Jim

2. Whistler's first letter to his beloved half-sister, Deborah Delano Haden, written on 1 January 1880:[5]

You are too nice and kind my dear little Sis and I got both your letters and enjoyed them as you may well imagine – and frozen I am and certainly feel that I also should live in conservatories with flowers and pines and the other luxuries that one is naturally meant for – the most charming people to say delightful things to you and in every way this absurd and ridiculous poverty effaced! – there! these are my sentiments – and I offer them to you on this New Year while je te la 'souhaite bonne et heureuse' and you must pass on to the dear Mother and Nellie this greeting from the generally-misunderstood-though-well-meaning-yet-difficult-to-explain brother Jim! – [...] There are some Reillys here with Lady Rowden who I believe sent me a cutting from the Daily News with a description of Xmas day in London in which it was regretted that Whistler should be etching in Venice instead of painting the fog so worthy of him at home! – There is but one thing that consoles me in my numbed state here and that is the total darkness you seem to live in over there – Of course if things were as they ought to be all would fit in well and I should be resting happily in the only city in the world fit to live in, instead of struggling on in a sort of Opera Comique country when the audience is absent and the Season is over! – I said the other night to the horror of the few listeners at the consul's where on me veut du bien though I fancy I am a trial, that an artist's only possible virtue is idleness! – and there are so few who are gifted with it. – Quite true – isn't it? – you understand me I am sure – you who see so many flooding the place with their vicious work. Look at the 'Uncle Johns' who rest on the Sunday as I once heard him say and who sin all the week as I told him – Ah well! nous ne sommes pas ici pour nous amuser – though I really believe we are, and the mistake is with the dull ones who arrange life for "us others" – they say this is right – and that is wrong – and know not – and we are poor when we ought [to] be rich, that we might sing and our songs not reek of the sweat of the brow, which they like and which is horrid and offensive like themselves – I shall bring back some things though I fancy that will delight a few – among others (I may confide in you) – myself! – at last! – [...] Tell Nellie I have received the World all right so far – by the way have you seen the Xmas number? but I wish Willie would forward them regularly now every week for I lend them to the Harrises (American Consuls) – Well Goodbye Sis – with much love to Annie,[6] and the nicest things to all – I know there will be a lot I shall think of directly I have sent this off – but I shall say it in my next to Nellie – probably tomorrow – probably not! I hear you say –
Always affectionately
Jimmie
Oh I shall look for the glass things Nellie and Miss Caird want[7]

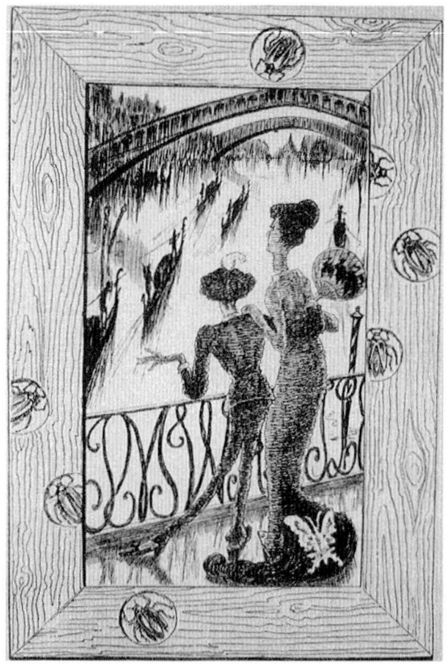

147
'Ididdlia on the Grand Canal'
The World, Christmas Number, 1879
Glasgow University Library

3. This letter was written to Whistler's sister-in-law, Helen, early in 1880:[8]

I hear that it is mild Spring over there with you my dear Nellie – while here the cold is fiercer than ever – and I am just a little down on my back for the moment – The native doctor has been and I am to gargle a throat that I am sure Willie would have stopped with nitrate of Silver – I have been working too hard, though keeping in tolerable health and spirits – but the cold has simply been quietly getting into my bones and so now I have to stay in for a couple of days – Every body seems to think that I have achieved wonderful results and that I might well rest for a while – but I am so impatient – However I am getting together things that are certainly very jolly and must mean gold – As to the etchings they are far away beyond the old ones – only I am barely able to touch a plate – litteraly [sic] – it is like ice – and for the last two months and more it has been the same thing – No winter like this known for at least thirty years, and at last I am getting very much depressed – By the way ask Willie if he tolerates 'Extract of Malt' – an English preparation which I have found really wonderful – for coughs and various – and very pleasant

to take – I wish I had some of those throat pastes of his though – couldn't you send me a few in the next World!! – . – . Of course you had my letter for Sis, and I wrote the other day to Way[9] – he will doubtless lend Willie the letter – so that altogether I don't think I am doing so badly in my new role of foreign correspondent – Now it is for all of you in your turn to write me lots of news and if you can find no scandal you must invent some – [...] Aleco you tell me is superb:[10] when I come home perhaps he may require some of the lovelinesses I bring with me – However I doubt much if they will go a begging this time – But I am not well tonight and just a leetle blue – don't be alarmed though for the doctor seemed to make light of it – Tell us about your Christmas – You went down I know to the Mother's – and how is she? – I went to a grand high mass in St Marcs and very swell it all was – but do you know I couldn't help feeling that the Peacock Room is more beautiful in its effect! – and certainly the glory and delicacy of the ceiling is far more complete than the decorations of the golden domes make them – That was a pleasant frame of mind to be in you will acknowledge – and I am sure you are not surprised at it! – I really rather thought that Elden owed me a letter – but when I next write it will I think be to him – Tell Ridley[11] when you see him that I hope he is keeping the printing press in good working order – for when I come back I shall retire to his studio to print all my proofs – [...] Has Willie seen Sutherland lately? – he should tell him that of course I had expected all sorts of attentions on the part of the P. and O. company resulting from instructions from head quarters – and am disappointed simply – [...]
Goodbye Nellie – With best love to both and all –
Ever affectionately
J A McN Whistler –

You will be glad to hear that I am now pretty well out of my cold again and my throat is nearly well [...]

4. Whistler wrote to Marcus Bourne Huish of the Fine Art Society in reply to a letter dated 14 January 1880:[12]

My dear Mr Huish –
I am shocked out of all my usual impassiveness by the suggestion I have this instant read with horror in your letter, that I could be neglecting the work, for which I had exiled myself, in order to trifle with plates, whose exaggerated size, not only partook of the character so generally accorded to all Howellian[13] assertion, but would have been proof enough in itself – were any needed – of the unlikelihood of the story! –
Little Mr Brown would have told you how Mr Whistler holds in contempt & derision the "big plate" – the advertisement of the ignorant – the inevitable pitfall of the amateur –

I am even astonished that Howell himself – in his desire to make statements – should have missed this tip – as he has often heard me scoff at the vulgarity of the pretence – and point out the gross condition of brain that could tolerate the offensive disproportion between the delicate needle of the etcher and the monster plate to be covered! – Perceive how inartistic is the undertaking – based as it is on the dullness which distinguishes not between mastery of manner, and "muchness" of matter! – From this pente ridicule the painter's science saves him – he <u>knows</u> that the dimensions of the work <u>must</u> be always in relation to the means used – and reaching the limit, unerringly lays aside the needle for the brush, that he may not find himself worming his weary way across a waste of copper – all quality lost – all joy of execution gone – nothing remaining but the doleful task for the dreary industry of the foolish – the virtue of the duffer! – Behold now the hardy though unconscious Amateur! – He hesitates not! – and so we have heads the size of soup plates – and landscapes like luncheon trays – while lines are bitten furiously until in the impression they stand out like the knotted veins on his own unthinking brow –

Poor meek Rembrant! – with his mild miniatures – beside such colossal deeds how dwarfed he becomes! how uninteresting his puny portraits of diminutive Burgomaster Siegmund Clement de Young – how weak his little windmill[14] ...... Ah well! nous avons changé tout celà! – ... But this is not a letter! – I shall find myself in the midst of another pamphlet so by the way you had better carefully keep this – for who knows – I may borrow it for an extract[15] – Meanwhile I am not sorry that in this moment of your anxiety you should find me enunciating theories and offering doctrines as a means of reference – for I wish you to see in this very preoccupation and certainty in what concerns my work a reason for rejecting doubtful suggestions from outsiders – The "Venice" my dear Mr Huish will be superb – and you may double your bets all round – only I can't fight against the Gods – with whom I am generally a favorite – and not come to grief – so that now – at this very moment – I am an invalid and a prisoner – because I rashly thought I might hasten matters by standing in the snow with a plate in my hand and an icicle on the end of my nose. – I was ridiculous – the Gods saw it and sent me to my room in disgrace. – For two weeks, with an ulcerated throat and a native doctor, have I been fought over by an attached friend with a faith in homœopathy – though an architect by profession – perhaps because an architect. – Sly doses of Aconite have counteracted gargles until at length refusing further experiments, I have asserted my right as a wreck – and now comes your letter of reproach. – I have not written to you for I hate writing – and couldn't tell you anything that you didn't already well know – Have you not read how the people in Monté Carlo fled before the snow – shrieking with fear at the unknown miracle? How Mount Vesuvius is frozen inside – and nothing but icicles come out? – How here in Venice there has been a steady hardening of every faculty belonging to the painter for the last two months and a half at least – during which time you might as well have proposed to etch on a block of Wenham Lake as to have done anything with a copperplate that involves holding it! Nevertheless be comfortable Huish – and put on an air of ease when you appear among the questioning philistines and unbelievers generally – for it is a good thing to have gone in for and will pay splendidly in the end – and after all it is even "for the best" that this inclemency should have interfered – for had there been nothing but ordinary weather to deal with, your twelve plates would have been finished & I should have been back in London before I had at all known the mine of wealth for both you and me in this place – You see when I promised to come here and complete a set of etchings within a given time, I undertook a Herculean task without knowing it – but as far as the mere plates went doubtless I should have carried out my contract had not Providence interfered greatly to the advantage of us both – and now I have learned to know a Venice in Venice that the others never seem to have perceived, and which, if I bring back with me as I propose will far more than compensate for all annoyances delays & vexations of spirit – Of course I should have found you something new in any case – but it would not have been so complete – and the trouvaille would not have been such a mine of wealth as I shall manage to make it – I have not been idle you may be sure – The etchings themselves are more delicate in execution, more beautiful in subject and more important in interest than any of the old set – Then I shall bring fifty or sixty if not more pastels totaly [sic] new and of a brilliancy very different from the customary watercolor – and will sell – I don't see how they can help it – But then my dear Huish the revers de la medaille: – I am frozen – and have been for months – and you cant hold a needle with numbed fingers – and beautiful work cannot be finished in bodily agony – also I am starving – or shall be soon – for it must be amazing even to you that I should have made my money last this long –

You had better send me fifty pounds at once and trust to a thaw which will put us all right – If I come back with pictures drawings and etchings the expedition will have exceeded beyond all hope and each item will go to increase the value of the other –

Please write and address, Café Florian, Place St. Marc. Venice –

[butterfly signature] Very sincerely Yours
J A McN. Whistler

The 57th day of hard unrelenting frost! Venetian method of counting – Send for Howell and read him my letter! –

5. On 26 January 1880 Whistler writes to his friend Charles Augustus Howell, nicknamed 'Owl' both because that was the cockney pronunciation of Howell and he was a wise old nightbird:[16]

It appears my dear old Owl that you are alive and of course kicking – kicking naturally! – How is the Show?[17] [...]

"Various" is going on amazingly here and I propose to bring back what will delight you – As to etchings I am the kind of thing that out swaggers all the collection – only mon cher I am frozen! – and I scarcely know exactly when I can finish [...] But tell us about yourself – What programe [sic] is there – and would you like to run anything? – I wish I could show you some of the lovely pastels I have done! I told you I should discover something new and of course you may be sure that a fresh condition of things have I stirred up – Money must come in this time without fail – You know this would be superb for your show – if you could only manage to work something here! – First the absence of cabs would make you a small income of itself – and then living is amazing – Arks could be moored and shows propped up on eighteenpence – For the rest "Various" is rife and Palma Vechio's for Leyland and his kind to be had for fivers or less – Seriously Venice is not to be neglected – and now that I have taken the habit of voyaging I don't see why Lisboa and the rest of it should not be turned to account – I tell you old chap that I am bound to turn everything I touch now into gold – I can't help it – The work I do is lovely and these others fellows have no idea! no distant idea! of what I see with certainty – Mind I shall not come back with sketches of Venice after the manner of Philip's [sic] return with sketches of Spain[18] – the whole thing with me will be just a continuation of my own art work, some portions of which complete themselves in Venice –

Now what in thunder have you been saying in Bond Street! – Huish has just written – quite upset by some report you have spread in his place to the effect of my working upon some huge plate not for him – not in the set! – How can you yield to this mania of yours? Why must you always go about inventing things – In this particular case too I should never have supposed you could have had the want of wisdom! – dropping matches about in my show! – However I have given you h— ! You go and ask Huish to read you my letter – It is too bad – when I am really working like a nigger and risking my health in the cold – Never mind – I will forgive you if you write me a long volume of yarns – Besides we all know you can't help it – so what is the use – –

… Give my kindest regards to Mrs Howell and my Goddaughter[19] – how is she? – I shall not forget your little black gondola […] I wrote the other day to Way – and shall write to Elden in a day or two – Now Goodbye – La bonne année to you all
Ever Yours
J A McN Whistler.
Always address to me Café Florian –
Place St Marc. Venice – [butterfly signature]

6. A business letter, to Ernest G. Brown, assistant manager of the Fine Art Society:[20]

Dear Mr Brown –
I forgot in my letter to Mr Huish to say that you might well send me some pieces of old Dutch paper for in Venice nothing can be had of any kind – You might see to this yourself for me as you know what I like – Where to look for it I can't exactly tell you – but perhaps Goulding may have some – You ought to send me about 20 or 30 pieces – rolled up properly and sent by post would be the way – Mr Way has sent me some Japanese paper and it arrived quite safely and in good condition – he had rolled it in a large Christmas number of the World – indeed he tells me that he has thought out some other safe method – so you might consult with him – for it would be a great pity if anything were to happen to what I value so much. Try and get me some of the tone and size of that on which the Putney Bridge was printed[21] –

The printing business itself is very primitive and difficult here and on another pilgrimage of the kind I should certainly bring out my own press –

Also pop a couple of little balls of varnish – ("etching ground" the proper name – and you get them at Hughes & Kimber, West Harding Street, Chancery Lane) into a little pasteboard box and send it by post –

While you are about it send 3 and a small bottle of "Stopping Out varnish". Quite a small one will do, for I still have some – you had better put it in a little flat one that will pack nicely – and then put it in a neat little wooden box which would be safer – and send by Post –

Always address Café Florian Place St. Marc – Venice.

If you think of any little news don't think that it will be uninteresting so pray write me anything you can remember in the way of "Etching and Etchers" –
Very truly yours,
J A McN. Whistler
Please lose no time about the varnish and paper –

7. Whistler to Helen Whistler, written in late February or March 1880:[22]

My dear Nellie
I do hope the Mother is better – and that you will write me at once another nice letter to say so – I got off a letter to Elden last night which as I had forgotten his address I sent to your care – Tell him to be sure and put his address on his answer in full – […] Now my dear Nellie I fell asleep over all this several times last night as I told you I should, for I do get so worn out after my days work that I am quite unfit for anything – This must go now as I know you are all anxious for my answer – Elden will read you what I have said about my work – for by dint of writing a scrap now and then I have told him something about it […] Well things are terribly provoking here with the hard bitter weather against which I can make very little head way – but I do hope when I get back to make a nice little haul of guineas and then I might be able to help my weeny bit towards the general merriment of the show where I was for such a long time so pleasantly entertained and tolerated

– The pastels you know Nellie I verily believe will be irresistable [sic] to buyers – in them I have found what Elden would call "the game" – as far as the pocket goes – I assure you the people – painter fellows – here, who have seen them are quite startled at their brilliancy – Besides you will be delighted with them yourself, and we shall have such a jolly time looking them all over – I have ordered the frames through the Fine Arts Society – so that they shall be all ready when I come – and we can put them in together – Dear me how I look forward to that day – If all goes well we might frame them all first and then have Huish round to breakfast with Elden and make a swell show afterwards – Oh and then the etchings – and hmm! .... something too perhaps for the Grosvenor ... who knows – and I shall have such a lot to say about the Ruskin lot ... and in short various! and I suppose you will find me very trying! Tell Willie to ask Huish to lend him the letter I wrote to him some time ago in which I had a shot at the Amateurs who do big plates – I need only tell you that it will satisfy even Elden! I wish Willie might find among my papers, my little book of addresses – "Where is it" – and send it to me by Post – also ask Miss Caird, to whom many amiable things, for the number and name of her Gondolier – I have forgotten them – And write at once Nellie and tell me that the Mother is better and tell me all the news [...]
Goodbye – love to the Mother and Sis –
Affectionately – Jimmie

8. Whistler to Helen Whistler:[23]

Well for once my dear Nellie I do not think that your news is as complete as I have always declared it to be! [...] Willie then writes, and upon the falacious plea that "Nellie has told me all the news" limits himself to statements in no way concerning the affair – while Elden from whom at least I still hoped – doesn't write at all! [...] Of course you have seen Miss Caird and heard all about her visit here! – also how amazed I was at suddenly seeing her – without the slightest preparing hint from you – for Willie's post card – and why post card? – only came the day after – She will tell you though – and you must write me an account of the tea taking and chatting and all – and anything else you can possibly think of – for you know I always look forward to your letters as the most perfect of the lot! – Do try and tell us all the scandal you know and any tit bits about everybody – for I am just a wee bit down again in comparison – A superb chap I had posing for me must needs get an awful cold, fall into the hands of a couple of the native doctors, who discover pleurisy or pneumonia or whatever it may be involving lungs and thereupon bleed him to within an inch of his life! The priest is sent for and he is going to leave me, with my unfinished picture, for another and a cheaper world when I come in one morning and give him a milk punch, throw open the windows and let in the sun which happened not to be frozen at the moment and persuade him to stay – but it will be some time before he is off his bed poor fellow – and my swell Gondolier must wait![24] – It is well nothing has been said about it – However you know I am irrepressible – and so have started something else – [...] – and could stay here forever only I am so homesick! – Never mind – all this is between you and me – and I daresay by the time I get another letter from Wimpole St – I shall be all jolly again. Huish is preparing fifty frames! for the pastels which are, and remain even in my present depression, lovely! Just think fifty – complete beauties! – and something so new in Art that every body's mouth will I feel pretty soon water – Tissot I daresay will try his hand at once – and others too – By the way has Woods called upon you yet? He promised me that he would – Willie would find him though every evening at the Arts Club [...] There is nothing like a good fight! It clears the air – and the only thing is not to have any half measures – for that gives a chance to the enemy who think you are showing signs of timidity, and so gather courage themselves for a general rush against you – The mistake I have sometimes made in my battles is that I have left my man alive! – He invariably gets better and worries you again, or at any rate remains a regret! – What in the world has that old Ass Ruskin been gabbing about now – really I must call him deliberately Ass – nothing else in English so describes him as I feel him to be – and what can dear Mme Coronio think she understands in his prattle![25] Ah well wait till I come back and I will explain this apparently violent language – Don't put off sending my address book Nellie – I want to try and remember a lot of my friends whose names I fear I have forgotten! – The Bronsons by the way have come back and I dined with them last night. They are very nice, and Bronson himself is very funny – Miss Chapman too with them – and very kind in visiting my sick Gondolier – Now Goodbye – This is a long letter again – I am so very glad to know that the Mother is better and I send her a note with this – Tell Elden to write – and any news there may be of Howell let me have –
Love to all –
Ever [Affectionately] Jim –
Tell Elden to address his letters to me Café Florian –

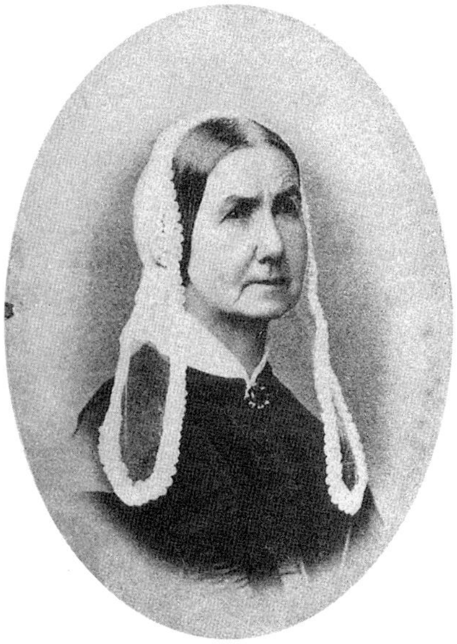

148
Anna McNeill Whistler
Photograph 1870s
Glasgow University Library

9. A rare letter from Whistler to his mother, Anna Matilda McNeill Whistler:[26]

My own dearest Mother –
I have been so grieved to hear of your being ill again – and now I am delighted to hear better news of you – Do not let any anxiety for me at all interfere with your rapidly getting quite well – for I am happy to tell you that my own health is capital and the weather alone in all its uncertainties retards my work – which however is now very nearly complete – so that I look forward to being with you soon. It has been woefully cold here – The bitterest winter I fancy that I ever experienced – and the people of Venice say that nothing of the kind has been known for quite a century – Mrs Bronson was telling me – by the way you will be pleased to hear that they have returned from their wanderings and are now settled in their palace on the Grand Canal – well she has told me that since it was known that she was here, her many pensioners have called to welcome her back and all said to her the same thing – "Look Signora they said, pointing to their white hair, look – I am old – and yet I have never seen such a Winter! – and I only wonder that I have lived through it to tell the Signora!" – At last the ice and snow have left us and now the rain is pouring down upon us! Today reminds me of our stay long ago at Black Gang Chyne![27] – After all though this evening the weather softened slightly and perhaps tomorrow may be fine – and then Venice will be simply glorious, as now and then I have seen it – After the wet, the colors upon the walls and their reflections in the canals are more gorgeous than ever – and with sun shining upon the polished marble mingled with rich toned bricks and plaster, this amazing city of palaces becomes really a fairyland – created one would think especially for the painter – The people with their gay gowns and handkerchiefs – and the many tinted buildings for them to lounge against or pose before, seem to exist especially for one's pictures – and to have no other reason for being! – One could certainly spend years here and never lose the freshness that pervades the place! But I must come back to you all now though – even if I return afterwards – Yes I hope now in a couple of weeks or so to pack all my works and see how the long hoped for etchings will look in London – Also you know, for I daresay Nellie has told you, – that I have fifty pastels! So you see Mother dear that I have not been idle – though I have found my labors terribly trying – It will be pleasant to talk them all over with you when I come back – I shall have plenty to tell you of all the beautiful things I have seen – and I hope you will like some of the pastels I have done – Nellie must tell you about them – They are much admired here – and I think rather well of them myself – though sometimes I get a little despondent – My kind friend Mr Graham whom you remember my writing to you about, has been away for some weeks in Rome – returning only the other day – I was glad to see him for he had been most courteous and persistent in his good services to me – He brought Mr Bronson with him a couple of mornings ago, and very jolly was our meeting – for I always like him – he is most original and amusing – I have dined with the Bronsons since – and they are most amiable and nice – Mrs Bronson who is the most generous woman possible has been so kind to a poor Gondolier I was painting, and who fell ill with dreadful cough and fever – I told her all about him – and she at once had all sorts of nice things made for him – and Miss Chapman[28] who is staying with the Bronsons has been herself to call on poor Giovanni – He is getting well now I hope and will soon be able again to pose for his picture – Mrs Harris the wife of the American Consul has been very charming – always asking me to her house and presenting me to all her best acquaintances – She is a dear old lady and I know you would like her – So you see I have not been without friends Mother, and notwithstanding the fearful climate, not absolutely forlorn and cheerless – I am so glad to hear that everything is happily arranged for Annie's future[29] – Give my love and congratulations to her when you see her, or send them through Sis – And now Goodbye my darling Mother – I do hope you will be quite well and strong again directly now – for I have accounts from England saying that the sun is shining

upon all there and that everything is warm and delightful! [...] I received your nice Christmas card Mama dear – and meant to have written at once to tell you how gratified I was – but it is the same old story my dear Mother I am at my work the first thing at dawn and the last thing at night, and loving you all the while though not writing to tell you [...]
your fond son Jimmie

10. Another letter to Helen Whistler, in which he was chiefly concerned with the fate of paintings left in London:[30]

My dear Nellie –
You are a brick! It is so nice of you to write me such a pleasant little letter, for after all – notwithstanding the lot of discomforting news it contained, it read capitally way out here, and as a proof of my appreciation I am answering it the evening of its arrival – I do hope and trust that the Mother will not be ill again – and dear me I have so meant every day to write but I am worked to death – up in the morning without exageration by half past six and "at it again" – though let me tell you it is bitterly cold still in the early part of the day – But you see I have been so put back by the ice and snow that I try not to lose a moment now – Well then you can easily imagine how utterly done up I am by the end of the day, in the evening I am simply hopelessly stupefied with sleep and fatigue – Hence my "behaviour" – which by the way, on reflection is not so bad as far as you and Willie are concerned for unless I mistake greatly, you owe me a letter! – Strange isn't it! – My last was to you though – or at any rate to Willie – and a good long one too [...] I will tell you more in my next about myself and the lovely things I am going to bring back –

This must go <u>at once</u> – not a moment to lose so Goodbye, with best love to the Mother and yourselves and all.
Ever affectionately yrs
Jim –
It was very nice in you to send me the cutting from the paper about Sara Bernhardt but you can fancy the shock it gave me when I found nothing about my own delightful self!! [...]

11. A letter to a close friend, the artist, Matthew Robinson Elden:[31]

If you only knew the real delight a long letter from you gives me I am sure old fellow you would sit down at once and write me another like the one I have just received – As a general thing people write one very unsatisfactory sort of letters – they have apparently a knack of leaving out or missing altogether the very pith of their news! – They tell you that which they ought not to have told! and they leave untold that which they ought to tell – and there is no joy in them! – so that one puts down their letters always with a "hang it! Why the deuce doesn't he say <u>who</u> or <u>what</u>!!"...! Now you my dear Elden, and my sister Mrs Doctor Willie are both charming and your letters a happiness – In return I have lots to talk to you about – but it is such difficulty to get simply the chance! – I mean the half hour which of course becomes an hour I never can place at either end of the day – for I am working with the kind of wildness that belongs to the sportsman! – I ought to say eagerness – so I am up early and off – and by the end of the day manage more or less to bring back some thing in my bag – and my work is charming to me – most absorbing – the only drawback being still the intense cold! The bitterness of the winter here has been beyond anything unfortunate for me – no – perhaps I am not just right there – for while it has prolonged my stay in Venice, it has opened for me a mine that I might otherwise have left undiscovered – simply rushing back to London with the etchings of infinitely less rare beauty that I doubtless should have completed in a few weeks had I not been made a prisoner by the ice and snow – that now if it would only be amiably warm! – It is so execrably cold! miserably wretchedly cold! and if you only knew how trying that is <u>here</u> – In Chelsea you see one could sit cowering over the fire and remain indifferent to all time lost – but here! When "all outdoors" means lovely work of the most fascinating – with every possible joy thereto attached – golden guineas among others – then you can fancy the rage of the pent up painter! – Now then last week I have stood, with frozen fingers that could scarcely hold needle or chalk, trying to put down what I could not help going out to look at – suffering most acutely but unable to remain in my cage – I can't tell you how intoxicating this place is – I mean it without any exageration [sic] – Lessor's photographs can I am sure give you no idea of Venice.[32] There is work for more than a lifetime in it and a delight in it all. I shall bring you back lots but I am greedy for so much more – I do so wish you were here that I might show you the marvels that wait for me at every turn – Indeed that is the danger of the place – You are perfectly bewildered with the entanglement of beautiful things! You say I will do this and I must do that and I ought to do the other! and if not carefull [sic], it all ends in dizziness and craze! – And mind you, all this while it is not merely the "Views of Venice" or the Streets of Venice, or the "Canals of Venice" such as you have seen brought back by the foolish sketcher – but great pictures that stare you in the face – complete arrangements and harmonies in color & form that are ready and waiting for the one who can perceive –

Dear me! one might pass a lifetime out here – not but what I am most anxious to get back – and am straining every nerve to complete my work and leave – I picture to myself the joy I shall have in showing you my pastels – Seriously I think you can form no idea of their bright beauty – their merry lightness and daintiness – I have today looked them all over and am quite in love with them myself – ! This you may smile at and believe to be nothing new – but I wonder what you will say to the drawing in them all – You can't imagine what I have taught myself by all this – I have worked very well – notwithstanding this awful weather – and shall bring, I hope, sixty pastels – my etchings – (and they are far away in quality beyond the old ones) – and a large painting – but this last you must keep quite for yourself and the doctor – I fancy the pastel business will become quite the fashion – that is lots of chaps will be sure to go in for pastels! We shall have Tissot and co going it.[33] They cant help it! – My dear fellow it is a great find – and we must keep it dark as long as we can – [...] Tell Howell that it will be cruel indeed if he continues this silence! – I wrote to him long ago – and certainly he received my letter as safely as every one else did theirs though doubtless he will explain to me that it never reached him – Go and ask Huish to read you my letter! – You will see what I said about the "big platists"! you will dance with delight [...] Write again at once and I will answer directly – I send this to the Doctor's for you for I have forgotten your exact address –
With kindest regards to all at home,
Always affectionately Yours
[butterfly signature]

12. Whistler wrote to his ten-year-old son, Charles James Whistler Hanson, on 2 May 1880:[34]

My dear little Charley –
I am very much pleased with your pretty letter which proves to me what an industrious nice little gentleman you have been during my long absence. – much longer has it turned out to be than ever I looked forward to – and very anxious am I to get back to you all and hear

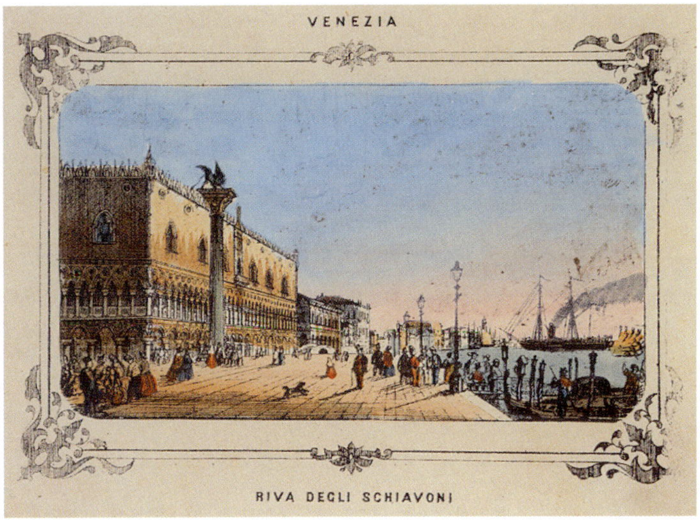

149
Riva degli Schiavoni
Hand-coloured engraving in Whistler's letter to Charles
Glasgow University Library

all the good accounts of you from Auntie Jo and see the tall fellow you have grown – It was very kind in you to send your first letter to me and very much I value it and shall put it away with my treasures – I send you in return a picture of this beautiful city – which much as I am charmed with it, I shall be only too glad to leave at last – possibly I hope within another week or two – but one of these days perhaps I may bring you out here and show you all the lovely things it contains. We will take a row in a gondola – one of the long black boats you see in the corner of the picture and which I think I have drawn better myself! – however you shall judge when you see my etchings and pastels – If your uncle Charley come too, I will teach him how to manage a Gondola – very different it is to his outrigger – and two or three Americans who have tried that sort of thing have fallen off into the canal! – I should have been home long ago had it not been for the terrible winter which has prevented my working – the weather has been of a severity unknown for centuries – snow and cold which has now given place to wind and rain so that I am still prevented completing my plates – Tell uncle Charlie what I am sure he will be pleased to hear that notwithstanding all this, I have worked very hard, and bring back with me a perfect gallery of beautiful pastel drawings – about sixty in all – which I fancy will represent nearly a thousand pounds! – The frames are already ordered and by this time probably made in London – where the collection will doubtless be exhibited – probably at the Fine Arts Society in Bond Street – Every body who has seen them here is very much struck by them and all acknowledge that I have found some thing quite new and entirely different from any views of Venice ever done before – Also the etchings are much finer and more important than the old ones – so that we may hope for a success at last that will repay for all this time and trouble –

I am so glad my dear boy to know that you are doing so well with your studies and are so obedient and attentive to your kind Auntie Jo – Tell her with my love that she must expect a letter from me at once – as I shall write tomorrow – indeed often would I have written to you all had I not each day been such a slave to my work – I get up Charlie every morning at six and labor away until dark. – and now my dear boy with much love to you all
Goodbye – Your fond papa
J A McN.Whistler –
[butterfly signature]

13. A letter from Whistler to his brother, William Gibbs Whistler, and sister-in-law, announces his imminent return:[35]

Dear Willie & Nellie –
Two words for I am awfully pressed –

I think I shall turn up at last in about a couple of weeks! .... – only keep it dark and on the strict QT. – for I dont want any body to know until I am in full blaze – I shall bring only my etchings – and my pastels – the pictures later on –

It is the result of letter from Huish – there is to be great Etching Game in Bond Street shortly – the Twelve greatest living etchers! though as I said to him where [the] devil do they all come from – and I have promised to turn up on condition that of course I have the centre of the whole thing for myself! – It will be great fun – and also a capital rentrée for me! – Huish is to be quiet about my return and the painter chaps are to suppose that things are unsatisfactory in Venice – But if Ridley is in town then you may tell him in strict confidence – and he must get the press ready and in perfect working order – having oils for ink and boards for pressing proofs all nicely prepared for me for I shan't have a day to lose –
love to both & all – [...]
Yours Affectly –
Jim –

Love to the Mother, I shall write to her at once –
What of Elden? Did you read him my letter –
Do get Nellie to write now a good cackly letter with <u>all</u> the bits in it – [...]

14. Whistler's last letter from Venice was written to M. B. Huish on 25 October 1880:[36]

The "Fine Arts Society" my dear Huish is, I suppose, a serious body, and has its own inscrutable reasons for its mysterious proceedings –

The Gentlemen of the board doubtless "know what they are about" in losing the ship for the proverbial ha'porth of tar – but to my unbusinesslike organisation they appear simply mad! with due deference be it said – and, if not too much to prophecy I should fancy their future reflections to be of the nature of the postprandial regrets of the saddened philosopher who said "There is a right way of doing a thing – and there is a wrong way – and (hic!) begad I've missed em both". – Understand clearly that I absolve you from all responsibility in the mismanagement of this matter – I really believe that the Committee are, as you say, united in their opposition – and if the fifty pounds are your own venture, I can only thank you for the courteous belief in my success that they show – and I regret for your sake that they are of no more use to me than Mr Montague Tigg's[37] "ridiculously small amount of eighteen pence." – and Messrs Blümenthal[38] had better return them to you at once –

I told you in my letter that I required £100 – and that "I could not do with less" – Did the Committee think I was joking?

I have, my dear Huish, scarcely the patience sufficient for this letter – Please to remember that since the <u>3rd. of February</u> I have not had a penny from the "Fine Arts Society" – and that, while working for their profit during these ten months, I struggled with all vexing difficulties, rather than ask for the assistance it should have been their duty and their pride to have extended, until the end – and now that I am ready to bring them a result far exceeding all their expectations, let me say it advisedly – they in return for this delicacy refuse me the means of leaving this place honorably and decently – and so destroy their own chances at the moment of triumphant success –

It is really incredible! – "The fool knoweth not his way to the City" – and for once I see Soloman's [sic] application to the hesitating business man –

What is the real meaning of this Exhibition of yours if it be not the production of your new publication? – I saw and entered warmly into your plan – The Venetian Etchings were to be the centre of the whole thing – and never could there have been a better arrangement for showing them in all their freshness & novelty than surrounded as they would have been – You rely on my cooperation and I would not have failed you – Why my good Huish I should have brought 40 etchings as an answer to your appeal – 40 etchings far exceeding in quality all that I had hitherto done – Yes – you backed me – and I meant to win for you – but at the last minute you hedge and save .... the peck of oats that might have gained you the race. –

What an amazing concentration of consistency is a "Company"! – Not a day to be lost, say you – and here you keep me still scribbling letters – "Gird up your loins – pay your hotel bill" – (how devilish lucky I didn't ask for it!) – "and bring me a boat load of plates" – and then you scuttle the boat that was to bring them.

Now there is no use writing more – the Game is up – I have labored for you with a devotion and absorption and a faith in yourselves that precluded my attending better to my own interests – having all the while only the perfection of the work in view – and I have had to deal with a body that has utterly failed to understand me – You yourself personally, have been charming – and I feel that we shall always stand well in each others consideration –

Kindly use your influence – though I fear you have but little – with the Committee to still refrain from seizing the parcel in your hands as security, for at least one month from this date – and meanwhile I propose refunding the £200 – advanced by the Society – with interest as agreed upon –

Always very sincerely Yours,
J. A. McN. Whistler
Monday – Venice Oct 25. 1880 –

P. S. I could quite understand the Fine Arts Society never engaging themselves with me at all – but, as a mere matter of curiosity, explain to me my dear Huish, the wisdom of their breaking with me now that the work is done –

1 Nd. [Nov/Dec 1879], GUL W680.
2 Collectors, like the Ionides, Coronios and Prinseps, and artists, like Leighton, Watts, Albert Moore, Fildes, and J. B. Yeats, lived in Holland Park, Kensington.
3 Probably Walter Théodore Watts (later Watts-Dunton), solicitor, novelist and poet.
4 Possibly Adam Scott Reid, surgeon, active in the Afghan war, 1879–80, and the Indian Medical Department in Bengal in 1881.
5 GUL H20.
6 Annie Harriet Haden, later Mrs Charles Thynne; Whistler's niece.
7 Miss Caird, a friend of the Leylands, posed to Whistler in the 1870s. The 'glass' would have been Murano glassware.
8 Nd. [late Jan/Feb 1880], GUL W681. This echoes Whistler's letter to Howell on 26 Jan 1880 (see below), although 'Spring' suggests a later date.
9 Thomas Way, lithographer.
10 Alexander ('Aleco') Ionides, businessman and patron.
11 Matthew White Ridley, painter and etcher.
12 Nd. [21/26 Jan 1880], GUL LB3/8.
13 Whistler wrote on the same subject to C. A. Howell (see below).
14 Rembrandt's *Clement de Jonghe* (1651, B.272) and *The Windmill* (1641, B.233).
15 This letter was refined, published as 'Propositions' with the 'Second Venice Set', *A Set of Twenty-six Etchings*, by Messrs Dowdeswell in 1886 and again in Whistler 1890, pp.76–7.
16 GUL LB 12/39, dated by postmark.
17 'Show', a term for business.
18 John 'Spanish' Phillip, artist.
19 Frances Kate ('Kitty') Howell, née Howell, cousin and wife of C. A. Howell and her daughter, Rosalind Blanche Catherine (b.1877).
20 Nd. [26/29 Jan 1880], GUL LB 9/1
21 *Old Putney Bridge* (K178) published by the FAS in 1879.
22 GUL W683. The original letter is lost and this is a typescript copy.
23 Nd. [20 Feb/March 1880], GUL W684.
24 *A Gondolier* (YMSM 216) was never completed.
25 Aglaia Coronio, née Ionides, wife of George Coronio.
26 Nd. [March/May 1880], copies, GUL LB 4/19–22, W559; Thorp 1994, pp.65–8, no.23.
27 His mother took her boys to the gorge called Black Gang Chine on the Isle of Wight in July 1848 (see M.20).
28 Possibly Rose, sister of Alfred Chapman, from Liverpool.
29 On 8 June 1880 Annie Haden married Charles Thynne.
30 Nd. [22 March 1880], GUL W682; dated from postmark; see YMSM 88–9.
31 Nd. [15/30 April 1880], GUL E61.
32 See preface, fig.2.
33 Jacques Joseph ('James') Tissot, painter and etcher.
34 GUL H55. Charlie was staying with Whistler's ex-mistress Joanna Hiffernan and her sister Agnes, who was living with, and later married, C. J. Singleton, at 5 Thistle Grove off the old Brompton Road, South Kensington. Charlie was not related to them.
35 Nd. [19/26 Oct 1880], GUL W988.
36 GUL F44; two drafts of the letter have survived, GUL F42–3.
37 Montague Tigg was a confidence trickster in Charles Dickens' *The Life and Adventures of Martin Chuzzlewit*, London, 1843–4.
38 Bankers in Venice.

Appendix: Whistler's Work in Venice

Etchings: *Venice, a Series of Twelve Etchings*, the 'First Venice Set', was published by the Fine Art Society in 1880; *Twenty-six Etchings*, the 'Second Venice Set', by Messrs Dowdeswell in 1886.

Title	Published
Little Venice (K.183)	1881
Nocturne (K.184)	1881
The Little Mast (K.185)	1881
The Little Lagoon (K.186)	1881
The Palaces (K.187)	1881
The Doorway (K.188)	1881
The Piazzetta (K.189)	1881
The Traghetto, No.1 (K.190)	–
The Traghetto, No. 2 (K.191)	1881
The Riva, No.1 (K.192)	1881
Two Doorways (K.193)	1881
The Beggars (K.194)	1881
The Mast (K.195)	1881
Doorway and Vine (K.196)	1886
San Biagio (K.197)	1886
Bead-Stringers (K.198)	1886
Turkeys (K.199)	1886
Fruit-Stall (K.200)	1886
San Giorgio (K.201)	1886
Nocturne: Palaces (K.202)	1886
Long Lagoon (K.203)	1886
The Bridge (K.204)	1886
Upright Venice (K.205)	1886
The Riva, No.2 (K.206)	1886
The Balcony (K.207)	1886

Title	Published
Fishing-Boat (K.208)	1886
Ponte del Piovan (K.209)	1886
Garden (K.210)	1886
The Rialto (K.211)	1886
Long Venice (K.212)	1886
Nocturne: Furnace (K.213)	1886
Quiet Canal (K.214)	1886
La Salute: Dawn (K.215)	1886
Lagoon: Noon (K.216)	1886
Glass-Furnace, Murano (K.217)	–
Fish-Shop, Venice (K.218)	–
The Dyer (K.219)	–
Little Salute (K.220)	–
Wool-Carders (K.221)	–
Islands (K.222)	–
Nocturne: Shipping (K.223)	–
Old Women (K.224)	–
Stables (K.225)	–
Nocturne: Salute (K.226)	–
Gondola under a bridge (K.227)	–
The Steamboat, Venice (K.228)	–
Shipping, Venice (K.229)	–
Venetian Court (K.230)	–
Venice (K.231)	–
Venetian Water-Carrier (K.232)	–
The Smithy (K.240)	–

Drawings, Pastels and Watercolours: This list is based on M. F. MacDonald's *James McNeill Whistler, Drawings, Pastels, and Watercolours*, Yale University Press, London and New Haven, 1995, with present collections. Titles follow Whistler's original titles wherever possible. Some of Whistler's titles have been corrected to conform with Italian spelling.

FAS 1881 Cat. No.	Titles	Collections
–	*Santa Maria della Salute, Venice* (M.725)	Private Collection
–	*Venice Harbour* (M.726)	Freer Gallery of Art, Washington, DC
32	*The Beggars – Winter* (M.727)	Freer Gallery of Art, Washington, DC
34	*The Old Bridge – Winter* (M.728)	Hunterian Art Gallery, University of Glasgow
–	*Venetian Palace* (M.729)	Whereabouts unknown
–	*Venetian Palace* (M.730)	Whereabouts unknown
–	*Venetian canal* (M.731)	Whereabouts unknown
–	*Bead-Stringers* (M.732)	Dr and Mrs John E. Larkin, Jr.
–	*The Rialto* (M.733)	Hunterian Art Gallery, University of Glasgow
–	recto: *Riva, Venice*; verso: *Heads and hats* (M.734)	Cleveland Museum of Art
–	*Santa Maria della Salute* (M.735)	Baltimore Museum of Art

–	*The Large Pool* (M.736)	Whereabouts unknown
27	*Campanile at Lido* (M.737)	Private Collection, USA
36	*The Cemetery* (M.738)	Frick Collection, New York
29	*The Giudecca – Winter; grey and blue* (M.739)	Fine Art Society, London
–	*Sunrise at Sea* (M.740)	Whereabouts unknown
–	*Venice at Sunset* (M.741)	Portland Art Museum
–	*View in Venice, looking towards the Molo* (M.742)	Private Collection
25	*Sunset, in red and brown* (M.743)	Freer Gallery of Art, Washington, DC
–	*Venetian scene* (M.744)	New Britain Museum of American Art
40	*The Salute; Morning; blue and rose* (M.745)	Whereabouts unknown
53	*The Brown Morning – Winter* (M.746)	Private Collection
–	*Sunset note* (M.747)	Whereabouts unknown
–	*Long Venice* (M.748)	Whereabouts unknown
3	*The Little Riva; in opal* (M.749)	Lauren Rogers Museum of Art, Laurel
–	*Boats at Venice* (M.750)	Whereabouts unknown
31	*From the Café Orientale* (M.751)	Private Collection, USA
–	recto: *Houses along a Venetian waterfront;* verso: *Buildings* (M.752)	Maier Museum of Art, Randolph-Macon Woman's College, Lynchberg
51	*Campo Sta. Marta – Winter Evening* (M.753)	Freer Gallery of Art, Washington, DC
–	*A Venetian canal* (M.754)	Private Collection, Great Britain
50	*Winter Evening* (M.755)	Freer Gallery of Art, Washington, DC
–	*Venetian Street* (M.756)	Private Collection, USA
30	*San Samuel* (M.757)	Whereabouts unknown
15	*The Palace; white and pink* (M.758)	Private Collection
14	*The Bridge; flesh colour and brown* (M.759)	Burrell Collection, Glasgow
44	*Fondamenta dei Mori* (M.760)	Private Collection
21	*Fish Market, San Barnaba* (M.761)	Private Collection
5	*The Tobacco Warehouse* (M.762)	Hirschhorn Museum and Sculpture Garden, Washington, DC
–	*A street in Venice* (M.763)	Private Collection
8	*Little Calle in San Barnaba; gold and brown* (M.764)	Private Collection
–	*A Venetian canal* (M.765)	Hirschhorn Museum and Sculpture Garden, Washington, DC
–	recto: *Venetian canal;* verso: *Bridge over canal* (M.766)	Private Collection, Great Britain
?	*A Street in Venice* (M.767)	Freer Gallery of Art, Washington, DC
41	*Note in flesh colour and red* (M.768)	Whereabouts unknown
1	*Sotto Portico, San Giacomo* (M.769)	Private Collection
33	recto: *The Palace in Rags;* verso: *Houses by a canal, with bridges* (M.770)	Private Collection, Great Britain
17	*Under the Frari* (M.771)	Private Collection
19	*San Rocco* (M.772)	Boston Public Library Print Department
2	*Campanile Santa Margarita* (M.773)	Addison Gallery of American Art, Phillips Academy, Andover
4	*The Zattere; harmony in blue and brown* (M.774)	Terra Museum of American Art, Chicago
–	*Calle San Trovaso, Venice* (M.775)	Private Collection
43	*A Red Note* (M.776)	Whereabouts unknown
42	*Little Canal, San Barnaba; flesh colour and grey* (M.777)	Private Collection
20	*Canal, San Cassiano* (M.778)	Westmoreland Museum of Art, Greensburg
7	*The Little Back Canal* (M.779)	Frick Collection, New York
–	*Maud Reading, in a Hammock* (M.780)	Fogg Art Museum, Harvard University
	recto: *Seven sketches of heads;* verso: *Chart* (M.781)	Freer Gallery of Art, Washington, DC
35	*The Staircase; note in red* (M.782)	Freer Gallery of Art, Washington, DC
12	*San Giovanni Apostolo et Evangelista* (M.783)	Freer Gallery of Art, Washington, DC
52	*Corte del Paradiso* (M.784)	Private Collection
–	*Archway, Venice* (M.785)	Private Collection, USA
23	*The Steps* (M.786)	Freer Gallery of Art, Washington, DC

26	*Note in pink and brown* (M.787)	Metropolitan Museum of Art, New York
45	*Bead-Stringers* (M.788)	Freer Gallery of Art, Washington, DC
–	*Door* (M.789)	Whereabouts unknown
11	*Courtyard on Canal; grey and red* (M.790)	St. Louis Art Museum
24	*Behind the Arsenal* (M.791)	Fogg Art Museum, Harvard University
–	*Venetian courtyard* (M.792)	Dr and Mrs John E. Larkin, Jr.
–	*Venetian courtyard* (M.793)	Dr and Mrs John E. Larkin, Jr.
22	*The Old Marble Palace* (M.794)	Freer Gallery of Art, Washington, DC
38	*The Red Doorway* (M.795)	Private Collection
–	*Venice* (M.796)	Whereabouts unknown
–	*Nocturnal note: Venice* (M.797)	National Gallery of Art, Washington, DC
–	*Gondolas by moonlight* (M.798)	Whereabouts unknown
10	*Nocturne – The Riva* (M.799)	Frick Collection, New York
–	*Riva, Nocturne* (M.800)	Private Collection, New York
–	*Nocturne: ships and gondolas, Venice* (M.801)	Hunterian Art Gallery, University of Glasgow
–	*Venice* (M.802)	Freer Gallery of Art, Washington, DC
18	*Nocturne – San Giorgio* (M.803)	Freer Gallery of Art, Washington, DC
39	*From the Steps of the Piazzetta* (M.804)	Whereabouts unknown
–	*The Church of San Giorgio Maggiore* (M.805)	Corcoran Museum of Art, Washington, DC
46	*Sunset; red and gold – The Gondolier* (M.806)	Fogg Art Museum, Harvard University
6	*The Riva – Sunset; red and gold* (M.807)	Yale University Art Gallery, New Haven, Conn.
28	*The Storm – Sunset* (M.808)	Fogg Art Museum, Harvard University
48	*Salute – Sundown* (M.809)	Hunterian Art Gallery, University of Glasgow
49	*Sunset; red and gold – Salute* (M.810)	Hunterian Art Gallery, University of Glasgow
–	*Venice: Sunset on harbour* (M.811)	Freer Gallery of Art, Washington, DC
–	recto: *Venice: Sunset*; verso: *Bead-Stringers* (M.812)	Freer Gallery of Art, Washington, DC
–	*Sunset: Venice* (M.813)	Private Collection
37?	*Sunset; blue and gold* (M.814)	Private Collection
–	*Santa Maria della Salute* (M.815)	Whereabouts unknown
–	*Venice* (M.816)	Private Collection, USA
13	*The Giudecca; note in flesh colour* (M.817)	Mead Art Museum, Amherst College, Amherst
9	*San Biagio; flesh colour and grey* (M.818)	Private Collection, USA
47	*Fishing Boats* (M.819)	Cincinnati Art Museum
–	recto: *Clouds and sky, Venice*; verso: *Buildings* (M.820)	St Louis Art Museum
–	*Sky study* (M.821)	Private Collection
–	*Blue and silver – The Islands, Venice* (M.822)	Freer Gallery of Art, Washington, DC
16	*Little Venice; in turquoise* (M.823)	Whereabouts unknown
?	*Venice* (M.824)	Whereabouts unknown
–	*Venice* (M.825)	Whereabouts unknown

Oils: This list is based on Young, A. M., MacDonald, M. F., Spencer, R. and Miles, H., *The Paintings of James McNeill Whistler*, New Haven and London, 1980 (YMSM).

Title	**YMSM**	**Collections**
Nocturne in Blue and Silver: The Lagoon, Venice	212	Museum of Fine Arts, Boston
Nocturne: Blue and Gold – St Mark's, Venice	213	National Museum of Wales, Cardiff
Portrait of a Girl	214	Whereabouts unknown
Sketch of a Girl	215	Private Collection
A Gondolier	216	Whereabouts unknown
Nocturne: Venice	217	Whereabouts unknown
Santa Maria della Salute, Venice	218	Whereabouts unknown
Nocturne of the Giudecca, Venice	219	Whereabouts unknown
Sunset, Venice	220	Whereabouts unknown
Grand Canal, Venice	221	Whereabouts unknown
The Riva and San Biagio, Venice	222	Whereabouts unknown
The Riva and San Marco, Venice	222a	Whereabouts unknown

Select Bibliography

Abbreviation	Manuscripts
FGA	Archives, Freer Gallery of Art, Washington, DC
GUL	Whistler Collection, Special Collections Department, Glasgow University Library, University of Glasgow, Scotland
LC PC	E. R. and J. Pennell Collection, Library of Congress, Washington, DC
LJR	Lessing J. Rosenwald Collection, Rare Books and Manuscripts Division, Library of Congress, Washington, DC

	Title
Bacher 1908	Bacher, O., *With Whistler in Venice*, New York, 1908, (based on 'With Whistler in Venice', *The Century Magazine*, vol.73, no.2, Dec 1906, pp.217–18 and 'Stories of Whistler', *The Century Magazine*, vol.74, no.1, May 1907, pp.100–11). The 1908 edition was suppressed and a revised edition published in 1909
Bell 1987	Bell, L., *Fact and Fiction: Whistler's Critical Reputation in England 1880–1892*, Ph.D. thesis, University of East Anglia, 1987
Bendix 1995	Bendix, D. M., *Diabolical Designs, Paintings, Interiors, and Exhibitions of James McNeill Whistler*, Washington, 1995
Bromberg 2000	Bromberg, R., *Walter Sickert: Prints. A Catalogue raisonné*, New Haven and London, 2000
Bunting 1995	Bunting, V., 'The Prints and Papers: Whistler's Venice Sets at the Freer Gallery of Art', report to the Conservation Analytical Laboratory of the Smithsonian Institution, Washington, DC, August 1995
Butlin and Joll 1977	Butlin, M. and Joll, E., *The Paintings of J. M.W. Turner*, New Haven and London, 1977
Cook and Wedderburn 1903–12	Cook, E. T. and Wedderburn, A. (eds), *The Works of John Ruskin*, London, 1903–12
Costantini and Zannier 1986	Costantini, P. and Zannier, I., *Venezia nella Fotografia Dell'Ottocento*, Venice, 1986
Curry 1984	Curry, D. P., *James McNeill Whistler at the Freer Gallery of Art*, Washington, New York and London, 1984
Dorment and MacDonald 1994	Dorment, R. and MacDonald, M. F., *James McNeill Whistler*, exh.cat., Tate Gallery, London; Musée d'Orsay, Paris; National Gallery of Art, Washington, DC; 1994–5 (print entries by R. E. Fine)
Faberman 1996	Faberman, H., 'Best shop in London, The Fine Art Society and the Victorian Art Race', in Casteras, S. P. and Denney, C. (eds), *The Grosvenor Gallery, A Palace of Art in Victorian England*, New Haven and London, 1996
Fildes 1968	Fildes, L. V., *Luke Fildes, RA, A Victorian Painter*, London, 1968
Filippi 1991	Filippi, L., *Vecchie Immagini di Venezia*, 3 vols, Filippi Editore, Venezia, 1991–3
Getscher 1970	Getscher, R. H., *Whistler and Venice*, Ph.D. thesis, Case Western Reserve University, 1970
Getscher 1977	Getscher, R. H., *The Stamp of Whistler*, exh.cat., Allan Memorial Art Museum, Oberlin, Ohio, et al., 1977–8
Getscher and Marks 1986	Getscher, R. H. and Marks, P., *James McNeill Whistler and John Singer Sargent, Two Annotated Bibliographies*, New York and London, 1986
Getscher 1991	Getscher, R. H., *James McNeill Whistler. Pastels*, London, 1991
Godwin 1881	Godwin, E. W., 'With Whistler's Critics', *British Architect*, 25 Feb 1881, pp.98–9
Grieve 1996	Grieve, A., 'The Sites of Whistler's Venice etchings', *Print Quarterly*, vol.13, no.1, March 1996, pp.19–39
Grieve 2000	Grieve, A., *Whistler's Venice*, New Haven and London, 2000
Heijbroek and MacDonald 1997	Heijbroek, J. F and MacDonald, M. F., *Whistler and Holland*, Amsterdam, 1997
Honour and Fleming 1991	Honour, H. and Fleming, J., *The Venetian Hours of Henry James, Whistler and Sargent*, London, 1991
Kennedy 1910 (K.)	Kennedy, E. G., *The Etched Work of Whistler*, The Grolier Club, New York, 1910 (reprint Alan Wofsy Fine Art, San Francisco, 1978)
Lochnan 1984	Lochnan, K., *The Etchings of James McNeill Whistler*, New Haven and London, 1984
Lovell 1989	Lovell, M., *A Visitable Past*, Chicago, 1989

MacDonald 1971	MacDonald, M. F., *Whistler in Venice: Etchings, Drypoints and Pastels*, University of Glasgow, 2–26 Feb 1971
MacDonald 1976	MacDonald, M. F., *Whistler. The Graphic Work: Amsterdam, Liverpool, London, Venice*, exh.cat., T. Agnew & Sons, London, Walker Art Gallery, Liverpool and Glasgow Art Gallery, 1976
MacDonald 1995 (M.)	MacDonald, M. F., *James McNeill Whistler. Drawings, Pastels, and Watercolours. A Catalogue Raisonné*, New Haven and London, 1995
Mansfield 1909	Mansfield, H., *A Descriptive Catalogue of the Etchings and Drypoints of J. M. Whistler*, Chicago, 1909
Menpes 1904	Menpes, M., *Whistler as I Knew Him*, London, 1904
Merrill 1992	Merrill, L., *A Pot of Paint: Aesthetics on Trial in Whistler v Ruskin*, Washington and London, 1992
Pennell 1908; Pennell 1911	Pennell, E. R. and J., *The Life of James McNeill Whistler*, London and Philadelphia, 2 vols, 1908; 5th (revised) ed., 1911
Ruskin 1851–3	Ruskin, J., *The Stones of Venice*, London, 1851–3, 3 vols; introductory chapters and local indices …, 2 vols, Orpington, 1879–81
Ruskin 1877–84	Ruskin, J., *St. Mark's Rest. The History of Venice, written for the help of the few travellers who still care for her monuments*, Orpington, 1877–84
Sitwell 1947	Sitwell, O. (ed.), *A Free House! The writings of Walter Richard Sickert*, London, 1947
Spencer 1989	Spencer, R., *A Retrospective*, New York, 1989
Stebbins 1992	Stebbins, T. (ed.), *The Lure of Italy, American Artists and the Italian Experience 1760–1914*, Boston and New York, 1992
Thomas 1874	Thomas, R., *A Catalog of the Etchings and Dry-Points of James Abbott MacNeil [sic] Whistler*, London and New York, 1874
Thorp 1994	Thorp, N., *Whistler on Art, Selected Letters and Writings, 1849–1903*, Manchester, 1994
Way 1912	Way, T. R., *Memories of James McNeill Whistler the Artist*, London, 1912
Weber 1985	Weber, B., *Robert Frederick Blum (1857–1903) and his Milieu*, Ph.D. thesis, City University of New York, 1985
Whistler 1883	Whistler, J. McN., *Etchings and Drypoints. Venice. Second Series*, exh.cat., The Fine Art Society, London, 1883
Whistler 1890	Whistler, J. McN., *The Gentle Art of Making Enemies*, London, 1890 (2nd ed., 1892)
Yriarte 1878	Yriarte, C., *Venise, Histoire, Art, Industrie, la Ville, la Vie*, Paris, 1878
YMSM 1980	Young, A. M., MacDonald, M. F., Spencer, R. and Miles, H., *The Paintings of James McNeill Whistler*, New Haven and London, 1980

Bibliography of Reviews

The majority of these presscuttings were kept in albums by the artist and are now in Glasgow University Library. Reviews are anonymous unless otherwise stated.

Abbreviation	Bibliographical ref.	GUL
1880		
Daily News, 2 Dec 1880	'Mr Whistler's Venice Etchings', *Daily News*, 2 Dec 1880	PC4/15, 15/11
British Architect, 3 Dec 1880	'Notes on Current Events', *British Architect*, XII, 3 Dec 1880, p.237	PC4/19
Globe, 3 Dec 1880	'Mr. Whistler's Etchings', *The Globe*, 3 Dec 1880	PC4/15, 15/11
World, 8 Dec 1880	*The World*, 8 Dec 1880	
St James' Gazette, 9 Dec 1880	'Mr. Whistler's Venice', *St James' Gazette*, 9 Dec 1880	PC4/17, PC15/13
British Architect, 10 Dec 1880	'Notes on Current Events', *British Architect*, XII, 10 Dec 1880, p.247	PC4/19
Spectator, 11 Dec 1880	[H. Quilter], 'Mr. Whistler's "Venice" at the Fine-Art Society, New Bond Street', *Spectator*, vol.53, no.2737, 11 Dec 1880, pp.1586–7	PC4/89
Times, 25 Dec 1880	[H. Quilter], 'Mr. Whistler's Etchings of Venice', *The Times*, 25 Dec 1880, p.4	PC4/11
1881		
Punch, 22 Jan 1881	'The Diffusion of Aesthetic Taste', *Punch*, vol.80, 22 Jan 1881, p.26	
Daily News, 31 Jan 1881	'Mr. Whistler's Venice Pastels', *Daily News*, 31 Jan 1881	PC4/37
Whitehall Review, Feb 1881	*The Whitehall Review*, Feb 1881	PC4/57
World, 2 Feb 1881	'Fine Arts. Mr. Whistler's "Venice Pastels"', *The World*, XIV, no.344, 2 Feb 1881, pp.9–10	PC4/49, PC15/31
British Architect, 4 Feb 1881	[E. W. Godwin], 'Notes on Current Events', *British Architect*, 4 Feb 1881, vol.15, pp.59-64.	PC4/37, 39; PC15/53-5
Daily Telegraph, 1 Feb 1881	[G. Turner], 'Venice Pastels', *Daily Telegraph*, 1 Feb 1881	PC4/48, PC15/33
Country Gentleman, 5 Feb 1881	*The Country Gentleman*, 5 Feb 1881	PC4/47, PC15/39, 55, 57
Pan, 5 Feb 1881	'W', 'Mr. Whistler's Venice Pastels', *Pan*, 5 Feb 1881	PC4/59
Times, 2 Feb 1881	'Mr Whistler's Venice Pastels', advertisement, *The Times*, 2 Feb 1881	PC4/67

Athenaeum, 5 Feb 1881	'Mr. Whistler's Pastels', *Athenaeum*, no.2780, p.206, 5 Feb 1881	PC4/47, PC15/27, 47
Pictorial World, 5 Feb 1881	'Mr. Whistler's Venice Pastels', *Pictorial World*, 5 Feb 1881, p.371	PC4/43
Observer, 6 Feb 1881	'Venice Pastels', *Observer*, 6 Feb 1881	PC4/45, 69
St James' Gazette, 9 Feb 1881	'Venice in Pastel', *St James' Gazette*, 9 Feb 1881, p.13	PC15/37
Pall Mall Gazette, 9 Feb 1881	'Mr. Whistler's Pastels on Venice', *Pall Mall Gazette*, 9 Feb 1881	PC4/68, PC15/29
Times, 9 Feb 1881	[H. Quilter], 'Mr. Whistler's Venice Pastels' *The Times*, 9 Feb 1881, p.4	PC15/27, PC4/35
Court Journal, 12 Feb 1881	*The Court Journal*, 12 Feb 1881	PC4/52-3, PC15/39
Queen, 12 Feb 1881	'Mr. Whistler's "Venice Pastels"', *Queen*, 12 Feb 1881	PC15/41
Punch, 12 Feb 1881	[F. C. Burnand], 'Whistler's Wenice; or, Pastels by Pastelthwaite', *Punch*, vol.80, 12 Feb 1881, p.69	PC4/41
Sun, 13 Feb 1881	*Sun* (New York), 13 Feb 1881	PC15/49
Academy, 19 Feb 1881	F. Wedmore, 'Fine Art: Mr. Whistler's Pastels', *The Academy*, 19 Feb 1881, vol.19, no.459, p.142	PC4/55
Weekly Times, 20 Feb 1881	'The Millais Collection', *Weekly Times*, 20 Feb 1881	PC4/53
British Architect, 25 Feb 1881	E. W. Godwin, 'With Whistler's Critics', *The British Architect*, XV, 25 Feb 1881, pp.98–9	
Fanfulla Sabato, 26 Feb 1881	*Fanfulla Sabato*, 26 Feb 1881	PC15/57
World, 9 March 1881	*The World*, 9 March 1881	PC15/57
Artist, 1 March 1881	'Mr Whistler's Pastels', *Artist*, 1 March 1881, p.72	
Punch, 19 March 1881	'London Paved with Gold', *Punch*, vol.80, 19 March 1881, p.132	
Punch, 26 March 1881	'The Millais-nium in New Bond Street', *Punch*, vol.80, 26 March 1881, p.133	
Art Journal, 1881, p.93	[T. R. Way], 'Art Notes and Reviews. Exhibitions: Venice Pastels and Etchings', *Art Journal*, vol.20, March 1881, p.93	

1883

World, 7 Feb 1883	'What the World says', *The World*, 7 Feb 1883	
Times, 17 Feb 1883	[H. Ward], 'Mr. Whistler's Etchings', *The Times*, 17 Feb 1883, p.5	
Pall Mall Gazette, 19 Feb 1883	'Mr Whistler's Latest "Arrangement"', *Pall Mall Gazette*, 19 Feb 1883	
Daily News, 20 Feb 1883	'Mr. Whistler's Etchings', *Daily News*, 20 Feb 1883	PC6/21
Bird o' Freedom, 20 Feb 1883	*Bird o' Freedom*, 20 Feb 1883	PC6/42
World, 21 Feb 1883	(probably 'Atlas', E. Yates), 'Caviare to the Critics', *The World*, XVIII, no.451, 21 Feb 1883, p.9	
Building News, 23 Feb 1883	'Mr Whistler's Etchings' *Building News*, XLIV, 23 Feb 1883, p.221	PC6/42
Catholic Times, 23 Feb 1883	*Catholic Times*, 23 Feb 1883	PC6/42
Coventry Standard, 23 Feb 1883	*Coventry Standard*, 23 Feb 1883	PC6/42
Saturday Review, 24 Feb 1883	'Mr Whistler's Exhibition', *Saturday Review*, vol.55, no.1426, 24 Feb 1883, pp.241–2	
Illustrated London News, 24 Feb 1883	'Fine Arts', *Illustrated London News*, vol.82, 24 Feb 1883, p.197	
Academy, 24 Feb 1883	F. Wedmore, 'Mr. Whistler's Exhibition', *Academy*, 24 Feb 1883, vol.23, no.564, pp.139–40	
Advertiser, 24 Feb 1883	'Mr. Whistler's Latest "Arrangement"', *Advertiser*, 24 Feb 1883	PC6/42
Ashton Standard, 24 Feb 1883	'Mr. Whistler's Latest "Arrangement"', *Ashton Standard*, 24 Feb 1883	PC6/41
Country Gentleman, 24 Feb 1883	*Country Gentleman*, 24 Feb 1883	PC6/43
Lady's Pictorial, 24 Feb 1883	'Art Gossip', *Lady's Pictorial*, 24 Feb 1883	
London Figaro, 24 Feb 1883	*London Figaro*, 24 Feb 1883	PC6/43
Rochdale Observer, 24 Feb 1883	*Rochdale Observer*, 24 Feb 1883	PC6/41
Society, 24 Feb 1883	'Mahlstick' [H. W. Sweny], 'An Arrangement in White and Yellow', *Society*, 24 Feb 1883	PC6/49
South Durham Herald, 24 Feb 1883	*South Durham Herald*, 24 Feb 1883	PC6/41
Weekly Register, 24 Feb 1883	*Weekly Register*, 24 Feb 1883	PC6/41
People, 25 Feb 1883	'H. W. S.' [Sweny], 'Venice and Whistler', *People*, 25 Feb 1883	PC6/44
Daily Chronicle, 26 Feb 1883	'The Fine Art Society, New Bond Street', *Daily Chronicle*, 26 Feb 1883	PC6/43
Bazaar, 28 Feb 1883	'Fine Art. Mr. Whistler's Exhibition', *Bazaar*, 28 Feb 1883	PC6/44
Artist, 1 March 1883	'Mr. Whistler at the Fine Art Society's Gallery', *Artist*, 1 March 1883, vol.4, p.70.	PC6/45

Pictorial World, 1 March 1883	J. Forbes-Robertson, *Pictorial World*, 1 March 1883	
Times, 1 March 1883	'Art Jottings', *The Times*, 1 March 1883	PC6/46
Western Morning News, 1 March 1883	*Western Morning News*, 1 March 1883	PC6/41
Echo, 2 March 1883	('X'), 'Mr. Whistler's Fiasco', *Echo*, 2 March 1883	PC6/46
Advertiser, 3 March 1883	'Our Ladies Column', *Advertiser*, 3 March 1883	PC6/47
Country Gentleman, 3 March 1883	*Country Gentleman*, 3 March 1883	PC6/47
Lady's Pictorial, 3 March 1883	*Lady's Pictorial*, 3 March 1883	PC6/44
London Figaro, 3 March 1883	*London Figaro*, 3 March 1883	PC6/47
Moonshine, 3 March 1883	'Still More Armies', *Moonshine*, 3 March 1883	PC6/45
Nottingham Advertiser, 3 March 1883	[A Lady], 'Lady's Column', *Nottingham Advertiser*, 3 March 1883	PC6/46
Punch, 3 March 1883	'Whistler in Venice: A Gavotte in Gamboge', *Punch*, vol.84, 3 March 1883, p.107	PC6/48
Western Morning News, 3 March 1883	*Western Morning News*, 3 March 1883	PC6/47
Architect, 10 March 1883	'Minor Exhibitions', *The Architect*, XXIX, 10 March 1883, p.155	PC6/48
Funny Folks, 10 March 1883	*Funny Folks*, 10 March 1883	PC6/48
Whitehall Review, 14 March 1883	*Whitehall Review*, 14 March 1883	PC6/50
Punch, 24 March 1883	'Notes from a Whistler', *Punch*, 24 March 1883, vol.84, p.133	
Pictorial World, 31 March 1883	John Forbes-Robertson, 'Mr Whistler, His Arrangement in White and Yellow, His Etchings and His Catalogue', *Pictorial World*, 31 March 1883	
Paper and Printing, March 1883	'Mr. Whistler's Etchings', 'Chit Chat', *Paper and Printing Trades Journal*, no.42, March 1883, p.60	PC6/48
Magazine of Art, 1 April 1883	'Art in March', *Magazine of Art*, 1883, vol.6, n.p.n	PC6/1
New York Daily News, 4 Oct 1883	'Art Babble', *New York Daily News*, 4 Oct 1883	PC3/75
New York Evening Telegram, 11 Oct 1883	'Whistler's Etchings and Drypoints', *New York Evening Telegram*, 11 Oct 1883	PC4/10
New York World, 11 Oct 1883	'Whistler's Queer Conceits. A Novel Arrangement in White and yellow', *New York World*, 11 Oct 1883	PC3/59, PC4/12
Boston Evening Transcript, 12 Oct 1883	'E.W.M.', 'Whistler's Arrangement. Etchings on Exhibition in New York in a "Yellow-and-White" Setting', *Boston Evening Transcript*, 12 Oct 1883	PC4/16
New York Mail and Express, 24 Oct 1883	'The Whistler Exhibition', *New York Mail and Express*, 24 Oct 1883	PC3/61
Daily News, 15 Nov 1883	'Something about the Artist Whistler', *The Daily News*, 15 Nov 1883	PC3/59
Critic, 26 Nov 1883	'The Fine Arts. An Exhibition of Mr. Whistler's Etchings', *The Critic*, 26 Nov 1883	PC4/14

1887

Academy, 30 April 1887	'Mr. Whistler 's New Series of Etchings', *Academy*, XXXI, no.782, 30 April 1887, pp.313–14	

Picture Credits: Aberdeen Art Gallery, f.143; © Addison Gallery of American Art, Phillips Academy, Andover, All Rights Reserved., f.17; Archivio Filippi, f.18, 56, 69, 87; Photograph © 2000 The Art Institute of Chicago. All rights reserved, f.120; The George A. Lucas Collection of The Maryland Institute, College of Art, on extended loan to the Baltimore Museum of Art. All rights reserved, f.14; Courtesy of Boston Public Library, Print Department, f.62; Trustees of the British Museum, f.139; R. Bromberg, *Walter Sickert: Prints, A Catalogue Raisonée*, New Haven and London 2000, (B.172 I), f.140; Canadian Centre for Architecture, Montréal, f.46; Carnegie Museum of Art, Pittsburgh, Museum Purchase, f.19; Cincinnati Art Museum, f.65 (Bequest of Mary Hanna), f.79 (The Albert P. Strietmann Collection and Deaccession Funds); Private Collection, photograph courtesy of Thomas Colville Fine Arts, f.16, 36, 45; © Copyright Reserved, f.142, 144, 145; © Estate of the Artist, f.143; The Fine Art Society, London, f.8, 9, 71, 76, 90, 99, 103, 106, 109, 125, 129–30; Freer Gallery of Art, Smithsonian Institution, Washington, DC, f.21–2, 25, 27, 39–40, 48, 57, 68, 70, 72, 84, 96, 111, jacket; The Frick Collection, New York, f.43, 67; Glasgow Museums, The Burrell Collection, f.41; Special Collections Department, Glasgow University Library, f.11–2, 118–19, 146–8; The President and Fellows of Harvard College, Harvard University, f.47, 60; Hunterian Art Gallery, University of Glasgow, f.5, 10, 13, 28, 38, 63–4, 74, 81, 83, 85–6, 91, 94–5, 101–2, 104–5, 107, 122, 128, 131, 133–4, 144; M. F. MacDonald, f.4, 26, 33–4, 42, 44–6, 49, 54, 59, 73, 77, 82, 141; Mead Art Museum, Amherst College, Gift of George D. Pratt, Class of 1893, acc.no. ACP. 1933.14, f.113; Copyright © 2000 The Metropolitan Museum of Art. All Rights Reserved, f.29; Courtesy of the City Libraries and Archives, Mitchell Library, Glasgow, f.15; Emily L. Ainsley Fund, Courtesy of Museum of Fine Arts, Boston, f.31; Ewan Mundy, Fine Art, f.123; National Galleries of Scotland, f.6, 121, 127, 142, 145; National Gallery of Art, Washington, DC, Photograph © 2000 Board of Trustees, f. 7 (John Hay Whitney Collection), f.88 (Gift of Mr and Mrs J. Watson Webb in memory of Mr and Mrs H. O. Havemeyer), f.92; National Museums and Galleries of Wales, Cardiff, f.35; New Britain Museum of American Art, Connecticut, Harriet Russell Stanley Fund 1950.12, Photographic credit E. Irving Blomenstrann, f.51; Private Collection, courtesy of David Nissensen Fine Art, f.116; Rijksmuseum, Amsterdam, f.37; Royal Institute of British Architects, Library Photographic Collection, f.115; The St. Louis Art Museum, f.61; © Estate of Walter R. Sickert 2001. All Rights Reserved, DACS, f.140; Sotheby's, New York, f.23; © Tate, London, 2000, f.32; Terra Foundation for the Arts, Daniel J. Terra Collection, 1992.162, photograph courtesy of Terra Foundation for the Arts, Chicago, f.55; Trustees of the Victoria and Albert Museum, f.2; Collections of the Westmoreland Museum of American Art, 221 North Main Street, Greensburg, PA 15601-1898, Gift of the William Coulter Fund, #1963.49, f.58; Witt Library, Courtauld Institute, London, f.24.

Index